Y0-AEZ-737

QuickBooks® 2007
The Official Guide

Custom Edition

About the Author

Elaine Marmel is President of Marmel Enterprises, LLC, an organization that specializes in freelance technical writing and consulting. Elaine has an MBA from Cornell University and has worked on projects to build financial management systems for New York City and Washington, D.C. This experience provided the foundation for Marmel Enterprises, LLC, which helps small businesses implement computerized accounting systems.

Elaine left her native Chicago for the warmer climes of Arizona (by way of Cincinnati, OH; Jerusalem, Israel; Ithaca, NY; Washington, D.C.; and Tampa, FL) where she basks in the sun with her PC and her cats Cato, Watson, and Buddy and her dog Josh, and sings barbershop harmony with the 2006 International Championship Scottsdale Chorus.

Elaine spends most of her time writing; she has authored and coauthored more than 30 books about *Microsoft Project, QuickBooks, Quicken for Windows, Quicken for DOS, Microsoft Excel, Microsoft Word for Windows, Microsoft Word for the Mac, Windows 98, 1-2-3 for Windows,* and *Lotus Notes.* From 1994 to 2006, she was also the contributing editor to the monthly publication *QuickBooks Extra.*

QuickBooks® 2007
The Official Guide

Custom Edition

Elaine Marmel

New York   Chicago   San Francisco
Lisbon   London   Madrid   Mexico City   Milan
New Delhi   San Juan   Seoul   Singapore   Sydney   Toronto

The McGraw·Hill Companies

McGraw-Hill books are available at special quantity discounts to use as premiums and sales promotions or for use in corporate training programs. For more information, please write to the Director of Special Sales, Professional Publishing, McGraw-Hill, Two Penn Plaza, New York, NY 10121-2298. Or contact your local bookstore.

QuickBooks® 2007 The Official Guide

Copyright © 2007 by The McGraw-Hill Companies. All rights reserved. Printed in the United States of America. Except as permitted under the Copyright Act of 1976, no part of this publication may be reproduced or distributed in any form or by any means, or stored in a database or retrieval system, without the prior written permission of publisher, with the exception that the program listings may be entered, stored, and executed in a computer system, but they may not be reproduced for publication.

1234567890 CUS CUS 019876

QuickBooks® 2007 The Official Guide For Premier Edition Users
ISBN-13:   978-0-07-226347-3
ISBN-10:   0-07-226347-4

QuickBooks® Enterprise Solutions 7.0 The Official Guide
ISBN-13:   978-0-07-226348-0
ISBN-10:   0-07-226348-2

Sponsoring Editor Megg Morin	**Indexer** Stephen Ingle
Editorial Supervisor Jody McKenzie	**Production Supervisor** George Anderson
Project Manager Vasundhara Sawhney	**Composition** International Typesetting and Composition
Acquisitions Coordinator Agatha Kim	**Illustration** International Typesetting and Composition
Technical Editor Tom Barich	**Art Director, Cover** Jeff Weeks
Copy Editor Saloni Narang	**Cover Designer** Pattie Lee
Proofreader Christine Andreasen	

Information has been obtained by McGraw-Hill from sources believed to be reliable. However, because of the possibility of human or mechanical error by our sources, McGraw-Hill, or others, McGraw-Hill does not guarantee the accuracy, adequacy, or completeness of any information and is not responsible for any errors or omissions or the results obtained from the use of such information.

Contents

Acknowledgments . . . . *xxiii*

Introduction . . . . *xxv*

Part One

Getting Started

1   Introducing QuickBooks   1

2   Setting Up Your Lists   5

   Adding Accounts to the Chart of Accounts   6

      Using Numbers for Accounts   6

      Naming Accounts   7

      Using Subaccounts   10

      Adding Accounts   12

      Editing Accounts   13

      Creating Subaccounts   13

      Merging Accounts   15

   Customers and Jobs   15

      Setting Up a New Customer   16

      Address Info Tab   18

      Additional Info Tab   19

      Payment Info Tab   22

      Editing Customer Records   23

Working with the Vendor List   24
Setting Up Payroll Lists   26
   Creating Pay Schedules   27
   Entering Payroll Items   27
   Establish Employee Default Information   30
   Entering Employees   31
   Workers Compensation Tab Set   36
Entering Items   36
   Understanding Item Types   36
   Entering the Data for Items   36
Entering Jobs   39
Setting Up Other Lists   40
   Fixed Asset Item List   41
   Price Level List   42
   Sales Tax Code List   43
   Class List   43
   Workers Comp List   44
   Other Names List   44
   Memorized Transaction List   44
   Sales Rep List   44
   Customer Type List   45
   Vendor Type List   45
   Job Type List   45
   Terms List   45
   Customer Message List   46
   Payment Method List   46
   Ship Via List   46
   Vehicle List   47
Using Custom Fields   48
   Adding a Custom Field for Names   48
   Adding a Custom Field for Items   49
Merging Entries in Lists   50
   Performing a Merge Operation   51
   Guidelines and Restrictions for Merging List Entries   51
Additional Features for Selected Editions of QuickBooks   52

Part Two
Bookkeeping

3   Invoicing   55

Customer Center   56

Creating Standard Invoices   58

Entering Heading Information   60

Entering Line Items   62

Applying Price Levels   63

Entering Discounts   64

Check Spelling   64

Add a Message   65

Add a Memo   66

Choose the Method for Sending the Invoice   66

Save the Invoice   66

Editing a Previously Entered Invoice   66

Voiding and Deleting Invoices   67

Behind the Scenes of Customer Invoices   68

Using Estimates   69

Setting Preferences   69

Creating an Estimate   70

Creating Invoices from Estimates   71

Estimates and Reporting   72

Memorizing Estimates   74

Creating Sales Orders   74

Preferences   75

Creating a Sales Order   76

Invoicing from a Sales Order   77

Checking on Customer Backorders   78

Issuing Credits and Refunds   79

Creating Credit Memos   81

Sending Invoices and Credit Memos   83

Printing Invoices and Credit Memos   83

Printing Mailing Labels   87

Printing Packing Slips   88

E-mailing Invoices and Credit Memos   90

Customizing Templates   94
    Editing a Predefined Template   94
    Designing a New Template   96
    Designing the Layout   100
Using Memorized Invoices   101
Additional Features for Selected Editions of QuickBooks   103
    Customized Templates   103
    Current Availability of Items   103
    Sales Order Fulfillment Worksheet   104

4   Receiving Payments   107
Receiving Payments for Invoices   108
    Recording the Payment   108
    Applying Payments to Invoices   110
    Working with the Undeposited Funds Account   111
    Handling Underpayments   112
    Applying Credits to Invoices   113
    Applying Credits to a Different Job   115
    Applying Discounts for Timely Payments   115
    Applying Discounts for Untimely Payments   117
    Behind the Scenes of Customer Payments   117
Handling Cash Sales   118
    Entering Cash Sale Information   119
    Customizing the Sales Receipts Template   120
    Handling Batches of Daily Cash Sales   123
    Handling a Cash Drawer   123
Depositing Income   124
    Choosing the Payments to Deposit   124
    Filling Out the Deposit Slip   126
    Printing Deposit Slips   129

5   Tracking Accounts Receivable   131
Reporting On Who Owes You Money   132
    Customizing Aging Reports   133
    Memorizing Aging Reports   137
    Exporting and Importing Memorized Reports   138
    Printing Reports   139

Using Finance Charges 140
　　Setting Up Finance Charge Preferences 140
　　Assessing Finance Charges 141
Sending Statements 144
　　Entering Statement Charges 144
　　Creating Statements 146
　　Previewing the Statements 148
　　Printing the Statements 149
　　Customizing Statements 149

6   Entering Accounts Payable Bills **151**
Vendor Center 152
Recording Vendor Bills 153
　　Easy One-Account Posting 155
　　Splitting Expenses among Multiple Accounts 157
Reimbursable Expenses 157
　　Options for Managing Reimbursable Expenses 158
　　Setting Up to Track Reimbursable Expenses 158
　　Recording Reimbursable Expenses 161
　　Invoicing Customers for Reimbursable Expenses 161
Managing Item Purchases 166
　　Using Purchase Orders 168
　　Receiving Inventory Items without a Bill 170
　　Recording Bills for Received Items 173
　　Receiving Items and Bills Simultaneously 174
　　Behind the Scenes of Item Receipts and Vendor Bills 176
Recording Vendor Credits 177
Entering Recurring Bills 178
　　Creating a Memorized Bill 178
　　Using a Memorized Bill 181
　　Creating Memorized Bill Groups 181
Tracking Mileage Expense 182
　　Entering Mileage Rates 182
　　Creating a Mileage Item 183
　　Entering Mileage 184
　　Creating Mileage Reports 184
　　Reimbursing Employees and Subcontractors
　　　for Mileage 186

7 Paying Bills 187
   Choosing What to Pay 188
      Viewing Your Unpaid Bills 188
      Selecting the Bills to Pay 189
      Selecting the Payment Amounts 190
      Saving the Pay Bills Information 195
   Preparing Manual Checks 196
   Printing Checks 196
      Purchasing Computer Checks 196
      Setting Up the Printer 197
      Printing the Checks 199
      Reprinting after a Problem 200
   Using Direct Disbursements 201
      Writing Direct Disbursement Manual Checks 201
      Printing Direct Disbursement Checks 205
      Behind the Scenes for Direct Disbursements 206
   Sending Sales Tax Checks and Reports 206
      Enabling Sales Tax Tracking 206
      Default Sales Tax Codes 207
      Sales Tax Payment Basis 209
      Sales Tax Payment Dates 209
      Sales Tax Items 209
      Assigning Codes and Items to Customers 210
      Creating Tax Groups 210
      Running Sales Tax Reports 212
      Remitting the Sales Tax 214
      Adjusting Sales Tax Amounts 214

8 Running Payroll 217
   QuickBooks Payroll Services 218
   The Employee Center 220
   Configuring Payroll Elements 222
      Vendors 223
      Payroll Items 224
      Creating Pay Schedules 224
      Employee Information 225
      Chart Of Accounts 226

Entering Historical Data 226
   Understanding How QuickBooks
      Handles Historical Data 226
   Entering the History 227
Using the QuickBooks Payroll Setup Wizard 227
   Setting Up Payroll Items in the Wizard 228
   Setting Up Employees in the Wizard 230
   Setting Up Payroll Taxes in the Wizard 231
   Scheduling Tax Payments 232
   Entering Payroll History in the Wizard 233
   Finishing Steps 236
Running Payroll 236
   Reviewing Employees to Pay 236
   Reviewing Paycheck Information 238
   Printing the Paychecks 239
   Sending Direct Deposit Information 240
   Editing a Paycheck 240
Additional Features for Enterprise Solutions Users 242
   Employee Organizer 242

9 Government Payroll Reporting 245
Making Payroll Tax Deposits 246
   Setting up Tax Liability Payment Schedules 246
   Paying Tax Liabilities 248
Paying Unscheduled Payroll Liabilities 251
Adjusting Payroll Liabilities 252
Handling Workers Compensation 252
   Setting Up Workers Compensation Tracking 253
   Payroll and Workers Compensation 256
   Reporting on and Paying Workers Compensation 257
Preparing Your Quarterly 941 Form 257
Preparing Annual Payroll Documents 258
   Preparing State and Local Annual Returns 258
   Preparing the 940 Report 258
   Printing W-2 Forms 258

10   Configuring and Tracking Inventory 261

Creating Inventory Items 262
    Setting Inventory Preferences 262
    Setting Up Units of Measure 263
    Creating New Items 267
    Creating Subitems 270
    Making Items Inactive 270
Creating Assemblies 271
    Creating an Assembly Item 271
    Assembling Finished Goods 273
    Pending Builds 273
    Disassembling Assemblies 275
    Printing the Components of Assemblies 275
Counting Inventory 276
    Printing the Physical Inventory Worksheet 276
    Making Inventory Adjustments 277
Running Inventory Reports 280

11   Managing Bank and Credit Card Accounts 283

Making a Deposit 284
Transferring Funds between Accounts 285
Handling Bounced Checks 286
    Setting Up to Handle NSF Checks 287
    Adjusting Your Accounts for the Bad Check 287
    Attempting to Redeposit the NSF Check 288
    Recollecting the Debt 288
Voiding Disbursements 290
Tracking Cash 290
    Creating a Petty Cash Account 290
    Putting Money into Petty Cash 291
    Recording ATM Withdrawals 291
    Recording Petty Cash Disbursements 291
Managing Your Credit Cards 292
    Treating Credit Cards as Vendors 292
    Treating Credit Cards as Liability Accounts 293

12   Reconciling Bank Accounts 297
  Establishing the Bank Account's Opening Balance 298
  Using the Begin Reconciliation Window 298
  Entering Interest Income and Service Charges 299
  Reconciling the Transactions 300
    Setting Up the Reconcile Window 300
    Clearing Transactions 301
    Adding Transactions during Reconciliation 301
    Editing Transactions during Reconciliation 302
    Deleting Transactions during Reconciliation 302
    Resolving Missing Check Numbers 303
    Pausing the Reconciliation Process 304
  Finishing the Reconciliation 304
  Printing the Reconciliation Report 304
    Deciding on the Type of Report 304
    Printing the Reports 305
  Troubleshooting Reconciliation Issues 305
    When the Ending Balance and the
      Cleared Balance Differ... 305
    Resolving Unexpected Differences
      in the Beginning Balance 306
    Viewing the Last Reconciliation Report 309
    Undoing the Last Reconciliation 310
    Giving Up the Search for a Reason 311
    Permitting an Adjusting Entry 312

13   Using Budgets and Planning Tools 313
  Budgets and QuickBooks 314
    Types of Budgets 314
    Deleting a Budget 314
    Understanding the Budget Window 315
    Tasks to Perform before You Start Your Budget 316
  Creating a Budget 316
    Enter Budget Amounts 317
    Copy Numbers across the Months 319
    Create a Budget from Last Year's Data 319

Customer:Job Budgets 322
Class Budgets 323
Budget Reports 323
Budget Overview 324
Budget vs. Actual 326
Profit & Loss Budget Performance 326
Budget vs. Actual Graph 327
Exporting Budgets 327
Analyzing Your Business 328

14   Using Journal Entries 331
The QuickBooks Journal Entry Window 332
Entering the Opening Balances 334
Entering Opening Balances for Bank
Accounts and Credit Card Accounts 335
Entering Opening Customer and Vendor Balances 337
Entering Opening Balances for Inventory Items 337
Entering Opening Balances for Payroll Liabilities 338
Making Adjusting Entries 338
Making Journal Entries for Changed Accounts 338
Making Depreciation Entries 339
Reversing Entries 341
Recording Payroll from Outside Payroll Services 342
Transferring Money to the Payroll Account 342
Recording the Payroll 342
Recording Employer Payments 343
Create Your Own Boilerplate 344
Reconciling the Payroll Account 345
Reporting on Journal Entries 345

15   Running Financial Reports 347
Reporting the Trial Balance 348
Changing the Appearance of the Trial Balance Report 348
Memorizing a Customized Report 354
Generating a Balance Sheet 354
Balance Sheet Standard Report 354
Balance Sheet Detail Report 355

Balance Sheet Summary Report 355

Balance Sheet Prev Year Comparison Report 356

Generating a Profit & Loss Report 356

Profit & Loss Standard Report 356

Profit & Loss Detail Report 357

Profit & Loss YTD Comparison Report 357

Profit & Loss Prev Year Comparison Report 357

Profit & Loss By Job Report 357

Profit & Loss By Class Report 357

Profit & Loss Unclassified Report 357

Creating an Accountant's Copy 358

Working during the Accountant's Copy 360

Merging the Accountant's Changes 360

Unlocking Your Files without Receiving a Review 364

Voided and Deleted Transactions Reports 364

Voided/Deleted Transactions Summary Report 364

Voided/Deleted Transactions Detail Report 365

Audit Trail Report 365

Cash Flow Reports 366

Statement of Cash Flows 367

Cash Flow Forecast 369

Net Worth Graph 369

Export and Import Memorized Reports 370

Process Multiple Reports 371

Consolidated Reports for Multiple Companies 372

ODBC Reporting 373

16 Using Online Banking Services 377

Understanding Online Banking 378

Setting Up a Connection 379

Dial-up Connections 379

Network or Always-on Connections 380

No Internet Connection 380

Setting Up Online Banking 380

Finding Your Bank Online 381

Using the QuickBooks Bill Pay Service 383

Using a QuickBooks Credit Card 383

Setting Up Online Access 383
Enabling Direct Connect Online Bank Accounts 384
Enabling Web Connect Online Bank Accounts 385
Getting Bank Account Data Online 385
Exchanging Data with Web Connect 385
Exchanging Data with Direct Connection 387
Creating Messages to Send to Your Bank 387
Connecting to Your Bank 387
Sending Data to Your Bank 387
Viewing the Received Data 388
Matching Transactions 389
Matching Unmatched Transactions 389
Transferring Money between Accounts Online 392
Paying Bills Online 393
Creating Online Transaction Reports 394
Receiving Customer Payments Online 395

17   Year-End Procedures 397
Understanding Year-End Tasks 398
Running Year-End Financial Reports 399
Year-End Profit & Loss Report 399
Year-End Balance Sheet 399
Issuing 1099 Forms 400
Checking 1099 Vendor Information 400
Checking 1099 Setup 401
Verifying Vendor 1099 Balances 402
Print 1099 Forms 403
Making Year-End Journal Entries 404
Running Tax Reports 405
Checking Tax Line Information 405
Calculating Officer Compensation 406
Using TurboTax 407
Closing Your Books 407
Understanding Closing in QuickBooks 407
Closing the Year 407
Closing Date Exception Report 408
Creating a Year-End Backup 409

Part Three

Tracking Time and Billing

18 Using Time Tracking 411

Setting Up Time Tracking 412

Setting Up Workers 413

Setting Up the Tasks 415

Using Timesheets 415

Tracking a Single Activity 416

Using Weekly Timesheets 419

Reporting Timesheet Information 420

Running Timesheet Reports 420

Editing Time Entries 422

Printing the Weekly Timesheets 422

Creating Invoices with Timesheets Data 424

Changing Invoicing Options for Time Charges 425

19 Using Timesheets for Payroll Job Costing 427

Linking Employee Time to Payroll or Job Costing 428

Modifying the Employee Record 428

Setting Payroll Preferences for Job Costing 429

Using Classes for Payroll Job Costing 430

Using Timesheets Efficiently 430

Running Payroll with Timesheet Data 430

Running Payroll Reports for Cost Information 432

20 Using QuickBooks Timer 435

Distributing the Timer Software to Others 436

Installing the Timer on a Recipient Computer 437

Exporting Data Lists to Timer Users 437

Using the Timer 439

Opening the Timer for the First Time 439

Setting Up an Activity 440

Editing the Activity 441

Timing Your Work 442

Setting Preferences in the Timer 442
Exporting Timer Files 443
Importing Timer Files into QuickBooks 445

Part Four
Managing QuickBooks

21 Customizing QuickBooks 449
Setting Preferences 450
    Setting My Preferences for the General Category 451
    Setting Company Preferences for the General Section 453
    Accounting Preferences 453
    Bills 455
    Checking Preferences 456
    Desktop View Preferences 457
    Finance Charge Preferences 459
    Integrated Applications Preferences 459
    Items & Inventory 459
    Jobs & Estimates Preferences 460
    Payroll & Employees Preferences 460
    Reminders Preferences 460
    Reports & Graphs Preferences 462
    Sales & Customers Preferences 464
    Sales Tax Preferences 467
    Send Forms Preferences 467
    Service Connection Preferences 467
    Spelling Preferences 468
    Tax:1099 Preferences 468
    Time Tracking Preferences 468
Using Classes 468
    Creating a Class 469
    Creating a Subclass 470
    Editing, Deleting, and Merging Classes 470
    Using a Class in Transactions 470
    Reporting by Class 470

Customizing the Icon Bar 472
    Changing the Order of Icons 472
    Display Icons without Title Text 473
    Change the Icon's Graphic, Text, or Description 473
    Separate Icons 473
    Removing an Icon 473
    Adding an Icon 474
Managing Multiple Users in QuickBooks Premier 475
    Creating, Removing, and Changing User Information 475
    Creating a New User 475
    Setting User Permissions 476
    Establishing Transaction Rights 478
    Multi-User Mode Restrictions 478
Managing Multiple Users in QuickBooks Enterprise 479
    Examining Users and Roles in Enterprise 480
    Creating a New Role 482
    Assigning an Administrator Password 483
    Creating a New User 483
    Reporting on Permissions 485
    Multi-User Mode Restrictions 485

22   **Managing Your QuickBooks Files** 487
Finding Transactions 488
    Performing a Simple Search 488
    Performing an Advanced Search 489
    Google Desktop Search 489
Creating Companies in QuickBooks 491
Backing Up and Restoring Files 493
    Backing Up 493
    Automatic Backups 496
    Restoring a Backup 499
Using a Portable Company File 500
    Creating a Portable Company File 501
    Restoring a Portable Company File 501

Cleaning Up Data 502
    Understanding What Happens When
      You Clean Up Data 502
    Running the Cleanup Utility 503
Updating QuickBooks 505
    Automatic Updates 506
    Manual Updates 506
    Setting Up the QuickBooks Update Service 506

Part Five
Appendices

A Fixed Asset Manager 509
Overview of Fixed Asset Manager 510
QuickBooks Files and Fixed Asset Manager 510
    QuickBooks Company Information 511
    Company Fixed Assets List 511
Fixed Asset Manager Client File Setup 511
Importing Data from Other Software 512
Working in Fixed Asset Manager 513
    Schedule Tab 513
    Asset Tab 514
    Disposal Tab 514
    Projection Tab 514
    Using the Section 179/40% Test 514
    Using the Client Totals Summary 515
Calculating Depreciation 515
Posting the Journal Entry to QuickBooks 515
Producing Reports 515
Exporting Depreciation Data 517
Tax Worksheets 518

B Financial Statement Designer 519
Overview of Features 520
FSD and QuickBooks Data Files 520

FSD Components 521
    Financial Statement Organizer 521
    Financial Statement Editor 522
    Supporting Document Editor 523
Previewing and Printing Financial Statements and Documents 524
Export Financial Statements and Supporting Documents 524
Save Financial Statements and Documents as PDF Files 524
E-mailing Financial Statements and Supporting Documents 525

Index 527

Acknowledgments

From the publisher: Thank you to Liane Freeman, Gary Wiessenger, Katherine Morris, Tracy Stinson, Jacint Tumacder, Dawn Hughan, Shane Hamby, John Wang, Andrew Holmes, Jim St. Leger, and all the Project Managers at Intuit, Inc., for their assistance and cooperation.

From the author: I'd like to thank Megg Morin for giving me the opportunity to write this book and for really good chocolate, Tom Barich for keeping me technically accurate, and Jacint Turnacder for cheerfully seeing that I got the information I needed to complete the book and that things stayed on track. I'd like to thank the technical support staff in Tucson, AZ, for taking time out of their busy schedules to help me. I'd like to say a special thank you to Nicholas Tolstoshev for his insightful comments and untiring dedication to helping me make this a better book and for the chuckles you provided at key moments to ease my tensions. And, last, but not in any way least, heartfelt thanks to my friend and QuickBooks expert Daniel Hodge, who, over the years of our association, helped me achieve the expertise to write this book.

Introduction

How to Use This Book

This book is organized with a certain amount of logic connected to the way you'll probably use your QuickBooks software. You can consult the table of contents, where you'll notice that the topics start with the tasks you perform immediately after installing the software, move on to the tasks you perform often, and then cover the tasks you perform less frequently.

The index guides you to specific tasks and features, so when you absolutely must know immediately how to do something, it's easy to find the instructions.

What's Provided in This Book to Help You

There are some special elements in this book that you'll find extremely useful.

- **Tips**   Give you some additional insight about a subject or a task. Sometimes they're shortcuts, and sometimes they're workarounds for QuickBooks restrictions.
- **Notes**   Provide extra information about a topic or a task. Sometimes they provide information about what happens behind the scenes when you perform a task, and sometimes they have additional information you might be curious about.
- **Cautions**   Are presented to help you avoid the traps you can fall into if a task has a danger zone.
- **Sidebars**   Are filled with facts you don't necessarily need to perform a task, but the information may be helpful. Some sidebars help you understand the way QuickBooks "thinks" (all software applications have a predictable thinking pattern); others are designed to point out the way certain procedures help you run your business.

You and Your Accountant

One of the advantages of double-entry bookkeeping software like QuickBooks is that a great many simple bookkeeping tasks are performed automatically. If you've been keeping manual books or using a check-writing program such as Quicken, your accountant will probably have less work to do now that you're using QuickBooks.

Many accountants visit clients regularly or ask that copies of checkbook registers be sent to the accountants' offices. Then, using the data from the transactions, a general ledger is created, along with a trial balance and other reports based on the general ledger (Profit & Loss Statements and Balance Sheets).

If you've had such a relationship with your accountant, it ends with QuickBooks. Your accountant will only have to provide tax advice and business-planning advice. All those bookkeeping chores are performed by QuickBooks, which keeps a general ledger and provides reports based on the data in the general ledger.

Throughout this book you'll find information about general ledger postings as you create transactions in QuickBooks, and you'll also find references to specific information that is going to be important to your accountant. Accountants tend to ask questions about how software handles payroll, inventory, accounts receivable, and accounts payable. There are also a number of places in this book where you're advised to call your accountant before making a decision about how to handle a certain transaction.

Don't worry, your accountant won't complain about losing the bookkeeping tasks. Most accountants prefer to handle more professional chores, and they rarely protest when you tell them they no longer have to be bookkeepers. Their parents didn't spend all that money on their advanced, difficult education for that.

Getting Started

ongratulations on deciding to use QuickBooks to track your business finances! Accounting software such as QuickBooks has to be set up and carefully tweaked before you begin using it.

Part One of this book has two chapters. In Chapter 1, you'll learn about the focus of the Premier and Enterprise Solution editions of QuickBooks. You'll also find a summary of the new features in QuickBooks 2007. Then, in Chapter 2, you'll learn how to set up lists that form the backbone for using QuickBooks.

Introducing
QuickBooks

Several years ago, the QuickBooks group at Intuit identified an increasing need to support the business management tasks of large and growing companies who are already Intuit customers, as well as those customers joining Intuit from outside of the QuickBooks installed base. The QuickBooks Enterprise Solutions and the QuickBooks Premier product lines are the result. You have in your hands one of the most robust QuickBooks products ever delivered to the marketplace.

Both QuickBooks Premier and QuickBooks Enterprise Solutions support all basic accounting functions needed by growing and larger businesses. You can invoice customers, pay employees, and manage bill payment and inventory quickly, easily, and efficiently. While QuickBooks Premier contains most of the features also available in QuickBooks Enterprise Solutions, QuickBooks Enterprise Solutions is aimed at the larger organization that must support more than five simultaneous QuickBooks users. For example, the level of security that you can set in QuickBooks Enterprise Solutions far exceeds that available in QuickBooks Premier. QuickBooks Enterprise Solutions offers features like ODBC reporting capabilities and the ability to produce combined financial reports for multiple companies (see Chapter 15) that aren't available in QuickBooks Premier.

In addition to the General Business edition of QuickBooks, both QuickBooks Premier and QuickBooks Enterprise Solutions are available in a number of industry-specific editions:

- Accountant
- Contractor
- Mfg/Wholesale
- Nonprofit
- Professional
- Retail

The 2007 version of QuickBooks continues to offer unique features for large and growing companies:

- The installation wizard places your new or existing QuickBooks data files in Microsoft Vista-compliant locations so you are ready for the next generation of the Windows operating system.
- Creating new general ledger accounts is easier because you get extra help selecting the correct type of account.
- Significant improvements help you include reimbursable expenses on invoices.
- Price levels are now available when you create estimates.
- Improvements to the Shipping Manager make it much easier to use.
- You can resize the panes of the Customer, Vendor, and Employee Centers to make them work better in your environment.
- QuickBooks "learns" from vendor bills you enter and suggests accounts when you create a new bill.

- Improvements to the bill-paying process make it easy to determine that you paid what you intended to pay when you intended to pay it.
- Significant improvements to payroll processing make it much easier to pay your employees.
- QuickBooks helps you set up payroll liability tax payment schedules to ensure that you pay your and your payroll liabilities on time. You also can schedule payments for other company-paid payroll liabilities, such as health insurance premiums.
- The new "dividing date" feature that you set when exchanging data with your accountant make it easy for both you and your accountant to work in your QuickBooks data simultaneously.
- Backing up your data is considerably easier with the new Backup wizard.
- In addition to the time tracking features already available in QuickBooks, you can use online subscription service, QuickBooks Time Tracker, to enter time in QuickBooks.
- The Unit of Measure Conversion inventory feature enables user to apply different units of measure when purchasing or selling the same item. You can buy an item in one unit of measure, and stock and sell it in another.
- Use the specially designed Google Desktop™ engine that comes with QuickBooks to search your QuickBooks data, your computer, or the Internet.

Welcome to QuickBooks!

Setting Up Your Lists

n this chapter:

- Adding accounts to the chart of accounts
- Entering data into lists
- Inventing your own fields to make your lists more useful

In this chapter, I'm going to cover a lot of basic chores. They aren't terribly exciting or creative, but if you do them now, you'll find your work easier later. So take the time now to get the basic data into the system to make future work faster and more efficient.

 TIP: QuickBooks has a spell checker, and, when you edit some list entries, you'll see a Spelling button. Click it to check the text you entered. Then you won't have to worry about spelling errors in transactions (for instance, invoices) because you've already checked the elements.

When you view the items in a list, you can sort the list by any column in the window. Just click the column heading to sort the list by the category of that column.

Adding Accounts to the Chart of Accounts

The first priority is your chart of accounts. QuickBooks created some accounts for you during the initial setup of your company, but most people need additional accounts to keep books accurately. You set up the Chart Of Accounts first because some of the other lists you create require accounts in the Chart Of Accounts. For example, you assign the items you sell to income accounts and you assign payroll items to liability and expense accounts.

Using Numbers for Accounts

As you go through the entry of accounts, remember that I'm using numbers as the primary element in my chart of accounts. There's a title attached to the number, but the primary method of sorting my account list is by number (see "How QuickBooks Sorts Accounts"). Even though the QuickBooks default is to use names, it's a simple matter to change the default and use numbers. If you prefer to stick to names, see the next section for some hints about creating account names.

To switch to a number format for your accounts, you just need to spend a couple of seconds changing the QuickBooks preferences:

1. Choose Edit | Preferences from the menu bar to open the Preferences dialog box.
2. Select Accounting from the scroll bar in the left pane.
3. Click the Company Preferences tab.
4. Select the Use Account Numbers check box.
5. Click OK to save the changes and assign the account numbers.

If you chose a built-in chart of accounts during the EasyStep Interview, those accounts are switched to numbered accounts automatically. You may want to change some of the numbers, and you can do so by editing the accounts (see "Editing Accounts" later in this chapter). Some accounts (those you added yourself during or after the interview) have to be edited manually to turn them into numbered accounts; QuickBooks doesn't automatically number them.

When you select the option to use account numbers, the option Show Lowest Subaccount Only becomes accessible (it's grayed out if you haven't opted for account numbers). This option tells QuickBooks to display only the subaccount on transaction windows instead of both the parent account and the subaccount, making it easier to see precisely which account is receiving the posting. (Subaccounts, and details about this feature to display them alone, are discussed later in the section "Using Subaccounts.")

If all your accounts aren't numbered and you select Show Lowest Subaccount Only, when you click OK QuickBooks displays an error message that you cannot enable this option until all your accounts have numbers assigned. After you've edited existing accounts that need numbers (any accounts that QuickBooks didn't automatically number for you), you can return to this Preferences window and enable the Show Lowest Subaccount Only option.

I believe that a numbered chart of accounts helps you, your bookkeeper, and your accountant work more efficiently and easily. If you assign ranges of numbers to account types, numbers can give you a quick clue about the type of account with which you're working. In QuickBooks, you'll find predefined charts of accounts that use a structure like the one shown in Table 2-1; this structure uses five-digit numbers and is friendly and easy to use.

 NOTE: Some companies use four-digit numbers in their structure and there's no "right" answer here. A five-digit structure like the one QuickBooks uses gives you more room to grow and add accounts.

Using a numbering scheme like this one leaves a lot of room (unused numbers) for further breakdowns, especially in the expenses. Most companies need more expense categories than any other category.

Usually, you should add accounts by increasing the previous account number by 100; if your first bank account is 10000, the next bank account is 10100, and so on. This gives you room to squeeze in additional accounts that belong in the same general area of your chart of accounts when they need to be added later.

I also try to alphabetize my accounts within any account type range; that is, all of my expense accounts appear in alphabetical order within the 60000 to 69999 range, and all of my income accounts appear in alphabetical order within the 40000 to 49999 range. Alphabetizing the accounts within an account number range makes finding a particular account easier when you view reports that don't list account numbers, such as the Profit & Loss report.

Naming Accounts

Even if you enable account numbers, you have to give each account a name. I suggest that you establish a company-wide standard for naming accounts.

Your standard should be clear, so that, when everyone follows the standard, the account naming convention is consistent. Why is this important? Because when

# Range		# of Accts	Acct Type
10000	14999	4999	Bank
15000	15999	999	Accounts Receivable
16000	16999	999	Other Current Asset
17000	18999	1999	Fixed Asset
19000	19999	999	Other Asset
20000	20999	999	Accounts Payable
21000	23999	2999	Credit Card
24000	26999	2999	Other Current Liability
27000	29999	2999	Long Term Liability
30000	39999	9999	Equity
40000	49999	9999	Income
50000	59999	9999	Cost of Goods Sold
60000	69999	9999	Expense
70000	79999	9999	Other Income
80000	89999	9999	Other Expense
90000	99999	9999	Nonposting

TABLE 2-1   Account Numbering Structure used by QuickBooks

I visit clients who haven't invented and enforced standards, I find accounts with names such as:

- Telephone Exp
- Exps-Telephone
- Tele Expense
- Telephone
- Tele

And, it isn't surprising to find that every one of those accounts has amounts posted to them. If you establish account naming standards, you can avoid the errors introduced by a variety of individuals making up names without realizing that accounts already exist.

Here are a few suggestions for your standards—feel free to amend them to fit your own situation or invent different standards that better suit your purposes. Consistency is the goal:

➡ **FYI**

How QuickBooks Sorts Accounts

- By default, QuickBooks sorts your chart of accounts by account type. That's why you can select the numbering schemes for the default account structures as you create a new company group account type within a number range. Assets:
- Bank
- Accounts Receivable
- Other Current Asset
- Fixed Asset
- Other Asset
- Liabilities
- Accounts Payable
- Credit Card
- Other Current Liability
- Long-Term Liability
- Equity
- Income
- Cost of Goods Sold
- Expense
- Other Income
- Other Expense
- Nonposting Accounts

QuickBooks automatically creates nonposting accounts when you enable features that use those account types: Estimates, Sales Orders, and Purchase Orders. Nonposting accounts store information but don't affect account balances in your company.

- Avoid apostrophes.
- Avoid abbreviations when possible.
- When abbreviations can't be avoided, set the number of characters for abbreviations. For example, if you permit four characters, telephone is abbreviated "tele"; a three-character rule produces "tel."
- Decide whether to use the ampersand (&) or a hyphen. For example, is it "repairs & maintenance" or "repairs-maintenance"?
- Decide whether spaces are allowed. For example, would you have "repairs & maintenance" or "repairs&maintenance"?

Using Subaccounts

Subaccounts provide a way to post transactions more precisely using subcategories for main account categories. For example, if you create an expense account for insurance expenses, you may want to have subaccounts for vehicle insurance, liability insurance, equipment insurance, and so on. Post transactions only to the subaccounts, never to the parent account. When you create reports, QuickBooks displays the individual totals for the subaccounts, along with the grand total for the parent account. To create a subaccount, you must first create the parent account, as described in the section, "Creating Subaccounts," later in this chapter.

If you're using numbered accounts, when you set up your main (parent) accounts, be sure to leave enough open numbers to be able to fit in all the subaccounts you'll need; plan to increment subaccount numbers by ten. For example, suppose you have the following parent accounts:

- 60100 Insurance
- 60200 Utilities
- 60300 Travel

You can create the following subaccounts:

- 60110 Insurance:Vehicles
- 60120 Insurance:Liability
- 60130 Insurance:Equipment
- 60210 Utilities:Heat
- 60220 Utilities:Electric
- 60310 Travel:Sales
- 60320 Travel:Seminars and Meetings

The colon in the account names listed here is added automatically by QuickBooks to indicate a relationship between a parent account and a subaccount—you only have to create the subaccount name and number.

In addition, QuickBooks supports two views of your lists: the hierarchical view and the flat view. In the Chart Of Accounts window, the difference between these views becomes apparent when you set up and view subaccounts. The flat view (see Figure 2-1) simply lists accounts while the hierarchical view provides a visual cue about the relationship of one account to another (see Figure 2-2). By clicking the Account button and selecting the desired view, you can switch between these two views.

 TIP: When you view the Customers & Jobs list in the Customer Center, the hierarchical view provides a visual cue about the relationship of jobs and a customer.

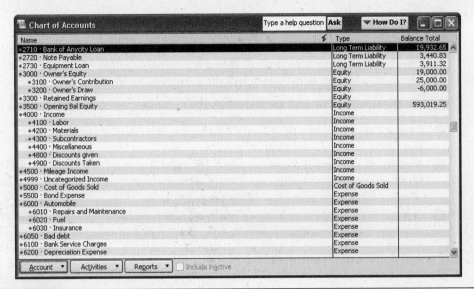

FIGURE 2-1 Viewing the Chart Of Accounts window in flat view lists your accounts

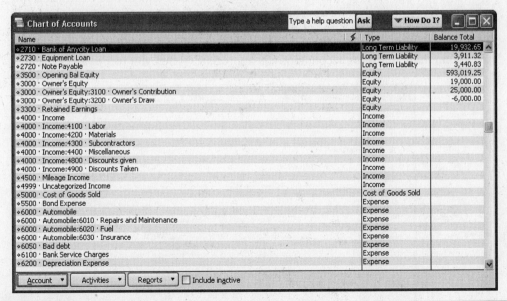

FIGURE 2-2 Viewing the Chart Of Accounts window in hierarchical view shows you the relationship between accounts and subaccounts

Adding Accounts

After you've done your homework, made your decisions, created your standards, and checked with your accountant, adding accounts is simple. When you add a new account, a wizard helps you select the correct account type.

Follow these steps to add an account:

1 Press CTRL-A (or click the Chart Of Accounts icon on the Home page) to open the Chart Of Accounts window.

2 Press CTRL-N to enter a new account. The New Account: Select Account Type window appears, providing more information about types of accounts to make it easier for you to select the correct account type.

3 Select a Type for the account you want to create and click Continue. The New Account dialog box appears for the type of account you selected (see Figure 2-3).

Because different types of accounts require different information, the dialog box you use to create a new account changes its appearance based on the account type you select. To create a new account, you must provide the account type, a name, and, if you've enabled account numbers, the account number. The Note field, which only appears on some account types, and the Description field are optional.

Some account types (for example, accounts connected to banks) have a field for an opening balance. I recommend that you not enter data in that field when you're creating an account; instead, see Chapter 14 for details on entering opening balances for various types of accounts. I recommend an alternate procedure for opening balances that helps you track the details of the opening balance—something that your accountant will appreciate. When you record an opening

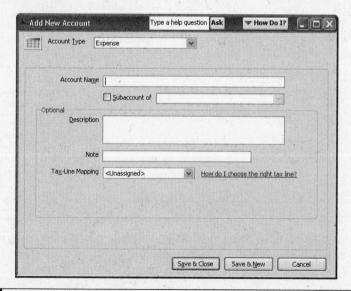

FIGURE 2-3   Use this window to complete creating a new account

balance using the Opening Balance field as you set up an account, QuickBooks posts the amount you enter to the account. Then, being a double-entry accounting system, QuickBooks needs to post the other side of the transaction to an account, and QuickBooks has no way of knowing what account to use, so QuickBooks uses a default account named Opening Bal Equity. Eventually, the amount in the Opening Bal Equity account becomes a huge number, and nobody can easily figure out what makes up that number. Accountants prefer being able to trace the balance of an account back to transactions, so please see Chapter 14 for details on entering opening balances for accounts.

As you finish entering each account, click Save & New to display another blank New Account window. When you're finished entering accounts, click Save & Close, and then close the Chart Of Accounts window by clicking the X in the upper-right corner.

 TIP: You can create up to 10,000 accounts in QuickBooks. To check to see how many accounts you have, press F2 while viewing the Chart Of Accounts window. In the List Information list box, you'll see the total number of accounts currently defined.

Editing Accounts

If you need to make changes to any account information (including adding a number after you enable numbered accounts), select the account in the Chart Of Accounts list, and press CTRL-E. The Edit Account window appears; this dialog box closely resembles the New Account window you used in the preceding section. In this window, you can select the Account Is Inactive option, which means the account won't be available for posting amounts while you're entering transactions; use this feature if you don't want anyone to post transactions to the account at the moment. Inactive accounts don't appear on the account drop-down list when you're filling out transaction windows. Make your changes and click OK to save them.

Creating Subaccounts

To create a subaccount, you must have already created the parent account.

Now take these steps:

1. Open the Chart of Accounts list.
2. Press CTRL-N to create a new account.
3. Select the appropriate account type.
4. In the drop-down box next to the check box, select the parent account.
5. If you're using numbered accounts, enter an account number.
6. Name the account.
7. Click the Subaccount Of check box to place a check mark in it (see Figure 2-4).
8. Click OK.

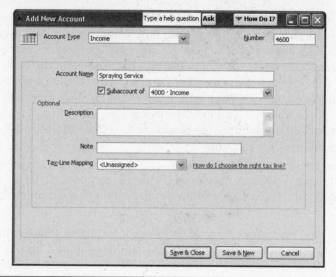

FIGURE 2-4   Use this window to create subaccounts

You can have multiple levels of subaccounts. For example, you may want to track income in the following manner:

Income

- Income:Consulting
  - Income:Consulting:Engineering
  - Income:Consulting:Training
- Income:Products
  - Income:Products:Technical
  - Income:Products:Accessories

You create the sub-subaccounts the same way you create the first level, making sure you've already created the first-level subaccounts (which are the parents of the sub-subaccounts). In the New Account dialog box, after you check the Subaccount check box, select the appropriate subaccount to act as the parent account.

When you view the Chart Of Accounts window, subaccounts appear indented under their parent accounts. When you view a subaccount in a transaction window, it appears in the following format:

- ParentAccount:Subaccount or
- ParentAccount:Subaccount:Subaccount.

For example, if you create a parent account named Income with a subaccount Consulting, and then use the combination in a transaction, the Account field shows Income:Consulting. If you've used numbers, the Account field shows 4000-Income: 4001-Consulting. Because many of the fields in transaction windows are small, you may not be able to see the subaccount names without scrolling through each account. It's much easier to work if only the subaccount name is displayed, and that's the point of enabling the preference Show Lowest Subaccount Only, discussed earlier in the section "Creating a Full Chart Of Accounts."

Merging Accounts

Sometimes you have two accounts that should be one. For instance, you may have accidentally created two accounts for the same purpose. As I discussed earlier in this chapter, I've been to client sites that had accounts named Telephone and Tele, with transactions posted to both accounts. You can merge those accounts to combine their balances into one account that you will use going forward. To merge accounts, they must be of the same account type and you must be working in single-user mode.

 N O T E : For a complete list of activities that must be completed in single-user mode, see Chapter 20.

Take the following steps to merge two accounts:

1. Open the Chart Of Accounts window.
2. Click the account that has the name you *do not* want to use going forward.
3. Press CTRL-E to open the Edit Account dialog box.
4. Change the account name and number to match the account you want to keep.
5. Click OK.
6. QuickBooks displays a dialog box telling you that the account number or name you've entered already exists for another account and asks if you want to merge the accounts. Click Yes to confirm that you want to merge the two accounts.

Customers and Jobs

QuickBooks handles customers and jobs together. You can create a customer and consider anything and everything you invoice to that customer a single job, or you can set up multiple jobs for the same customer.

Some businesses don't worry about jobs; they track only the customer. But if you're a building contractor or subcontractor, an interior decorator, a consultant, or some other kind of service provider who usually bills by the job instead of at an hourly rate for an ongoing service, you should track jobs.

Jobs don't stand alone as an entity; they are attached to customers, and you can attach as many jobs to a single customer as necessary. If you are going to track jobs, it's a good idea to enter all the customers first, and then attach the jobs later. If you enter your existing customers now, when you're first starting to use QuickBooks, all the other work connected to the customer is much easier.

TIP: Don't feel overwhelmed about getting all your customer information into QuickBooks. Many people enter just the customer name, company name, terms and sales tax information; the rest of the information is helpful but not required, so you can supply it later, as you have time.

Setting Up a New Customer

Every customer you create appears in a list of customers and jobs. To view this list of customers and jobs—and add to it—open the Customer Center (see Figure 2-5) by clicking the Customer Center icon on the Icon Bar.

 NOTE: Prior to QuickBooks 2006, this list appeared in a different format and was available on the Lists menu. The newer expanded format gives you more information about each customer in one place. You also won't find a Vendor List or an Employee List per se in QuickBooks 2007; they have been relocated to the Vendor Center and the Employee Center, respectively. Throughout the book, I'll refer to these lists; I'm using the term "list" to help you understand that I'm referring to the list that appears in the Customer Center, Vendor Center, or Employee Center.

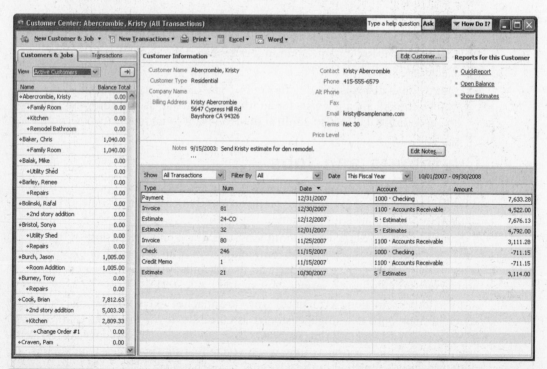

FIGURE 2-5   Your list of customers and their associated jobs appears in the Customer & Jobs tab of the Customer Center

In transaction windows and dialog boxes, any field that requires the entry of a customer or job is labeled Customer:Job.

You can open the Customer Center using any of the following methods:

- Click the Customer Center icon on the QuickBooks toolbar.
- Click the Customers icon on the left side of the Home page.
- Press CTRL-J.

Putting all your existing customers into the system takes very little effort. To create a new customer, follow these steps:

1 In the Customer Center, select the Customers & Jobs tab to display your list of customers.

2 Press CTRL-N (or click the New Customer & Job button above the Customers & Jobs tab and select New Customer) to open the New Customer dialog box (see Figure 2-6) and fill in the information.

The New Customer dialog box contains four tabs of information; in the sections that follow, I'm going to describe three of them: the Address Info tab, the Additional Info tab, and the Payment Info tab. I'm going to delay discussion of the Job Info tab until later in this chapter, in the section "Entering Jobs."

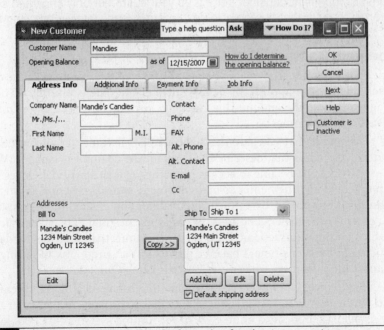

FIGURE 2-6   You can enter quite a bit of information for about your customer

NOTE: Some people prefer to enter just the customer name and company name when they're creating their customer lists and then fill in the rest of the information described in the following sections at their leisure or the first time they invoice the customer.

Address Info Tab

The New Customer window opens with the Address Info tab in the foreground. The first field to enter information is the Customer Name field. Consider this field a code rather than a customer name. It doesn't appear on your invoices or other sales transactions, but it does appear on QuickBooks reports. (The transactions use the data in the Company Name field.)

Customer Name Field

You should create a standard for the Customer Name field so that you set up every customer in the same manner; I suggest that you avoid punctuation. The information stored in the Customer Name field must be unique. And, although you have 41 characters in the Customer Name field, I suggest you keep the name recognizable but brief to minimize space used by the name on reports.

 NOTE: If you do a lot of different types of work for one customer named Johnson, you might consider setting up your customer only once and setting up different jobs for that customer. See "Entering Jobs" later in this chapter.

Opening Balance Field

QuickBooks makes an Opening Balance field available, along with the date for which this balance applies (by default, the current date is inserted). The field is designed to hold the amount this customer currently owes (if an open balance exists for the customer).

I recommend that you skip this field because, if you enter an amount, you'll have no detailed records that describe the basis for the customer's balance. Without these records, you won't be able to accept payments against specific invoices. It's better to skip this field and then enter as many invoices as necessary to post this customer's balance to your books, using the original dates you created those transactions when you enter those invoices and bills. By using the original date, you retain aging for the outstanding transactions. Entering transactions that describe the details associated with a customer's balance is the most accurate way of setting up existing balances for customers when you first start using QuickBooks.

As a side note, when you record an opening balance using the Opening Balance field on the customer record, QuickBooks posts the amount you enter to Accounts Receivable. Then, being a double-entry accounting system, QuickBooks needs to post the other side of the transaction to an account. QuickBooks has no way of knowing what income account to use, so QuickBooks uses a default account named Opening Bal Equity. Eventually, the amount in the Opening Bal Equity account becomes a huge number, and nobody can easily figure out what transactions make up the number. Accountants prefer being able to trace the balance of an account back to transactions, so please enter individual transactions for open balances.

Customer Address Info

In the Company and Addresses sections of the window, enter the company name, optionally enter a contact, and enter the billing address. Add any other contact information you want to track for this customer (telephone, e-mail, and so on).

Ship To Addresses

You can maintain multiple shipping addresses for your customers. Each shipping address has a name (title), so you can select it from a drop-down list when you're entering sales transactions.

If the shipping address isn't different from the billing address (or if you have a service business and never ship products), you can ignore the shipping address field, or use the Copy button to display the Add Ship To Address Information with address block information already filled in; click OK to copy that information into the Ship To field.

To add another shipping address, open the Ship To drop-down list and click Add New. QuickBooks displays the Add Ship To Address Information dialog box. Give this Ship To address a name, and enter the address information. QuickBooks enters the name Ship To 1, but that's merely a placeholder. Replace that text with a name that reminds you of the address location, which will make it easier to select this address from a drop-down list when you have to ship goods to this address.

Specify whether this address should be the default Ship To address, and click OK. Then, if necessary, enter another Ship To address for this customer.

Additional Info Tab

The information you enter on the Additional Info tab (see Figure 2-7) of any customer record ranges from essential to convenient. Prepopulating the fields with information makes your work go faster when you're filling out transaction windows, and it makes it easier to create in-depth reports. It's worth spending the time to design some rules for the way data is entered. (Remember, making rules ensures consistency, without which you'll have difficulty getting the reports you want.)

 N O T E :   The fields you see on the Additional Info tab may not be the same as the fields shown here. The preferences you configure (for example, whether you track sales tax) determine the available fields.

Let's spend a minute going over the fields in this tab. Most of the fields also appear in various QuickBooks lists, and if you haven't already entered items in those lists, you can do so as you fill out the fields in the New Customer dialog box. For each field that also appears in a list, you'll find an entry named <Add New>

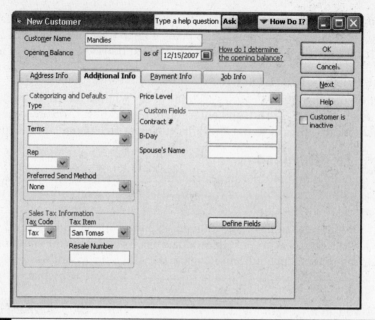

FIGURE 2-7   Entering additional customer information makes your work in QuickBooks go faster

when you click the drop-down arrow beside the field. Selecting the <Add New>
entry opens the appropriate new blank entry window.

Type

Use the Type field to sort your customers by a type you find important or
convenient when you create reports. QuickBooks maintains a Type list (see the
section "Customer Type List" later in this chapter). For example, you may want to
consider wholesale and retail customers as your customer types. To use the field,
click the arrow to select a type that you already entered, or click <Add New> to
create a new type.

Terms

Terms, of course, refers to payment terms. Click the arrow to the right of the text
box to see the terms that QuickBooks already defined, or choose <Add New> to
define a new one.

QuickBooks uses the terms in the Terms List for both customers and vendors,
and you may need to establish additional terms to meet your needs. See the section
"Terms List" later in this chapter to learn how to create different types of terms.

Rep

Use this field to assign a sales representative to your customer. It's useful to make this assignment whether you pay commissions or you just want to know who is in charge of this customer. Sales reps can be employees, vendors, or "other names" (which means the name is entered in the Other Names List). Select a rep from the list of reps or add a new rep by choosing <Add New>. See the section "Sales Rep List" for more information on populating this list.

Preferred Send Method

This field stores the default value for the way you want to send invoices, statements, or estimates to this customer. The choices are:

- None, which means no special features are used to send the documents. You print them and you mail them.
- E-mail, which means you e-mail the documents. This feature lets you attach the documents as PDF files to an e-mail message. The processes involved are managed within QuickBooks, using a QuickBooks server for sending the e-mail. Chapter 3 has the details.
- Mail, which lets you use a QuickBooks service to mail the invoices. The data is reproduced on a form that has a tear-off portion for your customers to enclose with their payment. See Appendix B for information about this QuickBooks service.

Regardless of the method you choose as your default, you can use any send method when you're creating a transaction.

Sales Tax Information

If you've configured QuickBooks to collect sales tax, the sales tax information uses three fields. If the customer is liable for sales tax, select the appropriate sales tax item for this customer, or create a new sales tax item. If the customer does not pay sales tax, select Non and enter the Resale Number provided by the customer (this is handy to have when the state tax investigators pop in for a surprise audit). See Chapter 7 for a complete discussion of sales tax codes and sales tax items.

Price Level

You can use price levels to create a pricing scheme, which usually involves special discounts that you want to use when you sell to this customer. Select an existing price level or create a new one. See the section "Price Level List" to learn about creating and assigning price levels.

Custom Fields

You can use custom fields to store specialized information and to sort and arrange your QuickBooks lists in various ways. See the section "Using Custom Fields" later in this chapter.

Payment Info Tab

Use the Payment Info tab to store the account number you assign to your customers (if you assign numbers), credit limit information, and preferred payment method information (see Figure 2-8).

Account No.

This is an optional field you can use to assign numbers to your customers.

Credit Limit

Use the *credit limit* field to set a threshold for a customer's unpaid balance. If the customer places an order, and the new order combined with any unpaid invoices exceeds the threshold, QuickBooks displays a warning. By default, QuickBooks won't prevent you from continuing to sell to and invoice the customer, but you should consider rejecting the order (or shipping it COD).

 T I P : If you aren't going to enforce the credit limit, don't bother to use the field.

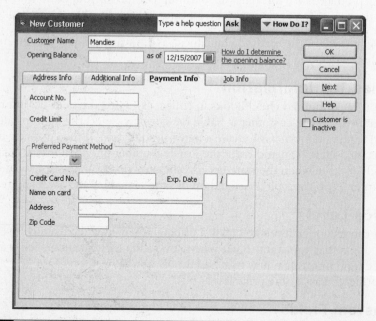

FIGURE 2-8 This tab puts all the important information about customer finances in one place

Preferred Payment Method

This field refers to the customer's preferred method for paying your invoices. A list of payment methods appears in the drop-down list. You can select the appropriate item from the list or add a new one by selecting <Add New>. See the section "Payment Method List" later in this chapter for more information.

 TIP: The payment method you select automatically appears in the Receive Payments window when you select this customer. You can change the payment method at that time, if necessary.

Credit Card No.

If the customer's preferred payment method is a credit card, you can use this field to store the customer's credit card number but not the credit card's three-digit security code—and there's a good reason that QuickBooks doesn't let you store the security code. In fact, I recommend that you not fill in the credit card field; in addition to the potential security problems posed by storing your customer's credit card numbers, the laws (both government and merchant-card providers) about keeping credit card numbers on file are changing. For the safety and protection of both you and your customer, I suggest that you skip this field.

I'm skipping the Job Info tab because there's a full discussion on entering jobs later in this chapter. When you have finished filling out the fields, choose Next to set up another customer. When you have finished setting up all of your customers, click OK.

Editing Customer Records

You can make changes to the information in a customer record quite easily. Click the Customer Center to display the Customers & Jobs List and double-click the customer record you want to change. You also can select the listing and click the Edit Customer button, or press CTRL-E.

In the Edit Customer dialog box, you can change any information or fill in data you didn't enter when you first created the customer.

The Edit Customer dialog box contains a Notes button that you can click to open a Notepad window dedicated to this customer. You can use this Notepad to store any information about the customer that you find useful. You can use the Notepad as a marketing tool recording notes to follow up on a promised order, track a customer's special preferences, or notify the customer when something special is available. When you view the Customers & Jobs List, an Edit Notes button appears in the Customer Information pane of the Customer Center. You can open the Notepad for the selected customer by clicking the button; you don't have to open the customer record to get to the note.

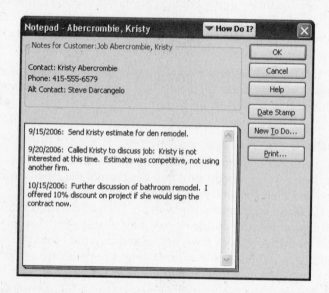

Working with the Vendor List

You'll find it easiest to enter the vendors from whom you purchase goods and services into QuickBooks when you first set up your QuickBooks company rather than when you want to enter a vendor bill or write a check.

To display the Vendor List, open the Vendor Center by clicking its icon on the toolbar, or by clicking the Vendor icon on the left side of the Home page. Click the Vendor tab to display the list. Press CTRL-N (or click the New Vendor button above the list) to open the New Vendor dialog box and fill out the fields (see Figure 2-9).

As with customers, you should have a set of standards about entering the information in the Vendor Name field. This field doesn't appear on checks or purchase orders, but QuickBooks uses it on reports and when sorting and selecting in the Vendor List. As with customers, I recommend that you avoid punctuation and use a name that will mean something to you while viewing reports.

As I discussed when setting up new customers, you should not enter anything into the Opening Balance field; instead, enter as many invoices as necessary to establish your current outstanding balance with the vendor. Using this technique, you have details about your outstanding opening balance with the vendor.

The Name and Address block is important if you're planning to print checks and the vendor doesn't enclose a return envelope. If you supply an address, QuickBooks prints that address on the check; you can then insert the check in a window envelope, and the vendor name and address block will appear in the right spots.

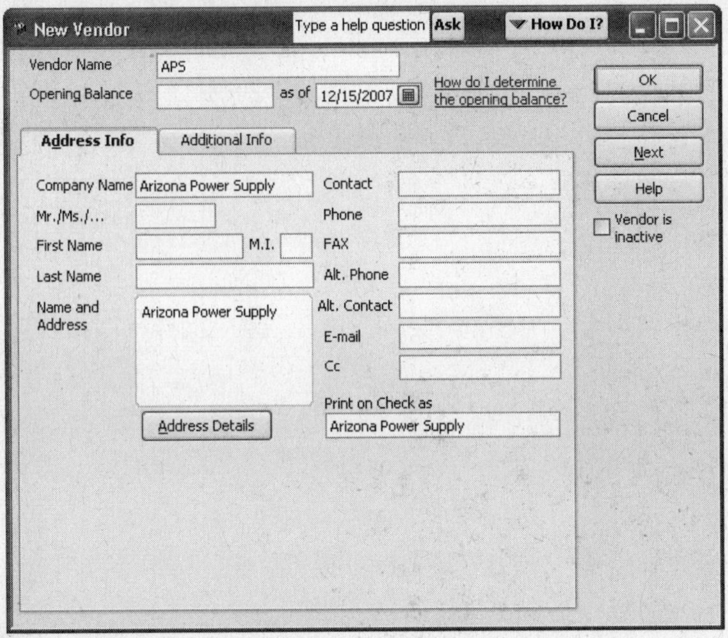

FIGURE 2-9   As with customers, you store vendor address information

The Additional Info tab for vendors has several important categories (see Figure 2-10):

- **Account No.**   Enter your account number with this vendor (to the vendor, it's your customer number), and the number will appear in the memo field of printed checks.

- **Type**   Select a type or create one. This optional field is handy if you want to sort vendors by type, which makes reports more efficient. For example, you can create vendor types for inventory suppliers, tax authorities, and so on.

- **Terms**   Enter the terms for payment this vendor has assigned to you.

- **Credit Limit**   Enter the credit limit this vendor has given you.

- **Tax ID**   Use this field to enter the social security number or EIN if this vendor receives a Form 1099.

- **Vendor Eligible For 1099**   If appropriate, select this check box.

- **Custom Fields**   As with customers, you can create custom fields for vendors (see the section "Using Custom Fields" later in this chapter).

- **Billing Rate Level**   If you use QuickBooks Enterprise or the Contractor, Professional, or Accountant Edition of QuickBooks Premier, you can assign a billing rate level. For more information, see the last section of this chapter.

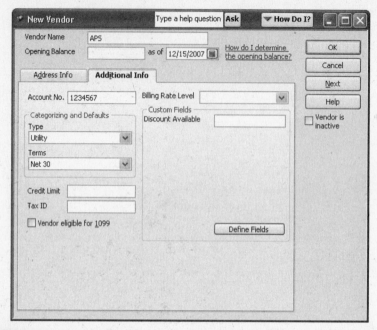

FIGURE 2-10   Add information to this tab to make producing checks and reports easier

After you fill in the information, choose Next to set up the next vendor. When you're finished, click OK.

When you view or edit a vendor's information by selecting the vendor's listing and pressing CTRL-E, you'll find a Notes button just like the one in the Edit Customer dialog box. You can use it in the same way.

Setting Up Payroll Lists

If you plan to use QuickBooks for payroll, you must enter all of your employees, including their pertinent tax information. To do that, you have to define the tax information, which requires you to define the items that make up the payroll check. This means you have three lists to create—the pay schedules, the payroll items and the employees.

For the following discussion, I'm assuming that you have set up all the vendors who receive checks from the payroll system in your Vendor List—the IRS, the state and local tax authorities, the medical insurance companies, pension providers, and so on. And, I'm assuming that you have set up all payroll accounts needed to process payroll on your Chart Of Accounts.

Creating Pay Schedules

Pay schedules, new to QuickBooks 2007, enable you to establish schedules on which you pay employees. You create a pay schedule from the Pay Schedule List; choose Lists | Pay Schedule List and then press CTRL-N to open the Edit Pay Schedule dialog box. For details on setting up pay schedules, see Chapter 8.

Create one pay schedule for each group of employees you need to pay; in most cases, you'll group your employees by pay frequency. QuickBooks displays each pay schedule that you create on the Payroll tab of the Employee Center to remind you when payroll is due, but the value of the pay schedule goes beyond serving as a reminder. In addition to creating the pay schedule, you also assign one pay schedule to each employee. Then, when you pay employees, you select a pay schedule and QuickBooks selects for payment only the employees assigned to that schedule. You assign a pay schedule to an employee when you enter or edit the employee's information, described later in this chapter in the section "Entering Employees."

Entering Payroll Items

The number of individual elements that go into a paycheck varies, depending on factors such as whether you pay salaried employees, hourly employees or both, whether you offer benefits, and which ones, and so on. Consider this list, which is typical of many businesses:

- Salaries
- Wages (hourly)
- Overtime
- Double-time
- Federal tax withholdings (including FIT, FICA, and Medicare)
- State tax withholdings
- State unemployment and disability withholdings
- Local tax withholdings
- Pension plan deductions
- Medical insurance deductions
- Life insurance deductions
- Garnishes
- Union dues
- Reimbursement for auto expenses
- Bonuses
- Commissions
- Vacation pay
- Sick pay
- Advanced Earned Income Credit

In addition, you have to track company-paid payroll items, such as matching FICA and Medicare, employer contributions to unemployment (both state and federal), state disability funds, pension and medical benefit plans.

To calculate payroll properly, you need to define each payroll item and link it to an account on the Chart Of Accounts. The vendors who receive payroll-related payments—for example, the government and insurance companies—should be set up as vendors so that you can assign them to the appropriate payroll item.

You cannot create payroll items until you've enabled payroll and signed up for a payroll service (covered in Chapter 8). During enrollment, some payroll items were added to the list automatically. Once you've completed enrollment, you can create payroll items. To view payroll items, choose Lists | Payroll Item List to open the Payroll Item List window (see Figure 2-11).

State and local taxes, medical benefits deductions, and other payroll items may not appear in the list, but you can add a new item by pressing CTRL-N while viewing the Payroll Item List to open the Add New Payroll Item wizard.

 TIP: You can use the Payroll Setup wizard, covered in Chapter 8, to walk you through setting up all the elements and components involved in setting up payroll.

Item Name	Type	Amount	Annual Limit	Tax Tracking	Payable To	Account ID
Salary	Yearly Salary			Compensation		
Sick Salary	Yearly Salary			Compensation		
Vacation Salary	Yearly Salary			Compensation		
Overtime Rate	Hourly Wage			Compensation		
Regular Pay	Hourly Wage			Compensation		
Sick Hourly	Hourly Wage			Compensation		
Vacation Hourly	Hourly Wage			Compensation		
Bonus	Bonus	0.00		Compensation		
Mileage Reimb.	Addition	0.32		Compensation		
Health Insurance	Deduction		-1,200.00	None	Sergeant Insu...	
Workers Compen...	Company Contr...			None	State Fund	
Advance Earned ...	Federal Tax			Advance EIC P...	Great Statewi...	00-7904153
Federal Unemplo...	Federal Tax	0.8%	7,000.00	FUTA	Great Statewi...	00-7904153
Federal Withhold...	Federal Tax			Federal	Great Statewi...	00-7904153
Medicare Company	Federal Tax	1.45%		Comp. Medicare	Great Statewi...	00-7904153
Medicare Employee	Federal Tax	1.45%		Medicare	Great Statewi...	00-7904153
Social Security C...	Federal Tax	6.2%	94,200.00	Comp. SS Tax	Great Statewi...	00-7904153
Social Security E...	Federal Tax	6.2%	-94,200.00	SS Tax	Great Statewi...	00-7904153
CA - Withholding	State Withholdi...			SWH	Employment D...	987-6543-2
CA - Disability E...	State Disability ...	0.8%	-79,418.00	SDI	Employment D...	987-6543-2
CA - Unemploym...	State Unemplo...	5.25%	7,000.00	Comp. SUI	Employment D...	987-6543-2
CA - Employee T...	Other Tax	0.1%	7,000.00	Co. Paid Other ...	Employment D...	987-6543-2
Direct Deposit	Direct Deposit			None		

FIGURE 2-11   The payroll items you create appear in the Payroll Item List window

Step through the Add New Payroll Item wizard, making selections and answering questions. Use the following guidelines as you enter payroll items:

- Check everything with your accountant.
- QuickBooks already has information on many state taxes, so check for your state before you add the information manually.
- You'll probably have to enter your local (city or township) taxes manually, because QuickBooks only has built-in information on a few cities.
- If your business is a C corporation or a Subchapter S corporation, you need to separate compensation for corporate officers from the compensation for other employees for tax-reporting purposes. To handle this need in QuickBooks, create a separate Earnings item called Officer Compensation and assign it to its own expense account. Then assign this Earnings item to each company officer.
- For deductions, company contributions, and federal, state, and local taxes, the wizard will ask for the agency to which you pay the liability; select the vendor that receives the money for the deduction.
- If you want the employer contributions to pension, health insurance, life insurance, and so on to appear on the payroll check stubs, you must enter those items as payroll items.
- When you enter a pension deduction, you must specify the taxes that QuickBooks should calculate *after* deducting the payroll item (see Figure 2-12). If you forget one, the paychecks and deductions may be incorrect. Some plans permit employees to choose between pre- and post-tax deductions. Some states have pre-tax deduction allowances.

When you have entered all your payroll items, you're ready to move on to the next step in entering your payroll information: employees.

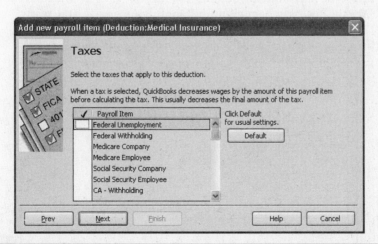

FIGURE 2-12 As you set up deduction payroll items, you'll see a screen like this one, where you determine whether a deduction is pre-tax or post-tax

Establish Employee Default Information

There is a great deal of information to fill out for each employee, and some of it is probably the same for all or most of your employees. For example, you may have many employees who share the same hourly wage or the same deductions for medical insurance.

To avoid entering the same information over and over, you can set up default information for QuickBooks to apply to all the employees you set up after establishing the defaults. You'll save yourself lots of time, even if some employees require you to edit one or two entries that differ from the defaults.

To display the Employee Defaults dialog box (see Figure 2-13), open the Employee Center by clicking the Employee Center icon on the toolbar, or choose Employees | Employee Center from the menu bar. Then, click the Manage Employee Information button at the top of the window, and choose Change New Employee Default Settings from the menu that appears.

The information you put into the template appears by default on the Payroll Info tab for each new employee you create (discussed in the next section, "Entering Employees"), so enter the data that applies to most or all of your employees in the Employee Defaults dialog box.

- Click in the Item Name column of the Earnings box, and then click the arrow to see a list of wage types that you've defined in your Payroll Items List. Select the one that applies to most of your employees.

- In the Hourly/Annual Rate column, enter a wage or annual salary figure if there's one that applies to most of your employees. If there's not, just skip it and enter each employee's rate on the individual employee record later.

- Use the arrow to the right of the Pay Period field to see a list of choices and select the payroll frequency you use most often. The available choices are Daily, Weekly, Biweekly, Semimonthly, Monthly, Quarterly, and Yearly.

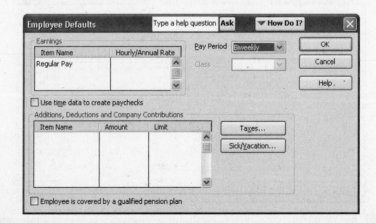

FIGURE 2-13   Establish payroll items that you assign to most of your employees

- Use the Class field if you've enabled classes to track data. (See Chapter 20 for information on using classes.)

- If you're using QuickBooks' time-tracking features to pay employees, you also see a check box labeled Use Time Data To Create Paychecks. Put a check mark in the check box to enable the feature if you pay most of your employees based on the hours they work. (See Chapter 19 to learn how to transfer time tracking into your payroll records.)

- If all or most of your employees have the same additional adjustments (such as insurance deductions, 401(k) deductions, or reimbursement for car expenses), click in the Item Name column in the Additions, Deductions And Company Contributions box, and then click the arrow to select the appropriate adjustments.

- Click the Taxes button to open the Taxes Defaults dialog, and select those taxes that are common and therefore suited for the template (usually all or most of them).

- Click the Sick/Vacation button to set the terms for accruing sick time and vacation time if your policy is similar enough among employees to include it in the template.

When you have finished filling out the template, click OK to save it.

Entering Employees

You're now ready to tell QuickBooks about each of your employees. Select the Employees tab in the Employee Center, and press CTRL-N to open the New Employee dialog box (see Figure 2-14).

 NOTE: You may see a message, asking if you want assistance adding the employee. If you click Yes, QuickBooks opens a browser window, where you can try out the Employee Organizer, service that helps you remain in compliance with state and federal employment laws. For Enterprise users, the Employee Organizer is included in the product. Premier users pay a fee to use the Employee Organizer service.

Personal Info appears in the Change Tabs drop-down list at the top of the dialog box.

 NOTE: Enterprise users automatically see the fields on the right side of this tab because they are associated with the Employee Organizer. By default, Premier users don't see these fields or the Marital Status, U.S. Citizen, or Ethnicity fields. The fields are added to the Premier Editions if a Premier user subscribes to the Employee Organizer service.

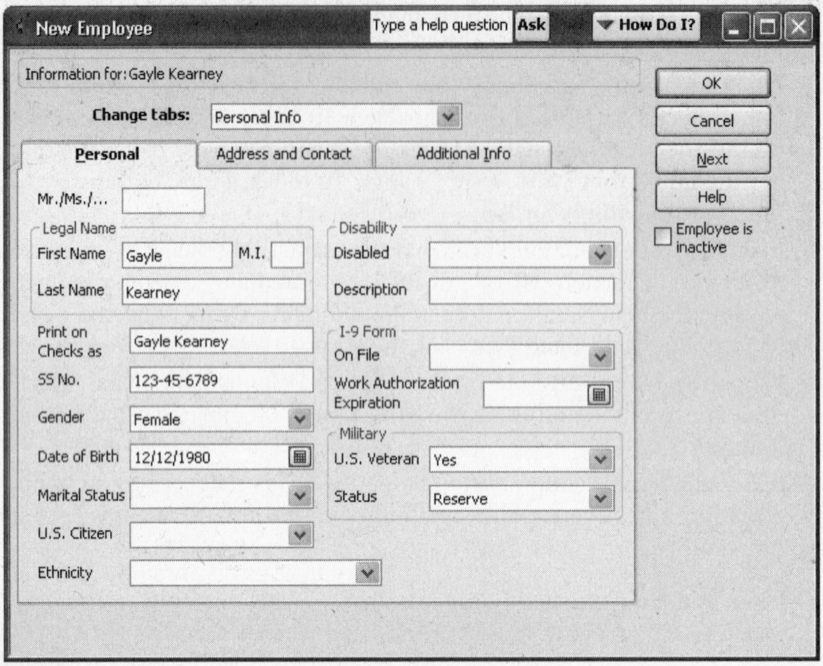

FIGURE 2-14   Use this dialog box to set up a new employee

Initially, you see three tabs in the New Employee dialog box: Personal, Address And Contact, and Additional Info. Use the drop-down list in the Change Tabs field at the top of the window to display other types of employee-related information:

- **Payroll And Compensation Info**, where you enter information about earnings, taxes, deductions, and other financial data.
- **Employment Info**, where you enter information about the employee's hiring date and other employment history.
- **Workers Compensation**, available only if you subscribe to the Enhanced Payroll Service.

Personal Info

While viewing Personal Info in the Change tabs list, you see three tabs associated with three categories of information.

Personal Tab   Enter the employee's name, social security number, and the way the name should print on paychecks. QuickBooks automatically inserts the data from the name fields, which is usually the way paychecks are written, but you may want to make a change (for instance, omitting the middle initial).

Enter the Gender and/or Date Of Birth if you have a company policy of recording this information, or if any tax or benefits agency requires it. For example, your state unemployment form may require you to note the gender of all employees; your medical or life insurance carrier may require the date of birth.

Address And Contact Tab   Use this tab to record the employee's address, as well as information about contacting the employee (phone number, e-mail, fax, and so on).

Additional Info Tab   Use this tab to enter the employee number (if your company uses employee numbers). This tab also contains a Define Fields button, so you can create custom fields for employee records (covered in the section "Using Custom Fields" later in this chapter).

Payroll And Compensation Info

On this tab, enter the information QuickBooks needs to pay employees (see Figure 2-15). If you set up employee defaults, QuickBooks fills in the information; make additions and changes as necessary for this employee.

 N O T E :   Premier users who have not purchased the Employee Organizer will not see a Raises and Promotions button.

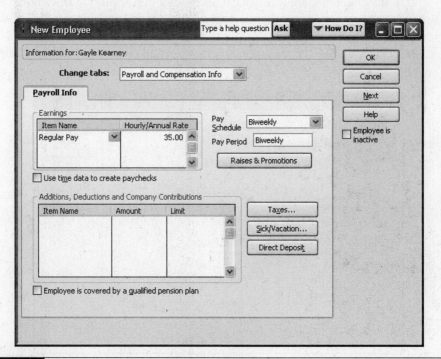

FIGURE 2-15   Enter pay-related information on this tab

If the amount of the earnings or the deduction payroll item remains constant from paycheck to paycheck, enter an amount. If the amounts vary, don't enter an amount. Instead, you'll enter that information when you create the payroll check.

Select the employee's pay schedule so that QuickBooks groups employees properly when you pay them.

Employee Tax Information   Click the Taxes button to open the Taxes dialog box (see Figure 2-16), which starts with Federal tax information. Fill in any data that wasn't automatically filled in from the Employee Template, and modify data that is different for this employee.

Click the State tab and set up the employee's state payroll information. Since this information varies from state to state, you should check with your accountant if you aren't sure of something you find there.

NOTE: QuickBooks has built in a great deal of state information. Depending on the state, you should see the appropriate withholdings and company-paid items. For example, states that don't deduct SUI from employees have a check box for SUI (Company Paid); states that collect disability funds will display the appropriate check box.

On the Other tab, apply any local payroll tax that applies to this employee. If you haven't already configured that tax in the Payroll Item List, you can click <Add New> to enter it now.

Click OK to save the tax status information and return to the Payroll Info tab.

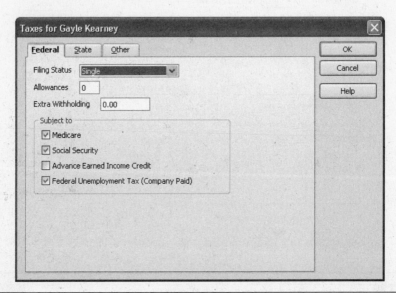

FIGURE 2-16   Set up employee federal, state, and local tax information

Sick and Vacation Pay Information Click the Sick/Vacation button and enter the configuration for this employee, which may include default information you established. When you are finished, click OK to return to the New Employee dialog box.

Direct Deposit The Payroll Info tab has a Direct Deposit button, which you can use to establish direct deposit of the employee's paycheck to his or her bank account. If you haven't signed up for direct deposit, the dialog box that appears when you click this button offers the chance to enroll. See Chapter 8 to learn how to use direct deposit.

Employment Info Tab Set

Select Employment Info in the Change Tabs drop-down list to see the Employment tab, from which you can track the following information about the employee:

- Hire date
- Release date (fill this in when an employee leaves your company)
- Employee type

The selection you make in the Type field has an impact on the way your tax returns are prepared. You should check with your accountant if you have any questions about the type you should assign to any employee. Table 2-2 explains your choices.

Type	Description
Regular	A person you hired for whom you deduct withholdings, issue a W-2, and so on. It's important to have every employee fill out a W-4 form every year.
Officer	An officer of a corporation. If your business isn't incorporated, you have no officers. On federal corporate tax returns, you are required to report payroll for officers of the corporation separately from the regular payroll amounts. Selecting Officer as the type has no impact on running your payroll (calculations, check printing, and so on); it only affects reports.
Statutory	Someone who works for you that the IRS has decided qualifies as an employee instead of as an independent contractor. Check the Circular E or with your accountant to make sure that you correctly classify someone as either a statutory employee or an independent contractor.
Owner	*Owner* and *Employee* are mutually exclusive terms to the IRS. If your company is a proprietorship or an unincorporated partnership, owners and partners are not employees; you should set them up in the Other Names list and pay them from the Write Checks window. If, however, you have already set up an owner or partner and cannot delete the record, set his or her Type to Owner so that the QuickBooks payroll services will not pay the owner or partner.

TABLE 2-2 Employee Types

TIP :   If you need extra W-4 forms, you can download them from the IRS at www.irs.gov. Go to the forms section, select W-4, and print or download the form. Then make as many copies as you need.

Workers Compensation Tab Set

If you subscribe to the Enhanced Payroll Service and you haven't disabled workers' compensation tracking in the Payroll & Employees category of the Preferences dialog box, choose Workers Compensation from the Change Tabs drop-down list. Assign the workers comp code that applies to the employee, or select Exempt. See Chapter 9 for more information.

Entering Items

Items are the things that appear on your invoices when you send an invoice to a customer. Do you charge sales tax? If you do, that's an item. Do you subtotal sections of your invoices? That subtotal is an item. Do you show prepayments or discounts? They're items, too.

Although you can issue an invoice that says "Net amount due for services rendered" or "Net amount due for items delivered" and enter one total in the invoice, the lack of detail will work against you when you try to analyze your business; you won't have enough information to determine where you're making lots of money and where you're making less money than you had expected.

This setup chore requires some planning. Each of your items must have a unique identification (QuickBooks calls that the Item Name/Number). Try to create a system that has some logic to it so that you can easily identify your items when you see them listed.

Understanding Item Types

In QuickBooks, you can define 11 different types of items, described in Table 2-3.

 TIP :   I've described all of the item types in terms of their use on your estimates, sales orders, and invoices, but you use many of them on your purchase orders and vendor bills, too.

Entering the Data for Items

You create new items from the Item List window; choose Lists | Item List from the menu bar. When the Item List window opens, any items that were created during your EasyStep Interview are listed.

Item Type	Description
Service	An intangible product that you provide to a customer. Selling a service doesn't affect any inventory accounts.
Inventory Part	A product you buy for the purpose of reselling. This item type isn't available unless you enable inventory using the EasyStep Interview or from the Items & Inventory section of the Preferences dialog box.
Inventory Assembly	Use this item type to describe inventory items that you sell that you create from (assemble) other inventory parts, noninventory parts, or service items. For example, the computer systems you sell include a CPU, a monitor, a keyboard, and a mouse, and you don't sell a system without all of its parts. Your computer system is an assembly. See Chapter 10 for more information on assemblies.
Noninventory Part	A tangible product you sell but don't track as inventory. Often, noninventory parts are items you buy specifically to resell to fill a customer's order. A home builder views windows as noninventory parts, purchased as needed to construct a home.
Other Charge	Use this item type for things like shipping charges or other line items that appear on your invoices.
Subtotal	This item type adds up everything that comes before it. It provides a subtotal before you add shipping charges or subtract any discounts or prepayments.
Group	This item type cleverly enables you to enter a group of items (all of which must exist in your Item ist) all at once. For example, if a service you sell consists of a charge for labor and charges for three different materials, you can group the items so that you don't have to enter each individually on the invoice.
Discount	Create a discount item so that you can give a customer a line item discount. You can create as many discount items as you need—for example, a discount for wholesale customers, a discount for a volume purchase, and a special holiday sale discount. When you use the item on an invoice, you can indicate a flat rate or percentage.
Payment	If you receive a prepayment (either a total payment or a partial payment as a deposit), you indicate it as a line item, using this item type.
Sales Tax Item	Create one of these item types for each sales tax authority for which you collect; this item type is available if sales tax is enabled.
Sales Tax Group	Use this item to group multiple sales taxes that appear on the same invoice; again, this item type is available if sales tax is enabled.

TABLE 2-3   Available Item Types

NOTE: Enterprise users see a set of search fields at the top of the Item List window that do not appear in Premier editions.

To create a new item, press CTRL-N. The New Item window opens, displaying a list of item types, as described previously in Table 2-2. Select an item type to display the appropriate fields in the blank New Item window; in Figure 2-17, you see the fields for an Inventory Part item. Other item types (such as Service items) have fewer fields.

The Item Name/Number field is the place to insert a unique identifier for the item. When you are filling out estimates, sales orders, invoices, purchase orders, or vendor bills, the Item Name/Number appears in the drop-down list.

 NOTE: After you've created an item, you can create subitems. For example, if you sell shoes as an item, you can create subitems for dress, shoes, sneakers, boots, and so on. Or use subitems for a parent item that comes in a variety of colors. You cannot create subitems for Subtotal items, Group items, Payment items, Sales Tax items, and Sales Tax Group items.

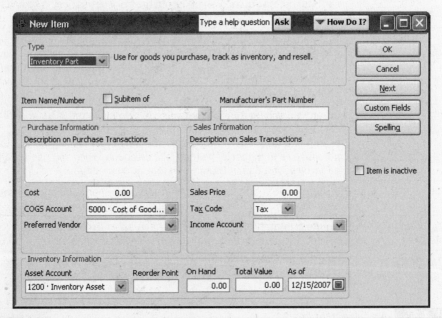

FIGURE 2-17   Creating a new Inventory Part item

Many of the rest of the fields in the New Item window change depending on the item type you select. Most of them are self-explanatory, but some are important enough to merit discussion:

- If you're entering an inventory item, fill in the cost of the item and enter the account to which you post the cost of goods sold (COGS). Optionally, fill in the name of the vendor from whom you purchase the item.
- In the Sales Price field, you can enter a rate for those items that you've priced; leave the rate at zero for the items you want to price when you are preparing the invoice. Don't worry—nothing is written in stone. You can change any rate that appears automatically when you include the item on a transaction.
- In the Income Account field, select an income account on your Chart Of Accounts.
- In the Tax Code field, choose Tax or Non to indicate whether the item is taxable. The Tax Code field is only available if you've configured your company to collect sales tax.

When you complete the window, choose Next to create another item. When you finish entering items, click OK.

Entering Jobs

Jobs are associated with customers; they can't stand alone. To create a job, press CTRL-J to open the Customer Center (or click the Customer Center icon on the toolbar) and select the Customers & Jobs tab.

Right-click the customer for whom you want to create a job, and choose Add Job to open the New Job window, the fourth tab in the New Customer window you saw earlier in this chapter; in the "Customers and Jobs" section, you read about the Address Info tab, the Additional Info tab, and the Payment Info tab.

Create a name for the job (you can use up to 41 characters) and make it descriptive enough for both you and your customer to understand.

If this job requires you to bill the customer at an address that's different from the address you entered for this customer, or to ship goods to a different shipping address than the one that's entered, make the appropriate changes on the Address Info tab. QuickBooks maintains this information only for this job and won't change the original shipping address in the customer record.

The Additional Info tab and the Payment Info tab are related to the customer rather than the job, so click the Job Info tab to set up this job (see Figure 2-18). All of the information on the Job Info tab is optional; the job may not require this data.

The Job Status drop-down list offers choices that you can change as the job progresses. You can change the text that describes each progress level to suit your own business.

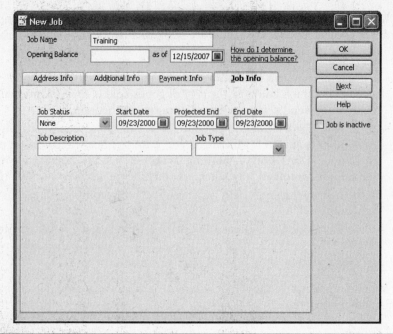

FIGURE 2-18   Set up job information on this tab

To accomplish this, follow these steps:

1. Choose Edit | Preferences to open the Preferences dialog box.
2. Click Jobs & Estimates in the left pane (see Figure 2-19).
3. Click the Company Preferences tab in the right pane to see the current descriptive text for each status level.
4. Change the text of any status level if you have a descriptive phrase you like better. For example, you may prefer "Working" to "In progress."
5. Click OK.

QuickBooks uses the new labels on every job in your company data file.

When you finish entering all the information about this job, choose Next to create another job for the same customer. Otherwise, click OK to close the New Job window. The jobs you create for a customer appear indented below the customer in the list of Customers & Jobs.

Setting Up Other Lists

There are a few items in the Lists menu that I haven't covered in detail. They don't require extensive amounts of data, and you may or may not choose to use them. If you do plan to use them, here's an overview of the things you need to know.

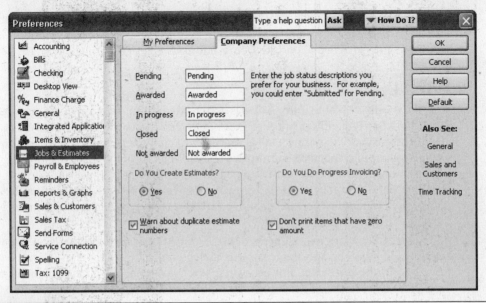

FIGURE 2-19 Set up job status labels

Some of these lists appear on the Lists menu, and some of them appear on a submenu of the Lists menu called Customer & Vendor Profile Lists.

 N O T E : One list, the Templates list, isn't covered here. The Templates list contains all of the invoice, purchase order, sales receipt, and other forms you use in transactions. I discuss working with and customizing those templates throughout this book in the appropriate chapters. I find that you can accomplish what you need in windows other than the Templates List window.

Fixed Asset Item List

Use the Fixed Asset Item List to store information about fixed assets. This list is meant to track data about the assets you depreciate. Each asset's record includes detailed information and even has fields to track the sale of a depreciated asset.

In all versions of QuickBooks Premier *except* the Accountant's Edition, the Fixed Asset Item List is a list designed to let you use QuickBooks to track your fixed assets as a QuickBooks list. The Accountant's Edition of QuickBooks Premier and all editions of QuickBooks Enterprise contain the Fixed Asset Manager, which uses the Fixed Asset Item List to help you track fixed assets and depreciation. See Appendix A for details.

Users of editions of QuickBooks Premier other than the Accountant's Edition can use the Depreciate Your Assets tool to determine depreciation rates in QuickBooks.

The Depreciate Your Assets tool is a planning tool that does not perform depreciation tasks. Instead, you depreciate your assets in regular QuickBooks transaction windows. You can learn about the Depreciate Your Assets tool in Chapter 13.

Price Level List

This list is only available if Price Levels are enabled in the Sales & Customers section of your Preferences (choose Edit | Preferences). The Price Level List is a clever and easy way to connect special pricing to customers and jobs. For example, you may want to create a discount price level for customers that are nonprofit organizations. Or, you may want to give excellent customers a special discount. On the other hand, you may want to keep your regular prices steady (assuming they're competitive) and only increase them for certain customers (perhaps customers who don't pay in a timely fashion).

To create a new price level, press CTRL-N; QuickBooks displays the New Price Level dialog box. The appearance of this dialog box changes, depending on the Price Level Type you select. For each price level, you establish a name, which can be anything you wish, and then select a type (see Figure 2-20). You can create percentage price levels or per item price levels. The Fixed % price level type allows you to specify the percentage amount by which the price level will increase or decrease all item prices.

Using the Per Item price level type (see Figure 2-21), you can increase or decrease the price of individual items that you select by either a percentage or a dollar amount. Per item price levels give you a great deal of flexibility in charging customers for products or services. You can use per item price levels to set multiple prices for the same item; for example, you can assign prices of $50.00, $40.00, and $30.00 to a single item (a product or a service).

You can assign a specific price for the item to a customer (or multiple customers), or to one or more jobs. In addition, if you wish, you can assign a specific price to an

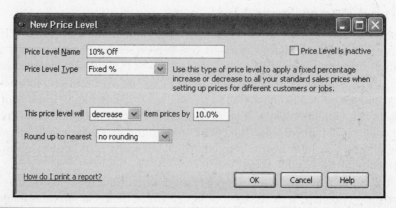

FIGURE 2-20   Setting up a new Fixed % price level

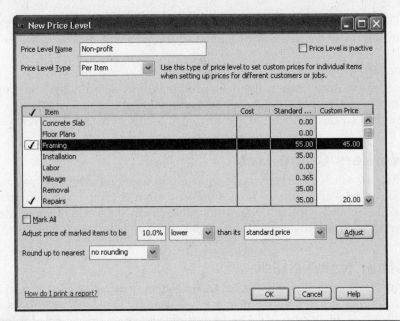

FIGURE 2-21   Setting up a new Per Item price level

item when you're creating an invoice. If the invoice contains an item that has price levels assigned, a drop-down list containing all the price levels is available in the Rate column of the invoice. Just select the price you want to charge for this item, for this invoice.

After you create price levels, you can apply a price level to customers. Open the Customers & Jobs List and select a customer. Press CTRL-E to edit the customer's information and select a price level on the Additional Info tab.

 T I P :   You can apply price levels to items in addition to customers, enabling you to provide discounts (or increases) while you're creating invoices.

Sales Tax Code List

This list is available if you configured your business to collect sales tax. Most businesses only need the two built-in sales tax codes: Tax and Non (meaning taxable and nontaxable). You can learn more about using sales tax codes effectively in Chapter 7.

Class List

The Class List appears in the Lists menu only if you've enabled the classes feature in the Accounting category of the Preferences dialog box. Classes provide a method of organizing your activities (income and disbursement activities) for reporting purposes. Often a well-designed chart of accounts will eliminate the need for classes, but if you do want to use them, you can create them ahead of time through the Lists menu.

Some business owners find it's a good idea to work with QuickBooks for a while. Then, if they feel they need a report that can only be produced by using classes, they can create classes at that point. Chapter 20 covers the use of classes.

Workers Comp List

This list, which appears if you're using QuickBooks Enhanced Payroll and have enabled workers comp tracking, stores the workers comp codes you create. Enter a code, optionally enter a description, and specify the workers compensation rate per $100.00 of gross wages. Also specify a start date for using the code.

Other Names List

QuickBooks provides a list called Other Names, which is the list of people whose names come up in transactions but whose activity you don't want to track. This list will appear when you write checks, but the names are unavailable for invoices, purchase orders, and any other QuickBooks transaction type.

If your business is a proprietorship or an unincorporated partnership, owners and partners belong on this list so that you can write draw checks.

When you press CTRL-N to open a New Name window, there are fields for the address (handy for printing checks), telephone numbers, and other contact information.

 TIP: Unless you're a proprietor or partner, it's totally possible to use QuickBooks efficiently without ever using this list.

Memorized Transaction List

This list is a collection of the transactions you memorize. You can tell QuickBooks to memorize any transaction at the time you create it, memorizing a transaction automatically adds the transaction to this list. You learn how to memorize specific types of transactions throughout this book in the chapters devoted to creating transactions.

Sales Rep List

This list appears in the submenu of Customer & Vendor Profile Lists. By common definition, a *sales rep* is a person who is connected to a customer, usually because he or she receives a commission on sales to that customer. However, it's frequently advantageous to track sales reps for other reasons. For example, you may want to know which noncommissioned person is attached to a customer (some people call this a *service rep*) or you may want to track the source of referrals.

To enter a new sales rep, press CTRL-N to open the New Sales Rep dialog box and select the person's name from the Sales Rep Name drop-down list. If that name doesn't already exist as an employee, vendor, or other name, QuickBooks asks you to add the name to one of those lists. QuickBooks fills in the Sales Rep Initials field and the Sales Rep Type field; click OK to save the sales rep.

Customer Type List

This list also appears in the submenu of Customer & Vendor Profile Lists. When you create your customer list, you may decide to use the Customer Type field as a way to categorize the customer. Setting up customer types gives you the opportunity to sort and select customers in reports, perhaps to view the total income from specific types of customers.

You can predetermine the customer types you want to track by opening this list item and creating the types you need during setup. Or you can create them as you enter customers.

Vendor Type List

This list appears in the submenu of Customer & Vendor Profile Lists. See the two preceding sections and substitute the word "vendor" for the word "customer."

Job Type List

This list appears in the submenu of Customer & Vendor Profile Lists. Use this list to set up categories for jobs. For example, if you're a plumber, you may want to separate new construction from repairs.

Terms List

This list appears in the submenu of Customer & Vendor Profile Lists. QuickBooks keeps both customer and vendor payment terms in one list, so the terms you need are all available whether you're creating a sales order, an invoice, a purchase order, or a vendor bill. To create a terms listing, open the Terms List window and press CTRL-N to open the New Terms window.

Use the Standard section to create terms that are due at some elapsed time after the invoice date:

- Net Due In is the number of days allowed for payment after the invoice date.
- To create a discount for early payment, enter the discount percentage and the number of days after the invoice date that the discount is in effect. For example, a 2 percent discount may be in effect for the first 10 days after the invoice date.

Use the Date Driven section to describe terms that are due on a particular date, regardless of the invoice date:

- Enter the day of the month the invoice payment is due.
- Enter the number of days before the due date that invoices are considered payable on the following month.
- To create a discount for early payment, enter the discount percentage and the day of the month at which the discount period ends. For example, if the standard due date is the 15th of the month, you may want to extend a discount to any customer who pays by the 8th of the month.

 TIP:　Date-driven terms are commonly used by companies that send invoices monthly, usually on the last day of the month. If you send invoices constantly, as soon as a sale is completed, it's very difficult to track and enforce date-driven terms.

Customer Message List

This list appears in the submenu of Customer & Vendor Profile Lists. If you like to write messages to your customers when you're creating an invoice, you can enter a bunch of appropriate messages ahead of time and then just select the one you want to use. For example, you may want to insert the message "Thanks for doing business with us" or "Happy Holidays."

Press CTRL-N to enter a new message to add to the list. You just have to write the text, which can't be longer than 101 characters, counting spaces. This is one of the easier lists to create.

Payment Method List

This list appears in the submenu of Customer & Vendor Profile Lists. You can track the way payments arrive from customers. This not only provides some detail (in case you're having a conversation with a customer about invoices and payments), but also allows you to print reports on payments that are subtotaled by the method of payment, such as credit card, check, cash, and so on. Your bank may use the same subtotaling method, which makes it easier to reconcile the bank account.

QuickBooks automatically populates the payment methods with common payment types. If you have a payment method that isn't listed, you can add that method to the list. To do so, press CTRL-N to open the New Payment Method dialog box. Name the payment method and select the appropriate payment type.

Ship Via List

This list appears in the submenu of Customer & Vendor Profile Lists. You can describe the way you ship goods on your invoices (in the field named Via), which many customers appreciate. QuickBooks automatically populates the list with a variety of shipment methods, but you may need to add a shipping method. To do so, press CTRL-N to add a new Ship Via entry to the list. All you need to do is enter the name, for example, Our Truck, or Sam's Delivery Service.

If you use one shipping method more than any other, you can select a default Ship Via entry, which appears automatically on your invoices; you can change it when the shipping method is different.

To perform this task, follow these steps:

1. Choose Edit | Preferences.
2. Select the Sales & Customers icon.
3. Select the Company Preferences tab.
4. In the Usual Shipping Method field, click the drop-down list and select the Ship Via entry you want as the default. (Select <Add New> if you want to enter a new shipping method for the default.)
5. Enter the FOB site you want to appear on invoices, if you wish to display this information.

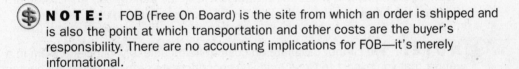 **NOTE:** FOB (Free On Board) is the site from which an order is shipped and is also the point at which transportation and other costs are the buyer's responsibility. There are no accounting implications for FOB—it's merely informational.

Vehicle List

This list appears in the submenu of Customer & Vendor Profile Lists. The Vehicle List lets you track mileage for vehicles used in your business. You can use the mileage information for tax deductions for your vehicles and to bill customers for mileage expenses. However, even if you don't bill customers for mileage or your accountant uses a formula for tax deductions, the Vehicle list is a handy way to track information about the vehicles (yours or your employees) used for business purposes.

To add a vehicle to the list, press CTRL-N to open a New Vehicle dialog box. The box has two fields:

- Vehicle, in which you enter a name or code for a specific vehicle. For example, you could enter Blue Truck, Mikes Toyota, Ford Mustang Convertible, or any other recognizable name.
- Description, in which you enter descriptive information about the vehicle.

While the Description field is handy for standard description terms (such as black, or blue/white truck), take advantage of the field by entering information you really need. For example, enter the VIN, the license plate number, the expiration date for the plate, the insurance policy number, or other "official" information. You can enter up to 256 characters in the field. You can learn how to track mileage and bill customers for mileage in Chapter 6.

Using Custom Fields

You can add your own fields to the Customer, Vendor, Employee, and Item records. Custom fields are useful if there's information you want to track but you can't find a QuickBooks field for it. For example, you may want to track the birthdays of your employees. Or perhaps you have two offices and you want to associate your customers to the office that services them. If you maintain multiple warehouses, you can create a field for items to indicate which warehouse stocks any particular item; similarly, you can track an item's bin location using a custom field.

You can create up to five custom fields for items and seven custom fields for customers, vendors and employees. Using one field on all three lists counts as one field; for example, if you add the Birthday field to the Vendor list, the Customer:Job list, and the Employee list, you can still add six more fields to each list.

 N O T E :   You cannot calculate on custom fields unless you include them in a report that you export to Excel, and you cannot create drop-down lists for custom fields.

Adding a Custom Field for Names

To add one or more custom fields to names, open any of the names lists (Customers & Jobs, Vendor, or Employee).

Now follow these steps:

1. Select any name on the list.
2. Press CTRL-E to edit the name.
3. Click the Additional Info tab.
4. Click the Define Fields button. The Define Fields dialog box appears (see Figure 2-22).
5. Name the field and indicate the list for which you want to use the new field.
6. Click OK to save the information.

When you save a new custom field, QuickBooks displays a message reminding you that if you customize your templates (forms for transactions, such as invoices), you can add these fields. Instructions for adding fields to transaction windows are found throughout this book in the chapters covering invoices, estimates, purchase

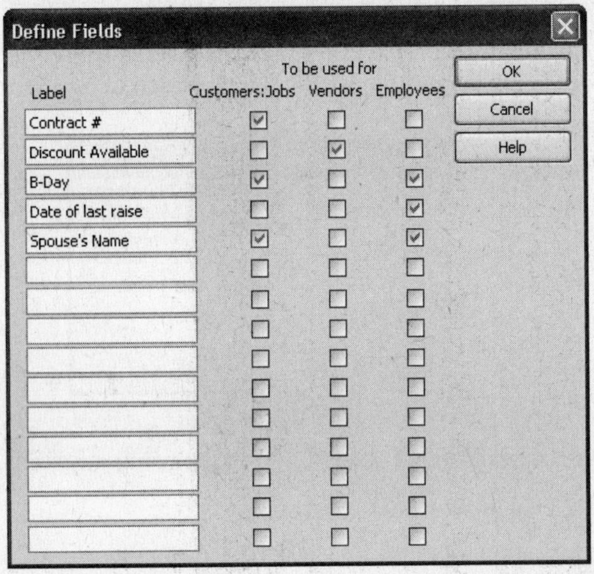

FIGURE 2-22   You can set up custom fields for customers, vendors, and employees in this dialog box

orders, and so on. When you click OK to close the message QuickBooks redisplays the Additional Info tab; the new custom field appears in the Custom Fields section of the Additional Info tab.

To add data to the custom fields, select a name on any list, press CTRL-E to edit the name, and add the appropriate data to the custom field.

Adding a Custom Field for Items

You can add custom fields to your items (except subtotal items and sales tax items) in much the same manner as you do for names. You can create up to five custom fields for items.

Use the following steps:

1. Open the Item List and select any item.
2. Press CTRL-E to edit the item.
3. Click the Custom Fields button.
4. If a message appears telling you that there are no custom fields yet defined, click OK.
5. When the Custom Fields dialog appears, choose Define Fields.

6 When the Define Custom Fields For Items dialog box appears, enter a label for each field you want to add. You can add fields that fit services, inventory items, and so on, and use the appropriate field for each item when you set up the item.

7 Click the Use box to use the field. (To stop using a custom field, you can uncheck the box.)

8 Click OK.

The first time you enter a custom field on an item, a dialog appears to tell you that you can use these fields on templates (forms such as Invoices, Sales Orders, Estimates, Purchase Orders, or Packing Slips). Click OK and optionally check the box to stop displaying this message in the future.

When you click Custom Fields in the Edit Item dialog box for any item, your existing custom fields appear. To enter data for the custom fields in an item, open the item from the Item List and click the Custom Fields button on the Edit Item window. Then enter the appropriate data.

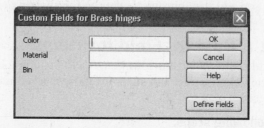

Merging Entries in Lists

After you've been working in QuickBooks for a while, you may find that some lists have entries that should be combined. For example, perhaps someone entered a vendor twice using different spellings, or perhaps you realize that several items in your chart of accounts are covering similar expenses. One common scenario is an Item List that's far too large and complicated. For example, an Item List invites errors when it contains inventory items such as Cable-cut to 2 ft long, Cable-cut to 3 ft long, and Cable-cut to 4 ft long. Users click the wrong item because all of the items look alike at first glance. It would be easier and smarter to have one item, named Cable, and then enter the length as a quantity in the Qty field or in the Description field.

You can only merge entries from the following lists:

- Chart Of Accounts
- Item
- Customers & Jobs
- Vendor
- Other Names

Performing a Merge Operation

To merge entries within a list, take the following steps:

① Select the list entry you want to eliminate and press CTRL-E to edit the entry.

② Change the entry's name to match the name of the entry you want to keep.

③ Click OK. QuickBooks displays a message telling you that the name is already in use and asks if you want to merge the two names.

④ Click Yes.

QuickBooks merges all of the information, including transaction data, into the entry you're keeping.

Guidelines and Restrictions for Merging List Entries

Bear in mind the following information when you decide to merge entries:

- You cannot "unmerge"—the process is not reversible. If you are unsure of the process, back up your data before you merge. See Chapter 21 for details on backing up.
- For accounts and items, you cannot merge entries that have subentries. Change the subentries to parent entries by removing the Subaccount Of or Subitem Of check mark. Merge the parent entries and then reapply the Subaccount Of or Subitem Of check mark (all of which will now be subentries of the new single, merged, parent entry).
- You can merge an item without subitems with an item that has subitems, but not the other way around.
- You can merge subentries of the same parent (which is in fact the most common type of merge).
- You can merge jobs that are subentries of the same customer.

Now that all your lists exist and they're fine-tuned, you can work quickly and easily in QuickBooks transaction windows. The following chapters walk you through those tasks.

Additional Features for Selected Editions of QuickBooks

For QuickBooks Enterprise users, the number of items you can store in the Items List and in the name lists (customers, vendors, employees, and other names) increases in QuickBooks 2007. At the time I wrote this, the final number hadn't yet been determined, but the number will be no less than 100,000 items. Similarly, QuickBooks Enterprise 2007 can store a total of no less than 100,000 names in all the name lists combined.

In addition to the lists covered in this chapter, the Contractor, Professional Services, and Accountant Editions of QuickBooks also have the ability to create a Billing Rate Levels List. This feature lets you assign a billing rate to a person performing a specific service. For example, on a given job, your senior consultants may be billable at one rate, while your junior consultants generate a different rate. You set up billing rate levels using the Billing Rate Level List, and associate billing rate levels with individual or all service items. Once you create the billing rates, you assign them to customers, vendors, employees, or someone listed on the Other Names List. To track services for each name and billing rate, use the QuickBooks Timesheet feature.

 TIP: See Chapter 18 to learn about using Timesheets.

When you invoice your customers, QuickBooks automatically adds the appropriate billing rate levels to the invoice from the Time and Costs dialog box that's available in the Invoice window. You can also apply any customer's percentage price level (usually a discount) to the billing rate invoice items.

Part Two

Bookkeeping

Part Two contains chapters about the day-to-day bookkeeping chores you'll be performing in QuickBooks. These chapters take you through everything you need to know about sending invoices to your customers and collecting the money they send back as a result. You'll learn how to track and pay the bills you receive from vendors. There's plenty of information about dealing with inventory—buying it, selling it, and counting it—and keeping QuickBooks up to date on those figures. Payroll is also discussed, both in-house payroll systems and outside services.

Part Two covers all the reports you can generate to analyze the state of your business as well as the reports you run for your accountant and for the government (tax time is less of a nightmare with QuickBooks).

Finally, you'll learn about budgets, general ledger adjustments, and all the other once-in-a-while tasks you need to know how to accomplish to keep your accounting records finely tuned.

Invoicing

In this chapter:

- Understanding the customer center
- Creating and edit invoices
- Working with estimates and sales orders
- Creating and edit credit memos
- Printing invoices and credit memos
- Creating pick lists and packing slips
- Customizing invoice forms

Chapter 3

For many businesses, the only way to get money is to send an invoice to a customer. Creating an invoice in QuickBooks is easy; in this chapter, you'll learn what all the parts of the invoice do and why they're there. In addition to invoices, you often have to create credits, packing slips, sales orders, and estimates.

After covering all those transaction documents, I'll describe the choices you have for getting those documents to your customers.

Customer Center

Throughout Chapters 3, 4, and 5, I refer you to the Customer Center, which quickly and easily displays information about your customers, their balances, and other important information. So, before we dive into creating invoices, let's take a moment to explore the Customer Center.

To open the Customer Center, take any of the following actions:

- Click the Customer Center icon on the toolbar.
- Click the Customers icon on the left side of the Home page.
- Press CTRL-J.
- Choose Customers | Customer Center from the menu bar.

As you can see in Figure 3-1, the layout of the Customer Center window is easy to understand and navigate.

The left pane of the Customer Center has two tabs: Customers & Jobs and Transactions. The Customers & Jobs tab actually replaces the Customer: Job list used in earlier versions of QuickBooks. As you click any customer or job on the Customers & Jobs tab, QuickBooks displays transactions for that customer on the right side of the screen. You can limit the transactions to a specific type to make the search easier, and you can filter the transactions; your filtering choices depend on the type of transaction you select in the Show list box. To further narrow the search, you can select a date range.

The Transactions tab (see Figure 3-2) lists all your customer-related transactions, and you can use this tab to find a particular transaction or transactions that meet certain criteria. On the left side of the screen, select the transaction type for which you are searching. Then, use the Filter By and Date list boxes to narrow the search.

You can use the toolbar buttons in the Customer Center window and the links in the right pane of the Customers & Jobs tab to open transaction windows and produce reports.

You can customize the Customer Center by resizing any of its panes. To resize a pane, move the mouse pointer over the edge of any pane; the mouse pointer changes to a vertical (or horizontal) bar with pointing arrows attached. Drag the pane left or right (up or down) to change its size. The other pane(s) will adjust to

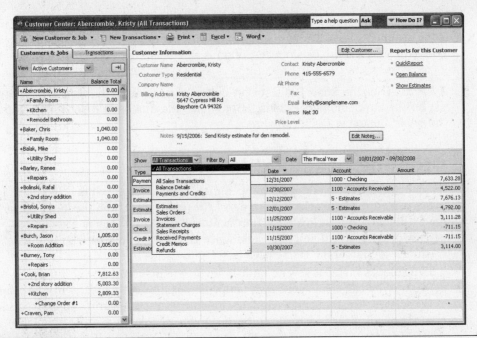

FIGURE 3-1 The Customer & Jobs tab provides a robust way to find information about a specific customer

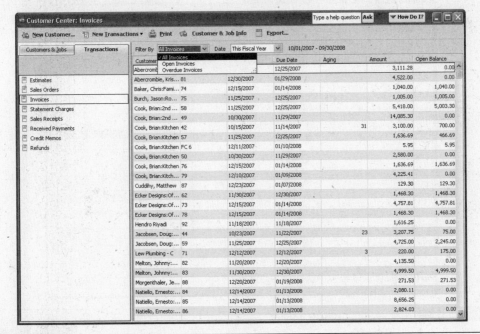

FIGURE 3-2 Use the Transactions tab to easily filter and find transactions

fill the space. In addition, you can choose the columns that QuickBooks displays in the Customer & Jobs List by right clicking on the list. QuickBooks displays a context menu; choose Customize Columns.

 TIP: Click the Show Full List Only button (it appears to the right of the View list box on the Customers & Jobs tab) to make the Customer & Jobs list fill up the entire Customer Center window.

Creating Standard Invoices

QuickBooks offers several ways to open the Create Invoices window. If you're a menu person, you can select Customers | Create Invoices from the menu bar or, in the Customer Center, click New Transactions | Invoices. If you're a keyboard person, press CTRL-I. If you like clicking icons, click the Invoice icon in the Customer section of the Home page (see Figure 3-3).

QuickBooks includes several built-in invoice templates that you can use. If necessary, you can create your own template, which is covered later in this chapter in the section "Customizing Templates." Before you start creating invoices, decide whether the displayed template suits you. You can look at the other templates

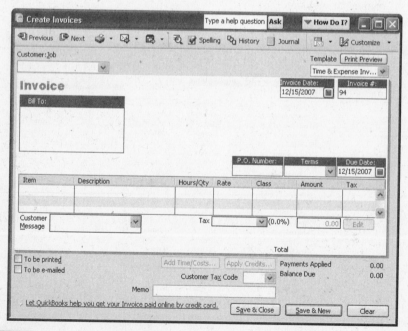

FIGURE 3-3   The Create Invoices window

before settling on the one you want to use by clicking the list box arrow beside the Template field and selecting another invoice template:

- The Attorney's Invoice, the Time & Expense Invoice, the Intuit Professional Invoice, the Custom Invoice template, and the Intuit Service Invoice templates are all very similar. They differ in the order of the columns. In addition, the Attorney's Invoice template and the Time & Expense Invoice template include an Hours/Qty column while same column is called "Quantity" on the other two invoice templates. The Service template, the Time and Expense Invoice template, and the Attorney's Invoice template have a field for a purchase order number. The Custom Invoice template contains a field for Contract #, but otherwise looks just like the Service template.

- The Intuit Product Invoice template has more fields and different columns than most of the other templates because it contains information about the items in your inventory.

- The Progress template and the Custom Progress Invoice template are designed specifically for progress billing against a job estimate. They appear in the Template list only if you have set your company preferences to use progress billing and contain columns that track prior invoicing as well as current invoicing; you'll read more about progress billing later in this chapter in the section "Using Estimates."

- The Custom S.O. Invoice template supports invoices created from sales orders. You'll read more about sales orders and using this invoice template later in this chapter in the section "Creating Sales Orders."

- The Fixed Fee Invoice template doesn't contain any columns for quantity and rate—the two fields you would usually use to calculate an amount. Instead, you simply supply an amount when you use this invoice template.

- The Intuit Standard Pledge template works best for nonprofit organizations. The customer is called "Donor" and the message box is called "Donor Message." Like the Fixed Fee Invoice template, this template doesn't contain any columns for quantity and rate—the two fields you would usually use to calculate an amount. Instead, you simply supply an amount when you use this invoice template.

- The Invoice from Proposal/Estimate template is a customized invoice form that you can use when you use a customized estimate template called "Proposal." As you'll see later in this chapter, you can create an invoice from an estimate. If you use the Proposal estimate template, QuickBooks fills in values from the estimate in the Proposal Amount column and the Prior Amount column of the Invoice from Proposal template.

- The Rock Castle Invoice template is the template used by default in the sample company Rock Castle Construction and supports selling a mixture of goods and services.

- The Finance Charge template appears if you enable finance charges in the Finance Charge category of the Preferences dialog. Information about finance charges is in Chapter 5.
- The Packing Slip template is discussed in the section "Printing Packing Slips" later in this chapter.

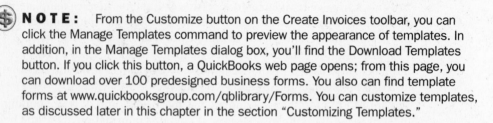

N O T E :   From the Customize button on the Create Invoices toolbar, you can click the Manage Templates command to preview the appearance of templates. In addition, in the Manage Templates dialog box, you'll find the Download Templates button. If you click this button, a QuickBooks web page opens; from this page, you can download over 100 predesigned business forms. You also can find template forms at www.quickbooksgroup.com/qblibrary/Forms. You can customize templates, as discussed later in this chapter in the section "Customizing Templates."

For this discussion, I'll use the Intuit Product Invoice template, because it contains the most fields. If you're using any other template, you'll still be able to follow along, even though your invoice form doesn't display some of the fields related to products.

The top portion of the invoice is for the basic information and is called the *invoice heading*. The middle section, where the billing items are placed, is called the *line item* section. The bottom section holds the totals and other details (such as customer messages).

Entering Heading Information

To create an invoice, first select the customer or the job. Click the arrow to the right of the Customer: Job field to see a list of all your customers. If you've created jobs for customers, those jobs are listed under the customer name. Select the customer or job for this invoice. If the customer isn't in the system, choose <Add New> to open a new customer window and enter all the data required for setting up a customer. See Chapter 2 for information on adding new customers.

If you've charged reimbursable expenses or time charges to this customer, QuickBooks displays a message reminding you to add those charges to this invoice. You can learn how to do that in Chapter 6.

N O T E :   If you have outstanding sales orders, QuickBooks displays the Available Sales Orders dialog box from which you can select a sales order on which to base your invoice. Read more about sales orders later in this chapter in the section "Creating Sales Orders."

The current date appears in the Date field. If you want to change the date, you can either type in a new date, or click the calendar icon at the right side of the field to select a date. If you change the date, the new date appears automatically in each invoice you create during this session of QuickBooks (the current date returns after you close, and then reopen the software).

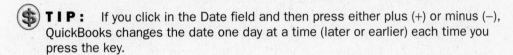

T I P : If you click in the Date field and then press either plus (+) or minus (–), QuickBooks changes the date one day at a time (later or earlier) each time you press the key.

N O T E : You can change the default behavior so that QuickBooks displays last date used on a transaction instead of today's date for the current session. Once the program has been closed and re-opened the date reverts to the current system date. Choose Edit | Preferences and click the General category. On the My Preferences tab, change the Default Date to Use for New Transactions option.

The first time you enter an invoice, fill in the invoice number you want to use as a starting point. From that point forward, QuickBooks increments the invoice number for each new invoice.

QuickBooks displays the Bill To address stored in the customer record. You can select a Ship To address from the drop-down list on the Product Invoice template, or add a new Ship To address by choosing <Add New> from the list.

If you have a purchase order from this customer, enter it into the P.O. Number field.

QuickBooks fills in the Terms field automatically with the terms you entered when you created the customer record. You can change the terms for this invoice if you wish. If terms don't automatically appear, then you didn't enter that information in the customer record.

➡ FYI

Finding Missing Invoice Numbers

Although QuickBooks numbers invoices incrementally, you can manually change an invoice number; if you do, it's possible that you'll end up with missing invoice numbers. Odd as this will sound, you can use the Missing Checks report to help you identify missing invoice numbers. To display the report, choose Reports, Banking, Missing Checks. QuickBooks prompts you for a bank account; select your Accounts Receivable account. When the report appears on-screen, its title will read "Missing Checks," but it will display invoices and missing invoice numbers. You can click the Modify button to change the report title. After you click OK, you can memorize the report; see Chapter 15 for details.

TIP: If you enter or change any information about the customer while you're creating an invoice, QuickBooks offers to add the information to the customer record when you save the invoice. If the change is permanent, click Yes; if the change is only for this invoice, click No.

In the Rep field, QuickBooks displays the salesperson assigned to this customer. You can click the arrow next to the field and choose any sales rep name from the drop-down list.

In the Ship field QuickBooks supplies the invoice date as the ship date.

Use the Via field to select a shipping method. Click the arrow next to the field to see the available shipping choices. (See Chapter 2 for information about adding to this list.)

Some companies use the FOB field to indicate the point at which the shipping costs are transferred to the buyer and the assumption of a completed sale takes place. If you use FOB terms, enter the applicable data in the field; it has no impact on your QuickBooks financial records and is there for your convenience only.

NOTE: FOB stands for Free On Board.

Entering Line Items

Now you can begin to enter the items for which you are billing this customer. Click in the first column of the line item section.

If you're using the Product invoice template, that column is Quantity. Enter the quantity of the first item you're selling.

In the Item Code column, an arrow appears on the right edge of the column—click it to see a list of the items you sell and select one. (See Chapter 2 to learn how to set up items.) QuickBooks automatically fills in the item's description and price using the information you provided when you created the item. If you didn't include the information when you created the item, you can enter it manually now. QuickBooks does the math, displaying the product of the quantity times the price in the Amount column. If the item and the customer are both liable for tax, the Tax column displays "Tax."

NOTE: QuickBooks warns you if you don't have enough items on hand and then asks if you want to learn how to track backorders, which are discussed later in this chapter.

You can add as many rows of items as you need to an invoice; if you run out of room, QuickBooks automatically adds pages to your invoice.

Applying Price Levels

If you're using the Price Levels feature (explained in Chapter 2), you can change the amount of any line item by applying a price level. Most of the time, your price levels are a percentage by which to lower (discount) the price, but you may also have created price levels that increase the price.

When you click in the Price Each column, an arrow appears; click the arrow to see a list of price level items, and select the one you want to apply to this item. As Figure 3-4 demonstrates, once you assign a quantity and price so that QuickBooks can calculate the amount, you see the name of your price level and the proposed item price at each price level. After you select a price level, QuickBooks changes the amount you're charging the customer for the item and adjusts the amount of the total for this item.

The customer sees only the price on the invoice; there's no indication that you've adjusted the price. This is different from applying a discount to a price (covered in the next section), where you include a separate line item to apply the discount.

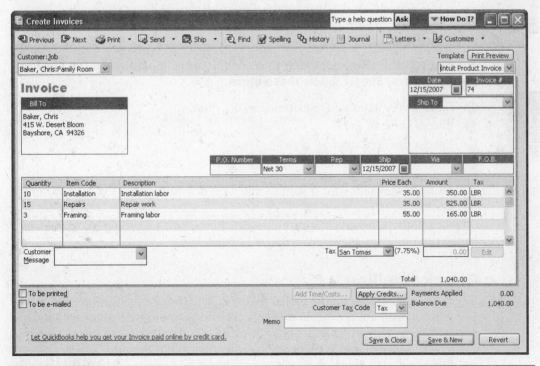

FIGURE 3-4   QuickBooks calculates the amount when you assign a quantity and price

Entering Discounts

Instead of using price levels, you can adjust individual lines of an invoice by applying discounts. Discounts are entered as line items, so the discount has to exist as an item in your Items List.

QuickBooks calculates the amount of a discount item based on the amount of the line item immediately above it. For example, let's suppose you have already entered line items as follows:

- Qty of 1 for Some Item with a price of $100.00 for a total line item price of $100.00
- Qty of 2 for Some Other Item with a price of $40.00 for a total line item price of $80.00

If you enter a 10 percent discount item on the next line, QuickBooks calculates the value of the discount as 10 percent of the last line you entered—and includes an $8.00 discount on the invoice.

To apply the discount to all the line items, first enter a subtotal item from the Items List that adds and calculates the total of all the lines on the invoice. Then enter the discount item as the next line item; QuickBooks calculates the discount based on the subtotal.

You can use the same approach to discount some line items on the invoice but not others. Simply follow these steps:

1. Enter all the items you're planning to discount.
2. Enter a subtotal item.
3. Enter a discount item.
4. Enter the remaining items (the items you're not discounting).

This method makes your discounts and your discount policies very clear to the customer.

When you're finished entering all the line items, you'll see that QuickBooks has kept a running total, including taxes (see Figure 3-5).

Check Spelling

Click the Spelling icon on the toolbar of the Create Invoices window to run the QuickBooks spell checker. If the spell checker finds any word in your invoice form that isn't in the QuickBooks dictionary, that word is displayed. You can change the spelling, add the word to the QuickBooks dictionary (if it's spelled correctly), or tell the spell checker to ignore the word.

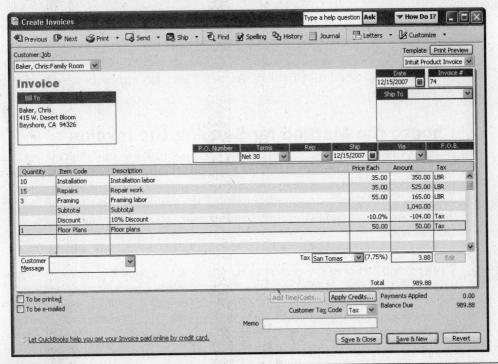

FIGURE 3-5 A completed and totaled invoice

TIP: If you check the spelling each time you create an item, you eliminate the need to worry about spelling on an invoice—everything is pre-checked before you insert the items in the invoice form. (The spell check ignores the data in the heading section of the invoice.)

NOTE: The spell checker is turned on by default. You can control the spell checker in the Spelling section of the Preferences dialog or from the Spell Options dialog box accessed by clicking the Options button in the Check Spelling on Form window.

Add a Message

You can include a message on the invoice by clicking the arrow in the Customer Message field to see all the available messages stored in the Customer Message List (see Chapter 2 for details). Or, you can type the message directly in the Customer Message window; when you use this approach, QuickBooks opens a Customer Message Not Found dialog box that offers you the chance to QuickAdd your new message to the Customer Message list, making it available for use in the future.

Add a Memo

You can add text to the Memo field at the bottom of the invoice. This text doesn't print on the invoice—it appears only on the screen (you'll see it if you reopen this invoice to view or edit it). However, the memo text *does* appear beside the invoice on statements.

Choose the Method for Sending the Invoice

At the bottom of the invoice template are two options for sending the invoice: To Be Printed and To Be E-mailed. Select the appropriate method if you're going to print or e-mail all your invoices after you finish entering them. You can also print or e-mail each invoice as you complete it. All of the options for printing and sending invoices are explained later in this chapter, in the section "Sending Invoices and Credit Memos."

 TIP: You can print the default packing slip at this point if you click the arrow next to the Print icon at the top of the Create Invoices window and select Print Packing Slip from the drop-down list. The Print Packing Slip dialog opens so you can select your printing options, which are the same as the options for printing invoices described later in this chapter.

Save the Invoice

Choose Save & New to save this invoice and move on to the next blank invoice form. If this is the last invoice you're creating, click Save & Close to save this invoice and close the Create Invoices window.

   You're ready to send the invoices to your customers. This is discussed later, in the section "Sending Invoices and Credit Memos."

 NOTE: It is not possible to print an invoice without saving it; QuickBooks automatically saves any invoice, sales order, estimate, credit memo, and sales receipt that you try to print before displaying the preview or the Print dialog box.

Editing a Previously Entered Invoice

To edit an invoice you created previously, you need to display it on-screen. You can click the Previous button to move back through all the invoices in your system. However, if you have a great many invoices, it's faster to use the Customer Center. As you click any customer or job on the Customers & Jobs tab, QuickBooks displays transactions for that customer on the right side of the screen. You can limit the transactions to a specific type to make the search easier, and you can filter the transactions; your filtering choices depend on the type of transaction you select in the Show list box. To further narrow the search, you can select a date range.

When you find the invoice you want to edit, double-click it; QuickBooks displays it in the Create Invoices window shown previously in this chapter.

 N O T E :   You also can use the QuickBooks Find feature (covered in Chapter 21).

Be aware of the following when you're editing a previously entered invoice:

- If the invoice has been paid, you should not edit the amount, date, or items. However, you can edit the memo field.
- If the invoice has not been paid, but has been mailed, you shouldn't edit anything, although it's probably safe to enter or modify text in the memo field if necessary.
- If the invoice has not yet been sent to the customer, you can make any changes you wish.

When you click Save & Close, QuickBooks displays a message dialog box asking whether you want to save the changes you made. Click Yes.

Voiding and Deleting Invoices

There's an enormous difference between voiding and deleting an invoice. Voiding an invoice makes the invoice nonexistent to your accounting and customer balances. However, the invoice number continues to exist (it's marked "VOID") so you can account for it—missing invoice numbers are just as frustrating as missing check numbers.

Deleting an invoice, on the other hand, removes all traces of it from your transaction registers and reports. Accountants will tell you that it's always best to leave the trail of a mistake that you correct rather than deleting the mistake; that way, auditors know that you made and corrected an honest mistake.

To void an invoice, follow these steps:

1. Display the invoice you want to void using the Customer Center and the techniques described in the preceding section.
2. Open the Edit menu and choose Void Invoice. QuickBooks changes all quantities on the invoice to 0, and enters "Void:" in the Memo field.
3. Click Save & Close.

 N O T E :   When you void an invoice, QuickBooks marks the status of the invoice as Paid. This means nothing more than the fact that the invoice is no longer "open and available for payment."

While you can delete invoices, I don't recommend the practice. You can accomplish the goal of canceling the effects of the invoice in some other way that leaves a trail of your actions that others can understand. For example, you can void an invoice or you can enter a credit memo to cancel the invoice. Voiding an invoice produces the same results as deleting an invoice but leaves a trail of your actions for your accountant. Using a credit memo to cancel the effects of an invoice provides both your accountant and your customer with the trail of your actions.

If you must delete an invoice, display the invoice, open the Edit menu, and click Delete Invoice. You'll have to confirm the deletion.

Behind the Scenes of Customer Invoices

It's important to understand what QuickBooks is doing behind the scenes because everything you do has an impact on your financial reports. Let's look at the effects of an imaginary invoice that has these line items:

- $500.00 for services rendered
- $30.00 for sales tax

Because QuickBooks is a full, double-entry bookkeeping program, it makes a balanced posting made to the general ledger. For this invoice, QuickBooks makes the following entries to the general ledger:

Account	Debit	Credit
Accounts Receivable	530.00	
Sales Tax		30.00
Income—Services		500.00

If the invoice includes inventory items, the entries are a bit more complicated. Suppose that an invoice sold and shipped ten widgets to a customer. The widgets cost you $50.00 each, you sold them for $100.00 each, and you charged tax and shipping.

Account	Debit	Credit
Accounts Receivable	1,077.00	
Income—Sales of Items		1,000.00
Sales Tax		70.00
Shipping		7.00
Cost of Good Sold	500.00	
Inventory		500.00

➡ **FYI**

Handling Shipping Costs

There are two theories on accounting for shipping costs:

- Separate your own shipping costs (an expense) from the shipping you collect from your customers (revenue).
- Post everything to the shipping expense.

To use the first method, create an income account for shipping and link that account to the shipping item you created to use in invoices.

If you use the latter method, at the end of the year you may find that QuickBooks reports your shipping expense as a negative number; that means that you collected more than you spent for shipping.

Using Estimates

An estimate is an educated guess of the potential sale of goods or services; you can print and present an estimate to your customer. Most people associate estimates with businesses that use job costing. In particular, the construction industry leaps to mind when most people think of estimates. But estimates can have a wider use than you might first imagine. For example, estimates can be used as work orders in businesses where you need to keep a list of promised items or services prior to actually invoicing the customer. Once work for the customer has been completed, you can use the estimate to create an invoice for the customer.

Estimates do not update your QuickBooks data; as such, you can think of them as placeholder documents that contain information you will need in the future when invoicing a customer. The invoice will update your QuickBooks data.

For certain customers or certain types of jobs, it may be advantageous to create estimates. An estimate isn't an invoice, but it can be the basis of an invoice. You can also create multiple invoices to reflect the progression of the job.

Setting Preferences

To use estimates, you must turn on the feature. Open the Edit menu and click Preferences. On the left side of the Preferences dialog box, click Jobs & Estimates. On the right side, click Company Preferences. Then click Yes in the Do You Create Estimates? box and in the Do You Do Progress Invoicing? box (see Figure 3-6). Click OK to save the changes.

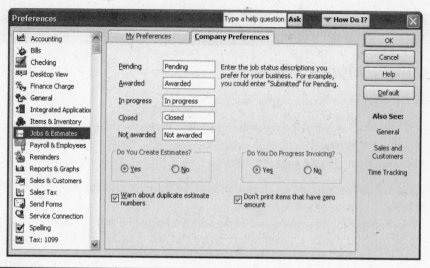

FIGURE 3-6   Set preferences for estimates

Creating an Estimate

To create an estimate, click the Estimates icon on the Home page, or choose New Transactions | Estimates in the Customer Center to display the Create Estimates window, which closely resembles the Create Invoices window. Fill out the fields in the same manner you use for invoices (see Figure 3-7).

 N O T E :   Starting in QuickBooks 2007, price levels are available on estimates.

On an estimate, you can mark up the cost of each line by entering the cost and indicating the markup in dollars or a percentage in the Markup column. If you decide to change the total of the item, QuickBooks will change the markup to make sure your math is correct.

You can create multiple estimates for a customer or a job. When you create multiple estimates for the same job, the Estimate Active option is checked by default. If a customer rejects any estimates, you can either delete them or remove the check from the Estimate Active box, effectively closing the estimate.

You can also duplicate an estimate, which provides a quick way to create multiple estimates with slightly different contents. While viewing the estimate you want to duplicate—you can use the Customer Center to find the estimate and double-click it to display it—right-click and choose Duplicate Estimate. The Estimate # field changes to the next number, while everything else remains the same. Make the required changes, and then click Save & Close.

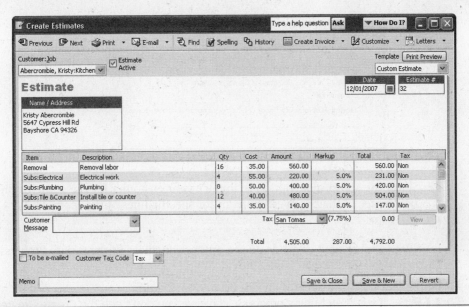

FIGURE 3-7   The Create Estimates window closely resembles the Create Invoices window

Creating Invoices from Estimates

If the customer accepts the estimate, you can convert it to a regular invoice or a progress invoice, which bills for part of an estimate rather than the entire estimate. When the job will take quite a while to complete and you need to collect money as you finish portions of the job, you can "bill as you go," charging either a percentage of the entire estimate or percentages of each line item.

When you convert an estimate to an invoice, you are actually creating an invoice to send to your customer, asking for payment. Unlike the estimate, the invoice does affect your accounting data; it reduces your inventory, increases cost of goods sold, increases accounts receivable and increases your income.

 T I P :   You also can create purchase orders automatically from estimates.

Follow these steps to create an invoice from an estimate:

1 In the Customer Center, find and double-click the estimate you want to use to create an invoice. QuickBooks displays the estimate in the Create Estimates window.

2 Click the Create Invoice button at the top of the window. QuickBooks displays the Create Progress Invoice Based on Estimate dialog box, from which you can decide whether to invoice the customer for the entire estimate or only part of the estimate.

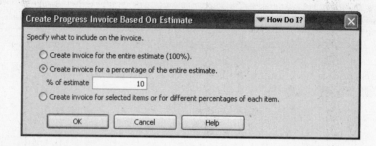

③ Select the appropriate option to invoice your customer for the entire estimate, a percentage of the entire estimate, or for specific lines of the estimate.

④ Click OK.

What happens next depends on the option you chose in the Create Progress Invoice Based on Estimate dialog box.

TIP: If you aren't using progress invoicing, you don't see the Create Progress Invoice Based On Estimate dialog box; instead, QuickBooks copies the entire estimate into the Create Invoices window.

If you chose to create an invoice for the entire estimate, QuickBooks copies the entire estimate into the Create Invoices window, which will look just like the Create Invoices window you saw earlier in this chapter.

If you chose to create an invoice for a percentage of the entire estimate, QuickBooks creates an invoice that contains all lines of the estimate and the appropriate dollar amount for each line, based on the percentage you supplied. For example, if you chose to bill for 10 percent of the estimate, QuickBooks lists all lines on the estimate and the dollar amount for 10 percent of each line (see Figure 3-8).

If you chose to invoice for specific lines of the estimate, QuickBooks displays the Specify Invoice Amounts for Items on Estimate dialog box shown in Figure 3-9. Use this dialog box to specify which lines you want to invoice and how much of them you want to invoice. You can specify an amount or a percentage on any line; the total appears at the bottom of the box. Once you fill in the appropriate information and click OK, QuickBooks displays the Create Invoices window with the correct information in it.

Estimates and Reporting

QuickBooks contains several reports that help you with estimate information. You'll find all these reports if you open the Reports menu and point to Jobs, Time, & Mileage. The Estimates by Job report lists all estimates for all jobs.

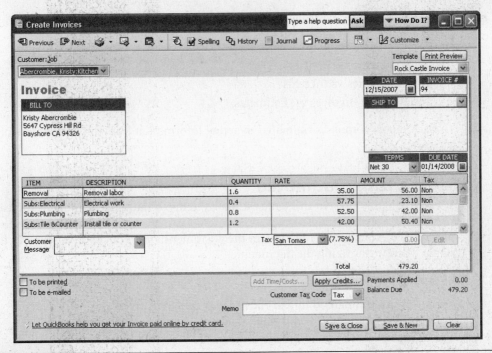

FIGURE 3-8   This invoice is for 10 percent of the estimate shown in Figure 3-7

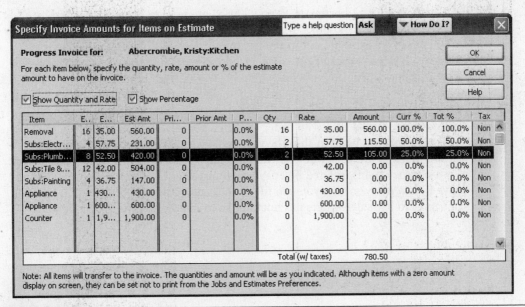

FIGURE 3-9   Select specific lines of an estimate to invoice

QuickBooks also contains reports that help you compare estimates to actuals:

- Job Estimates vs. Actuals Summary
- Job Estimates vs. Actuals Detail
- Item Estimates vs. Actuals
- Job Progress Invoices vs. Estimates

Each report compares estimated to actual information from different points of view.

Memorizing Estimates

If you frequently present the same estimated items to multiple customers, you can use the Memorize Estimate feature to create boilerplate estimates for future use. Memorized estimates do not contain the customer name; QuickBooks removes the name when memorizing the document.

Follow these steps:

1. Create an estimate, filling in the items that belong on this type of estimate. Don't fill in amounts (quantities, prices, or both) that usually change.
2. Press CTRL-M to memorize the estimate.
3. Give the estimate a name that reminds you of its contents.
4. Select the option Don't Remind Me.
5. Click OK.

To use the memorized estimate, press CTRL-T, or choose Lists | Memorized Transaction List. QuickBooks displays the Memorized Transaction List window. Double-click the estimate, fill in the Customer: Job information, and save it. QuickBooks doesn't change the memorized estimate; it creates a new estimate.

Creating Sales Orders

A customer calls and places an order for three items—and you only have two of the items in stock. You want to ship the two items you have now, but you'll need to wait for stock to arrive before you can ship the third item. How do you keep track of out-of-stock items ordered by customers? You'll need to know when the items arrive in inventory so that you can fill the customer's order—and avoid losing the sale. You can use sales orders in QuickBooks to handle situations like this one.

Many inventory-based businesses use sales orders as the first step in selling products to a customer. Think of a sales order as a "request"—if you can fill the request immediately, you'll ship the item and invoice the customer. If you can't fill the request immediately, you'll hold it until you can fill it—and *then* ship the item and invoice the customer.

Like an estimate, a sales order doesn't affect your inventory or the general ledger. You must create an invoice containing the information that appears on a sales order before QuickBooks reduces your inventory and updates the general ledger. Just as you could create an invoice from an estimate, you can create an invoice from a sales order. You also can create a purchase order from a sales order—particularly handy when you need to buy the item that you intend to resell to your customer. Like sales orders, purchase orders do not affect your QuickBooks data. You can read more about purchase orders in Chapter 6.

Preferences

To use sales orders, you must set preferences appropriately. Follow these steps:

1. Open the Edit menu and click Preferences.
2. Click Sales & Customers.
3. Click Company Preferences.
4. In the Sales Orders section on the right, place a check in the Enable Sales Orders box (see Figure 3-10).

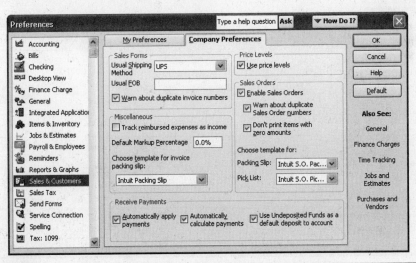

FIGURE 3-10   Enable sales orders and set other sales order preferences

⑤ Optionally, check the other two boxes in the Sales Orders section; I suggest that you check these boxes to avoid confusion later.

⑥ If your edition of QuickBooks offers options, select templates for the Packing Slip and the Pick List forms.

⑦ Click OK.

Creating a Sales Order

Create a sales order when you get a request from a customer for merchandise. "Why don't I just create an invoice?" you ask. Well, typically, you don't invoice a customer for merchandise unless you are providing the merchandise ordered. If you start to create an invoice and discover you don't have the merchandise on hand, you will end up creating a sales order for that merchandise so that you can track the backordered items. And, since you can easily create an invoice from a sales order, as you'll see in the next section, creating a sales order really isn't an extra step; it's actually a more efficient way to function.

To create a sales order, click New Transactions in the Customer Center and then click Sales Orders. The Create Sales Orders window appears (see Figure 3-11); fill in this window the same way you would fill in the Create Invoices window.

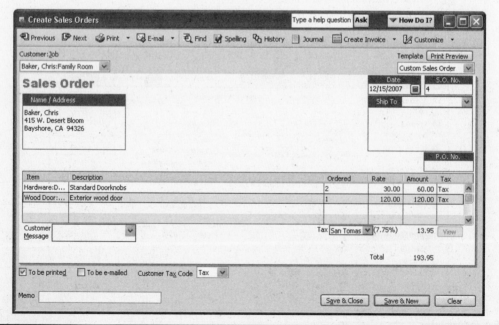

FIGURE 3-11   The Create Sales Orders window closely resembles the Create Invoices window

In the Ordered box, type the quantity your customer wants to order. In certain editions of QuickBooks, you may be able to display the Current Availability window, which shows you how many of the selected item you have on hand, on sales orders, reserved for assemblies, on purchase orders and available. See "Additional Features for Selected Editions of QuickBooks" at the end of this chapter.

QuickBooks may display a warning if you try to sell more than you have available or on hand; you can save the sales order anyway by clicking OK.

 T I P :   QuickBooks doesn't create and track back orders until you invoice, so you won't see the Back Order column on the sales order at this point.

Invoicing from a Sales Order

Typically, when you have some items in stock and some items that must be backordered, you want to ship the items you have and invoice the customer for those items at the time you fill the order. You want the remainder of the order to stay open until you receive the customer's goods.

To create an invoice for part of a sales order, redisplay the sales order in the Create Sales Orders window (you can use the Customer Center to find the sales order and double-click it to display it in the Create Sales Orders window) and click the Create Invoice button. QuickBooks displays the Create Invoice Based On Sales Order(s) dialog box.

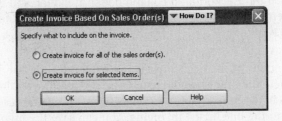

 T I P :   To create a purchase order for one or more items on the sales order that you need to buy to sell to your customer, click the down arrow beside the Create Invoice button and select Purchase Order. QuickBooks displays windows similar to the ones about to be described here, letting you save a purchase order. See Chapter 6 for details on working with purchase orders.

Select the Create Invoice For Selected Items option and click OK. QuickBooks displays the Specify Invoice Quantities for Items on Sales Order(s) window (see Figure 3-12), where you can select the items and the quantities that you want to include on the invoice. In the To Invoice column beside each item, type the number for which you want to invoice the customer.

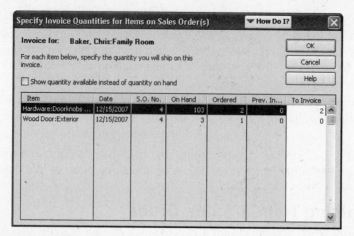

FIGURE 3-12 Use this window to select the items and the quantities that you want to include on the invoice

When you click OK, QuickBooks displays the Create Invoices window, containing all the information you provided on the sales order and in the Specify Invoice Quantities for Items on Sales Order window. You also can see the quantity ordered, the quantity invoiced, and the quantity backordered (see Figure 3-13).

($) **TIP:** If the Backordered column doesn't appear, you can customize the invoice template to display it. See "Customizing Templates" later in this chapter for details.

Notice that the invoice contains two lines but only one line will be invoiced. Don't delete the other line; it represents the backordered item. If you checked all the boxes in the Sales Order section when you set sales order preferences, QuickBooks won't print the line it isn't invoicing. You can save the invoice.

($) **TIP:** If you redisplay the sales order, QuickBooks shows the quantities invoiced and backordered.

Checking on Customer Backorders

QuickBooks contains two reports that you can use to track backorders you need to fulfill for customers: the Open Sales Orders By Item report and the Open Sales Orders By Customer report.

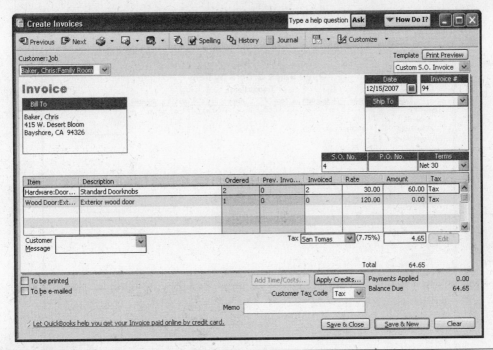

FIGURE 3-13 An invoice created from a sales order

You'll find the Open Sales Orders By Item report shown in Figure 3-14 most useful as stock that you have ordered arrives; you can check the report to see if any of the items you receive appear on the report. The report also shows you the customer for whom the items were ordered. You can drill down on the report to display the sales order and create an invoice from it.

The Open Sales Orders By Customer report shown in Figure 3-15 becomes very useful when you are trying to find a particular customer's order. Again, you can drill down on the report to display a sales order in the Create Sales Orders window.

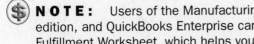 **N O T E :**   Users of the Manufacturing and Wholesale edition, the Retail edition, and QuickBooks Enterprise can take advantage of the Sales Order Fulfillment Worksheet, which helps you plan which sales orders to fill and the impact filling those sales orders will have on your inventory. See the end of this chapter for details.

Issuing Credits and Refunds

Sometimes you have to give money to a customer. You can do this in the form of a credit against current or future balances, or you can write a check and refund money you received from the customer.

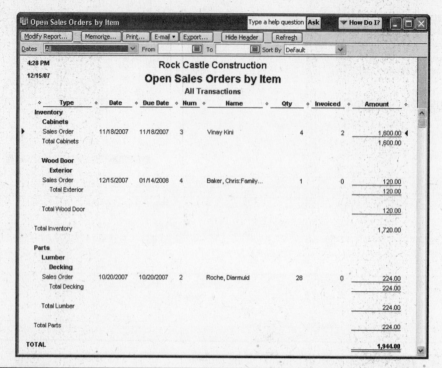

FIGURE 3-14   Use this report to check for the arrival of items on sales orders

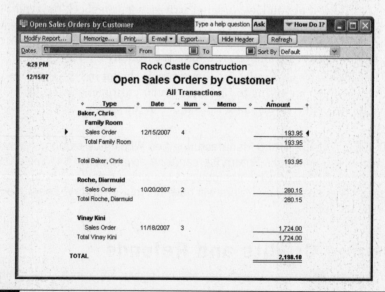

FIGURE 3-15   Use this report to monitor backorders for a particular customer

➡ FYI

When You Need to Issue a Credit But You Don't Receive Merchandise Back from the Customer

If the goods were damaged, your customer won't be returning goods to you but you'll need to issue a credit memo to reduce the customer's balance. In this case, don't use the items you sold on the credit memo—if you do, you'll return the items to inventory for resale. Instead, create an Other Charge item called Returns and Allowances. Make it a taxable item and assign it to an income account or to a Sales Returns and Allowances account, which you use to reduce income as needed. Use this Returns and Allowances item on the credit memo. Without affecting your inventory accounts, the credit memo will reduce the customer's balance and your total Accounts Receivable balance. It will also reduce income or increase the Sales Returns and Allowances account. And, by making the Returns and Allowances item taxable, QuickBooks will also adjust your sales tax liability.

Creating Credit Memos

A credit memo reduces a customer balance. Issue a credit memo when a customer returns goods, when you have invoiced the customer for goods that were lost or damaged in shipment, or when you agree to adjust a price on an invoice you issued to a customer.

You usually send the credit memo to the customer to let the customer know the details about the credit that's being applied. QuickBooks updates your accounting records for credit memos the same way it updates your accounting records for invoices, except there's an inherent minus sign next to the number.

Creating a credit memo is similar to creating an invoice:

1. Click the Refunds & Credits icon on the Home page or choose New Transactions | Credit Memos/Refunds in the Customer Center to open a blank Create Credit Memos/Refunds window (see Figure 3-16).
2. Select a customer, and then fill out the rest of the heading.
3. Move to the line item section and enter the item, the quantity, and the rate for the items in this credit memo. You don't need to use a minus sign.
4. Remember to insert all the special items you need to give credit for, such as shipping.
5. You can use the Customer Message field to add any short explanation that's necessary.
6. Click Save & Close or Save & New to save the credit memo.

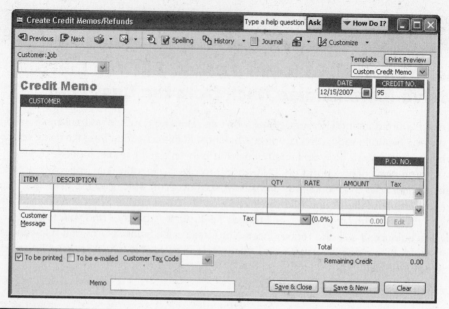

FIGURE 3-16   Create a credit memo in this window

NOTE: See the section "Sending Invoices and Credit Memos" later in this chapter to learn about delivering your credit memos.

When you save the credit memo, QuickBooks displays a dialog box where you can choose the way to apply this credit, explained in the following sections.

Retaining the Credit

Choose Retain As An Available Credit to let the credit amount stay with the customer. You can apply the credit to a future invoice, or apply it to an open invoice later, depending on what the customer wants to do. When you create invoices, or apply customer payments to existing invoices, the credit is available. If the credit is for a job, and the job doesn't have any outstanding invoices, you should retain the credit, because you can apply it against a different job for the same customer.

Issuing a Refund for the Credit

Choose Give A Refund to send the amount of the credit back to the customer. When you click OK, the Issue A Refund window opens (see Figure 3-17).

In the Issue This Refund Via field if you choose Cash or Check, QuickBooks deducts the amount from the bank account. Be sure to select the appropriate bank account in the Account field.

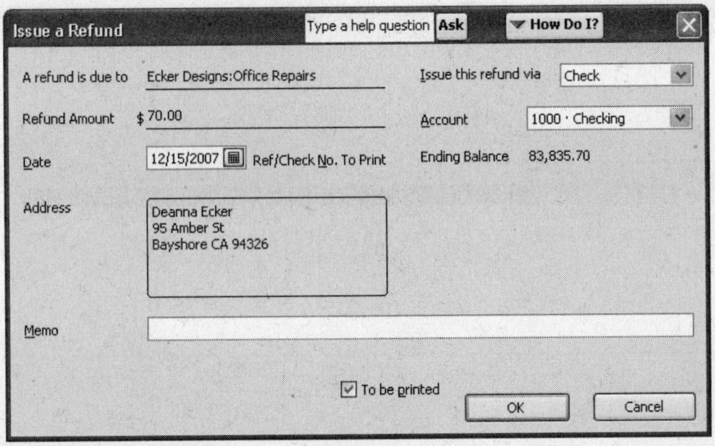

FIGURE 3-17 Issue a refund from this window

In addition, if you choose Check, QuickBooks adds the To Be Printed check box, checked by default. If you print checks, leave the check mark in the check box and click OK, and QuickBooks adds the check to the list of checks to be printed when you print checks. The check also appears in the bank account register with the notation "To Print."

If you write checks manually, remove the check mark in the To Be Printed check box, and click OK. QuickBooks adds the check to your bank account register, using the next available check number.

Applying the Credit to an Invoice

Choose Apply To An Invoice to apply the credit to an existing invoice. When you click OK, QuickBooks displays a list of open invoices for this customer or job, and automatically selects the oldest invoice (see Figure 3-18).

If the credit is larger than the oldest invoice, QuickBooks applies the remaining amount of the credit to the next oldest invoice. If there are no additional invoices, the remaining amount of the credit is held in the customer's record, and is treated as a retained credit. Click Done to close the window.

Sending Invoices and Credit Memos

You have several choices about the method you use to send invoices and credit memos. You can print and mail them, or send them via e-mail.

Printing Invoices and Credit Memos

You can print invoices and credit memos on blank paper, preprinted forms on a single sheet of paper, preprinted multipart forms, or on your company letterhead.

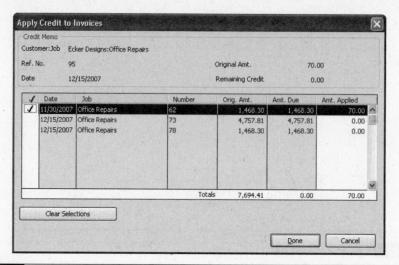

FIGURE 3-18   You can choose the invoice to which you want QuickBooks to apply the credit

The first time you print invoices and credit memos, you need to set up your printer for invoices and credit memos.

Setting Up the Printer for Forms

If you have multiple printers attached to your computer or accessible through a network, you have to designate one of them as the invoice printer. If you use multipart forms, you should have a dot matrix printer. Printers are set up in Windows, not QuickBooks, and QuickBooks will use those printers.

 TIP: You can assign different printers to different forms, which is a nifty time-saver.

Follow these steps to tell QuickBooks about the printer and the way you want to print invoices:

1. Choose File | Printer Setup from the menu bar to open the Printer Setup dialog box (see Figure 3-19) and select Invoice from the Form Name drop-down list.

2. If you have multiple printers available, select the printer you intend to use for invoices in Printer Name box.

3. In the bottom of the dialog, select the type of form you're planning to use for invoices from the following options:

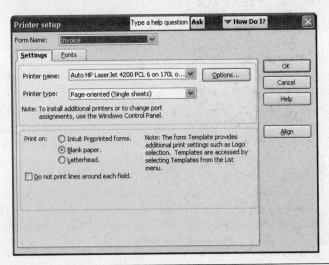

FIGURE 3-19 Use this dialog box to describe how you want to print invoices

- **Intuit Preprinted Forms:** These are templates with all your company information, field names, and row and column dividers already printed. These forms need to be aligned to match the way your invoice prints. Selecting this option tells QuickBooks that only the data needs to be sent to the printer because the fields are already printed.
- **Blank Paper:** Selecting this option tells QuickBooks that everything, including your company name and address, field names, and the like, must be sent to the printer. This is easiest, but it may not look as attractive as a printed form.
- **Letterhead:** Selecting this option tells QuickBooks not to print the company information when it prints the invoice because you'll be printing the invoice on your company letterhead, which already contains this information.

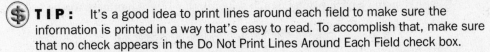 **TIP:** It's a good idea to print lines around each field to make sure the information is printed in a way that's easy to read. To accomplish that, make sure that no check appears in the Do Not Print Lines Around Each Field check box.

Setting Up Form Alignment

To test the QuickBooks output against the paper in your printer to make sure everything prints in the right place, click the Align button in the Printer Setup dialog, select the invoice template you're using (e.g., Service, Product, etc.), and then click OK. The dialog box that you see to set up alignment differs, depending on the type of printer you've selected.

Aligning Dot Matrix Printers

If you're using a continuous-feed printer (dot matrix using paper with sprocket holes), you'll see a dialog box that lets you perform both coarse and fine adjustments to allow you to set the placement of the top of the page, which you don't have to do with a page printer (laser, inkjet).

Start by clicking the Coarse button. A dialog box appears telling you that a sample form is about to be printed; you shouldn't make any physical adjustments to your printer after the sample has printed because QuickBooks displays another dialog box where you can make any necessary adjustments. Make sure the appropriate preprinted form, letterhead, or blank paper is loaded in the printer. Click OK.

The sample form prints to your dot matrix printer and QuickBooks displays a dialog box asking you to enter pointer line position. You can see the pointer line at the top of the printed sample. Enter the number of the pointer line in the dialog box and click OK (the printout numbers the lines). QuickBooks will walk you through any adjustments that might be needed.

If you want to tweak the alignment a bit further, choose Fine. (See the information on using the Fine Alignment dialog in the section "Aligning Laser and Inkjet Printers" that follows this section.) Otherwise, choose OK.

When the form is printing correctly, QuickBooks displays a message telling you to note the position of the form in your printer now that the form is properly aligned. You should note where the top of the page is in relation to the print head and the bar that leans against the paper.

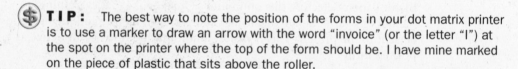 **TIP:** The best way to note the position of the forms in your dot matrix printer is to use a marker to draw an arrow with the word "invoice" (or the letter "I") at the spot on the printer where the top of the form should be. I have mine marked on the piece of plastic that sits above the roller.

Aligning Laser and Inkjet Printers

If you're using a page printer, you'll see only this Fine Alignment dialog.

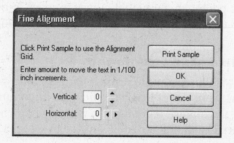

Click Print Sample to send output to your printer. Then, with the printed page in your hand, make adjustments to the alignment in the dialog. Use the arrows next to the Vertical and Horizontal boxes to move the positions at which printing occurs.

Click OK, and then click OK in the Printer Setup dialog. QuickBooks saves your settings for printing invoices.

Repeat this process to create settings for credit memos.

Batch Printing

If you didn't print each invoice or credit memo as you created it, and you made sure that the To Be Printed check box was selected on each invoice you created, you're ready to print invoices and credit memos. Place the correct paper in your printer and, if it's continuous paper in a dot matrix printer, position it properly. In the steps below, I'll show you how to print invoices; you use the same steps to print credit memos, except, in Step 1, choose File | Print Forms | Credit Memos.

Then, follow these steps:

1. Choose File | Print Forms | Invoices. In the Select Invoices To Print window, all your unprinted invoices appear selected with a check mark.

2. If there are any invoices you don't want to print at this time, click the check marks to remove them.

NOTE: If you want to print mailing labels for these invoices, you must print them first (see the next section).

3. Click OK to print your invoices.

The Print Invoices dialog appears, and you can change or select printing options. Click Print to begin printing. Repeat the steps to print your credit memos.

Printing Mailing Labels

If you need mailing labels, QuickBooks will print them for you. You must print the mailing labels before you print the invoices.

In the Select Invoices To Print window, click the Print Labels button to display the Select Labels To Print dialog box.

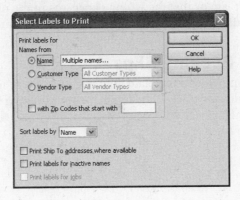

➠ FYI

The Shipping Manager

You can use the Shipping Manager in QuickBooks to ship products to your customers via either Federal Express or UPS. You can use the Shipping Manager from the Create Invoices window to create a shipment for one invoice; click the down arrow on the Ship button that appears on the window's toolbar.

Or, you can work in the Shipping Manager window to create shipments; choose File | Shipping and then select either Ship FedEx Package or Ship UPS Package. In all editions of QuickBooks 2007, the Shipping Manager has an improved interface and supports:

- Multipackage shipments
- Rate mark-up options
- Thermal printers
- Third party billing
- Drop shipping
- Return services
- Shipment declared value
- Electronic scales

QuickBooks preselects the option to produce labels for multiple customers, and the customers selected are those customers who have invoices waiting to be printed. Click OK to open the Print Labels dialog box (see Figure 3-20).

Select the appropriate printer and label format; in the drop-down list, you'll see a selection of Avery labels as well as preprinted labels from Intuit. Click Print.

After the labels print, QuickBooks redisplays the Select Invoices To Print dialog. Choose OK to open the Print Invoices dialog and begin printing your invoices.

After you've finished printing invoices, review the invoices to make sure that the printer didn't jam or that the wrong paper was in the printer. If anything went amiss, QuickBooks gives you an opportunity to reprint the forms.

Printing Packing Slips

QuickBooks provides a template for a packing slip, which is basically an invoice that doesn't display prices. The theory behind packing slips is that the warehouse personnel who manage and pack products don't need to know the dollars associated with those products.

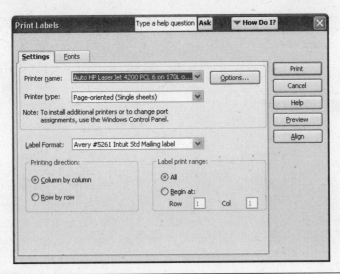

FIGURE 3-20   Use this dialog box to select the appropriate label format

Print the Default Packing Slip

To print the default packing slip, complete the invoice. Then click the arrow next to the Print icon at the top of the Create Invoices window and select Print Packing Slip from the drop-down list. The Print Packing Slip dialog opens so you can select your printing options (which are the same as the options described earlier for printing invoices).

Change the Default Packing Slip

If you create your own customized packing slip template, you can select it each time you print a packing slip.

You can also make that new form the default packing slip by following these steps:

1. Choose Edit | Preferences to open the Preferences dialog box.
2. Go to the Sales & Customers section and click the Company Preferences tab.
3. In the Choose Template For Invoice Packing Slip field, select your new packing slip form from the drop-down list.
4. Click OK.

If you have multiple packing slips, you can choose any of them for printing. With the completed invoice in the Create Invoices window, instead of selecting Print Packing Slip from the Print button's drop-down list, select a packing slip template from the drop-down list in the Template field. The Create Invoices window changes to display the packing slip (see Figure 3-21).

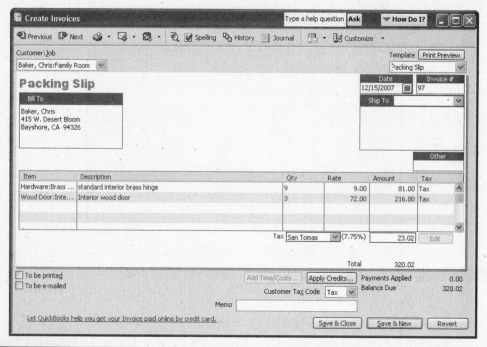

FIGURE 3-21   A packing slip

Although amounts appear on the packing slip in the illustration, they won't print. This particular packing slip is set up so that amounts appear on-screen but not when you print—a handy feature, as you'll learn when you read the section on customizing templates later in this chapter.

To see what the printed version of the packing slip looks like, click the Print Preview button. Click Close to return to the Create Invoices window.

E-mailing Invoices and Credit Memos

QuickBooks provides a free service that you can use to send invoices and credit memos as e-mail attachments to customers. In the following discussion, I'll refer to invoices in the discussion, but all the same instructions apply to credit memos and other customer forms.

You can use the Customer Center to find the invoice and double-click it to display it.

To e-mail an invoice, make sure the completed invoice appears in the Create Invoices window and follow these steps:

1 Click the arrow to the right of the Send icon on the Create Invoices window toolbar and select E-mail Invoice to save the invoice and open the Send Invoice dialog box.

2 In the Send Invoice dialog(see Figure 3-22), select E-mail, and make sure the e-mail addresses in the To and From fields are correct; QuickBooks fills them in using the data you entered for your company and your customers. If you didn't enter e-mail address data for your company or your customer, you can enter the e-mail address manually.

N O T E :   If you manually enter an e-mail address, QuickBooks notifies you that the address doesn't match the current stored data and offers to update the customer's record, providing you with an easy way to update the customer's record.

3 If you want to send a copy of the invoice to another recipient, enter the e-mail address in the CC field. For multiple recipients, separate each address with a comma.

4 Make any needed changes to the text of the e-mail message.

5 Click Send Now to e-mail the invoice immediately, or click Send Later to save the invoice and e-mail it with other invoices in a batch.

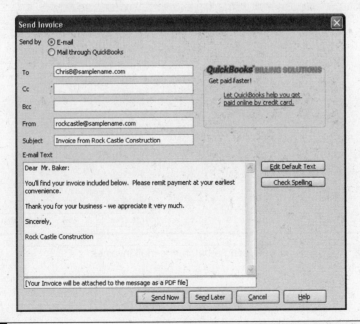

FIGURE 3-22   Double-check the e-mail address information before you e-mail an invoice

E-mail the Invoice Immediately

If you click Send Now to e-mail this invoice immediately, QuickBooks opens a browser window and takes you to the Business Services section of the Intuit web site. Your regular e-mail software doesn't open; this is all done by QuickBooks through the Internet. Follow the prompts to complete the sign up process; the service is free. When your e-mail is sent, QuickBooks displays a message indicating that your e-mail was sent successfully.

E-mail Invoices in a Batch

If you click Send Later, QuickBooks saves the e-mail message so that you can send it later as part of a group of messages.

When you want to e-mail all the invoices, choose File | Send Forms to open the Select Forms To Send dialog box (see Figure 3-23). You can also open this dialog by selecting Send Batch from the Send icon drop-down list in the Create Invoices window.

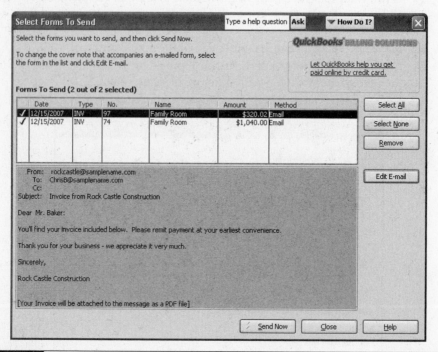

FIGURE 3-23   Use this window to send a batch of e-mail invoices

Here are some guidelines for working with the Select Forms To Send dialog box:

- By default, all e-mails are selected. Deselect an e-mail by clicking the check mark in the leftmost column of its listing. Click again to put the check mark back.
- You can delete any item by selecting it and clicking Remove. You're not deleting the invoice, you're deleting the e-mail. You can return to the invoice and send it anytime.
- To edit the message text of any e-mail, double-click its listing, or highlight it and click the Edit E-mail button. Make your changes and click OK.

Click Send Now to e-mail all the selected items. Your regular e-mail software doesn't open; this is all done by QuickBooks through the Internet. Follow the prompts to complete the sign-up process (the service is free).

Change the Default Message

If you want to change the default message that appears in the e-mail message, choose Edit | Preferences and click the Send Forms icon on the left side of the Preferences dialog box (see Figure 3-24). On the Company Preferences tab, make changes to any part of the message header or text.

You can use this dialog to customize the e-mail for all QuickBooks forms that can be sent by e-mail, which includes a wide variety of forms. Select the appropriate form from the drop-down list in the Change Default For field.

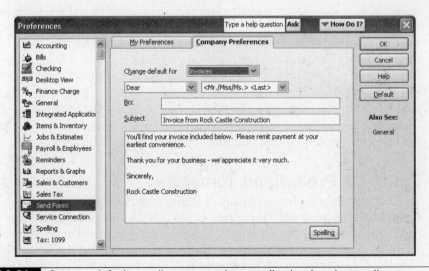

FIGURE 3-24 Set up a default e-mail message when sending invoices by e-mail

You can change the way the salutations are inserted in the message, change the text of the Subject field, and change the text in the message. You can also perform a spell check.

The Customer Side of E-mailed Invoices

When the customer receives your e-mail invoice, the invoice is a PDF attachment. In addition to the message text you sent, below your signature, the e-mail message includes a statement that the recipient needs Acrobat Reader to open the attached invoice file.

If your customer doesn't have Acrobat Reader (now called Adobe Reader) installed, clicking the "Acrobat Reader" link sends your customer to the Adobe web site, where the customer can download the software for free.

Additional Send Features for Forms

The Send drop-down list on the invoice form (and other forms) includes a choice named Mail Invoice. This refers to a fee-based feature for which you can sign up to let Intuit print and mail your invoices. The printed form has a tear-off remittance slip, a return envelope, and other features.

You can also add a "pay online" feature for customers, available, for a fee, from Intuit. Information about both additional services is available on the QuickBooks web site (www.quickbooks.com).

Customizing Templates

QuickBooks makes it very easy to customize the templates you use to create transactions such as invoices, purchase orders, and statements. You can use an existing template as the basis of a new template, copying what you like, changing what you don't like, and eliminating what you don't need. In the following discussion, I'm using invoice templates, but you can customize other templates just as easily.

Customizing a template impacts the printed look and feel of the selected form and adds fields to the on-screen version of the form. You can preview the form in the Manage Templates dialog box that appears later in this section.

Editing a Predefined Template

You can make minor changes to any of the built-in templates provided by QuickBooks; because these templates come with the software, Intuit helps you maintain what you got in the box by limiting what you can change on a built-in template. If you want to make more extensive changes, QuickBooks creates a new template for you by copying the template; then you can edit it using the techniques described later in this chapter in the section "Designing a New Template."

To make minor changes to a built-in template, open the transaction window—in this example, the Create Invoices window—and select the template from the Template drop-down list and then click the Customize button above the Template list. QuickBooks displays the Basic Customization dialog box (see Figure 3-25).

You can change the fonts that QuickBooks uses on the form. You also can remove or add your company name, company address, phone number, fax number, e-mail address, or web site address. In addition, you can add or remove the status stamp from the printed transaction; the status stamp indicates, for example, if an invoice is paid. If you want to add a logo to your printed form, check the Use Logo box. In the Select Image dialog that appears, navigate to the folder that has your logo file, select it, and click Open. Click OK to confirm the use of this file.

QuickBooks positions the logo in the upper-left corner of your invoice form. You cannot change the positioning of the logo when you're working in Edit mode. See the section "Designing the Layout" to learn how to change the location of your logo on your invoices.

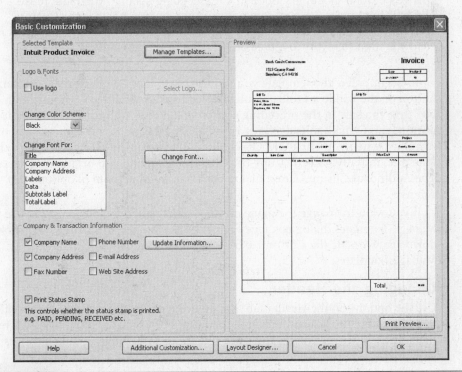

FIGURE 3-25   You can make limited changes to a template in this dialog box

TIP: QuickBooks copies your logo file to an image folder located below the folder containing your data file.

Designing a New Template

If you want to add, remove, or reposition elements in your invoice and you use any of the built-in templates, you have to design a new template. You also can add any custom fields you may have created for any of your lists to the transaction form.

To create a new template, you make a copy of an existing template. This approach works well because you leave the original template intact and you can easily revert to it, providing you with a good way to experiment with template configuration.

 NOTE: In earlier versions of QuickBooks, you could choose to edit a built-in template or duplicate the template. In QuickBooks 2007, if you want to make changes beyond those described in the preceding section, you must make a copy of a built-in template *except* templates whose names begin with "Custom." I suggest you make a copy of any template before you make changes, just in case you want to revert to a previous version of the template.

To begin, select the template you want to customize and click the Customize button on the window toolbar. QuickBooks displays the Basic Customization dialog box that you saw in the preceding section. Click the Additional Customization button, and QuickBooks displays a message indicating it will make a copy of the template; when you click OK, QuickBooks automatically creates a copy of the template, initially named "Copy of" whatever template you originally selected. The Additional Customization dialog box contains a plethora of options that you can use.

If you want to change the name of the template after you customize it, use the Manage Templates dialog box (see Figure 3-26). To open this dialog box, click the down arrow beside the Customize button on the window toolbar and choose Manage Templates.

Changing the Header

Use the options on the Header tab, shown in Figure 3-27, to change information that appears in the header section of the form. For example, you can add or remove the Ship To block, or change the word Invoice to something else like Services Rendered.

 TIP: As you add fields, watch the Preview window; you'll see QuickBooks add the field to the layout.

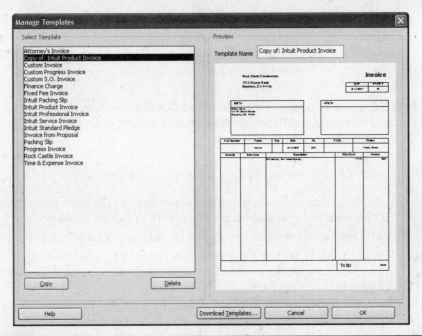

FIGURE 3-26 Use this dialog box to begin customizing a template

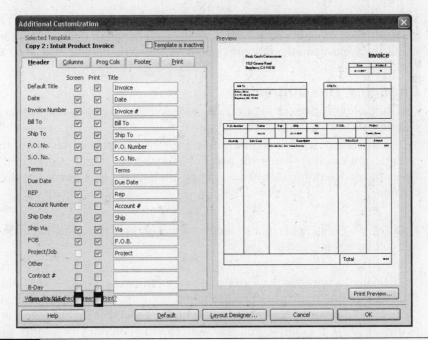

FIGURE 3-27   Change the information that appears in the header section of the form

Notice that two columns of check boxes appear for each field. These check boxes control *where* the field appears—on-screen, when you print the form, or both. For example, in the illustration, the Project field will appear on the printed invoice for the customer, but not on the screen.

 N O T E :   It's important to understand QuickBooks does not report on fields that you do not display in a transaction window, even if you provided information for the field on the customer record.

Here are some common changes you might want to make:

- Add a field that is displayed on the screen copy of the form to the printed copy (if you want the customer to see the new field and its information).
- Add a field to the screen copy to display data not currently displayed on the screen (a way to provide information to the person who is entering the data).
- Add a field to both the printed form and the screen display if it's appropriate for everybody to see the data.
- Remove fields from the printed copy of the form, the screen display, or both, if it's appropriate to skip that data.
- Add custom fields you created (as discussed in Chapter 2) to the printed form, the on-screen display, or both.

 T I P :   The custom fields that are available are the custom fields you created for Name lists (Customer:Job, Vendor, Employee). Custom fields created for items are available in the Columns tab, covered in the next section.

Changing the Columns

Use the Columns tab (see Figure 3-28) to modify the columns that appear in the line item section of the invoice.

You can add or remove columns from the screen or printed version of the form or both. You can also change the order of columns; the numbers displayed in the Order boxes determine the left-to-right position on the form, with 1 as the leftmost column.

 N O T E :   Some columns can only be removed from the printed version of the form, not the on-screen display.

QuickBooks provides two extra columns for your use, Other 1 and Other 2. Check the appropriate boxes to add these columns to the screen or print version of the invoice (or both). Then enter the text for the Label that should appear at the top of the column. For example, you may want to add a column for Quantity Shipped,

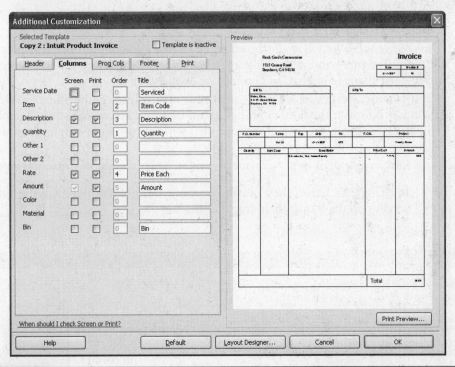

FIGURE 3-28 Change the line item columns or the order in which they appear

in which you enter the number of items you're shipping with this order. The number of items ordered appears in the Quantity column, and in this case you could change the text for the Quantity column to Qty Ordered.

 NOTE: Be aware that, while you can add these columns to an invoice template, you cannot search your company file or produce any reports that display information you enter into these fields.

Changing Data in the Other Tabs

Both the Prog Cols tab and the Footer tab work just like the Header tab and the Columns tab; you can go through these tabs, making changes as needed.

The Prog Cols tab provides customization options for invoices you send if you're using the Progress Billing feature (covered earlier in this chapter).

In the Footer tab, you can add information to the invoice, such as the current balance due or the payments received.

On the Print tab, you'll find self-explanatory options that control printer settings for printing invoices.

Designing the Layout

To change the layout of the form, click the Layout Designer button to display the Layout Designer window (see Figure 3-29). From this window, you can move elements, change margins, and build your own layout.

If you use window envelopes to mail your invoices, select the Show Envelope Window option at the bottom of the Layout Designer before you start. QuickBooks highlights in green the area of the form that will appear in the envelope windows, helping you avoid moving any fields into that area.

Select any element to put a frame around it. Then, do any of the following:

- To change the size of the element, position your pointer on one of the sizing handles on the frame, then drag the handle.

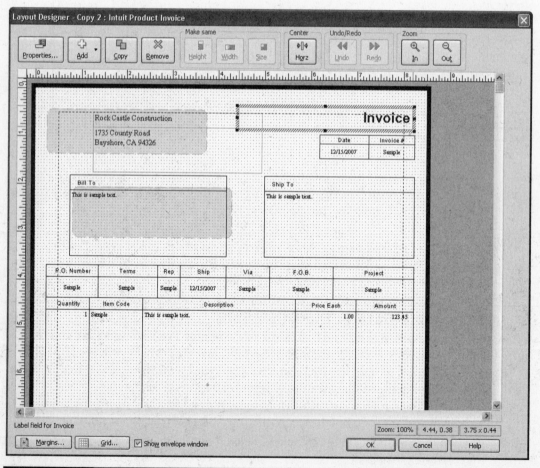

FIGURE 3-29   The Layout Designer window

- To move an element, position your pointer inside the frame and, when your pointer turns into a four-headed arrow, drag the frame to a different location on the form.
- Double-click an element's frame to see a Properties dialog that permits all sorts of option changes for the selected element.

- To change the margin measurements, click the Margins button at the bottom of the Layout Designer.
- Click the Grid button to show or hide the dotted-line grid on the screen, to change the spacing between grid lines, or to turn off the Snap To Grid option, which automatically aligns objects to the nearest point on the grid.
- Use the toolbar buttons to align, resize, and zoom into the selected elements. There's also an Undo/Redo choice. When you finish with the Layout Designer, click OK to redisplay the Basic Customization window.

Once everything is just the way you want it, save your new template by clicking OK. This new template name appears on the Template drop-down list when you create invoices.

 TIP: You can also use this new template as the basis for other customizations.

Using Memorized Invoices

If you have a recurring invoice—for example, if you have a retainer agreement with a customer—you can automate the process of creating it. Recurring invoices are those that are sent out at regular intervals, usually for the same amount.

Create the first invoice, filling out all the fields. If there are any fields that will change each time you send the invoice, leave those fields blank and fill them out each time you send the invoice. Then press CTRL-M to open the Memorize Transaction dialog.

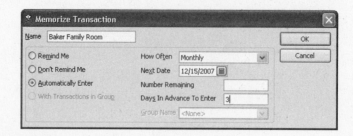

Fill in the fields using the following guidelines:

- Change the title in the Name box to reflect what you've done. It's easiest to add a word or phrase to the default title (which is the customer or job name), such as Retainer. You can use up to 31 characters, including spaces, in the Name box.
- Choose Remind Me and specify how and when you want to be reminded in the How Often and Next Date fields. The reminder will appear in the QuickBooks Reminder window.
- Choose Don't Remind Me if you only use this memorized invoice occasionally.
- Choose Automatically Enter if you want QuickBooks to issue this invoice automatically. If you opt for automatic issuing of this invoice, you must fill in the fields so that QuickBooks performs the task accurately, as follows:

  - The How Often field is where you specify the interval for this invoice, such as monthly, weekly, or so on. Click the arrow to see the drop-down list and choose the option you need.
  - The Next Date field is the place to note the next instance of this invoice.
  - The Number Remaining field is a place to start a countdown for a specified number of invoices. This is useful if you're billing a customer for a finite number of months because you only have a one-year contract.
  - The Days In Advance To Enter field is for specifying the number of days in advance of the next date you want QuickBooks to create the invoice.

Click OK when you have finished filling out the dialog. Then click Save & Close in the Invoice window to save the transaction. Later, if you want to view, edit, or remove the transaction, you can select it from the Memorized Transaction List by pressing CTRL-T.

Additional Features for Selected Editions of QuickBooks

Some of the editions of QuickBooks have some additional features available, above and beyond the features covered in this chapter.

Customized Templates

QuickBooks Enterprise and the Professional Services Edition of QuickBooks Premier contain customized invoice and estimate templates, and QuickBooks Enterprise and the Manufacturing & Wholesale Edition contains customized quote and sales order templates.

In the following editions of QuickBooks, you have the option to save modifications to estimates as change orders, which identify what changed on the estimate.

- QuickBooks Enterprise
- QuickBooks Premier: Contractor Edition
- QuickBooks Premier: Accountant Edition

Current Availability of Items

In the Accountant Edition, the Manufacturing and Wholesale Edition, and the Retail Edition, you'll see an icon in the Quantity column when you select an inventory item in the Item Code column while preparing an invoice. If you click the icon, QuickBooks displays the Current Availability window (see Figure 3-30), which shows the number of the selected item on hand, on sales orders, reserved for assemblies, on purchase orders and available. If the selected item appears on any purchase orders, you can click the Show Details button (which changes to Hide Details after you click it) to see the purchase order information.

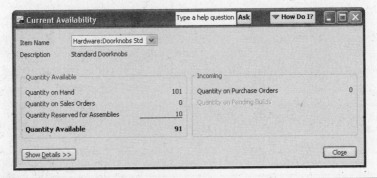

FIGURE 3-30   The Current Availability window

TIP: Displaying the Current Availability window is very handy if you are on the phone with a customer and want to check stock. You'll also find this window available from the Item List window.

Sales Order Fulfillment Worksheet

Fulfilling sales orders is one of the most difficult tasks in managing inventory. You can use the Sales Order Fulfillment Worksheet to help you:

- Plan the sales orders to fulfill and view the effects on inventory based on your selections.
- Process sales orders.
- Print pick lists, packing slips, and sales orders.

 NOTE: To use the Sales Order Fulfillment Worksheet, you need to set Preferences (choose Edit | Preferences) to enable inventory, purchase orders, and sales orders.

The Sales Order Fulfillment Worksheet (see Figure 3-31) is primarily a planning tool; you use it to test what will happen if you fill selected sales orders. Use the Sort dropdown list in the upper right corner to order the sales orders that appear in the top portion of the window.

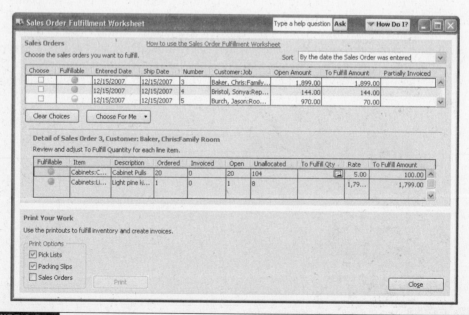

FIGURE 3-31   Use the Sales Order Fulfillment Worksheet to see how filling selected sales orders will affect your inventory

Sales orders containing inventory items appear in the top portion of the window. If you have enough in inventory to fill the entire sales order, a green icon appears in the Fulfillable column. If you have enough in inventory to fill only part of a sales order, QuickBooks displays a yellow icon in the Fulfillable column. If you don't have enough in inventory to fill any of a particular sales order, QuickBooks draws an X through the icon in the Fulfillable column.

You click a sales order in the top portion of the window to see the details of the sales order in the bottom of the window. If you click in the Choose column beside a sales order, QuickBooks fills in the updates the quantities in the To FulFill Qty column with the quantities you need to fill each inventory item on the sales order. QuickBooks also updates the Unallocated column using the numbers on the sales order to reflect how many of each inventory item you'll have left after you fill the sales order.

You can change the quantity in the To Fulfill Qty column to see the effect on inventory if you filled only part of the sales order. You also can click the Choose For Me button and let QuickBooks select sales order for you to fill. You can have QuickBooks fill:

- All orders with the earliest order date
- Full orders with the earliest order date
- All orders with the earliest ship date
- Full orders with the earliest ship date
- All orders with the largest potential revenue
- Full orders with the largest potential revenue

Once you've identified the sales orders you want to fill, you can use the Print button to print pick lists, packing slips, or sales orders. Warehouse personnel can use the pick list to pull the items for the order from you shelves. When they return the pick list to you, notated with quantities pulled for the order, you can print the packing slip. You may also want to print the sales order.

 T I P :   Print pick lists first to keep your inventory quantities accurate.

When you click the Print button, QuickBooks displays the Print dialog box for the type of form you selected. Select a printer and paper type and click the Print button to produce the printed copies.

Using the pick lists, packing slips, or sales orders, create invoices from the sales orders for the items you are filling. When you create an invoice from a sales order as described earlier in this chapter, QuickBooks updates the quantities on the sales order to keep your company information accurate.

Receiving Payments

In this chapter:

- Applying customer payments
- Applying credits and discounts to invoices
- Handling cash sales
- Depositing payments and cash sales into your bank account

Chapter 4

The best part of accounting is receiving payments. You need to make sure you apply customer payments correctly so that you and your customers have the same information in your records. In this chapter, we'll cover the tasks you'll perform when you receive money from customers.

Receiving Payments for Invoices

When you receive payments from customers, you use the Receive Payments window in QuickBooks to record them. There are actually several cases that can arise when you receive a customer payment, and in this section, we'll consider:

- The basics of recording a payment
- Handling underpayments
- Applying outstanding credits, and
- Handling discounts

Recording the Payment

When you record a payment from a customer, you use the Receive Payments window in QuickBooks.

When a check arrives from a customer, follow these steps to apply the payment:

1. Click the Receive Payments icon on the Home page or choose New Transactions | Receive Payments from the Customer Center menu bar. QuickBooks displays the Receive Payments window (see Figure 4-1).
2. Click the arrow to the right of the Received From field and select the customer or job from the drop-down list using the following criteria:
   - If you received a payment from a customer for whom you're not tracking jobs or for an invoice that wasn't related to a job, select the customer. The current balance for this customer automatically appears in the Customer Balance field.
   - If you received a payment for a job, select the job. The current balance for this job automatically appears in the Customer Balance field.
   - If you received a payment that covers multiple jobs, select the customer. The current balance for this customer automatically appears in the Customer Balance field, and QuickBooks displays all invoices for all of the customer's jobs.

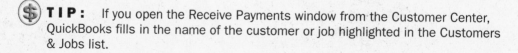 **TIP:** If you open the Receive Payments window from the Customer Center, QuickBooks fills in the name of the customer or job highlighted in the Customers & Jobs list.

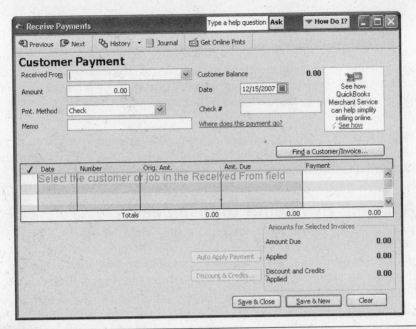

FIGURE 4-1 Use the Receive Payments window to record payments from customers

③ In the Amount field, enter the amount of the payment.

TIP: You can skip the Amount field and select invoices at the bottom of the Receive Payments window; QuickBooks calculates the total of the invoices you select and places it in the Amount field. You can disable this option in the Sales & Customers category of the Preferences dialog box. If you disable the option and you select an invoice listing without entering the amount of the payment first, QuickBooks displays an error message.

④ Click the arrow to the right of the Pmt. Method field and select the payment method:
- If the payment method is a credit card, complete the Card No. and Exp. Date fields. If you have a merchant account with the QuickBooks Merchant Account Service, click the option Process <*credit card name*> Payment When Saving.
- If the payment method is a check, enter the check number in the Check # field.

⑤ The Memo field is optional; if there's some important memorandum you want to attach to this payment record, this is the place to record it.

If the Deposit To field appears on-screen, select the bank account into which you'll deposit the payment, or select the Undeposited Funds account (see the section "Turning Payments into Bank Deposits" later in this chapter for more information on the Undeposited Funds account). If the Deposit To field doesn't appear on-screen, you've set your Sales & Customers Preferences to automatically deposit payments to the Undeposited Funds account.

 NOTE: You can add any additional payment methods you need by choosing <Add New> in the Pmt. Method drop-down list (see Chapter 2 to learn about adding items to QuickBooks lists).

Applying Payments to Invoices

If you enter a payment amount (Step 3 above), then, by default, QuickBooks automatically applies the payment to the oldest invoice, unless the amount of the payment exactly matches the amount of another invoice; in which case, QuickBooks applies the payment to that invoice (see Figure 4-2).

You can change this behavior so that you select the invoices to which QuickBooks should apply payments. If you prefer to enter a payment amount and then select the invoices to which the payment applies, choose Edit | Preferences and click the Sales

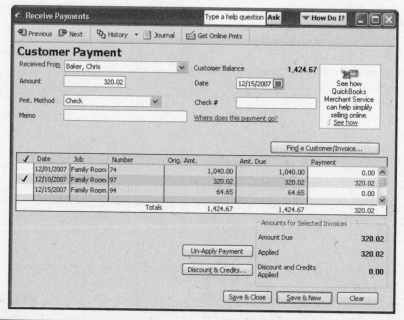

FIGURE 4-2　By default, QuickBooks applies payments to the oldest invoice or to an invoice whose amount matches the payment

& Customers icon in the left pane. On the Company Preferences tab, remove the check from the Automatically Apply Payments check box.

You can easily identify the invoice a customer is paying when the payment amount matches one specific invoice, but that isn't always the case. For example, the customer may have one or more unpaid invoices and send you a payment for an amount lower than any single invoice. Or, the customer may have several unpaid invoices and send you a payment for an amount greater than any one invoice but not large enough to cover two or more invoices.

The rule of thumb is "apply payments according to the customer's wishes" so that your records match your customer's records, making it easier for you and your customer to discuss open account balances. When the customer's intention isn't clear, I suggest that you call the customer and ask how the customer wants the payment applied. In QuickBooks, you can manually enter the amount you're applying against any invoice in the Payment column.

If the customer sent a copy of the invoice with the payment or indicated the invoice number on the check or stub, apply the payment to that invoice, even if an older invoice remains unpaid. Customers sometimes deliberately pay a newer invoice and not an older one, usually because they are disputing a charge on the older invoice.

Working with the Undeposited Funds Account

Ultimately, money you receive from your customers will end up in your bank account, but, in QuickBooks, you determine the path the money takes to get there. QuickBooks offers you two approaches. You can place each customer payment:

- Directly into a bank account
- Into the Undeposited Funds account

QuickBooks offers these two approaches so that you can choose the method that will best make your bank deposits match the entries in QuickBooks, which will make your bank account reconciliation easier.

Let's suppose that you prepare a deposit ticket for six checks totaling $10,450.25. Most banks list a single deposit of $10,450.25 on your bank statement instead of listing the individual checks that made up the deposit. A few banks, however, will list each of the six checks on your statement rather than listing the sum of the deposit.

To accommodate the few banks that list the checks individually, you should deposit each customer payment directly into a bank account. When you use this approach in QuickBooks, each payment appears as a separate entry when you reconcile your bank account in QuickBooks, so your deposits in QuickBooks will match the deposits that appear on your bank statement.

However, if your bank lists the sum of the deposit—the $10,450.25—you should deposit customer payments into the Undeposited Funds account and then use the Make Deposits window to select the checks that you will include in the deposit you make at your bank. Think of the Undeposited Funds account as a "holding tank" for money you have not yet deposited in your account at the bank. This approach groups individual checks into a single bank deposit that appears in the Reconcile window so that your bank deposits in QuickBooks will match the deposits that appear on your bank statement. See Chapter 12 for detailed instructions on reconciling bank accounts.

Even if your bank is one of the few that lists, on bank statements, individual checks as deposits instead of the sum of a deposit, I recommend that you *not* change the default in the Sales & Customers category of the Preferences dialog box. When you don't change the default setting, you allow QuickBooks to always deposit cash into the Undeposited Funds account, making the payment and deposit distinct and separate transactions.

Handling Underpayments

If a customer sends a payment that isn't sufficient to completely pay an invoice, after you apply the customer's payment, the Receive Payments window changes, displaying an area where you can decide how to handle the underpayment (see Figure 4-3).

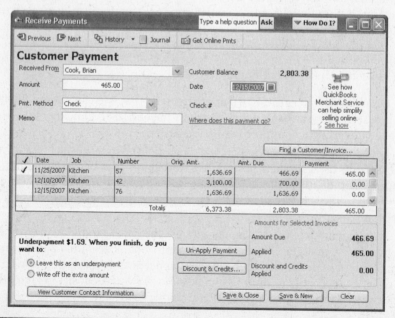

FIGURE 4-3   Using the lower-left corner of the Receive Payments window, decide how to handle an underpayment

If you select Leave This As An Underpayment, QuickBooks applies the payment to the selected invoice adjusting the open balance of the invoice by the amount of the payment you applied.

If you select Write Off The Extra Amount, QuickBooks takes no action until you click Save & Close or Save & New. Then, QuickBooks opens the Write Off Amount dialog box so you can choose the posting account, and, if applicable, apply a class to the transaction.

Discuss the account to use for a write-off with your accountant. You can create an Income or Expense account for this purpose, depending on the way that you and your accountant agree you should track receivables you've decided to forgive.

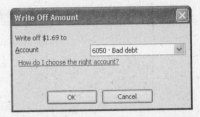

Applying Credits to Invoices

You can apply any existing credits to an open invoice, in addition to applying the payment that arrived. If credits exist, you'll see a notation in the Receive Payments window below the list of invoices (see Figure 4-4).

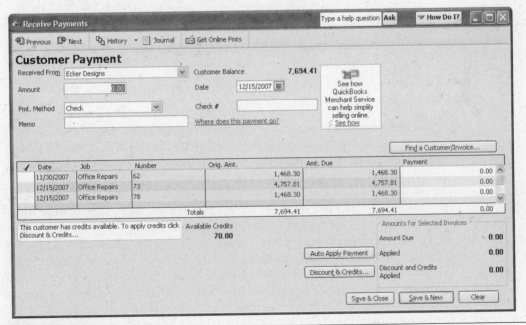

FIGURE 4-4   QuickBooks notifies you in the Receive Payments window if credits exist for the selected customer

To apply a credit balance to an invoice, select the invoice—click anywhere *except* the leftmost column, where you place a check to apply a payment—and then click the Discount & Credits button on the Customer Payment window; QuickBooks displays the Discount And Credits dialog box.

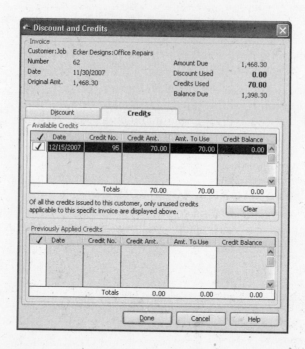

Select the credit you want to apply. Depending on the circumstances, here's how QuickBooks handles the credits:

- When the credit total equals or is less than the unpaid amount of the selected invoice, QuickBooks reduces the balance due on the selected invoice. If the customer sent a payment that reflects a deduction for the amount of his or her credits, so that the credit total is equal to the unpaid amount, QuickBooks zeroes out the balance of the invoice. If applying the existing credit along with the payment doesn't pay off the invoice, QuickBooks reduces the balance due on the invoice by the total of the payment and the credit.

- If the amount of credit exceeds the amount needed to pay off an outstanding invoice, QuickBooks retains the balance of the credit so that you can apply it to another invoice. To apply a credit to more than one invoice, repeat the process of selecting an invoice and clicking the Discount & Credits button as many times as necessary to use up the balance of the credit. You don't need to use the entire credit balance at one time; QuickBooks retains any unused credits for future use.

You can send a statement to the customer to reflect the current, new invoice balances as a result of applying the payments and the credits; see Chapter 5 for details on creating statements in QuickBooks.

Applying Credits to a Different Job

Suppose that you have created two jobs for a single customer and the customer has already paid the invoices for one of the jobs but has an outstanding balance on the other job. Further suppose that you and the customer agreed that you needed to issue a credit for the job that has no outstanding balance and you entered that credit. Later, the customer called you and pointed out that he owes you money for one job but has a credit balance on the other job. It's likely that the customer will tell you to apply the credit balance to another job.

To move the credit from one job to another, open the credit memo in the Create Credit Memos/Refunds window—you can display it on-screen by finding it using the Customer Center—and change Customer:Job from the current job to the one you and the customer agree to credit.

Applying Discounts for Timely Payments

If you offer your customers terms that include a discount if they pay their bills promptly (for instance, 2% 10 Net 30), you'll need to apply the discount to the payment if it's applicable.

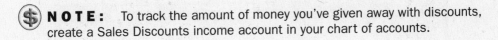 **N O T E :**   To track the amount of money you've given away with discounts, create a Sales Discounts income account in your chart of accounts.

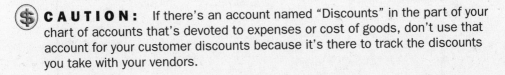 **C A U T I O N :**   If there's an account named "Discounts" in the part of your chart of accounts that's devoted to expenses or cost of goods, don't use that account for your customer discounts because it's there to track the discounts you take with your vendors.

Figure 4-5 shows the Receive Payments window for a customer who has been offered a discount for timely payment; QuickBooks displays a message below the list of invoices that tells you the customer has discounts available.

QuickBooks doesn't apply the discount automatically; select the invoice and click the Discount & Credits button to see the Discount And Credits dialog box for the selected invoice.

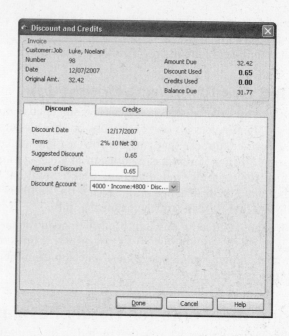

QuickBooks inserts the amount of the discount to use; select a discount account and click Done.

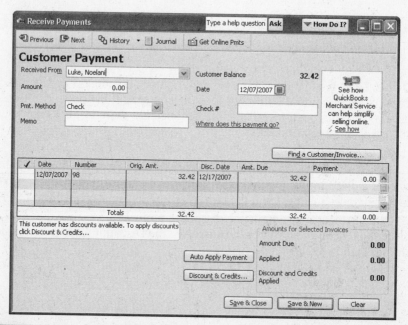

FIGURE 4-5   When a discount for early payment applies, QuickBooks displays a message in the Receive Payments window

N O T E :   If the customer only made a partial payment and you want to give a proportionately smaller discount, you can change the amount of the discount in the Discounts And Credits dialog box.

When QuickBooks redisplays the Receive Payments window, you'll see that a Discount column appears, displaying the amount of the discount for the selected invoice.

Applying Discounts for Untimely Payments

Sometimes customers take the discount even if the payment arrives after the discount date. You can apply the payment to the invoice and leave a balance due for the discount amount that was deducted by the customer, but most companies give the customer the discount even if the payment is late, as a good will gesture.

When you select the invoice and click the Discount Info button, QuickBooks does not automatically fill in the discount amount in the Discount & Credits dialog box, but you can enter the amount, select the discount account, and click Done to apply the discount to the invoice.

Behind the Scenes of Customer Payments

To understand what happens behind the scenes of a customer payment, let's first review what QuickBooks does when you record an invoice for a customer who has terms that permit a 1% discount. Let's assume the sale was for $100.00. QuickBooks records the following amounts:

Account	Debit	Credit
Accounts Receivable	$100.00	
Income		$100.00

The customer's terms don't come into play until you record the customer's payment. When you enter the customer payment in the amount of $99.00, QuickBooks makes the following entries:

Account	Debit	Credit
Undeposited Funds or Bank Account	$99.00	
Accounts Receivable		$100.00
Discounts Given	$1.00	

Let's also take a moment to review what happens behind the scenes when you deposit customer payments directly into a bank account compared to when you deposit customer payments into the Undeposited Funds account.

If you deposit a customer payment directly to a bank account, QuickBooks makes the following entries:

Account	Debit	Credit
Bank	Individual customer payment	
Accounts Receivable		Individual customer payment

In addition, when you make the actual bank deposit, you don't use the Make Deposits window in QuickBooks; in fact, you won't find them in the window when you open it.

If you place customer payments in the Undeposited Funds account, QuickBooks makes the following entries:

Account	Debit	Credit
Undeposited Funds	Total of cash receipts	
Accounts Receivable		Total of cash receipts

When you make the actual deposit, using the Make Deposits window, QuickBooks makes the following entry:

Account	Debit	Credit
Bank	Total of deposit	
Undeposited Funds		Total of deposit

Handling Cash Sales

A *cash sale* is a sale for which the exchange of product and payment occurred simultaneously; no time elapses during which you have provided goods and services but have not yet been paid. A cash sale doesn't necessarily involve cash; it can involve a check or a credit card.

You can easily handle the occasional cash sale in any edition of QuickBooks Premier or Enterprise. But, if cash sales are your normal method of doing business—that is, you're running a retail store—you should use the Retail Edition of QuickBooks Premier or QuickBooks Enterprise.

You can record a cash sale for a Customer: Job if a customer pays you on the spot for goods or services. More commonly, people record cash sales to account for sales of goods or services to customers you are not tracking in QuickBooks—typically "occasional" customers with whom you don't do business regularly.

To record a cash sale, click the Create Sales Receipts icon on the Home page, or choose New Transactions | Sales Receipts from the Customer Center. QuickBooks displays the Enter Sales Receipts window (see Figure 4-6), which closely resembles the Create Invoices window.

Entering Cash Sale Information

If you made this sale to a customer that you already set up in your Customer: Job list, select the name in the Customer: Job drop-down list. If you make a sale to a customer who doesn't appear in the Customer: Job list and you want to start tracking sales for this customer, you can add a new customer by choosing <Add New>.

TIP: If you make regular sales to customers who always pay at the time of the sale, you should set these customers up in QuickBooks and you might want to consider creating a customer type such as "Cash" for this group. You can then easily report on this group or identify them for marketing and advertising campaigns.

For sales to customers you don't track in QuickBooks (and don't want to track in QuickBooks), click <Add New> to set up a customer named "Cash Sale" and select that customer for the sale.

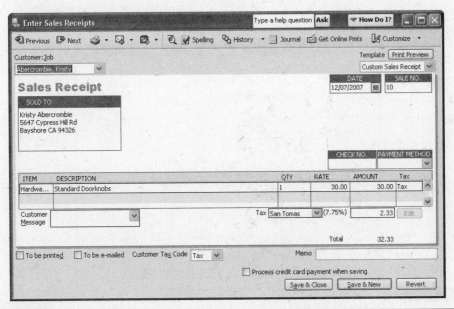

FIGURE 4-6   Use this window to record a sale for which you receive cash at the time you supply goods or render services

You can fill in the rest of the fields in the Enter Sales Receipts window the same way you complete them in the Create Invoices window, with one exception: If you have turned off the Undeposited Funds option in the Sales & Customers category of the Preferences dialog box, you need to select an account in which to deposit the cash you receive. For the same reasons I presented earlier in this chapter, in the section "Working with the Undeposited Funds Account," I suggest that you deposit the cash into the Undeposited Funds account.

Some cash customers want a receipt. When you finish filling out the form, click the Print button on the Enter Sales Receipts window toolbar to open the Print One Sales Receipt window, shown in Figure 4-7. If you're not printing to a dot matrix printer with multipart paper and you want a copy of the receipt for your files, be sure to change the value in the Number Of Copies box from 1 to 2.

Click Save & New to start a sales receipt or click Save & Close to close the Enter Sales Receipts window.

Customizing the Sales Receipts Template

You may want to modify the appearance of the Enter Sales Receipts window to include information suited to your business. For example, you may want to include a field for the Sales Rep in the Sales Receipts window if you want to track the person who made the sale or to help if you pay commissions on cash sales. You may also want to include the Ship To address and the Ship Via field for customers who pay cash and want you to deliver the goods.

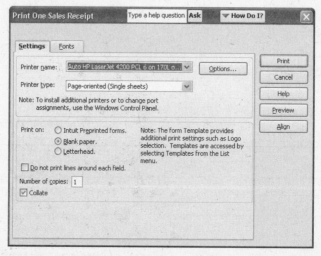

FIGURE 4-7   Use this dialog box to select a printer and paper type and specify the number of copies to print

Customize the Custom Sales Receipts form using these steps:

① Click the Customize button on the Enter Sales Receipts window toolbar. QuickBooks displays the Basic Customization dialog box shown in Figure 4-8, with the Custom Sales Receipt selected.

NOTE: To customize a different template or to make a copy of the selected template, click Manage Templates, highlight the template you want to copy, click Copy, edit the Template Name, and then click OK.

② Make basic changes, such as adding a logo or company information or changing fonts in the Basic Customization dialog box.

③ Click Additional Customization to display the Additional Customization dialog box (see Figure 4-9).

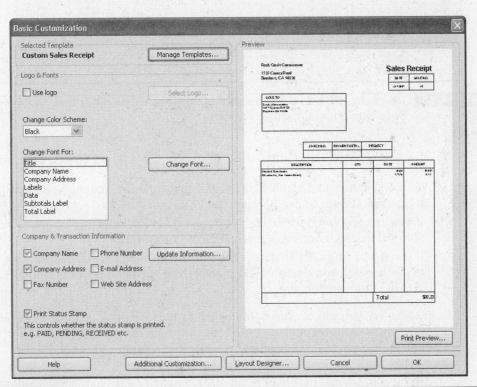

FIGURE 4-8   Use this dialog box to make basic changes to the Enter Sales Receipt window

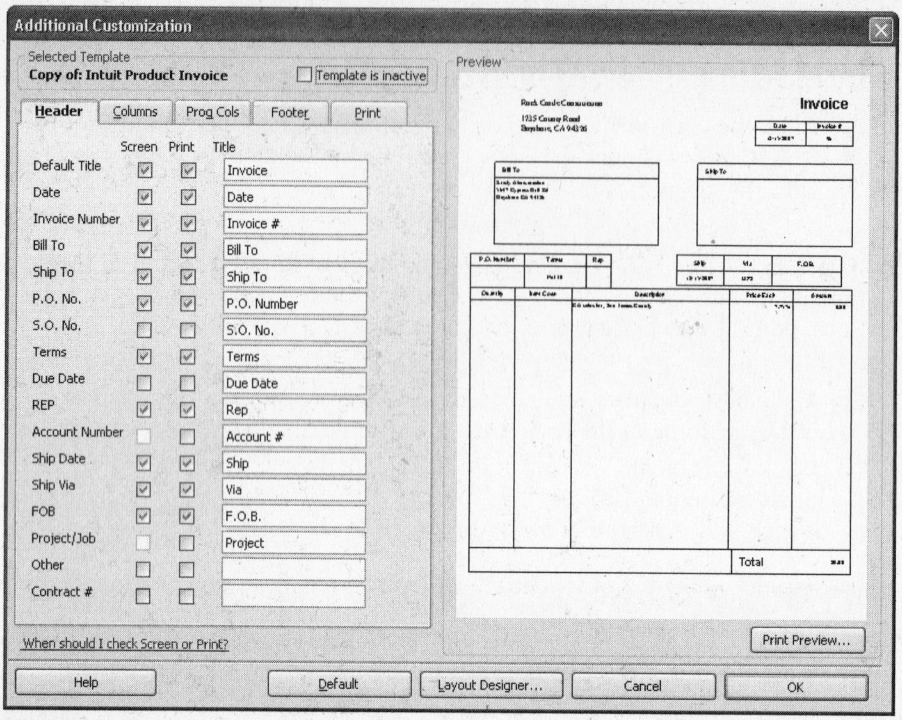

FIGURE 4-9   You can use the tabs in this dialog box to add and remove fields from the Enter Sales Receipt window and printed form

You may want to consider doing any of the following on the Header tab:

- You can change the Default Title to anything you want; you might prefer the term Cash Receipt or just Receipt.
- If you ever ship products to cash customers, add the Ship To, Ship Date, and Ship Via fields for both the Screen and the Print forms.
- If you're tracking salespersons (either for commission or just to know who made the sale), add the REP field to the screen version; optionally, you can add it to the print version, too.

If necessary, you can use the Columns tab to add or remove columns in the line item section of the form or change the order in which the columns appear. For example, you may prefer to display Qty in the first column instead of the Item number.

After you finish making changes, click OK twice to return to the Enter Sales Receipts window, where your changes are incorporated into the template.

Handling Batches of Daily Cash Sales

If you have a business in which sales and service personnel return to the office each day with customer payments in hand, you might want to consider batching these cash sale transactions. This technique works well if you don't care about maintaining information about the customers and no customer expects a receipt.

Create a customized form using the steps described in the previous section, minimizing the fields in the top portion of the form to make data entry quick and easy. For example, on the Header tab of the Additional Customization dialog box, keep only the Date and Sale Number fields in the heading and remove optional fields such as Payment Method.

Each day, at the beginning of the day, open the new customized Enter Sales Receipts window and record one sales receipt transaction that includes all sales made the preceding day. Use a customer named "Cash" or "Cash Sale." In the line item section, enter each item sold on a new line, ignoring the customer who purchased the item and the individual sales made to separate customers. The idea here is to record the sale of items without worrying about who bought the items or how the items were grouped when they were sold. Click Save & Close when you finish the transaction.

Handling a Cash Drawer

If you deal in cash regularly, have a cash register, and aren't using the Retail Edition of QuickBooks Premier or QuickBooks Enterprise, you can account for cash register transactions easily, using the Enter Sales Receipts window and the Undeposited Funds account.

To place money in the cash drawer initially, use the Write Checks window to write a check from your operating account; on the Expenses tab of the Write Checks window, select your petty cash account. If you get the money for your petty cash account using an ATM withdrawal, you can use the Transfer Funds window instead of the Write Checks window.

 N O T E :   If you want, you can create a bank account for the Cash Register to use instead of your petty cash account, but be aware that putting the money into the cash register is, essentially, a one-time event and you won't use the cash register bank account again.

Record cash sales as previously discussed in this chapter, making sure that you select the Undeposited Funds account if you are selecting a deposit account; otherwise, don't change the defaults in QuickBooks and simply allow QuickBooks to automatically record your sales receipt transactions in the Undeposited Funds account.

When you want to deposit cash collected in the cash register, leave the original startup money—in this example, $100.00—in the drawer. Count the rest of the money and deposit that money into your checking account. See the next section, "Depositing Income," for details on creating the deposit that moves the cash from the Undeposited Funds account to your bank account.

Depositing Income

If you use the Undeposited Funds account, a "holding tank" for money you have not yet deposited in your account at the bank, then you need to move money out of this account and into appropriate accounts when you take the money to the bank—and this section shows you how to move the money. If you've been depositing every payment and cash receipt to a specific bank account, you don't need to read this section and you don't need to do anything special in QuickBooks when you make a bank deposit.

Choosing the Payments to Deposit

As you've been entering payment and cash sales transactions, QuickBooks has been recording them in the Undeposited Funds account. When you make a bank deposit, you move the dollars associated with these transactions from the Undeposited Funds account to the appropriate bank account.

To record a bank deposit in QuickBooks, click the Record Deposits icon on the Home page or choose Banking | Make Deposits from the menu bar. QuickBooks displays the Payments To Deposit window (see Figure 4-10).

The Payments To Deposit window displays only the payments you've entered using the Receive Payments window or the Enter Sales Receipts window in QuickBooks. As you walk through this process, you'll see another window where you can record other types of deposits, such as refunds, loan proceeds, or capital infusion.

In the Payments To Deposit window, the Type column identifies the window where you recorded the transaction—PMT for transactions recorded in the Receive Payments window and RCPT transactions recorded in the Enter Sales Receipts window.

The Payment Method column lists whether the payment was cash, check, a specific credit card, and so on. You can use this information to group transactions on a bank deposit so that they will match the deposits you see on the statement your bank sends you, making bank reconciliation easy.

Select the items you want to include in a single bank deposit by clicking to the left of the item; QuickBooks places a check mark in the column beside each item you click. Click Select All to include all payments in a single deposit. When you finish selecting, click OK. The following sections describe some techniques you might consider using while selecting items to include in a deposit.

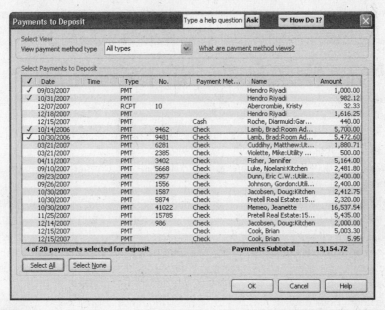

FIGURE 4-10 Use this window to identify the transactions you want to include in a bank deposit

Separate Deposit Items by Payment Method

You can easily create bank deposits segregated by Payment Method; select a payment method from the View Payment Method Type drop-down list at the top of the Payments To Deposit dialog box. You can choose Selected Types to open the Select Payment Types dialog box and choose several payment types to include in the same deposit.

 N O T E :   You may use the Other category to deposit a money order or a traveler's check. If you plan to print deposit slips, use only the Cash or Check category.

After making a selection from the View Payment Method Type drop-down list, QuickBooks displays only the transactions that match the selected payment method in the Payments To Deposit window.

This feature is particularly useful if the money you deposit comes from a cash bag. You can use the View Payment Method Type drop-down list to display only cash and create one deposit; then you can view only checks and create a second deposit. Segregating the deposits is particularly helpful if the bank notifies you that its automatic counting machine produced a total different from the total on your cash deposit slip. You can you can easily edit the correct cash bank deposit in your bank account register.

➡ FYI

Some Notes About Credit Card Deposits

You can't record credit card deposits into QuickBooks until your merchant bank notifies you that it has placed the funds into your bank account.

If you have QuickBooks online banking, the deposit shows up in the QuickReport (see Chapter 16 to learn about managing online banking transactions).

If you have online access to your merchant card account, the transfer will appear on the activities report on the web site.

If you don't have any form of online access, you'll have to wait for the monthly statement to arrive (or contact the bank periodically to see if anything showed up in your account).

QuickBooks 2007 allows "negative" deposits, which helps businesses that take payment by credit card. When you select deposits for a credit card using that credit card's Payment Method, and the credit card returns exceed the credit card sales, QuickBooks will make your deposit, which will be negative.

If your merchant bank deducts fees before transferring funds, learn how to deposit the net amount in the section "Calculating Merchant Card Fees" later in this chapter.

Separate Deposits by Bank Account

If you're depositing money into multiple bank accounts, select only the transactions that go into the same account. After you complete the deposit for one account, start this process again and create another deposit for another bank account.

Filling Out the Deposit Slip

When you click OK in the Payments To Deposit window, QuickBooks displays the Make Deposits window (see Figure 4-11).

Select the bank account you're using for this deposit. Then make sure the date matches the day you're physically depositing the money so that you can easily match QuickBooks bank deposits to the ones that appear on the bank statement.

Adding Items to the Deposit

To add deposit items that weren't in the Payments To Deposit window, click anywhere in the Received From column, click the arrow, and select an existing name or click <Add New> to enter a name that isn't in your system.

In the From Account column, enter the account that QuickBooks should use for the other side of the transaction (QuickBooks automatically uses the bank account you selected at the top of the window for one side of the transaction). For example, if you're depositing a check you received as a bank loan, select the liability account

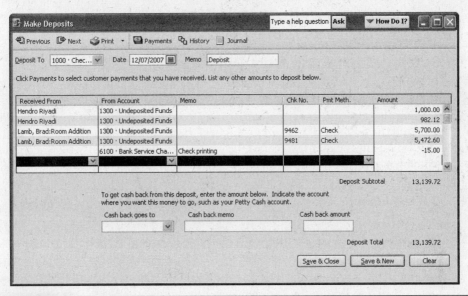

FIGURE 4-11 Use the Make Deposits window to complete the bank deposit

for that bank loan (you can create it here by choosing <Add New> if you didn't set up the account earlier). If you're depositing a check that represents an infusion of capital from you, use the owner's capital account in the Equity section of your chart of accounts. Fill in the other fields, which are self-explanatory.

Handling Merchant Card Fees

If your merchant card bank deposits the gross amount of each transaction and charges your bank account for the total fees due at the end of the month, you don't have to do anything special to deposit credit card payments. You can deal with the fees when you reconcile your bank account.

If your merchant card bank deducts fees from transactions and deposits the net proceeds to your account, you can use the following steps to deposit the correct amount:

1. Select the credit card transactions in the Payments To Deposit window. These represent the full amount the customer paid you.
2. Click OK to display the transactions in the Make Deposits window.
3. On the first empty line, select the merchant in the Received From column.
4. In the Account column, select the expense account to which you post merchant card fees.
5. Move to the Amount column and enter the fee as a negative number.

When you make this entry, the net amount of the QuickBooks deposit matches the amount that the merchant card bank deposited in your bank account.

Getting Cash Back from Deposits

To get cash back from a bank deposit and account for it, use the fields at the bottom of the Make Deposits window.

Enter the account, usually a petty cash account, to which you want to assign the cash and the amount of cash you want back from this deposit. As you spend the cash for business expenses, record the expenses against the petty cash account, which you typically set up as a bank account, using the Write Checks window.

 C A U T I O N :   Many banks will not cash checks made out to a company.

Handling Overages and Shortages for a Cash Drawer

If you collect cash for cash sales, when you count the money in the cash register at the end of the day, you may find that the recorded income doesn't match the cash you expected to find in the cash register. You can use the Make Deposits window to resolve an overage or a shortage.

To handle overages and shortages, set up an income account called "Overage-Shortage" and a customer called "Over-Short."

After selecting the cash and check items to deposit, enter the overage or shortage on the next available line of the Make Deposits window. In the Received From column, select the "Over-Short" customer, and in the From Account column, select the "Overage-Shortage" account. Enter an overage as a positive amount to increase your deposit to the amount of cash you plan to deposit. Enter a shortage as a negative amount, reducing the deposit to the amount you plan to deposit.

 T I P :   By creating a customer to which you assign overages and shortages, you can view that customer's register to see all your overages and shortages.

While you may be tempted to try to use the Cash Back boxes at the bottom of the Make Deposits window to handle overages and shortages, you can't, for two reasons:

- Using those fields only decreases the deposit, so you cannot use them to record overages.
- You can assign the amount for the Cash Back Amount field only to Balance Sheet accounts, and you typically want to track overages and shortages using either an income or an expense account.

Printing Deposit Slips

You can print a deposit slip or a deposit summary if you click the Print button in the Make Deposits window. QuickBooks displays the Print Deposit dialog box, asking whether you want to print a deposit slip and deposit summary, or just a deposit summary.

If you want to print a deposit slip that your bank will accept, you must order printable deposit slips from QuickBooks. Visit its web site, www.quickbooks.com, and search for Printable Deposit Slips.

The QuickBooks deposit slips are guaranteed to be acceptable to your bank, and you use them with either a laser printer or inkjet printer. When you print the deposit slip, there's a tear-off section at the bottom of the page that has a deposit summary that you can keep for your own records. You take the rest of the page to the bank along with your money.

If you don't have QuickBooks deposit slips, select Deposit Summary Only and fill out your bank deposit slip manually. On-screen, QuickBooks displays a Print dialog box so that you can change printers, adjust margins, or even print in color. Choose Print; when QuickBooks redisplays the Make Deposits window, click Save & Close to save the deposit.

Tracking Accounts Receivable

In this chapter:

- Running A/R aging reports

- Setting up finance charges

- Printing customer statements

Collecting the money owed to you is one of the most important tasks in running a business. Successfully tracking and managing your accounts receivable can mean the difference between a healthy business and one that won't survive.

You can track overdue invoices and then send statements as reminders to your customers to pay. And, you can use finance charges to encourage your customers to pay on time. In this chapter, I review the tools and features QuickBooks provides to help you track and collect the money your customers owe you.

Reporting On Who Owes You Money

Aging reports list the customers that owe you money. You produce them as often as you feel it's necessary to know the extent of your receivables; many companies run an aging report every morning, while other companies run the report weekly. You'll want to consider producing the report before you charge finance charges or produce customer statements.

QuickBooks provides two versions of the aging report: the A/R Aging Summary Report, shown in Figure 5-1, and the A/R Aging Detail Report, shown in Figure 5-2.

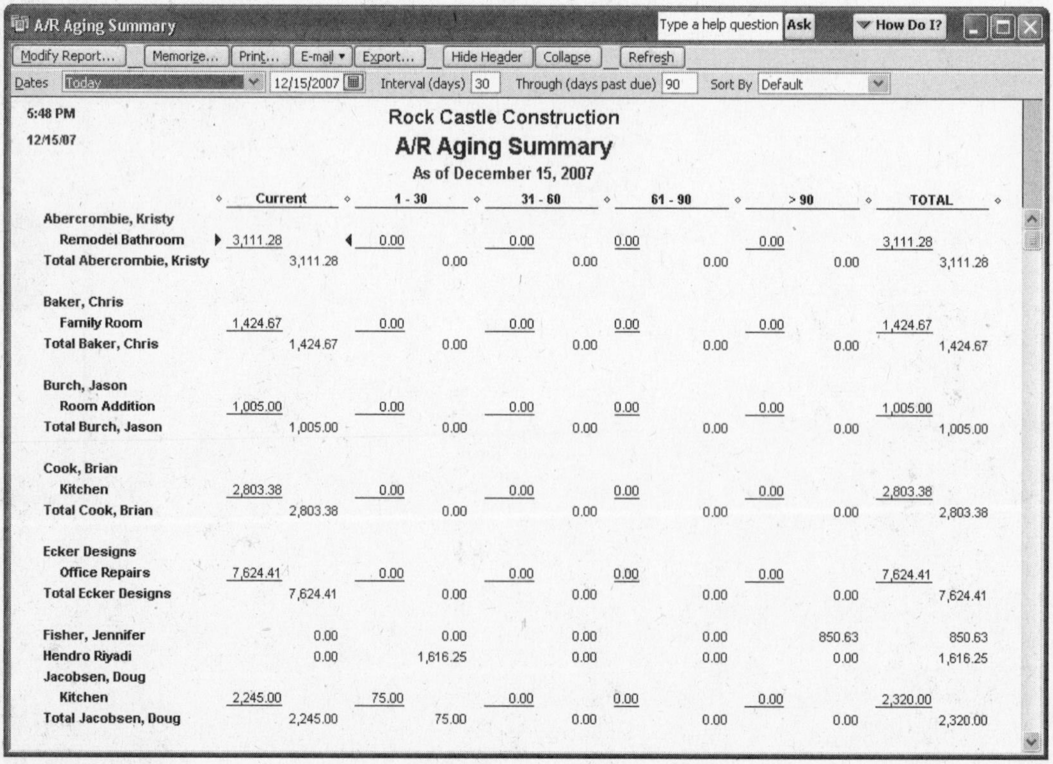

Rock Castle Construction
A/R Aging Summary
As of December 15, 2007

	Current	1 - 30	31 - 60	61 - 90	> 90	TOTAL
Abercrombie, Kristy						
Remodel Bathroom	3,111.28	0.00	0.00	0.00	0.00	3,111.28
Total Abercrombie, Kristy	3,111.28	0.00	0.00	0.00	0.00	3,111.28
Baker, Chris						
Family Room	1,424.67	0.00	0.00	0.00	0.00	1,424.67
Total Baker, Chris	1,424.67	0.00	0.00	0.00	0.00	1,424.67
Burch, Jason						
Room Addition	1,005.00	0.00	0.00	0.00	0.00	1,005.00
Total Burch, Jason	1,005.00	0.00	0.00	0.00	0.00	1,005.00
Cook, Brian						
Kitchen	2,803.38	0.00	0.00	0.00	0.00	2,803.38
Total Cook, Brian	2,803.38	0.00	0.00	0.00	0.00	2,803.38
Ecker Designs						
Office Repairs	7,624.41	0.00	0.00	0.00	0.00	7,624.41
Total Ecker Designs	7,624.41	0.00	0.00	0.00	0.00	7,624.41
Fisher, Jennifer	0.00	0.00	0.00	0.00	850.63	850.63
Hendro Riyadi	0.00	1,616.25	0.00	0.00	0.00	1,616.25
Jacobsen, Doug						
Kitchen	2,245.00	75.00	0.00	0.00	0.00	2,320.00
Total Jacobsen, Doug	2,245.00	75.00	0.00	0.00	0.00	2,320.00

FIGURE 5-1 The A/R Aging Summary Report

Type	Date	Num	P. O. #	Name	Terms	Due Date	Aging	Open Balance
Current								
Invoice	11/15/2007	51		Pretell Real Estate:...	Net 30	12/15/2007		1,072.50
Invoice	12/15/2007	72		Robson, Darci:Rob...		12/15/2007		12,420.98
Credit Memo	12/15/2007	95		Ecker Designs:Off...		12/15/2007		-70.00
Invoice	12/09/2007	67		Smallson, Fran:Off...	Net 15	12/24/2007		1,665.00
Invoice	11/25/2007	57		Cook, Brian:Kitchen	Net 30	12/25/2007		466.69
Invoice	11/25/2007	59		Jacobsen, Doug:K...	Net 30	12/25/2007		2,245.00
Invoice	11/25/2007	75		Burch, Jason:Room...	Net 30	12/25/2007		1,005.00
Invoice	11/25/2007	80		Abercrombie, Kris...	Net 30	12/25/2007		3,111.28
Invoice	12/11/2007	70		Teschner, Anton:S...	Net 15	12/26/2007		1,225.00
Invoice	11/30/2007	62		Ecker Designs:Off...	Net 30	12/30/2007		1,468.30
Invoice	11/30/2007	83		Melton, Johnny:De...	Net 30	12/30/2007		4,999.50
Invoice	12/01/2007	63		Pretell Real Estate:...	Net 30	12/31/2007		12,412.18
Invoice	12/01/2007	74		Baker, Chris:Family...	Net 30	12/31/2007		1,040.00
Invoice	12/07/2007	98		Luke, Noelani	2% 10 N...	01/06/2008		32.42
Invoice	12/10/2007	42		Cook, Brian:Kitchen	Net 30	01/09/2008		700.00
Invoice	12/10/2007	69		Pretell Real Estate:...	Net 30	01/09/2008		1,715.00
Invoice	12/10/2007	97		Baker, Chris:Family...	Net 30	01/09/2008		320.02
Invoice	12/15/2007	73	A905-01	Ecker Designs:Off...	Net 30	01/14/2008		4,757.81
Invoice	12/15/2007	76		Cook, Brian:Kitchen	Net 30	01/14/2008		1,636.69
Invoice	12/15/2007	77		Pretell Real Estate:...	Net 30	01/14/2008		12,412.18
Invoice	12/15/2007	78		Ecker Designs:Off...	Net 30	01/14/2008		1,468.30
Invoice	12/15/2007	94		Baker, Chris:Family...	Net 30	01/14/2008		64.65
Invoice	12/05/2007	66		Violette, Mike:Work...	Net 60	02/03/2008		4,735.73
Total Current								70,904.23
1 - 30								
Invoice	11/18/2007	92		Hendro Riyadi		11/18/2007	27	1,616.25
Invoice	11/18/2007	93		Vinay Kini		11/18/2007	27	862.00
Invoice	10/23/2007	44		Jacobsen, Doug:K...	Net 30	11/22/2007	23	75.00

Rock Castle Construction
A/R Aging Detail
As of December 15, 2007

5:49 PM
12/15/07

FIGURE 5-2   The A/R Aging Detail Report

The A/R Aging Summary Report presents an overview of what your customers owe you, and it breaks out each customer's balance to indicate how old the balance is. The A/R Aging Detail Report presents a different view of the same information, focusing on the age of the balance and listing each invoice in each age bracket.

To produce an aging report, choose Reports | Customers & Receivables, and then choose either A/R Aging Summary or A/R Aging Detail. You can customize these reports so that they display information the way you want to see it.

Customizing Aging Reports

You can customize both reports using basically the same techniques. In the following sections, I'll work in the A/R Aging Detail Report since you can modify that report more than you can modify the A/R Aging Summary Report. While viewing the A/R Aging Detail Report, click the Modify Report button. QuickBooks displays the Modify Report window that appears in Figure 5-3.

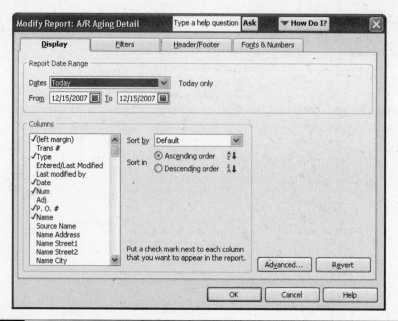

FIGURE 5-3   Use the Display tab of the Modify Report dialog box to control the fields that appear on the report

Controlling the Columns

You can control the columns that appear on the A/R Aging Detail Report but not on the A/R Summary Report.

You can add a column to the report; for example, if you want to call customers to discuss outstanding invoices, you can add the customer's phone number to the report. To add a column, click to place a check mark beside an entry in the Columns list.

You can remove any column on the report that doesn't interest you. For example, you may not want to view the purchase order number on the A/R Aging Detail report. To remove a column, click to remove the check mark that appears beside it in the Columns list. When you click OK, QuickBooks reproduces the report without the column.

 TIP: While viewing the report (not the Modify Report dialog box) you can remove any column if you place the mouse pointer over the diamond in the column heading area at the right edge of the column and then drag left to the diamond on the left side of the column.

Filtering Information

When you filter a report, you limit the information that appears on it by specifying criteria for one or more particular fields; typically, you filter a report to help you highlight a particular issue. For example, you may want to focus only on outstanding invoices that are at least 30 days old. You can filter the report to show only those invoices.

To filter the report, click the Filters tab of the Modify Report dialog box.

Select a filter in the Filter list on the left side of the box; the conditions you can set for that filter appear beside it. Set the conditions, and QuickBooks moves the filter and its conditions into the Current Filter Choices box on the right side of the Filters tab. In Figure 5-4, I set a filter to limit the report's information to only those invoices that are at least 30 days old.

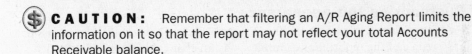 **CAUTION:**   Remember that filtering an A/R Aging Report limits the information on it so that the report may not reflect your total Accounts Receivable balance.

You can remove any filter if you click it in the Current Filter Choices box and then click Remove Selected Filter, and you can return to the default filters settings by clicking the Revert button.

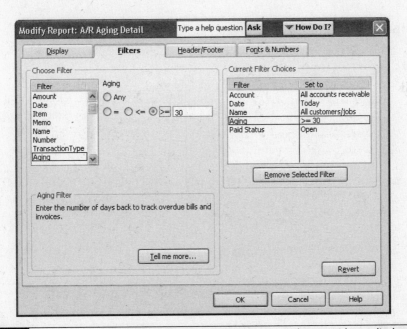

FIGURE 5-4   Use this tab to limit the information that appears on the report by a criteria you set

Changing Header/Footer Information

You can customize the text that appears in the header and footer of the report by making changes on the Header/Footer tab (see Figure 5-5).

 N O T E : The Date Prepared field is not really displaying a date; it is displaying a date format. Click the arrow to the right of the field to see the other formats for inserting the date. The Page Number field works in the same way.

You can eliminate a Header/Footer field by removing the check mark from the field's check box. For fields you include, you can change the text. You can also change the layout by choosing a different Alignment option from the drop-down list.

Customizing the Appearance

From the Fonts & Numbers tab (see Figure 5-6), you can control the cosmetic appearance of the report. For example, you can change the way QuickBooks displays negative numbers, and you can change the fonts for any or all of the individual elements in the report.

When you click OK in the Modify Report dialog box, QuickBooks applies all changes you made on all tabs.

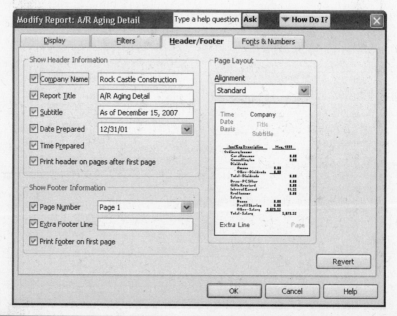

FIGURE 5-5   Use the Header/Footer tab to decide what information should be printed in those areas

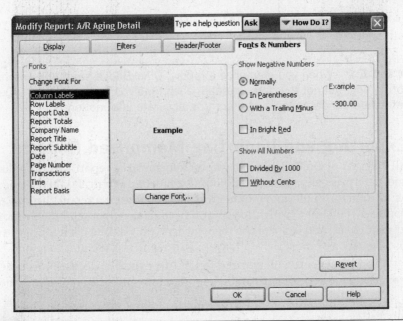

FIGURE 5-6   Use the Fonts & Numbers tab to change the cosmetic appearance of the report

When you close the report window, QuickBooks may ask if you want to memorize the report with the changes you made. Or, before you close the report, you can click the Memorize button and then follow the instructions in the next section.

Memorizing Aging Reports

Memorizing a report helps you avoid reinventing the wheel; when you memorize a report, you save all the settings you establish in the Modify Report dialog box.

Click the Memorize button in the report window. In the Memorize Report window that appears, enter a new name for the report, optionally save it within a report group, and click OK.

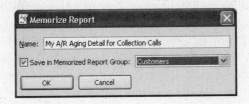

When you choose Reports | Memorized Reports from the menu bar, your report will appear in the group you selected.

 N O T E :   When you memorize a report, QuickBooks saves the criteria and formatting, but not the data. Instead, each time you open the report, QuickBooks refreshes the data, so you get current, accurate information.

Exporting and Importing Memorized Reports

All versions of QuickBooks can import a memorized report. QuickBooks Premier and Enterprise users also can export a memorized report. If you're an accountant using a Premier edition, you can create and memorize a report that has exactly what you need, laid out exactly the way you need it, and then send the memorized report to your client. You can run the report when you visit the client or have your client run the report, export the contents to Excel, and then send it to you.

When you export a memorized report, the exported document is called a *template*, and the template can be imported into any edition of QuickBooks.

To export a memorized report template, follow these steps:

1. Choose Reports | Memorized Reports | Memorized Report List.
2. Click the report you want to export.
3. Click the Memorized Report button at the bottom of the window and select Export Template. QuickBooks displays the Specify Filename For Export dialog box.
4. Navigate to the drive and folder where you want to save the report.
5. Click Save. QuickBooks saves the report template.

You can now send the report template to a QuickBooks user via e-mail or via disk.

If you receive an exported report template, the process of importing it converts the template into a memorized report that's added to the currently open company file.

To import a template, follow these steps:

1. Choose Reports | Memorized Reports | Memorized Report List.
2. Click the Memorized Report button at the bottom of the window, and select Import Template. QuickBooks displays the Select File To Import dialog box.
3. Navigate to the drive and folder that contains the template file you received, and double-click it. QuickBooks displays the Memorize Report dialog box.
4. Enter a name for the report or accept the displayed name, which is the name used by the person who exported the template.

⑤ You can place the report in an existing memorized report group; check the Save In Memorized Report Group box and use the drop-down arrow to select the group.

⑥ Click OK. The report now appears in the Memorized Report List.

Printing Reports

You can print any report by first displaying it in a report window. Then, click the Print button at the top of the window to display the Print Reports window. If the report is wide, use the Margins tab to set new margins, and use the options on the Settings tab to customize other printing options.

In addition to the aging reports, QuickBooks contains customer and job reports designed to give you information about the selected customers/jobs instead of providing information on the totals for your business. There are plenty of customer reports available from the menu that appears when you choose Reports | Customers & Receivables.

Report	Description
Customer Balance Summary Report	Lists current total balance owed for each customer
Customer Balance Detail Report	Lists every open accounts receivable transaction for each customer with a net subtotal for each customer
Open Invoices Report	Lists all unpaid invoices, sorted and subtotaled by customer and job
Collections Report	Includes the contact name and telephone number, along with details about invoices with balances due. Use this report to call the customer to discuss past due balances
Accounts Receivable Graph	Shows a graphic representation of the breakdown of your accounts receivable, helping you focus on where to start collection efforts if appropriate
Unbilled Costs By Job	Tracks job expenses you haven't invoiced
Transaction List By Customer	Displays individual transactions of all types for each customer
Online Received Payments	Shows payments received from customers who pay you online (if you've signed up for online payments)
Customer Phone List	Displays an alphabetical list of customers along with the telephone number for each if you entered the telephone number in the customer record
Customer Contact List	Displays an alphabetical list of customers along with the telephone number, billing address, and current open balance for each
Item Price List	Lists all your items with their prices and preferred vendors

Using Finance Charges

Once you've reviewed your A/R Aging reports, you may decide that you need to speed up the process of collecting the money due to you. One way to speed up collections is to impose finance charges for late payments.

Setting Up Finance Charge Preferences

To use finance charges, you need to establish the rate and circumstances under which QuickBooks should assess finance charges. QuickBooks stores these settings in the Preferences dialog box. Choose Edit | Preferences to open the Preferences dialog box. Then, click the Finance Charge icon in the left pane and select the Company Preferences tab on the right (see Figure 5-7).

In the Annual Interest Rate field, entering any positive number enables the Finance Charge feature. The interest rate you enter should be the annual rate, not the monthly rate. So, to charge 1.5% a month, enter 18% in the Annual Interest Rate field.

NOTE: QuickBooks calculates the finance charge by taking the annual rate, dividing it by 365, and then multiplying that percentage by the number of days overdue. Because the number of days per month varies, February's charges will not be the same as January's charges when all other conditions remain the same.

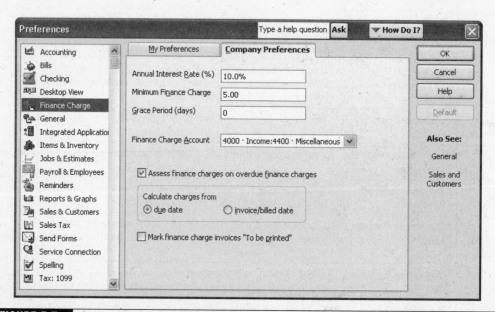

FIGURE 5-7   Set up Finance Charge option here

▶ FYI

Assessing Finance Charges on Overdue Finance Charges

The issue of assessing finance charges on overdue finance charges is a sticky one. The practice is illegal in many states. If you select this option, here's how QuickBooks behaves:

Suppose that a customer owed $100.00 last month and QuickBooks assessed a finance charge of $2.00, giving the customer a current outstanding balance of $102.00. When you check the Assess Finance Charges On Overdue Finance Charges box, QuickBooks calculates the next finance charge on the balance of $102.00 instead of on the original overdue balance of $100.00.

Regardless of state law, the fact is that very few businesses opt to use this calculation method.

You can assess a minimum finance charge for overdue balances. QuickBooks will calculate the finance charge, and if it's less than the minimum you establish in the Preferences dialog box, QuickBooks will charge the minimum charge you specify here.

Use the Grace Period field to enter the number of days your customer can be late paying an invoice before QuickBooks considers an invoice eligible for finance charges, and use the options in the Calculate Charges From box to choose whether to calculate the finance charge from the due date or the invoice date.

When you assess finance charges, QuickBooks creates invoices for each finance charge; by default, QuickBooks doesn't mark these invoices for printing. Instead, they will appear, along with other invoices, as a line item on a monthly statement. If you want to mail finance charge invoices separately, check the Mark Finance Charge Invoices "To Be Printed" box.

Click OK to save your settings after you've filled out the window.

Assessing Finance Charges

You should assess finance charges just before you produce customer statements. Click the Finance Charges icon on the Home page or choose Customers | Assess Finance Charges from the menu bar. QuickBooks displays the Assess Finance Charges window (see Figure 5-8) with a list of all the customers with overdue balances.

Before the window appears, QuickBooks may display a message if you have any customers that have credits that you haven't yet applied to an invoice. This message is not necessarily connected to the customers who are due to have finance charges assessed; it's a general statement that somewhere in your company data file, there's an unapplied credit. If an asterisk appears beside the name of any customer or job

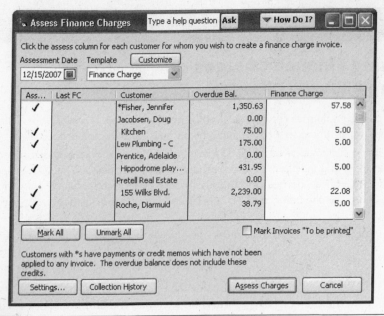

FIGURE 5-8   Use this window to assess finance charges

in the Assess Finance Charges window, close the window, correct the situation, and then reopen the window.

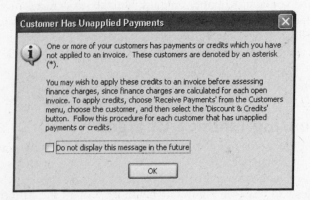

Choosing the Assessment Date

Change the Assessment Date field to the date on which you want the finance charge to appear on customer statements. It's common to assess finance charges on the last day of the month. When you press TAB to move out of the date field, QuickBooks recalculates the finance charges to reflect the new date.

N O T E :   QuickBooks uses the Last FC column to calculate the number of days overdue. When calculating the number of days overdue, QuickBooks starts counting using the date you last assessed finance charges. If an invoice is 60 days overdue, and you assessed charges 30 days ago, QuickBooks assesses new finance charges only on the 30 days since the last assessment.

Selecting the Customers

By default, QuickBooks selects all customers with overdue balances when assessing finance charges. You can eliminate a customer from the process by clicking in the Assess column to remove the check mark.

 N O T E :   Some customers on the list may display a zero balance. These customers have an A/R balance that isn't older than the grace period you specified when you set up finance charge preferences. QuickBooks doesn't select these customers.

If you have only a few customers for whom you want to assess finance charges, choose Unmark All and then reselect the customers you want to include.

Checking the History

To make sure that you don't erroneously assess a charge that isn't really due, you can display a collection report for a customer from the Assess Finance Charges window. Click a customer and click the Collection History button; QuickBooks displays a Collections Report for the selected customer (see Figure 5-9). As you move your mouse over a transaction in the report, the pointer turns into a magnifying glass with the letter "z" (for "zoom"). You can double-click any transaction to display the transaction in the window where you created it if you need to examine the details.

Selecting Printing Options

If you want to print the finance charge invoices, select the Mark Invoices "To Be Printed" check box in the Assess Finance Charges window. If you prefer to display the finance charge on the monthly statement—the common method for most businesses—you don't need to select the Mark Invoices "To Be Printed" check box.

 N O T E :   After you assess finance charges, if you opted to print them, choose File | Print Forms | Invoices. The list of unprinted invoices appears, and the list includes the finance charge invoices—all finance charge invoice numbers begin with "FC."

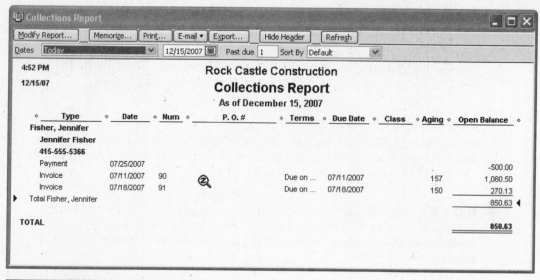

FIGURE 5-9   Double-check the details behind a proposed finance charge

Saving the Finance Charge Invoices

When all the figures are correct, click Assess Charges in the Assess Finance Charges window, and QuickBooks creates and saves finance charge invoices. When you create your customer statements, the finance charges will appear. Each finance charge invoice number begins with FC.

Sending Statements

On a periodic basis, typically once each month, most businesses send statements to customers. Statements remind customers of outstanding balances, and they help ensure that your records and your customers' records reflect the same information.

Entering Statement Charges

Before creating statements, you should create any transactions that should appear on the statements. Invoices and payments appear automatically, but you may want to add statement charges. A *statement charge* is a charge you want to pass to a customer for which you don't create an invoice. You can use statement charges for special charges for certain customers, such as a general overhead charge, or a charge you apply instead of using reimbursements for expenses incurred on behalf of the customer. You can also use statement charges for discounts for certain customers, such as reducing the total due by a specific amount, instead of creating and applying discount rates or price levels.

NOTE: Some companies, typically professional service companies like lawyers and architects, don't use invoices at all; instead, they enter statement charges for services performed and then send statements monthly.

You must add statement charges before you create the statements so that the charges appear on the statements. Statement charges use items from your Item list, but you cannot use any of the following types of items:

- Items that are taxable because the statement charge can't apply the tax
- Items that have percentage discounts because the statement charge can't look up the discount percentage to apply
- Items that represent a payment transaction because those are negative charges, which a statement charge doesn't understand

To record a statement charge, you work directly in the register of a customer or a job:

1. In the Customer Center, right-click a customer on the Customers & Jobs tab and choose Enter Statement Charges from the shortcut menu. QuickBooks opens the register for the selected customer (see Figure 5-10).
2. Select an item from the Item drop-down list or use <Add New> to create a new item. See Chapter 2 for details on adding items.
3. Enter a quantity in the Qty field if the item is invoiced by quantity.

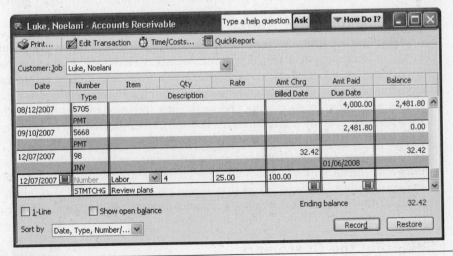

FIGURE 5-10   A customer register

④ If you're using the Qty field, enter a rate or accept the default rate if one exists. QuickBooks calculates the amount using the Qty field and the Rate field.

⑤ Enter the amount charged if you didn't supply values in the Qty and Rate fields.

⑥ Enter a description for the statement charge.

⑦ Optionally, enter the billed date, which does not have to match the transaction date in the first column of the register. Postdating or predating this field determines the statement on which the charge appears.

⑧ Enter the due date, which affects your aging reports and your finance charge calculations. If you don't enter a date, QuickBooks uses the customer's terms to determine the date.

⑨ Click Record to save the transaction.

If your statement charges are recurring charges, you can memorize them to have QuickBooks automatically create them. After you create the charge, right-click it in the register and select Memorize Stmt Charge from the shortcut menu. This works exactly like memorized invoices (covered in Chapter 3).

To create a statement charge for a different customer or job, use the drop-down list at the top of the register window to select the customer or job.

Creating Statements

Before you start creating your statements, make sure that you've entered all of the transactions that should appear on the statements. To create statements, click the Statements icon on the Home page or choose Customers | Create Statements from the menu bar. QuickBooks displays the Create Statements window (see Figure 5-11).

Selecting the Date Range

The statement date range determines which transactions appear on the statement. The printed statement displays the previous balance, which is the total due before the "From" date, and includes individual lines for each transaction created within the date range. You should set the day after the last date of your last statement run as the starting date. If you do monthly statements, choose the first and last days of the current month for the date range; if you send statements quarterly, enter the first and last dates of the current quarter—and so on.

If you choose All Open Transactions As Of Statement Date, the printed statement shows only unpaid invoices and statement charges and unapplied credits. You can reduce the number of transactions that appear on the statement if you select Include Only Transactions Over X Days Past Due Date, where X is a number of days that you specify.

Selecting the Customers

It's normal procedure to send statements to all customers, but if that's not the plan, you can change the default selection.

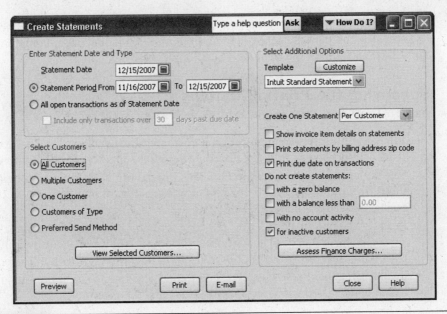

FIGURE 5-11 Use this window to create statements

If you want to send statements to a group of customers, click the Multiple Customers option to display a Choose button beside it. Then click the Choose button to display a list of customers and select each customer you want to include. You can manually select each customer, or select Automatic and then enter text to tell QuickBooks to match that text against all customer names and select the matching customers. The automatic match option only matches exact text, not partial text, and therefore only matches one customer at a time.

Click OK when you have selected all the appropriate customers.

If you're sending a statement to one customer only, select One Customer, and open the list box to select the customer.

You also can select customers by customer type.

Finally, you can select customers based on the preferred send method you established in each customer's record. Select the Preferred Send Method option, and then select the send method for this batch from the drop-down list that appears:

- **E-mail**   Sends the statements by e-mail, using the QuickBooks e-mail services feature.
- **Mail**   Sends the statements to QuickBooks services, a fee-based service, where the statement is created with a tear-off slip that the customer can return with payment. QuickBooks mails the invoice.
- **None**   Means no special handling. You print the statements, put them in envelopes, and mail them.

TIP: After you select customers using any of the methods described above, you can click the View Selected Customers button to display a list of customers for whom QuickBooks will produce statements.

Specifying the Printing Options

In the Select Additional Options section, you can make the following choices:

- You can print one statement for each customer, listing all transactions for all that customer's jobs, or you can print a separate statement for each job.
- You can opt to show invoice item details instead of listing one line for each invoice on the statement. If your invoices have a lot of line items, this could make your statements very long.
- Printing statements in order by ZIP code is handy if you're printing labels that are sorted by ZIP code. This option is also important if you use a bulk mail permit, because the post office requires bulk mail to be sorted by ZIP code.
- By default, QuickBooks displays the original due date for each transaction on the statement; you can choose not to print this information.

Specifying the Statements to Skip

You can skip producing statements for customers who meet the criteria you set in the Do Not Create Statements section of the dialog. For example, you may not want to send statements to customers with $0 balances.

Last Call for Finance Charges

If you haven't assessed finance charges and you want them to appear on the statements, click the Assess Finance Charges button. The Assess Finance Charges window opens, showing customers selected for finance charges. Follow the steps listed earlier in this chapter in the section "Assessing Finance Charges" to create finance charge invoices that will appear on customer statements.

If you've already assessed finance charges, QuickBooks will warn you that finance charges have already been assessed as of the selected date. Don't ignore the message, because QuickBooks will add another round of finance charges.

Previewing the Statements

Before you print statements, you can click the Preview button to get an advance look (see Figure 5-12).

Use the Zoom In button to see the statement and its contents close up. Click the Next Page button to move through all the statements. Click Close to redisplay the Create Statements window.

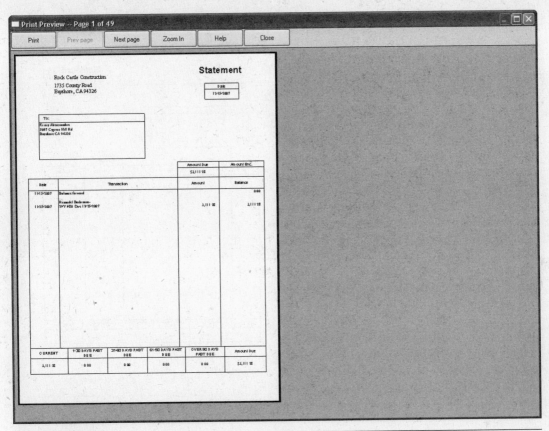

FIGURE 5-12 You can preview customer statements before printing them

Printing the Statements

You can print the statements by clicking the Print button in either the Print Preview window or the Create Statements window. If you clicked Close in the Preview window, QuickBooks redisplays the Create Statements window—click Print to open the Print Statement(s) window. Then change the printing options as needed.

Customizing Statements

You don't have to use the standard statement form—you can design your own. In the Create Statements window, click the Customize button to open the Basic Customization window (see Figure 5-13); from this window, you can make basic changes to the template, such as adding a logo or changing company information.

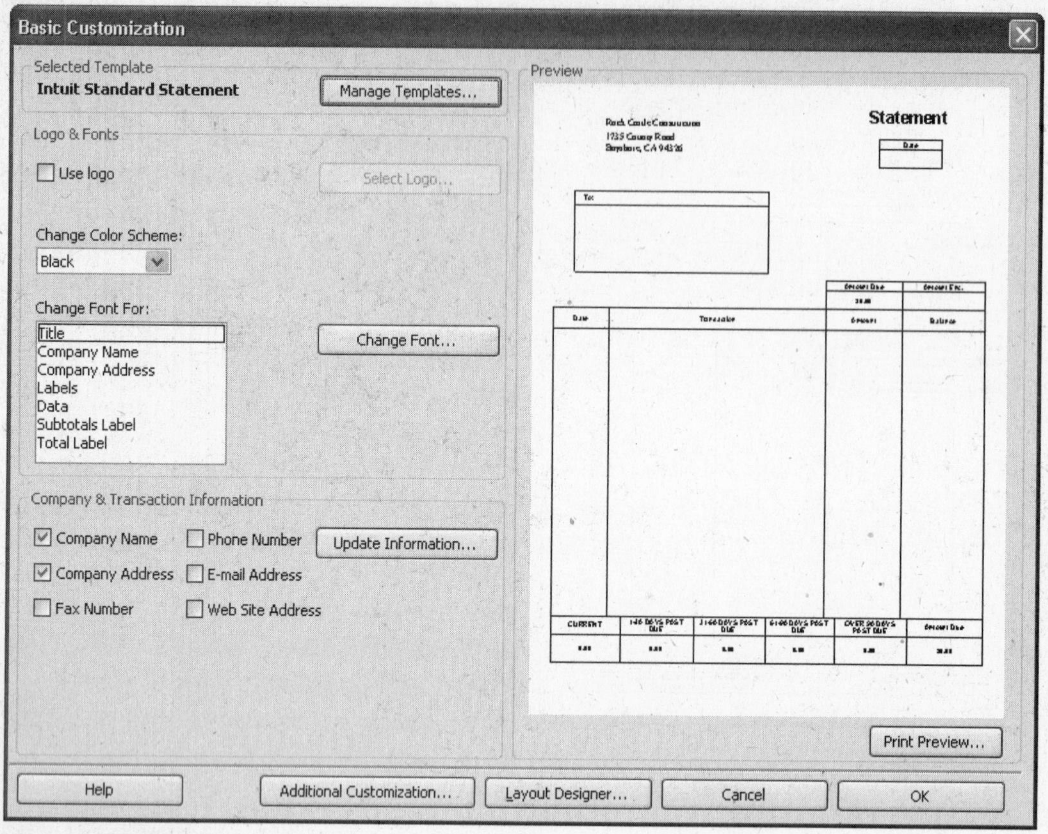

FIGURE 5-13   Make basic changes to the template

To make more extensive changes, click the Additional Customization button. QuickBooks automatically makes a copy of the template—to help you preserve the original form—and adds "Copy of" to the original template's name. You can rename the template, but first, let's finish our work in the Additional Customization dialog box.

From the Additional Customization dialog box, you can use the Header tab to add or remove fields or change the titles of fields in the header portion of the statement. From the Columns tab, you can add, remove, or reorder the columns of the statement. And, you can use the Footer area to add a text message to each statement.

Click OK to redisplay the Basic Customization dialog box. If you want to rename the template to something more meaningful to you, click the Manage Templates button and edit the template name. When you have finished, click OK to redisplay the Create Statements window. Click Close to save your changes.

Entering Accounts Payable Bills

In this chapter:

- Understanding the vendor center

- Entering vendor bills

- Tracking reimbursable expenses

- Entering item purchases

- Using purchase orders

- Entering vendor credit memos

- Entering recurring bills

- Managing mileage costs

Chapter 6

QuickBooks can help you track and pay bills in a timely fashion. You can enter bills that affect accounts, such as utility bills, and you can enter bills for items (inventory and noninventory) and services you purchase. If appropriate, you can assign portions of bills to customers as reimbursable expenses. You also can use purchase orders to help track items you order.

In this chapter, you'll learn how to handle all these tasks and more; you'll also learn how to account for vendor credits, reduce the data entry work of entering bills by creating recurring bills, and manage mileage costs.

Vendor Center

The Vendor Center works much like the Customer Center, quickly and easily displaying information about your vendors, your balances with them, and other important information.

To open the Vendor Center, take any of the following actions:

- Click the Vendor Center icon on the toolbar.
- Click the Vendors icon on the left side of the Home page.
- Choose Vendors | Vendor Center from the menu bar.

As you can see in Figure 6-1, the layout of the Vendor Center window is easy to understand and navigate.

 SECURITY NOTE: Users who do not have access permissions for vendor information do not see financial information when they open the Vendor Center window.

The left pane of the Vendor Center has two tabs: Vendors and Transactions. The Vendors tab actually replaces the Vendor List used in earlier versions of QuickBooks. As you click any Vendor on the Vendors tab, QuickBooks displays transactions for that vendor on the right side of the screen. You can limit the transactions to a specific type to make the search easier, and you can filter the transactions; your filtering choices depend on the type of transaction you select in the Show List box. To narrow the search further, you can select a date range.

The Transactions tab (see Figure 6-2) lists all your vendor-related transactions, and you can use this tab to find a particular transaction or transactions using criteria you specify. On the left side of the screen, select the transaction type for which you are searching. Then, use the Filter By and Date List boxes to narrow the search.

You can use the toolbar buttons in the Vendor Center window and the links in the right pane of the Vendors tab to open transaction windows and produce reports.

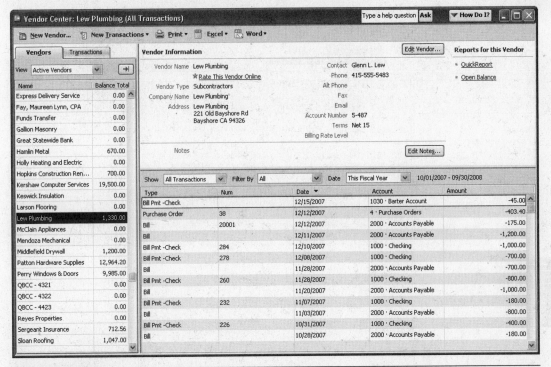

FIGURE 6-1   The Vendors tab provides a robust way to find information about a specific vendor

You can customize the Vendor Center by resizing any of its panes. To resize a pane, move the mouse pointer over the edge of any pane; the mouse pointer changes to a vertical or horizontal bar with pointing arrows attached. Drag the pane left or right (up or down) to change its size. The other pane(s) will adjust to fill the space. In addition, you can choose the columns that QuickBooks displays in the Vendor List by right clicking on the list. QuickBooks displays a context menu; choose Customize Columns.

 TIP: Click the Show Full List Only button (it appears beside the View List box on the Vendors tab) to make the Vendor list fill the entire Vendor Center window.

Recording Vendor Bills

When bills arrive, you should enter them into QuickBooks; that way, QuickBooks can begin to age the bills based on the terms your vendor extends to you, and help ensure that you pay your bills on time. Paying your bills either late or early can cost

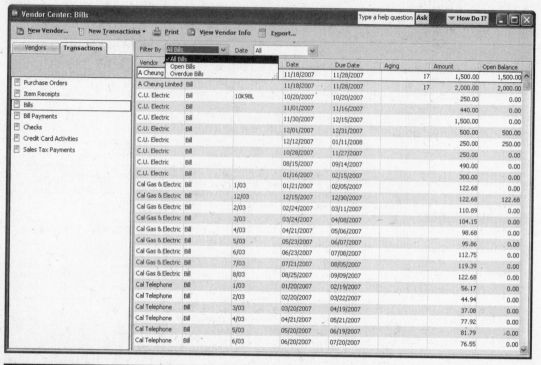

FIGURE 6-2 Use the Transactions tab to easily filter and find transactions

you money. If you pay your bills late, you may lose discounts offered by your vendors or incur finance charges from your vendors. And, if you pay your bills too early, you lose the opportunity to use cash to earn money.

 NOTE: A quick reminder: You established your terms with your vendor when you set up the vendor in QuickBooks. You'll find the details in Chapter 2.

To enter your bills, click Enter Bills in the Vendor section of the Home page or choose New Transactions | Enter Bills from the Vendor Center. When the Enter Bills window opens (see Figure 6-3), you can fill out the information from the bill you received.

The window has two sections: the top of the window, generally called the Heading section, contains information about the vendor and the bill, and the bottom of the window, generally called the Details section, records the information related to your general ledger accounts. The Details section has two tabs: Expenses and Items.

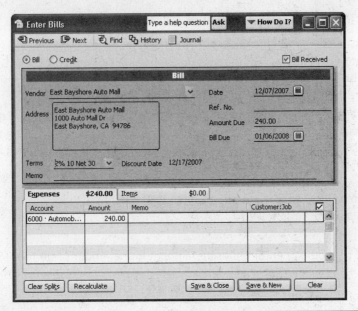

FIGURE 6-3 Use this window to enter a bill you receive from a vendor

In this section, I'll cover bills that you record using the Expenses tab; I'll cover entering bills using the Items tab later in this chapter in the section "Managing Item Purchases."

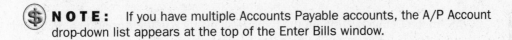 **NOTE:** If you have multiple Accounts Payable accounts, the A/P Account drop-down list appears at the top of the Enter Bills window.

Depending on the bill, you may be able to assign the entire bill to one expense account, or you may have to split the bill among multiple expense accounts. For example, your utility bills are usually posted to the appropriate utility account (electric, heat, and so on). However, you typically split credit card bills among numerous expenses, and loan repayments between interest (an expense account) and principal (a liability account).

Easy One-Account Posting

In the Vendor field, click the arrow to choose a vendor from the list that appears.

NOTE: If the vendor isn't on the list, choose <Add New> to add this vendor to your QuickBooks Vendor List.

Now fill out the rest of the bill as follows:

1 Enter the bill date. In the Bill Due field, QuickBooks fills in the due date automatically, based on the terms you set up with this vendor. You can change this date if you wish.

($) NOTE: If you didn't set up terms for this vendor, QuickBooks fills in the due date automatically using the default number of days (10) for paying bills. You can change the default by choosing Edit | Preferences and then clicking Bills on the left side of the Preferences dialog box.

2 Enter the vendor's invoice number in the Ref. No. field.

3 Enter the amount due.

($) TIP: You can enter either the amount in the Amount Due field (Step 3) or in the Amount column (Step 5). QuickBooks fills in the field in which you made no entry.

4 In the Terms field, click the arrow to display a list of terms and select the terms that reflect your agreement with your vendor. QuickBooks changes the due date to reflect the terms.

($) NOTE: If you don't see the terms you have with this vendor, choose <Add New> to create a new Terms entry.

5 In the Details section on the Expenses tab, click in the Account column, and then click the arrow that appears to display your chart of accounts. Select the account to which you want to assign this bill. QuickBooks automatically assigns the amount you entered in the Amount Due field to the Amount column.

($) TIP: You can set preferences so that QuickBooks "learns" the account you choose most often for the selected vendor. Choose Edit | Preferences and click the General category. Then, on the My Preferences tab, check the Automatically Remember Account Or Transaction Information check box and select the Prefill Accounts For Vendor Based On Past Entries option.

6 If you wish, enter a note in the Memo column.

7 In the Customer: Job column, enter a customer or job if you're paying a bill that you want to track for job costing, or if this bill is a reimbursable expense. See "Reimbursable Expenses" later in this chapter for details.

8 If you're tracking classes, a Class column appears; enter the appropriate class.

9 When you're finished, click Save & New to save this bill and display another blank Enter Bills window. When you've entered all your bills, click Save & Close.

Splitting Expenses among Multiple Accounts

Some bills, like credit card bills or bills to an insurance carrier for different kinds of insurance, need to be split among multiple accounts in your general ledger instead of being neatly assigned to one account.

 NOTE: Although I mention that you can split credit card expenses among accounts, you use this approach *only if* you don't use the Credit Card account type to track credit card expenses. For a full treatment of tracking credit card expenses, see Chapter 11.

Here's how to split a bill among multiple general ledger accounts:

1 Complete Steps 1 through 4 in the preceding section.

2 On the first line of the Expenses tab, click in the Account column to display the arrow you use to see your chart of accounts and select the first account to which you want to assign some portion of this bill.

3 Type the amount you want to assign to the account you selected.

4 On a new line of the Expenses tab, repeat Steps 2 and 3 until you have entered all the lines needed to sum to the total of the bill.

As you add each additional line to the bill, QuickBooks updates the Amount column on the Expenses tab with the total remaining amount based on the amount you entered in the Amount Due field in the header section. This updating process provides you with a visual cue if the last line item does not make the total of the line items match the amount of the bill (see Figure 6-4).

Reimbursable Expenses

A reimbursable expense is one that you incurred on behalf of a customer. Even though you pay the vendor bill, there's an agreement with your customer that you'll send an invoice to recover your costs. There are two common types of reimbursable expenses:

- General expenses you incur as a cost of doing business with the customer, such as long-distance telephone charges, parking and tolls, and other incidental expenses. When you enter the vendor bill, you record separately those portions of the bill that apply to customer agreements for reimbursement.
- Specific goods or services that you purchase for a customer that you would not have purchased otherwise.

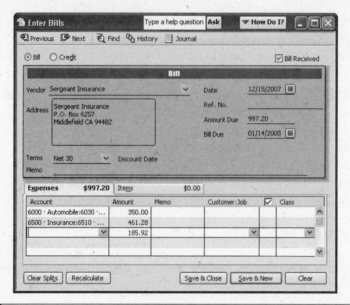

FIGURE 6-4　Record a line on the Expenses tab for each account in the general ledger affected by the bill

Options for Managing Reimbursable Expenses

You can manage reimbursable expenses in two ways:

- Let QuickBooks automatically post the reimbursable expense to the same expense account that you use to record your portion of the expense. This approach cancels the original expense and reduces the expense total in your Profit & Loss statements.
- Let QuickBooks automatically post the reimbursable expense to an income account that you create for reimbursable expenses. This approach lets you track totals for both the original expense and the reimbursement.

You may want to discuss these choices with your accountant. Many businesses prefer the second option—tracking reimbursable expenses separately—because it's more accurate when you're analyzing your expenses and income. I'll therefore go over the steps you should take to set up to track reimbursable expenses. You can ignore the instructions if you prefer to reduce your expense totals by posting reimbursable expenses to the same expense account you use when you enter the vendor's bill.

Setting Up to Track Reimbursable Expenses

To track reimbursable expenses, you need to set preferences. To track them separately from your expenses, you must also create income accounts that you'll use when collecting reimbursable expenses.

Setting Preferences to Track Reimbursable Expenses

You tell QuickBooks that you want to track reimbursable expenses in the Preferences dialog box.

Use the following steps:

1. Choose Edit | Preferences to open the Preferences dialog box.
2. Select the Sales & Customers icon in the left pane.
3. Click the Company Preferences tab.
4. Check the Track Reimbursed Expenses As Income box.
5. Click OK.

 N O T E :   You'll notice a field to enter a markup percentage right below the option to Track Reimbursed Expenses As Income. See the section "Marking Up Reimbursable Expenses" later in this chapter to learn about the markup feature.

When you enable this option, QuickBooks adds a new field to the window you use when you create or edit an expense account so that you can set up an expense account to assign reimbursable expenses to an income account of your choice. Whenever you post a vendor expense to this account and also indicate that the expense is reimbursable, QuickBooks automatically posts the amount you charge on the customer's invoice to the income account linked to this expense account. To assign an income account for reimbursable expenses to an expense account, press CTRL-A to open the Chart Of Accounts window, highlight the expense account, and press CTRL-E. In the Edit Account window that appears, check the Track Reimbursed Expenses In box and then use the Income Account drop-down list to select the income account you want to use for reimbursable expenses.

Set Up Income Accounts for Reimbursement

You may have numerous expense accounts that you want to use for reimbursable expenses; in fact, that's the common scenario. Portions of telephone bills, travel expenses, subcontractor expenses, and so on are frequently passed on to customers for reimbursement.

QuickBooks expects a one-to-one relationship between a reimbursable expense and the reimbursement income from that expense. So if you have more than one expense account for which you may receive reimbursement, you must create an income account for accepting reimbursed expenses for each of these expense accounts.

To easily view totals for income received from reimbursed expenses, set up the income accounts as subaccounts; you can name the parent account Reimbursements or Reimbursed Expenses. That way, your reports will show the total amount of income due to reimbursed expenses, and you can ignore the individual account totals unless you have some reason to audit a number.

Depending on the company type you selected during the EasyStep Interview, QuickBooks may have already created a Reimbursed Expenses account in the Income section of your chart of accounts. If so, you can use that account as the parent account; the steps below show you how to create both the parent account and the subaccounts.

Use these steps to set up a parent account and subaccounts for tracking reimbursed income:

1. Open the chart of accounts by pressing CTRL-A.
2. Press CTRL-N to open a New Account window.
3. Select Income as the account type.
4. Enter an account number (if you use numbers) and name the account Reimbursements (or something similar).

You've created the parent account—now create the subaccounts using these steps:

1. Click Next.
2. If you're using numbered accounts, assign a number to the subaccount that leaves 10 numbers between the subaccount number and the number you used for the parent account. Also enter a name for the account, such as Telephone Reimbursements.
3. Select the Subaccount Of check box and link it to the parent account you created.
4. Click Next to create the next account.

Repeat this process as many times as necessary, clicking OK in Step 5 when you finish. For example, my chart of accounts has the following accounts for this purpose:

- 4200 Reimbursements
- 4210 Equip Rental Reimbursements
- 4220 Telephone Reimbursements
- 4230 Travel Reimbursements
- 4240 Subcontractor Reimbursements

My reports show information for the subaccounts as well as a total of all transactions for the parent account.

Don't forget to edit your existing expense accounts to link the income accounts you just created to the appropriate expense account. Check the box to track reimbursed expenses and select the appropriate income account.

Recording Reimbursable Expenses

To be reimbursed by customers for expenses you incurred on their behalf, you enter the appropriate information while entering the vendor's bill on which the expense appears. After you enter the account and the amount, click the arrow in the Customer: Job column and select the appropriate customer or job from the drop-down list.

Entering data in the Customer: Job column automatically places a check mark in the column to the right of the Customer: Job column. The check mark means that you're tracking this expense to invoice the customer for reimbursement.

If you don't want to bill the customer for the expense but you do want to track what you're spending for the customer, you can click the check mark. QuickBooks removes the check mark and doesn't create a reimbursable expense for which you can invoice the customer, but continues to associate the expense with the customer. You use this technique when tracking costs for jobs.

A vendor's bill may not be entirely chargeable to a customer; some of the amount may be your own responsibility. In addition, multiple customers may owe you reimbursement for the amount; this is often the case with telephone expenses when your customers reimburse you for long-distance charges.

Here's how to enter the transaction:

1. Select the expense account and enter the portion of the bill that you are charging back to a customer.
2. Enter an explanation of the charge in the Memo column. When you create the invoice, the customer sees the text in the Memo column.
3. In the Customer: Job column, choose the appropriate customer or job.
4. If you're only tracking expenses and don't want to include the amount in your invoice to this customer, click the check mark beside the customer's name to remove it.
5. Repeat Steps 1 through 4 to include any additional customers for this expense account.
6. In the next line, select the same account and enter the portion of the bill that is your own responsibility.

When you're finished, the total amount you entered on-screen should match the amount on the vendor's bill (see Figure 6-5).

When you save the vendor bill, QuickBooks creates reimbursable expense entries for the amounts you assigned to customers.

Invoicing Customers for Reimbursable Expenses

Chapter 3 has complete information about creating invoices for customers, but in this section I'll discuss the particular steps you take when you create an invoice that includes reimbursable expenses.

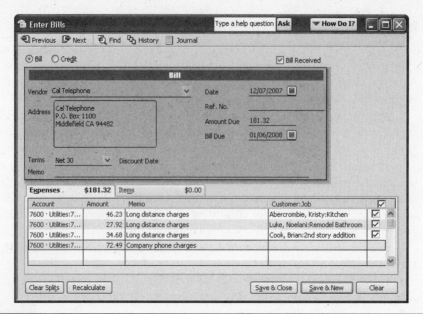

FIGURE 6-5   Entering a bill that includes reimbursable expenses

As soon as you select a customer in the Create Invoices window, QuickBooks checks to see if that customer has any outstanding billable time or costs; if such outstanding entries exist, QuickBooks displays a message alerting you of that fact and asking how you want to handle the outstanding billable time or costs.

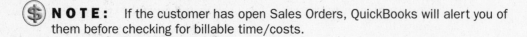

N O T E :   If the customer has open Sales Orders, QuickBooks will alert you of them before checking for billable time/costs.

If you select the second option, QuickBooks doesn't place any of the outstanding time and cost entries on the invoice, but you can click the Add Time/Costs button on the invoice to add them later.

If you select the first option, QuickBooks displays the Choose Billable Time And Costs window (see Figure 6-6).

T I P :   You can set your preferences (choose Edit | Preferences) so that QuickBooks automatically opens the Choose Billable Time And Costs window when you select a customer with outstanding reimbursable expenses.

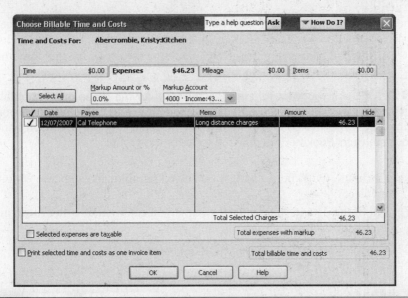

FIGURE 6-6   Use this window to decide how you want QuickBooks to handle outstanding reimbursable expenses

Use the following steps to include reimbursable expenses on a customer invoice:

1. Click the Expenses tab to display the reimbursable amounts you posted for this customer when you entered vendor bills.

2. Click in the Use column to place a check mark next to the expense(s) you want to include on the invoice you're currently creating. Some notes about including reimbursable expenses:

   - You don't have to include all available reimbursable expenses; the ones you don't select will be available the next time you invoice this customer.

   - To charge sales tax for a reimbursable expense (assuming the customer is not tax-exempt), check the Selected Expenses Are Taxable box.

   - If you need to charge sales tax on some but not all reimbursable expenses, add them to the invoice in two groups. Click the Add Time/Costs button in the Create Invoices window and add the nontaxable items to the invoice. Then, click the Add Time/Costs button in the Create Invoices window again to reopen the Choose Billable Time And Costs dialog box and add the taxable items, making sure that you also check the Selected Expenses Are Taxable box. If you prefer, you can add both taxable and nontaxable expenses at the same time and then change the tax status in the Tax column on the invoice.

- If you include more than one reimbursable expense on an invoice, QuickBooks places an item called Reimb Group on the invoice, lists the individual items in the group, and enters the total for the reimbursable items (see Figure 6-7).

NOTE: If you want to print only the total for the group of reimbursable expenses, you can check the Print Selected Time And Costs As One Invoice Item. On-screen, the invoice looks like the one in Figure 6-7, but when you print the invoice, QuickBooks prints only the total for the group.

③ Click OK. QuickBooks adds the selected reimbursable expense(s) to the invoice.

④ Fill in the data in the invoice heading; you can include other lines on the invoice in addition to reimbursable costs.

⑤ Click Save & Close.

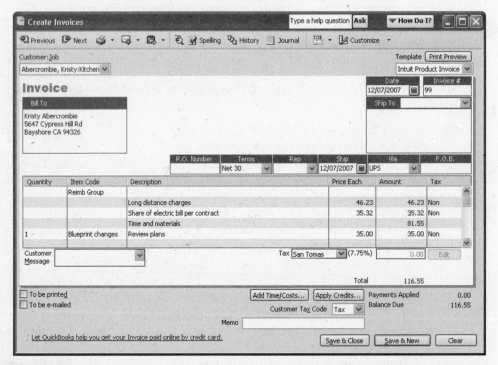

FIGURE 6-7   QuickBooks adds a line to the invoice for the reimbursable expense.

Notice that QuickBooks uses the text you entered in the Memo column when you entered the vendor's bill for the description of the reimbursable item. If you don't enter information into the Memo column when you enter the bill, you'll have to enter text manually in the Description column of the invoice—and that could turn out to be a real test of your memory. If you don't enter anything, the customer sees only an amount and no explanation for it.

Removing a Reimbursable Expense from the List

As explained earlier, when you're entering a vendor's bill and assigning expenses to customers and jobs, you can track the expense but mark it as not reimbursable by clicking the Reimbursable Expense icon.

Let's suppose that you entered the expense as reimbursable. Further suppose that you decide while invoicing the customer that you don't want to ask the customer to pay this expense; you've changed your mind.

To remove an expense from the Choose Billable Time And Costs dialog box, place a check mark in the Hide column beside the item. This action has the same effect as clicking the Reimbursable Expense icon in the Enter Bills window— QuickBooks continues to track the expense and assign it to a Customer: Job, but QuickBooks no longer considers the expense reimbursable.

Changing the Amount of a Reimbursable Expense

You can change the amount of a reimbursable expense in either the Choose Billable Time And Costs dialog box or in the Amount column of the Create Invoices window.

If you reduce the amount, QuickBooks does not keep the remaining amount on the Billable Time And Costs window. Instead, QuickBooks assumes that you're not planning to pass the remaining amount to your customer in the future.

You may want to increase the charge for some reason (perhaps to cover overhead); in this case, you should mark up the expenses, as described in the next section.

Marking Up Reimbursable Expenses

Many companies mark up expenses they invoice to cover any additional costs incurred such as handling or time. You apply a markup in the Choose Billable Time And Costs dialog box. Check the items you want to mark up and enter a markup in the Markup Amount or % field. You can enter an amount or a percentage (enter a percentage by typing a number followed by the percent sign).

In the Markup Account list, select the account to which you post markups. You can create an account specifically for markups or use an existing income account.

The individual reimbursable expense amounts and their total don't change when you apply the markup; you'll see the change in the Total Expenses With Markup and Total Billable Time And Costs fields of the Choose Billable Time And Costs dialog box (see Figure 6-8).

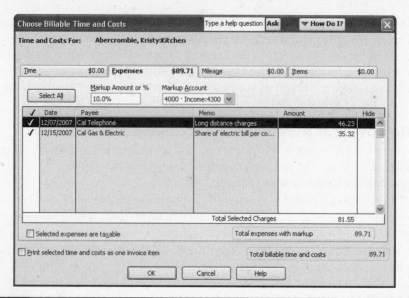

FIGURE 6-8   Applying a markup changes the Total Expenses With Markup and Total Billable
Time And Costs fields

When you click OK and QuickBooks transfers the reimbursable expenses to the customer's invoice, you'll see the reimbursable expenses and the markup as separate items (see Figure 6-9).

Although it would be unusual for you to be marking up items without having discussed this with your customer, if you don't want your customer to see the markup amounts, check the Print Selected Time And Costs As One Invoice Item box in the Choose Billable Time And Costs dialog box. You'll see the breakdown on the screen version of the invoice, but the printed invoice will contain only the grand total.

The difference between using the markup function and just changing the amount of the reimbursable expense in the Amount column is the way QuickBooks posts amounts to your general ledger. If you use the markup function, the difference between the actual expense and the charge to your customer is posted to the markup account. If you change the amount of the expense, the entire amount is posted to the income account you linked to the reimbursable expense account.

Managing Item Purchases

You record a vendor bill that includes items you purchase—whether to replenish your inventory or to resell to a customer—a little differently than a bill that doesn't include items. When you buy items, the transaction really consists of two parts:

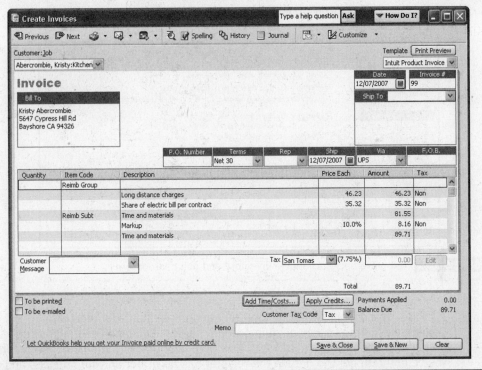

FIGURE 6-9   QuickBooks places the markup on a separate line on the invoice

you receive the items and you receive the bill for the items, and while those two events can coincide, they don't always happen at the same time. It's certainly possible for the bill to arrive after the items, and sometimes the bill comes before the items. In this section, I'll go over all three situations.

In addition, some companies like to start the process of purchasing items using a purchase order. I'll start this section by showing you how to use the purchase order feature in QuickBooks.

To use the Inventory and Purchase Order features, you must enable them. Choose Edit | Preferences to open the Preferences dialog box (see Figure 6-10). Then, click the Items & Inventory category, click the Company Preferences tab, and check the Inventory And Purchase Orders Are Active box and the Warn About Duplicate Purchase Order Numbers box. I suggest that you also check the rest of the boxes and select the When The Quantity I Want To Sell Exceeds The Quantity Available option. Selecting the When The Quantity I Want To Sell Exceeds The Quantity On Hand option tells QuickBooks to warn you if you try to sell more than you have in stock. Selecting the When The Quantity I Want To Sell Exceeds The Quantity Available option tells QuickBooks to also consider items on sales orders and items reserved for assemblies along with quantity on hand when warning you.

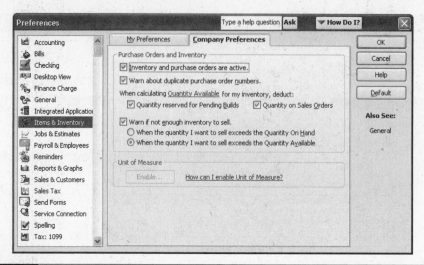

FIGURE 6-10   Set preferences to enable inventory and purchase orders

TIP: When you enable the Inventory and Purchase Order features, QuickBooks creates a non-posting account named Purchase Orders. You can double-click the account's listing to view and drill down into the purchase orders you've entered, but the data in the register has no effect on your finances and doesn't appear in financial reports.

Using Purchase Orders

You can use purchase orders to order items from your suppliers to help you track what you've ordered against what you've received. Creating and saving a purchase order has no effect on your financial information. When you create a purchase order, QuickBooks stores the transaction in a nonposting account that you'll find listed in the Chart Of Accounts window; you can double-click the account to view and drill down into the purchase orders you've entered, but the transactions don't affect your financial information.

TIP: You can automatically create a purchase order when you create a sales order or estimate involving items. This handy feature saves you the data entry time of creating a sales order and then retyping the same information in the Create Purchase Orders window. To create the purchase order, open the sales order transaction, click the arrow to the right of the Create Invoice icon on the toolbar, and select Purchase Orders.

Here's how to create a purchase order:

1 Choose Purchase Orders on the Home page, or choose New Transactions | Purchase Orders from the Vendor Center to open a blank Create Purchase Orders window.

2 Fill in the Purchase Order fields, which are easy and self-explanatory (see Figure 6-11).

($) TIP :   If you're purchasing something on behalf of the customer, select the customer or job in the Customer column, and QuickBooks will treat the line as a reimbursable expense when you enter the vendor's bill for this purchase order. You covered reimbursable expenses earlier in this chapter.

3 Click Save & New to save the purchase order and move on to the next blank purchase order form, or click Save & Close if you have created all the purchase orders you need right now.

You can print the purchase orders as you create them by clicking the Print button as soon as you complete a purchase order. Or, you can print them all in a batch; make sure a check appears in the To Be Printed box on each purchase order. Then, enter all your purchase orders and, just before you save the last one, click the arrow to the right of the Print button and select Print Batch. QuickBooks displays the Select Purchase Orders To Print dialog box, where you can remove purchase orders from the batch by clicking them. When you're ready to print, click OK.

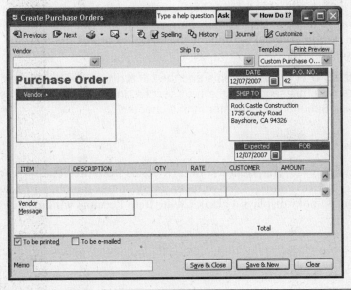

FIGURE 6-11   A purchase order resembles a vendor bill

You can also e-mail the purchase orders as you create them, or as a batch by selecting Send Batch from the drop-down list next to the E-mail icon on the toolbar in the Create Purchase Orders window. If you intend to e-mail purchase orders in a batch, be sure that you check the To Be E-Mailed box on each purchase order you intend to include in the batch.

 TIP: Many companies don't send physical purchase orders; instead, they create the purchase and then provide the vendor with the purchase order number when placing the order over the telephone, via e-mail, or by logging into the vendor's Internet-based order system.

When you order something from a vendor and receive less than you ordered, QuickBooks tracks the backordered items and displays the Backordered column in the Create Purchase Orders window, the Create Item Receipts window, and the Enter Bills window. You can track open purchase orders using the Open Purchase Orders report and the Open Purchase Orders by Job report. You can print both reports by choosing Reports | Purchases and then clicking the appropriate report.

When you receive the items and the bill, you can use the purchase order to create automatically the appropriate transactions in QuickBooks. In each of the following cases, the windows and your actions change slightly if you use a purchase order to create a transaction. As I explain how to enter these transactions, I'll describe the differences between using and not using a purchase order.

Receiving Inventory Items without a Bill

If the items you ordered arrive before you receive a bill from the vendor, you can receive the items so that they become available for sale—particularly useful if you have a customer order waiting for the arrival of one of these items.

 CAUTION: If the items and the bill arrive at the same time, don't use the steps in this section or the next section. Instead, refer to "Receiving Items and Bills Simultaneously" later in this chapter.

Follow these steps:

1. Choose New Transactions | Receive Items from the Vendor Center or choose Receive Inventory | Receive Inventory Without Bill on the Home page. QuickBooks displays a blank Create Item Receipts window (see Figure 6-12).

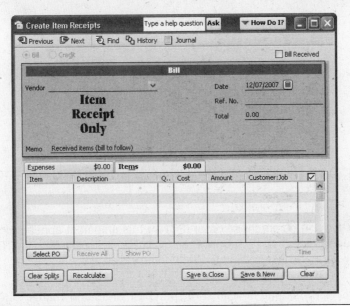

FIGURE 6-12   Use this window to record receiving items without a bill

2. Enter the vendor name, and if open purchase orders exist for this vendor, QuickBooks notifies you:

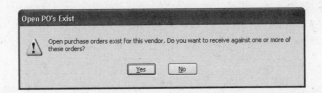

3. If you know there isn't a purchase order for this particular shipment, click No, and fill out the Create Item Receipts window manually; click in the Item column to select an item, supply the quantity you received, fill in a cost, if necessary and, if appropriate, assign the line to a customer to make the receipt a reimbursable expense. If a purchase order exists, click Yes. QuickBooks displays all the open purchase orders for this vendor (see Figure 6-13).

4. Place a check beside the appropriate purchase order(s) and click OK. QuickBooks fills in the Create Item Receipts window using the information on the purchase order (see Figure 6-14).

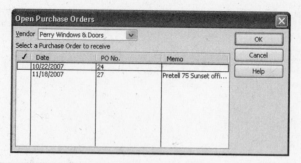

FIGURE 6-13   Use this dialog box to select a purchase order

$ **N O T E :**   If no purchase order (PO) for this shipment appears on the Open Purchase Orders list, click Cancel and QuickBooks redisplays the Receipts window, where you can fill in the item information manually.

⑤ Check the shipment against the purchase order and change any quantities that don't match.

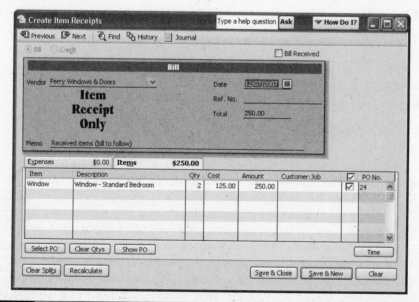

FIGURE 6-14   When you receive items against a purchase order, QuickBooks fills in the purchase order information for you

T I P :   You can click the Select PO button to redisplay the Select Purchase Order dialog box and add other purchase orders for the selected vendor to the Create Item Receipts window. You can click the Show PO button to display the purchase order associated with the last line shown in the Create Item Receipts window.

6 Click Save & New to receive the next shipment into inventory, or click Save & Close if this takes care of all the receipts of goods.

QuickBooks posts the amounts recorded on the purchase order to your Inventory and Accounts Payable account. The entry to the Accounts Payable account is not a typical method for handling receipt of goods before a bill arrives, but, ultimately, the accounting entries QuickBooks makes are correct; I'll explain what QuickBooks does in the section "Behind the Scenes" later in this chapter.

Recording Bills for Received Items

After you receive the items, eventually the bill comes from the vendor and you need to enter it because you now officially owe the vendor money. Before you record this bill, see the FYI "Resolving Date Issues When Converting Item Receipts to Bills."

 C A U T I O N :   If the bill and the items arrive at the same time, don't use the steps in this section or the preceding section. Instead, refer to "Receiving Items and Bills Simultaneously" later in this chapter.

To enter the bill, follow these steps:

1 Choose New Transactions | Enter Bill For Received Items to open the Select Item Receipt window. QuickBooks displays the Select Item Receipt window shown in Figure 6-15.

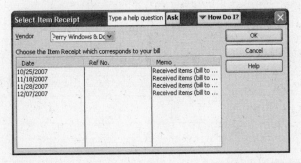

FIGURE 6-15   Use this window to select the Item Receipt for which you have now received a bill

2 Select the vendor, and QuickBooks displays the current items receipt information for the vendor.

3 Select the appropriate item and click OK. QuickBooks opens the Enter Bills window (see Figure 6-16) and fills it in using the information from the item receipt.

4 Change anything that needs to be changed. For example, the bill may specify a different cost per unit than the purchase order contained. Or, the bill may contain taxes and shipping costs that didn't appear on the purchase order. If you make any changes, click the Recalculate button so QuickBooks can match the total in the Amount Due field to the changed line item data.

5 Click Save & Close. QuickBooks displays a message asking if you're sure you want to save the changes. Click Yes, and QuickBooks replaces the original entry to Accounts Payable made when you received the items with the updated bill information.

Receiving Items and Bills Simultaneously

If the items and the bill arrive at the same time, tell QuickBooks about those events simultaneously. Do not use the steps in either of the two preceding sections. Instead, choose New Transactions | Receive Items And Enter Bill or click the Receive Inventory icon on the Home page and select Receive Inventory With Bill.

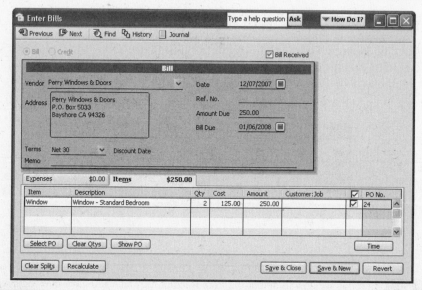

FIGURE 6-16   QuickBooks fills in this window with information from an Item Receipt transaction

▶ **FYI**

Resolving Date Issues When Converting Item Receipts to Bills

When QuickBooks replaces the original entries recorded when you used the Create Item Receipts window with the entries on the bill, QuickBooks changes the date that the item enters inventory—remember, you entered the item receipt earlier and waited for a bill to arrive.

Suppose that you've already sold an item or used it to build an assembly item before you receive the bill. When you enter the bill, QuickBooks changes the date the item enters inventory to match the bill date; you could possibly end up with negative inventory. While QuickBooks will let you have negative inventory, the condition doesn't make QuickBooks happy; the situation can cause bogus average cost calculations or, at worst, data damage. If you've used the item to build an assembly, the bill becomes pending (nonposting), and this situation can escalate to create other problems.

The easy workaround is to backdate the bill to the date of the item receipt. Be aware, though, that this approach has drawbacks. First, it changes the aging on the bill, affecting discounts from vendors; to accommodate the date change, check the due date of the bill and adjust it accordingly. Second, suppose that the items arrive at the end of one month and the bill arrives at the beginning of the next month. In this case, you may have completed work and printed financial statements for the month in which the items arrived. If you change the date on the bill to match the item receipt, you affect the balance of Accounts Payable for the earlier month.

There is another, more complex workaround, but it has the benefit of properly maintaining all your records:

1. When you receive the items, enter the Item Receipt and use the date the Items arrived.
2. When you receive the bill, enter it as described in this section, using the Item Receipt date on this bill.
3. Enter a Vendor Credit, described later in this chapter, using the date that appears on the paper copy of the bill and apply the Vendor Credit to the bill you entered in Step 2.
4. Finally, enter another bill—the one you will track and pay—using the date the bill that appears on the paper copy of the vendor's bill.

This approach maintains any assemblies you may have built using items that arrived before the bill; it also maintains your ability to properly age vendor bills and track vendor discounts without affecting the balance of Accounts Payable across months.

QuickBooks displays the Enter Bills window you saw previously in Figure 6-16. When you select the vendor's name, a message appears if open purchase orders exist for the vendor, asking if you want to receive goods and record a bill against an open purchase order.

If you click No, QuickBooks displays an empty Enter Bills window; on the Items tab, fill in the items that arrived using the cost information shown on the bill. Click Save & Close to save the transaction.

If you click Yes, QuickBooks displays the Open Purchase Orders window shown earlier in this chapter in Figure 6-14; from this window, select the appropriate purchase order and click OK. QuickBooks fills in the Enter Bills window using the line items on the purchase order. Correct any quantity or price difference between your original purchase order and the bill. When you save the transaction, QuickBooks receives the items into inventory in addition to posting the bill to A/P.

Behind the Scenes of Item Receipts and Vendor Bills

QuickBooks records the same entries, whether you receive items along with a bill or separately from a bill; if the amount involved is $400 worth of items, QuickBooks makes the following entries:

Account	Debit	Credit
Accounts Payable		$400.00
Inventory	$400.00	

QuickBooks makes this entry even if you use the Create Item Receipts window to receive items without recording a bill for the items. QuickBooks assigns a transaction type of ITEM RCPT to these transactions to track them, and you can see them in the Accounts Payable register. To view the Accounts Payable register, double-click your Accounts Payable account in the Chart Of Accounts window.

When you enter the bill that arrived separately from the items, QuickBooks does not record a new transaction in the Accounts Payable register. Instead, QuickBooks changes the transaction type of the Item Receipt entry in the Accounts Payable register from ITEM RCPT to BILL; if you made changes to any amounts when you recorded the bill, QuickBooks replaces the original amounts with the updated amounts. This practice ensures that you don't have duplicate entries for the same vendor transaction.

 C A U T I O N :   If you first enter an Item Receipt from a vendor and then try to use the Enter Bills command to enter the bill from the vendor, QuickBooks warns you that pending Item Receipts exist for the vendor and instructs you to use the Enter Bill for Received Items if you're trying to record a bill for items you received previously. You should not ignore this message. If the bill you want to enter is indeed for items you already received into QuickBooks, using the wrong command will result in double entries for the same amount in your Accounts Payable account.

Recording Vendor Credits

If you receive a credit from a vendor, you should record it in QuickBooks; you can apply a vendor credit to an open vendor bill, or you can leave it in the system to apply against your next order from the vendor. (See Chapter 7 for information about paying bills, which includes applying vendor credits to bills.)

To create a vendor credit, you use the Enter Bills window; follow these steps:

1 Click the Enter Bills icon on the Home page or choose New Transactions | Enter Bills from the Vendor Center. QuickBooks displays the Enter Bills window.

2 Select the Credit option. QuickBooks changes the available fields in the form (see Figure 6-17).

3 Select the vendor from the drop-down list that appears when you click the arrow in the Vendor field.

4 Enter the date of the credit memo.

5 In the Ref. No. field, enter the vendor's credit memo number.

6 Enter the amount of the credit memo.

7 If the credit is not for items, use the Expenses tab to assign an account and amount to this credit.

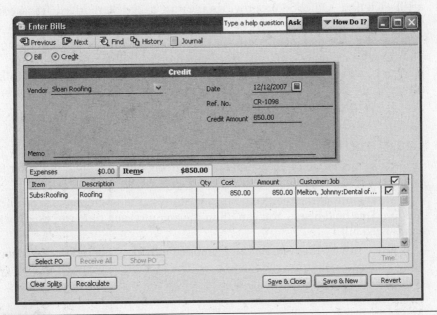

FIGURE 6-17   You create a vendor credit in the Enter Bills window

8 If the credit is for items, use the Items tab to enter the items, along with the quantity and cost, for which you are receiving this credit.

9 Click Save & Close to save the credit.

 N O T E :   If you've agreed that the vendor pays the shipping costs to return items, don't forget to enter that amount in the Expenses tab.

Here are the entries QuickBooks makes to your general ledger when you save a vendor credit:

Account	Debit	Credit
Inventory Asset		Amount of returned items
Applicable expense account(s)		Amounts of expenses in the credit
Accounts Payable	Total credit amount	

Entering Recurring Bills

You pay some bills on a regular basis. For example, you make rent or loan payments every month. You can easily pay those bills every month without entering a bill each time. QuickBooks provides a feature called Memorized Transactions, and you can put it to work to make sure your recurring bills are covered.

You can create memorized bills for bills you pay with any frequency—not just monthly. For example, you can create a memorized bill for auto insurance payments, which typically occur quarterly. You also can use memorized bills for transactions that occur with some regular frequency but the amount varies—like your telephone bill or your electric bill.

Creating a Memorized Bill

To create a memorized transaction for a recurring bill, first open the Enter Bills window and fill out the information (see Figure 6-18).

If the amount of the recurring bill isn't always exactly the same, leave the Amount Due field blank. You can fill in the amount each time you use the memorized bill.

Before you save the transaction, memorize it by pressing CTRL-M (or choose Edit | Memorize Bill from the menu bar). The Memorize Transaction dialog box appears (see Figure 6-19).

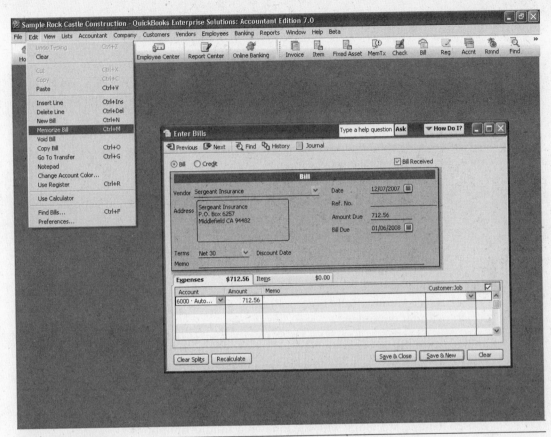

FIGURE 6-18   Create a bill that you want to memorize

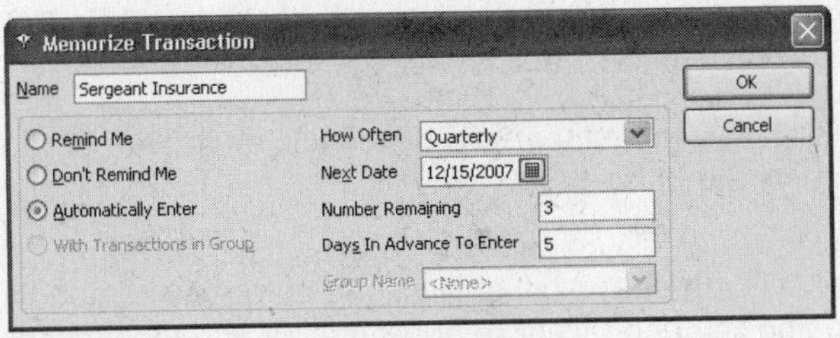

FIGURE 6-19   Use this dialog box to memorize the bill

You can make the following choices when you complete the Memorize Transaction window:

- Use the Name field to enter a name for the transaction. QuickBooks automatically enters the vendor name, but you can change it. Use a name that describes the transaction so you don't have to rely on your memory.

($) **CAUTION:** Reminders appear only if you've enabled reminders in QuickBooks. Choose Edit | Preferences and click the Reminders category icon to view or change Reminders options.

- Choose one of these options to specify how QuickBooks should handle entering the memorized bill:
  - a) Select Remind Me (the default) to tell QuickBooks to remind you when you open your company that you need to enter this bill.
  - b) Select Don't Remind Me if you want to enter the bill without being reminded.
  - c) Select Automatically Enter to have QuickBooks enter this bill automatically, without reminders.

  If you chose Remind Me, you have the following additional options to set.

- From the How Often list, select the interval for this bill.
- Enter the Next Date this bill is due.

If you chose Automatically Enter, you can set the same options as if you had chosen Remind Me, along with the following additional options:

- If you plan to pay this bill a finite number of times—loans fall into this category—use the Number Remaining field to specify how many times QuickBooks should pay this bill.
- Specify the number of Days In Advance To Enter this bill into the system. At the appropriate time, the bill appears in the Select Bills To Pay List you use to pay your bills (covered in Chapter 7).

Click OK to save the memorized bill. Then, click Save & Close in the Enter Bills window to save the bill.

($) **TIP:** If you created the bill only for the purpose of creating a memorized transaction and you don't want to enter the bill into the system for payment at this time, after you save the memorized transaction, close the Enter Bills window using the Close button in the top right corner, and respond No when QuickBooks asks if you want to save the transaction.

Using a Memorized Bill

If you've opted to enter the memorized bill yourself, you use the Memorize Transaction List window to enter the bill. Press CTRL-T or choose Lists | Memorized Transaction List from the menu bar.

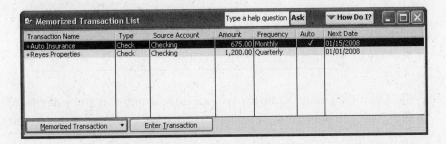

Double-click the appropriate listing to open the bill in the usual Enter Bills window with the next due date showing.

If the amount is blank, fill it in and click Save & Close. QuickBooks saves the bill; it will appear in the list of bills that must be paid when you write checks to pay your bills. (See Chapter 7 for information about paying bills.)

Creating Memorized Bill Groups

Suppose that you have a whole bunch of memorized transactions that are due the first of the month. You don't have to select them for payment one at a time; instead, you can create a group that QuickBooks will enter simultaneously.

To create a group, follow these steps:

1. Press CTRL-T to display the Memorized Transaction List.

2. Right-click any blank spot in the Memorized Transaction window and choose New Group from the shortcut menu. The New Memorized Transaction Group dialog box appears. This window looks almost identical to the Memorize Transaction dialog box (shown earlier in Figure 6-19).

3. Type a name for the group (I called mine "1st of the Month") and fill out the fields to specify the way you want QuickBooks to handle the bills in this group.

4. Click OK to save this group. QuickBooks places a bold entry in the Memorized Transaction List window.

Once you've created the group, you can add memorized transactions to it as follows:

1. In the Memorized Transaction List window, right-click the first memorized transaction you want to add to the group and choose Edit Memorized Transaction from the shortcut menu. QuickBooks opens the Schedule Memorized Transaction window for this transaction.

② Select the option With Transactions In Group option.

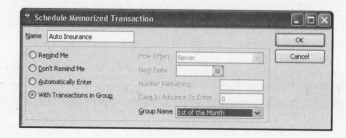

③ Open the Group Name list and select the group that you just created.

④ Click OK and repeat these steps for each bill you want to add to the group.

In the future, you can assign new memorized bills to this group as you create the new memorized bill by selecting the With Transactions In Group option and choosing the group.

Tracking Mileage Expense

QuickBooks provides a way to track the mileage of your vehicles. You can use the mileage information to track the expenses connected to vehicle use, to use mileage as part of your job-costing efforts, or to bill customers for mileage expenses.

 TIP: Your accountant may be able to use the vehicle mileage data on your income tax return.

To track a vehicle, you must add that vehicle to the Vehicle List (covered in Chapter 2). Then, you can begin tracking its mileage. If more than one person uses the vehicle, you may want to create a form that contains the following information to track mileage on the vehicle effectively:

- Trip Start Date
- Trip End Date
- Starting Odometer
- Ending Odometer
- Customer: Job or Purpose of the Trip

Entering Mileage Rates

To track the cost of mileage, make sure you have accurate mileage rates in your system. These change frequently; to get the current rate, check with the IRS (www.irs.gov) or ask your accountant. QuickBooks calculates the cost of mileage based on the information you enter.

Use the following steps to enter the rate:

1 Choose Company | Enter Vehicle Mileage to open the Enter Vehicle Mileage window.

2 Click the Mileage Rates button on the toolbar to open the Mileage Rates window.

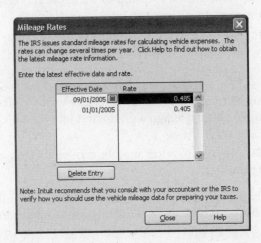

3 In the Effective Date column, select a date from the calendar.

4 In the Rate column, enter the IRS rate for that date.

5 Click Close.

Notice that you can continue to add dates and rates and QuickBooks will use the appropriate rate, based on the date of your mileage entry, to calculate costs.

Creating a Mileage Item

If you plan to use mileage expenses for job costing, or to bill customers for mileage, create a service item called mileage or travel or something similar. Attach an income account such as Mileage Income to the item.

It's important to understand that QuickBooks doesn't automatically transfer the mileage rate you established in the Mileage Rates window to the item you create for mileage. Therefore, you must independently fill in the rate for the item and update it when the IRS rate changes. You can use the same rate you used in the Mileage Rates window or enter a different rate to create a markup (or a markdown, if you wish to take that approach).

Entering Mileage

Use the following steps to enter mileage:

1. Choose Company | Enter Vehicle Mileage. QuickBooks displays the Enter Vehicle Mileage window (see Figure 6-20).
2. Select the vehicle from the drop-down list in the Vehicle field.
3. Enter the dates of the trip.
4. Enter the odometer readings—QuickBooks calculates the total miles.
5. If you want to bill the customer for mileage, place a check mark in the Billable check box and select the Customer: Job, the item you created for mileage, and the Class (if you're tracking classes). If you don't want to bill a customer but you want to track job costs, do not place a check mark in the Billable check box, but go ahead a assign a Customer: Job, the Mileage Item, and a Class.
6. Optionally, enter a note.
7. Click Save & New to enter another trip, or click Save & Close if you're finished entering mileage.

To add the billable mileage to a customer's invoice, follow the instructions for including reimbursable expenses on customer invoices in the section "Invoicing Customers for Reimbursable Expenses" earlier in this chapter.

Creating Mileage Reports

QuickBooks includes four vehicle mileage reports; you can print these reports by choosing Reports | Jobs, Time & Mileage, and selecting the appropriate mileage report from the submenu. If you're working in the Enter Vehicle Mileage dialog box,

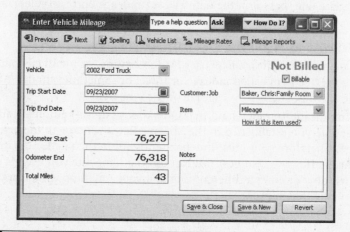

FIGURE 6-20   Recording a mileage tracking transaction

the reports are available in the drop-down list you see if you click the arrow next to the Mileage Reports button.

Mileage By Vehicle Summary

Use the Mileage By Vehicle Summary report to see the total miles and the mileage expense for each vehicle you're tracking. You can run this report for any date range that you want to check, helping you to determine whether vehicles need servicing. For example, you may need to change the oil and filter every 6000 miles, or schedule a 50,000-mile checkup. If you deduct mileage expenses on your income tax form, use the entire year as the date range.

Mileage By Vehicle Detail

Use the Mileage By Vehicle Detail report to view details about each mileage slip you created. For each vehicle, the report displays the following information:

- Trip End Date
- Total Miles
- Mileage Rate
- Mileage Expense

No customer information appears in the report, but you can add the Customer and Billing Status fields to the report from the Display tab of the Modify Report dialog box or you can double-click any listing to open the original mileage slip; either method shows you whether the trip is linked to a job and whether it's marked billable.

Mileage By Job Summary

Use the Mileage By Job Summary report to view the total number of miles linked to customers or jobs. The report displays total miles for all customers or jobs and displays billable amounts for any mileage entries you marked billable.

Mileage By Job Detail

Use the Mileage By Job Detail report to see the following information about each trip for each customer or job:

- Trip End Date
- Billing Status
- Item
- Total Miles
- Sales Price
- Amount

You can modify the report to display additional information by clicking the Modify Report button on the report window. On the Display tab of the Modify Report dialog box, select additional columns to add to the report. For example, you may want to add columns for the Mileage Rate, the Mileage Expense or both. You may even want to add the start date for the trip. If you modify the report and like the results, memorize the report so you don't have to repeat the modifications next time.

Reimbursing Employees and Subcontractors for Mileage

You can use the vehicle mileage-tracking feature to reimburse mileage expenses that you, your employees, or your subcontractors incur. Enter each person's car in the Vehicle List (use the person's name for the vehicle), and have everyone keep mileage logs.

If you're doing your own payroll, QuickBooks cannot transfer mileage reimbursements directly to paychecks the way QuickBooks transfers time, but you can modify the Mileage By Vehicle Detail report so that you can reimburse each individual and simultaneously provide the individual with a copy of the report.

Use the following steps to create a copy of the Mileage By Vehicle Detail report for each individual:

1. Open the Mileage By Vehicle Detail report.
2. Enter the date range for which you're reimbursing individuals.
3. Click the Modify Report button; QuickBooks displays the Modify Report dialog box.
4. On the Filters tab, open the Vehicle drop-down list and select the first person's car.
5. Click OK to return to the report window, which now displays information about that person's mileage only.
6. Memorize the report, naming it person mileage (substitute the real name for person).
7. Repeat the process for each remaining person.
8. Print each person's report and attach it to the reimbursement check.

Paying Bills

In this chapter:

- Choosing bills to pay
- Applying discounts and credits
- Writing checks
- Making direct disbursements
- Setting up sales tax payments

The expression "writing checks" doesn't have to be taken literally. You can let QuickBooks do the "writing" part by buying computer checks and printing them. Except for signing the check, QuickBooks can do all the work and save you considerable time.

Choosing What to Pay

You don't have to pay every bill that you've entered, nor do you have to pay the entire amount due for each bill. Your current bank balance and your relationships with your vendors have a large influence on the decisions you make.

Viewing Your Unpaid Bills

Start by examining the A/P Aging Summary report or Unpaid Bills Detail report. The A/P Aging Summary looks exactly like the A/R Aging Summary—listing bills you owe to vendors based on their age—and you print the report by choosing Reports | Vendors & Payables | A/P Aging Summary. The Unpaid Bills Detail report lists the bills that are due by vendor. Choose Reports | Vendors & Payables | Unpaid Bills Detail (see Figure 7-1).

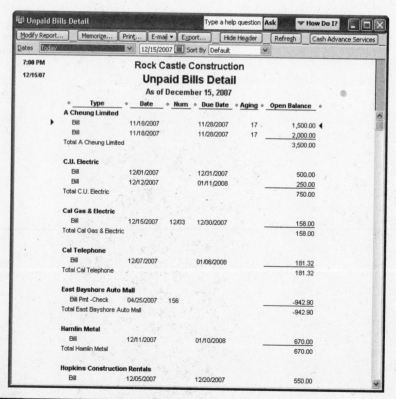

FIGURE 7-1   Use this report to identify unpaid bills

You can double-click any entry to see the line items of the original bill you entered. You can filter the report to display only certain bills if you click Modify Report and change the settings on the Filters tab. For example, you might want to:

- Filter for bills that are due today (or previously), eliminating bills due after today
- Filter for bills that are more or less than a certain amount
- Filter for bills that are more than a certain number of days overdue

Selecting the Bills to Pay

When you're ready to tell QuickBooks which bills you want to pay, click New Transactions | Pay Bills in the Vendor Center or choose Vendors | Pay Bills from the menu bar. The Pay Bills window appears (see Figure 7-2).

You can use the options in the window to show only some bills, sort the bills in various orders, and apply discounts or credits, as described in Table 7-1.

If you change the selection fields described in Table 7-1, your list of bills to be paid may change. If you plan to pay all the displayed bills either in full or in part,

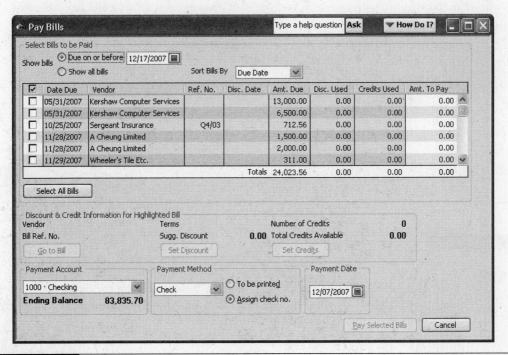

FIGURE 7-2   Use this window to select bills to pay

Option	Purpose
Due On Or Before	Displays all the bills due within ten days by default, but you can change the date to an earlier or later date. If your vendors offer discounts for timely payments, this selection is more important than it seems, because the due date isn't the same as the discount date. Consider a bill with terms of 2% 10 Net 30 that is dated April 2. It is due on May 2 and won't appear on the list if the due date filter you select is April 30, even though the discount date is April 12. If you want to use a due date filter, go out at least 60 days. (See the section "Applying Discounts" later in this chapter.)
Show All Bills	Shows all the outstanding bills in your QuickBooks company, regardless of when they're due. This is the safest option, because you won't accidentally miss a discount date because the list might be rather long.
A/P Account	If you have multiple A/P accounts, select the account to which the bills you want to pay were originally posted. If you don't have multiple A/P accounts, this field doesn't appear in the window.
Sort Bills By	Determines the order in which QuickBooks displays your bills in the Pay Bills window. The choices are Due Date (the default), Discount Date, Vendor, and Amount Due.
Payment Account	The checking or credit card account you want to use to pay these bills.
Payment Method	Displays the available methods of payment: Check and Credit Card appear by default, but if you've signed up for QuickBooks online bill payment services, that payment method also appears in the list. If you are printing your checks, be sure to select the To Be Printed option. If you're writing checks manually, select Assign Check No., and when you finish selecting bills to pay, QuickBooks opens the Assign Check Numbers dialog so you can specify the starting check number.
Payment Date	The date that appears on your checks. By default, the current date appears in the field, but if you want to predate or postdate your checks, you can change that date. If you merely select the bills today and wait until tomorrow (or later) to print the checks, the payment date set here still appears on the checks. You can tell QuickBooks to use "today" as the date on checks by changing the Checking Preferences.

TABLE 7-1   Options you can set to pay bills

you're ready to move to the next step. If some bills appear on the list that you don't plan to pay right now, you can just select the ones you do want to pay by clicking the leftmost column to place a check mark in it.

Selecting the Payment Amounts

If you want to pay in full all the bills that appear in the Pay Bills window and you don't need to worry about any credits or discounts, click the Select All Bills button at the bottom of the window to select all the bills for payment; after you click this button, the Select All Bills button changes its name to Clear Selections. When you pay all bills in full, QuickBooks makes the following entries in your general ledger:

Account	Debit	Credit
Accounts Payable	Total bill payments	
Bank		Total bill payments

QuickBooks doesn't make any entries to expense accounts when you pay bills because QuickBooks made those entries when you entered the bills. You only need to update expense accounts if you don't enter a bill but you write a check, as described later in this chapter in the section "Using Direct Disbursements."

Making a Partial Payment

If you don't want to pay a bill in full, you can easily adjust the amount.

Click the check mark column on the bill's listing to select the bill for payment. Then, click in the Amt. To Pay column and replace the amount QuickBooks entered with the amount you want to pay.

When QuickBooks enters the transaction in the general ledger, QuickBooks posts the amount of the payment as a debit to the Accounts Payable account and as a credit to your bank account; the unpaid balance of the bill remains in the Accounts Payable account.

Applying Discounts

Bills with discounts for timely payment display the Discount Date in the Disc. Date column. If you don't see a date in the Disc. Date column, the bill has no discount associated with it (see Figure 7-3).

Select the bill by clicking the check mark column, and the discount is automatically applied. You can see the amount in the Disc. Used column, and the Amt. To Pay column adjusts accordingly as long as the date in the Due On Or Before field is equal to or earlier than the discount date. If QuickBooks doesn't apply the discount automatically, check your preferences. If you want QuickBooks to apply discounts and credit automatically, choose Edit | Preferences, click the Bills category on the left, and, on the Company Preferences tab, check the Automatically Use Discounts and Credits check box. Also select a Default Discount Account and click OK.

 TIP: If the deadline for the discount has passed, you can still take the discount—see the next section "Taking Discounts After the Discount Date."

If you're making a partial payment and want to adjust the discount, click the Set Discount button to open the Discount And Credits window, and enter the amount

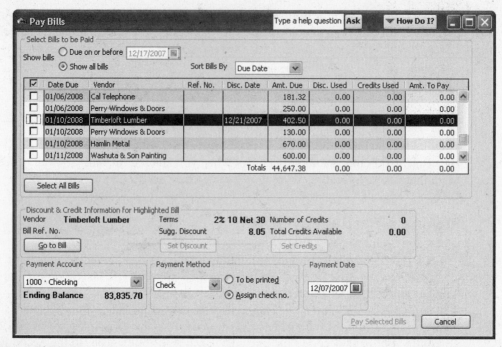

FIGURE 7-3   You'll see dates in the Disc. Date column for bills that offer discounts for timely payment

of the discount you want to take. Click Done to redisplay the Pay Bills window, where QuickBooks has applied the discount and adjusted the Amt. To Pay column.

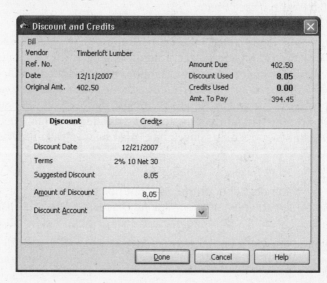

Taking Discounts After the Discount Date

Many businesses fill in the discount amount even if the discount period has expired. The resulting payment, with the discount applied, is frequently accepted by the vendor.

To take a discount after the discount date, use the same steps explained in the preceding section for applying a discount. When you click the Set Discount button to open the Discount And Credits window, the amount showing for the discount is zero. Enter the discount you would have taken if you'd paid the bill in a timely fashion, and click Done.

Understanding the Discount Account

The account for the discounts you take, sometimes called *earned discounts*, can be either an income or expense account; there's no right and wrong here. If you think of the discount as income because it is money you've brought into your company by paying your bills promptly, make the account an income account. If you think of the discount as a reverse expense because it is money you've saved by paying your bills promptly, make the account an expense account; it posts as a negative amount, which means it reduces total expenses.

If the only vendors who offer discounts are those from whom you buy inventory items, consider putting the discount account in the section of your chart of accounts that holds the Cost Of Goods Sold accounts.

Here's what QuickBooks posts to your general ledger when you take a discount. For this example, suppose the original amount of the bill was $484.00, the discount was $9.68, and the check amount was $474.32. Remember that QuickBooks originally posted the bill for the total amount without considering the discount.

Account	Debit	Credit
Accounts Payable	$484.00	
Bank		$474.32
Discounts Taken		$9.68

Applying Credits

If you click a bill in the Pay Bills window without selecting it, you'll see available credits in the Total Credits Available field below the list of unpaid bills. If you have set Bill preferences (choose Edit | Preferences, select the Bills category and click the Company Preferences tab) to automatically apply credits and you select any bill from a vendor for whom credits exist, QuickBooks automatically applies the credit(s). The amount of the credit appears in the Credits Used column, and QuickBooks adjusts the Amt. To Pay column (see Figure 7-4).

If you haven't set preferences to automatically apply credits or if you don't want to take the credit, click Set Credits to open the Discount And Credits window.

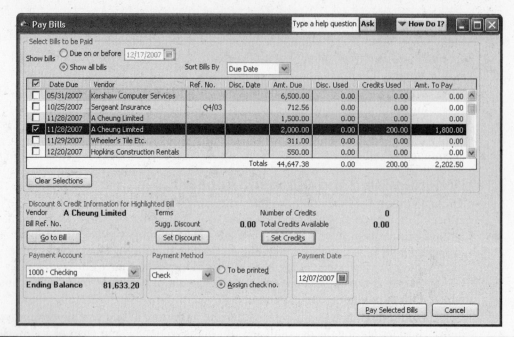

FIGURE 7-4   QuickBooks can automatically apply outstanding credits when you pay bills

Make the appropriate changes and click Done to change the Amt. To Pay column to reflect your adjustments.

If your total credits with the vendor are equal to, or exceed, the bill(s) you select, QuickBooks displays a message telling you no check will be created, because the bill is paid in its entirety with credits.

It's possible that you'll have several bills to pay from one vendor and a credit that you can use to pay one bill entirely. If you choose to use the credit to completely pay one bill, you may want to inform the vendor that you took this action, since the check you send won't include any reference to the bill paid entirely by a vendor credit.

To inform the vendor that you're paying a bill using a credit, print the history of the bill and include it with the payment. To print a bill's history, display the bill in the Enter Bills window—you can find the bill in the Vendor Center—and then click the History button to display a record of how the bill was paid. When QuickBooks displays the bill's history, click Print.

If you don't like this solution, don't use the credit to completely pay one or more bills. Instead, spread the credit out among the bills so that no bill is entirely paid by credit. That solution will be apparent to your vendor without any other effort on your part.

Saving the Pay Bills Information

When you're finished selecting bills to pay, click Pay Selected Bills. What you see next depends on whether you selected the Assign Check No. option or the To Be Printed option in the Pay Bills window.

If you selected the Assign Check No. option because you manually write checks, the Assign Check Numbers dialog box appears, enabling you to decide whether QuickBooks should assign check numbers or whether you will assign check numbers. If you want to assign check numbers, type them in the Check No. column and click OK.

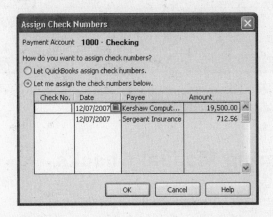

If you selected the To Be Printed option, the Assign Check Numbers dialog box doesn't appear.

Regardless of the option you selected, QuickBooks displays the Payment Summary window, which lists the checks you created in the Pay Bills window. From the Payment Summary window, you can click Print Checks to start the process of printing checks or you can click Done; for more information on printing checks, see the upcoming section "Printing Checks." QuickBooks also transfers all the information about the checks you created to the general ledger, and records the payments in your checkbook account register or credit card account register. You can see those checks in the bank account register (see Figure 7-5); press CTRL-R or click the Register icon on the Icon Bar and select the bank account.

If you select the Assign Check No. option, the checks appear with the numbers you assigned. If you selected the To Be Printed option, your bank account register displays To Print as the check number. See the upcoming section "Printing Checks."

$ TIP: If you pay bills online, QuickBooks records the payment information in the register using SEND as the check number and then retains the payment information until you go online.

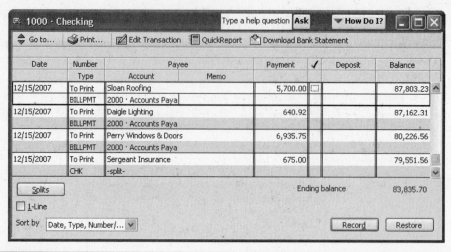

Date	Number	Payee		Payment	✓	Deposit	Balance
	Type	Account	Memo				
12/15/2007	To Print	Sloan Roofing		5,700.00	☐		87,803.23
	BILLPMT	2000 · Accounts Paya					
12/15/2007	To Print	Daigle Lighting		640.92			87,162.31
	BILLPMT	2000 · Accounts Paya					
12/15/2007	To Print	Perry Windows & Doors		6,935.75			80,226.56
	BILLPMT	2000 · Accounts Paya					
12/15/2007	To Print	Sergeant Insurance		675.00			79,551.56
	CHK	-split-					

Ending balance   83,835.70

FIGURE 7-5   Checks you intend to print for bills you paid appear in your checking account register

Preparing Manual Checks

If you're not printing checks, you must make sure the check numbers in the register are correct. In fact, it's a good idea to print the register and refer to it as you write the checks. To print the register, open the register by pressing CTRL-R and selecting the correct bank account. Then, click the Print icon at the top of the register window. When the Print Register dialog opens, select the date range that encompasses the checks you plan to write—usually, they're all dated the same day—and click OK. QuickBooks opens the Print Lists dialog box, where you can select print options before clicking Print to print.

Printing Checks

Printing your checks is far easier and faster than using manual checks and leaves less room for error. Before you can print, however, you have some preliminary tasks to take care of. You have to purchase computer checks and set up your printer.

 CAUTION: Lock the cabinet in which you keep the checks.

Purchasing Computer Checks

You can purchase computer checks for dot matrix printers or for laser and inkjet printers from many vendors. Investigate the prices and options available from the following sources:

- Intuit, the company that makes QuickBooks, sells checks through its Internet marketplace, which you can reach at www.intuitmarket.com.
- Business form companies; there are several well-known national companies, such as Safeguard and NEBS.
- Office supply stores, such as Staples, Office Depot, and others.
- Check with your bank; some banks have a computer-check purchasing arrangement with suppliers.

If you purchase checks from any supplier except Intuit, make sure you tell them that you use QuickBooks. All check makers know about QuickBooks and offer a line of checks that are designed to work perfectly with the software.

Computer checks come in several varieties (and in a wide range of colors and designs). For QuickBooks, you can order any of the following check types:

- Plain checks.
- Checks with stubs on which QuickBooks prints information.
- Checks with special stubs for current check and year-to-date information about wages and withholding for payroll checks.
- Wallet-sized checks.

Setting Up the Printer

Before you print checks, QuickBooks needs to know about the type of check you're using; you supply the information in the Printer Setup window. Choose File | Printer Setup from the menu bar and select Check/PayCheck as the form in the Printer Setup window (see Figure 7-6). Choose the printer name and type that match the printer you're using for checks.

Choosing a Check Style

Select the check style that matches the check style you purchased:

- **Voucher checks**   These checks are the same width as the standard check, but they have a detachable section at the bottom of the check. QuickBooks prints voucher information if you use voucher checks, including the name of the payee, the date, and the individual amounts of the bills being paid by this check.
- **Standard checks**   These checks are the width of a regular #10 business envelope. Laser printer checks come three to a page. Checks for a dot matrix pin-feed printer come on a continuous sheet with perforations separating the checks.
- **Wallet checks**   These checks are narrower than the other two check styles. The paper size is the same as the other checks, but there's a perforation on the left edge of the check, so you can tear off the check.

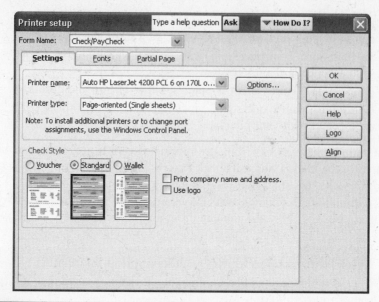

FIGURE 7-6   Set up your printer for check printing

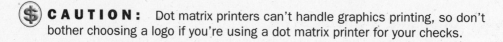

Adding a Logo

If your checks have no preprinted logo and you have a digital file of your company
logo, select the Use Logo option or click the Logo button to open the Logo dialog
box. Click the File button to locate the digital file, which must be a bitmapped
graphic (the file extension is .bmp).

$ C A U T I O N :   Dot matrix printers can't handle graphics printing, so don't
bother choosing a logo if you're using a dot matrix printer for your checks.

You can check the Print Company Name And Address check box, but when you
buy checks, that information is preprinted.

Changing Fonts

Click the Fonts tab in the Printer Setup window to choose different fonts for the
check information, such as the spelled-out amounts or the payee's address block.
Click the appropriate button and then choose a font, a font style, and a size from
the dialog that opens.

$ C A U T I O N :   Before you change fonts, make a note of the current settings.
No Reset or Default button exists in the Fonts tab. If you make changes and they
don't work properly, knowing the original settings will get you back to where you
started quickly and easily.

Handling Partial Check Pages on Laser and Inkjet Printers

If you're printing to a laser or inkjet printer, you don't always have the luxury of printing the exact number of checks that come on a page of checks. QuickBooks has a nifty solution for this problem, found on the Partial Page tab (see Figure 7-7). Click the option that matches the way your printer prints envelopes.

Click OK in the Printer Setup window to save the check printing setup information. You're ready to print your checks.

Printing the Checks

Place your checks in your printer; if you use a laser or inkjet printer and either standard or wallet checks and the first page of checks contains fewer than three checks, place that page in the manual feed tray.

 TIP: Voucher checks for laser and inkjet printers are one to a page, so you don't have to worry about using remaining checks on a page.

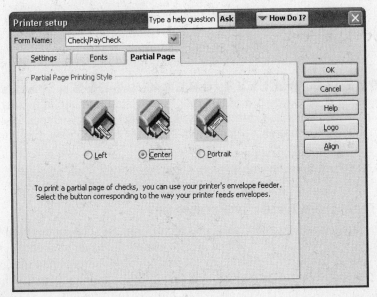

FIGURE 7-7   The Partial Page solution is based on the way your printer handles envelopes

Choose File | Print Forms | Checks from the menu bar to display the Select Checks To Print window.

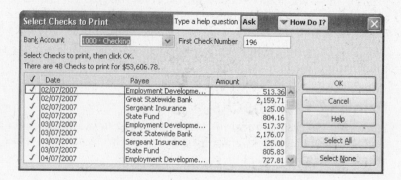

By default, QuickBooks selects all the unprinted checks. The first time you print checks, the first check number is 1; replace that number with the first check number you intend to print. After you select checks to print and establish the first check number, click OK to open the Print Checks window.

If you use a laser or inkjet printer and either standard or wallet checks, fill in the Number Of Checks On First Page box. If you indicate there are three checks on the page, printing starts with the checks in the standard letter tray.

 NOTE TO WALLET CHECK USERS: Make sure that you select the correct type of wallet check from the Wallet Check Type list box. If you're using Check 21 wallet checks, select Wallet Check (Check 21 image-compatible). If you aren't using Check 21 wallet checks, select Traditional Wallet.

Click Print to begin printing your checks.

Reprinting After a Problem

Sometimes things go awry when you're printing. The paper jams, you run out of toner, the ribbon has no ink left, the dog chews the paper as it emerges, the paper falls off the back tray and lands in the shredder—all sorts of bad things can occur. QuickBooks asks you to confirm whether checks printed properly before updating your company data file with the check number information.

If everything printed fine, click OK. If anything untoward happened, click the number(s) of the problematic check(s) and click OK. Place more checks in the printer and choose File | Print Forms | Checks. Your unprinted checks appear once again in the Select Checks To Print dialog box, and QuickBooks increments the first check number to the next available check number. Repeat the printing process to print your checks.

➡ **FYI**

Missing Check Numbers

If you have to restart the print run with the next available check number, QuickBooks does not track the number(s) of the checks that were misprinted. Those numbers are missing from your bank register, and auditors are always happier when they see sequential numbers.

To create this audit trail, enter the check number, the payee, and an amount of $0, and post the transaction to an account. Then right-click the transaction line, choose Void, and then choose Record.

The void check carries the payee and account information permanently, and it appears on reports for the payee and the account. You can use this technique to track check numbers for checks that aren't used for any reason: they failed to print, you sent them as samples when buying checks or when setting up electronic fund transfers, they accidentally fell into the shredder, or your dog ate them.

 T I P : When you send sample checks, be sure to write the word VOID across the check.

Using Direct Disbursements

You make a *direct disbursement* when you make a payment, usually by check, without matching the payment to an existing bill. Stated another way, you write checks without entering bills.

Even though you enter vendor bills and then issue checks as I described previously in Chapter 6 and in this chapter, you sometimes need to write a quick check without entering a vendor bill. For example, when the UPS delivery person is standing in front of you waiting for a COD check, you don't typically enter a bill and then pay it; you simply write the check.

 N O T E : You should *not* use either the register or the Write Checks window to write a check that pays a bill, because neither method associates the check with the outstanding bill. Stated another way, you'll mess up your payables if you try to pay a bill using either of the following methods.

Writing Direct Disbursement Manual Checks

If you write your checks manually, you can write your checks and then tell QuickBooks about it later, or you can bring your checkbook to your computer and enter the checks in QuickBooks as you write them. You have two ways to enter your checks in QuickBooks: in the bank register or in the Write Checks window.

Both approaches accomplish the same thing; work in the window that you find easiest to use.

Using the Register

The bank account register resembles the register you use in a manual check book to make a record of the checks you write (see Figure 7-8). To use the bank register, open the bank account register either by clicking the Check Register button on the Home page or pressing CTRL-R; then select your bank account.

N O T E : You cannot record a check that purchases items using the register. Use the Write Checks window instead (see the next section).

When the account register opens, you can enter the check on a transaction line as follows:

1 Enter the date.

2 Press the TAB key to move to the Number field. QuickBooks automatically fills in the next available check number.

T I P : If you intend to print this check, type "T" and press TAB. QuickBooks replaces the check number with "To Print."

3 Press TAB to move through the rest of the fields, filling in the name of the payee, the amount of the payment, and the expense account you're assigning to the transaction.

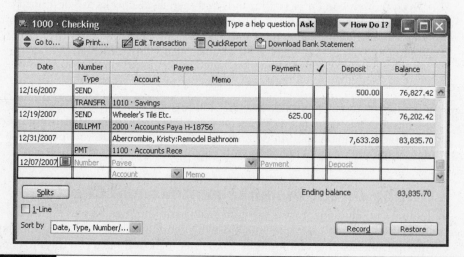

FIGURE 7-8 The QuickBooks bank account register looks like your checkbook register

④ Click the Record button to save the transaction.

⑤ Repeat the steps for the next check and continue until all the manual checks you've written are entered into the register.

If you want to assign a check to more than one expense account, click the Splits button. QuickBooks changes the appearance of the register (see Figure 7-9). In the Account box on the second line of the check's register entry, "-split-" appears. QuickBooks also displays lines where you can assign more than one account to the check. In this new area, select the appropriate accounts and fill in the amount for each account; QuickBooks enters the total for the check in the Payment column on the first line of the check's register entry. Click Close when you finish making account assignments.

Using the Write Checks Window

If you prefer or if you need to write a check for items you purchased, you can use the Write Checks window, which resembles the manual check you write. To open the window, click the Write Checks icon on the Home page or press CTRL-W. When the Write Checks window opens (see Figure 7-10), select the bank account you're using to write the checks.

QuickBooks automatically fills in the next available check number unless you check the To Be Printed box. If the box is checked, click it to remove the check mark and type the check number. QuickBooks warns you if you enter a check number that's already been used when you try to save the check.

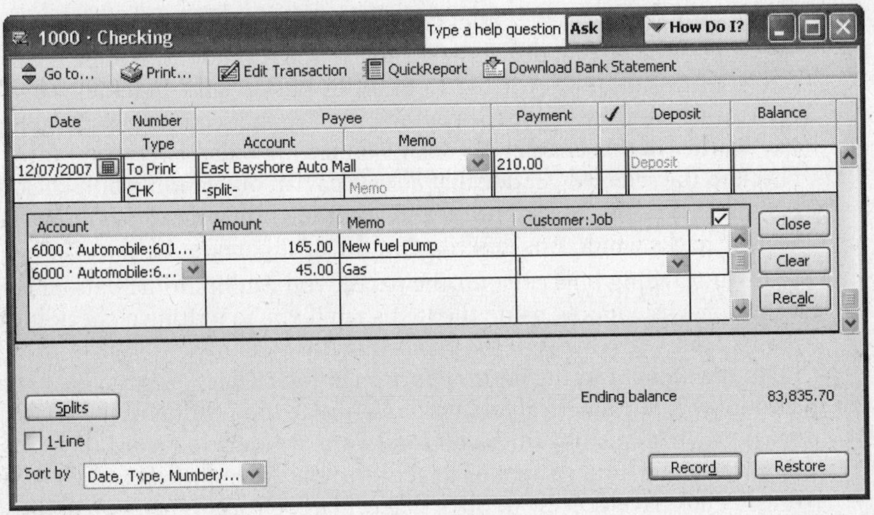

FIGURE 7-9   When you need to assign a check to more than one account, click the Splits button

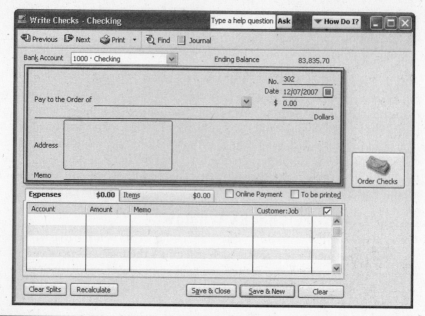

FIGURE 7-10   The Write Checks window looks like a check you would write by hand

Select a name from the Pay To The Order Of list; QuickBooks checks to determine whether outstanding bills exist for the payee:

- If outstanding bills exist, QuickBooks displays the Open Bills Exist window, which lists the outstanding bills for the selected vendor. If you're trying to pay one of those bills, click the Go To Pay Bills button, and QuickBooks will open the correct window to use for paying bills; see the section "Selecting the Bills to Pay" earlier in this chapter for details on paying bills. If you want to write a check to the selected vendor that *doesn't* pay an outstanding bill, click the Continue Writing Check button and continue filling out the bottom area of the Write Checks window as described in the next paragraph.

- If no outstanding bills exist for the payee, you can fill in the bottom area of the Write Checks window using the Items tab if you're writing a check for items or the Expenses tab to assign the check directly to an expense account. When you fill in the amount in the bottom portion of the check, QuickBooks updates the amount—both numerical and written—in the top portion of the check. You can use more than one line in the bottom of the window to record the purpose of more than one kind of item or to split the check between accounts. When you finish, click Save & New to open a new blank check. When you're through writing checks, click Save & Close to close the Write Checks window. Any checks you write in this window also appear in the bank account register.

Printing Direct Disbursement Checks

If you wrote a check to pay the UPS person for a COD delivery, you typically don't print that check. But, you can print checks written either in the register or through the Write Checks window.

Printing a Single Check Quickly

You can print checks as you create them in the Write Checks window.

Follow these steps to print a single check:

1. Click the Write Checks icon on the Home page, or press CTRL-W to open the Write Checks window.
2. Make sure the To Be Printed option is selected.
3. Fill in the fields in the check and then click Print. QuickBooks saves the check and opens a small window to display the next available check number.
4. Make sure that number agrees with the number of the check you're loading in the printer, and then click OK. QuickBooks displays the Print Checks window.
5. Follow the instructions for printing described earlier in this chapter.
6. When QuickBooks redisplays the Write Checks window, click Save & New to write another quick check, or click Save & Close if you're finished printing checks.

NOTE: You cannot print checks directly from the register, but you can print them in batches; see the next section.

TIP: You can use the Print button in the register to print the register, not checks in the register.

Printing Direct Disbursement Checks in Batches

You can print checks in a batch instead of one at a time from either the Write Checks window or the register. When you enter the checks, make sure you check the To Be Printed box in the Write Checks window or type To Be Printed in the Number column for checks you write from the register.

Then, you can print the checks using either of the following methods.

- Choose File | Print Forms | Checks from the menu bar.
- Click the arrow to the right of the Print button at the top of the Write Checks window, and choose Print Batch.

Regardless of the method you choose, QuickBooks displays the Select Checks To Print window shown earlier in this chapter in the section "Printing Checks." Follow the directions in that section to complete the process.

Behind the Scenes for Direct Disbursements

QuickBooks makes the following entries in the general ledger when you write a direct disbursement check:

Account	Debit	Credit
Bank account		Amount of the check
Each expense account	Amount of the check	

If you split the check among multiple accounts, QuickBooks posts multiple debits—one for the sum of the amount posted to each expense account—so that the debits equal the credit.

Sending Sales Tax Checks and Reports

If you collect sales tax from your customers, you have to turn that money over to the state taxing authorities. To charge sales tax, track it, and report on it, you have to turn on and set up sales tax collections in QuickBooks.

Your tracking and reporting needs may not be limited to state-based activities. In recent years, many states have created multiple sales tax authorities within the state, usually a specific location such as a county, a city, or a group of ZIP codes, each having its own tax rate. Businesses in those states may have to remit the sales tax they collect to both the state and the local sales tax authority or to multiple local sales tax authorities. As a result, tracking sales tax properly has become a very complicated process.

Because this subject can be a complex one, I'll present a rather comprehensive discussion in the following sections. If your sales tax issues aren't complicated, you should be able to pull out what you need from this discussion.

Enabling Sales Tax Tracking

When you set up the sales tax feature in QuickBooks, you set up tax codes that you assign to your customers to identify whether a customer is liable for sales tax. You also set up sales tax items so that you can set a percentage rate to charge for sales tax and link the sales tax item to a taxing authority.

If you didn't enable sales tax tracking during the EasyStep Interview, choose Edit | Preferences, click the Sales Tax icon in the left pane and select the Company Preferences tab. Choose Yes for the option "Do You Charge Sales Tax?" and then continue reading in the next section, where we'll review the other options on this tab.

If you did enable sales tax tracking during the EasyStep Interview, start your sales tax setup by clicking the Sales Tax Manager button on the Home page or by choosing Vendors | Sales Tax | Sales Tax Manager from the menu bar. From this window, you can:

- Watch a video on setting up sales taxes in QuickBooks
- Set Sales Tax Preferences
- Print sales tax reports
- Pay your sales tax liability

Click the Sales Tax Preferences button to display the Company Preferences tab for the Sales Tax category in the Preferences dialog box and continue reading in the next section where we'll review the other options on this tab.

Default Sales Tax Codes

To handle calculating, tracking, and reporting on sales tax, QuickBooks uses sales tax codes, sales tax items, and sales tax groups. I'll start by describing sales tax codes.

A sales tax code provides a way to group sales taxes for reporting purposes. Sales tax codes contain no information about the tax rate or the taxing authority. When you turn on the sales tax feature, QuickBooks automatically creates two sales tax codes: Tax and Non; these titles represent taxable and non-taxable. Many of you don't need any additional sales tax codes.

You will need additional sales tax codes if your sales taxing authorities require that you report on sales in other categories besides taxable and non-taxable; in this case, create codes that match the reporting categories required by your taxing authorities. You can assign one sales tax code to every customer and one sales tax code to every item. QuickBooks uses the codes to determine whether to charge sales tax for each item and each customer. Even if a customer pays sales tax, you don't necessarily charge the customer sales tax for every item the customer buys—because some items aren't taxable. Similarly, you don't charge sales tax if a sales tax-exempt customer buys a taxable item.

You may need additional sales tax codes for nontaxable customers, because some states want to know why a nontaxable customer doesn't pay sales tax. For example, do the rules in your state indicate that you don't have to collect taxes for out-of-state sales, nonprofit organizations, or government agencies? If your state wants to know the breakdown of non-taxable sales, you should create tax codes for each category of non-taxable sales to match the reporting needs of the taxing authorities in your jurisdiction (see "Creating Sales Tax Codes" for details on setting up sales tax codes).

For taxable customers, you may want to use tax codes to identify out-of-state customers from whom you collect sales tax if you remit taxes to that state's taxing authority.

In some states, the customer's residence determines the tax rate the customer pays; in other states, the location of the business selling the item determines the tax rate the customer pays. You don't handle these scenarios with sales tax codes because the codes don't determine the tax rate; instead you use sales tax items, which I'll discuss later in this chapter.

Some states have multiple tax rates, where a portion of the sales tax you charge belongs to the state and another portion belongs to a local taxing authority—a city or a county. In some cases, you may need to remit sales tax to the state, the county, and the city. Again, you don't use sales tax codes to handle these situations; you use sales tax items and sales tax groups for these situations. I'll also discuss sales tax groups later in this chapter.

If you need to create codes to track customer sales tax status in a manner more detailed than "taxable" and "nontaxable," follow these steps to add a new sales tax code:

1. Choose Lists | Sales Tax Code List.
2. Press CTRL-N to open the New Sales Tax Code window.

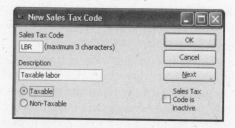

3. Enter the name of the new code, using up to three characters.
4. Enter a description to make it easier to interpret the code.
5. Select Taxable if you're creating a code to track taxable sales or nontaxable if you're entering a code to trace nontaxable sales.
6. Click Next to set up another tax code.
7. Click OK when you've finished adding tax codes.

If your taxing authorities require that you break down nontaxable sales, use sales tax codes. You might consider creating the following sales tax codes:

- NPO for nonprofit organizations
- GOV for government agencies
- WSL for wholesale businesses
- OOS for out-of-state customers if you aren't required to collect taxes from out-of-state customers

For taxable customers, the permutations and combinations are much broader, of course. If you're required to collect and remit sales tax for some additional states, just create codes for customers in those states using the postal abbreviations for each state.

Sales tax codes alone don't handle taxable customers. You may also need to assign a sales tax item to the customer. I'm going to save sales tax items for later in this chapter and finish covering the rest of the preferences you set for sales tax tracking.

Sales Tax Payment Basis

There are two ways to remit sales tax to the taxing authorities:

- **As Of Invoice Date**, which is accrual-based tax reporting
- **Upon Receipt Of Payment**, which is cash-based tax reporting

Check with your taxing authority (the payee for the check you write when you remit the sales tax you collected) and your accountant to identify the method you need to select; the method is dictated by your state and has nothing to do with your own tax reporting status.

Sales Tax Payment Dates

Select the frequency you use to remit sales tax to the taxing authority in the Pay Sales Tax section. Again, the sales taxing authority specifies the frequency they expect you to use to remit sales tax. Many states base the frequency on the amount of tax you collect, usually looking at your returns for a specific period of time. If the sales tax authority notifies you that the frequency with which you must remit sales tax changes, don't forget to return to the Preferences dialog box to change the interval.

Sales Tax Items

Sales tax items contain information about the tax rate and the taxing authority to which you remit taxes and reports. You need to set up one sales tax item for each taxing authority to which you report and remit sales tax.

Most Common Sales Tax

The Sales Tax category of the Preferences dialog box has a field named Most Common Sales Tax, and you must enter a sales tax item in that field. So, you must create at least one sales tax item before you can save your sales tax preferences. The item you create and assign in the Preferences dialog box becomes the default sales tax item for any customers you create from this point forward, but you can change any customer's default sales tax item.

Creating Sales Tax Items

You can create a sales tax item in either of the following ways:

- In the Sales Tax category of the Preferences dialog box, click the arrow next to the Most Common Sales Tax field and choose <Add New> from the drop-down list.
- Choose Lists | Item List from the menu bar to open the Item List. Then Press CTRL-N.

Either action opens the New Item dialog box.

Follow these steps to create the new sales tax item:

1. Select Sales Tax Item as the item type.
2. In the Sales Tax Name box, enter a name for the item.
3. Enter a description to describe this sales tax on your transaction forms.
4. Enter the tax rate as a percentage. QuickBooks automatically adds the percent sign to the numbers you type (for instance, enter 6.5 if the rate is 6.5 percent).
5. From the Tax Agency (vendor that you collect for) list, select the tax agency to whom you pay the tax.
6. Click OK.

Assigning Codes and Items to Customers

When you turn on the sales tax feature in the Preferences dialog box, QuickBooks asks if you want to make all existing customer items, inventory items, and non-inventory items taxable. If you make your customers and items taxable, QuickBooks assigns the Tax (taxable) sales tax code to all your customers and the default sales tax item you specify in the Sales Tax category of the Preferences dialog box to all existing items. These fields appear on the Additional Info tab of the customer's record or in the Edit Item dialog box, and you can edit each record to change the fields.

If you already created a great many customers and items, opening each record to make changes can be onerous, and you might want to wait until you use a customer in a sales transaction. Then, in the transaction window, select a new sales tax code on the line item or for the customer or sales tax item from the Tax drop-down list. When you save the transaction, QuickBooks cooperates with this approach by asking you if you want to change the customer's and/or item's sales tax information permanently and then updates the customer record and the item record. From this point forward, QuickBooks uses the new tax information in any transaction window for this customer and this item.

Creating Tax Groups

In some states, you collect sales tax for multiple taxing authorities. You remit the tax in a single check but you must report on the breakdown of the amount in the reports you send. For example, in Florida, the state sales tax is 6 percent, but businesses in Tampa must charge an extra 1.5 percent for Hillsborough County, the county in which Tampa is located. The customer pays 7.5 percent, and you send a check for 7.5 percent of taxable sales to the state's revenue department, but the report that you send along with the check must break down the remittance into the individual taxes—the 6 percent collected for the state, and the 1.5 percent collected for the county. In other states, you send the state's portion of the tax to the state and the locality portion of the tax to the local taxing authority.

The challenge is to display and calculate a single tax for the customer and report multiple taxes to the taxing authorities—and you use tax groups in QuickBooks to meet this challenge. A sales tax group is an item that groups sales tax items together. You use the sales tax group on the sales transaction, but QuickBooks calculates the tax amount by adding each of the individual sales tax items in the group and displaying the total on the sales transaction. The customer pays the combined rate but sees a single entry for sales tax.

If you remit your sales tax to one taxing authority, you can create one sales tax item for the combined amount—7.5 percent in my example—as long as you *never* need to report on the sales taxes separately, including at the end of the year. If, however, you need to report on the sales taxes separately at any time, then set up separate items and use a sales tax group to combine them. Sales tax reports in QuickBooks will break down the sales tax collected so that you can report on each sales tax item, and QuickBooks calculates the total liability you owe to the sales tax vendor(s) correctly.

To create a tax group, you must first create the individual tax items, and then use the following steps to create the group item:

1. Open the Item List by Choosing Lists | Item List.
2. Press CTRL-N to open the New Item dialog box.
3. From the Type List, select Sales Tax Group.
4. Enter a name for the sales tax group.
5. Enter a description; this description appears on your sales forms.
6. In the Tax Item column, choose the individual tax code items you need to create in this group. As you move to the next item, QuickBooks fills in the rate, tax agency, and description of each tax you already selected. The calculated total appears at the bottom of the dialog box (see Figure 7-11).
7. When you've added all the required tax code items, click OK.

Select this item for the appropriate customers when you're creating sales transactions. If a different tax item exists on the customer's record, QuickBooks will offer to replace the current sales tax item for the customer with the new sales tax group.

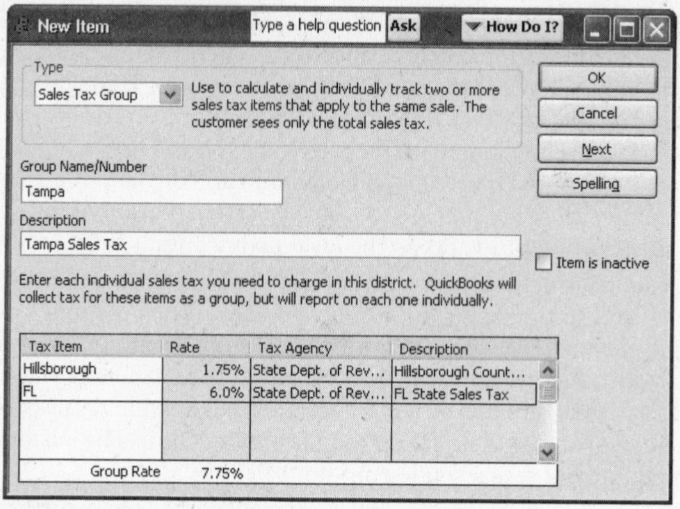

FIGURE 7-11   Setting up a Sales Tax Group

Running Sales Tax Reports

At some interval determined by your taxing authority, you need to remit the sales tax you've collected, along with a report of your total sales, your nontaxable sales, and your taxable sales, along with any other required breakdowns.

Sales Tax Liability Report

You can use the Sales Tax Liability report, shown in Figure 7-12, to help you prepare the report(s) required by your taxing authorities. To display the report, use the menu bar to choose Vendors, Sales Tax, Manage Sales Tax, and then click Sales Tax Liability or choose Reports | Vendors & Payables | Sales Tax Liability.

Use the Dates drop-down list to select an interval that matches the way you report to the taxing authorities. By default, QuickBooks chooses the interval you configured in the Preferences dialog, but that interval may only apply to your primary sales tax. If you collect multiple taxes, due at different intervals, you must create a separate report with the appropriate interval to display those figures.

Tax Code Reports

If you have to report specific types of taxable or nontaxable sales, you can print the Sales Tax Revenue Summary report shown in Figure 7-13. To display the report, use the menu bar to choose Vendors, Sales Tax, Manage Sales Tax, and then click Sales Tax Liability or choose Reports | Vendors & Payables | Sales Tax Revenue Summary.

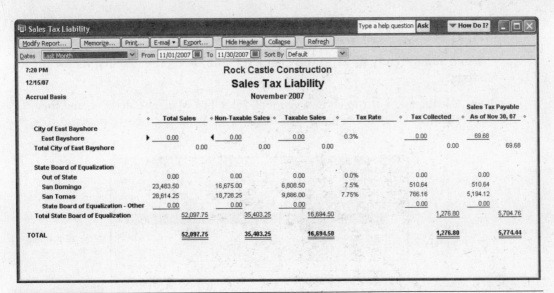

FIGURE 7-12 The Sales Tax Liability report breaks down sales tax into taxable and nontaxable sales

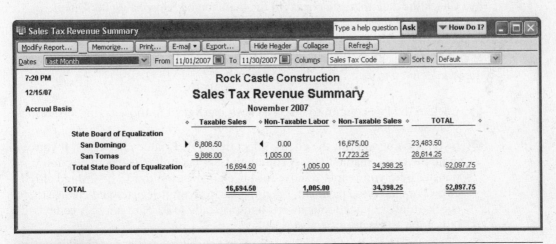

FIGURE 7-13 The Sales Tax Revenue Summary report breaks down sales tax by sales tax code

Remitting the Sales Tax

When you're ready to write the check for your sales tax liability, follow these steps:

1 Use the menu bar to choose Vendors, Sales Tax, Manage Sales Tax, and then click Pay Sales Tax. QuickBooks displays the Pay Sales Tax window.

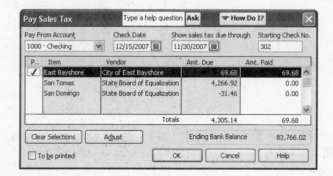

2 Select the bank account to use if you have more than one bank account.

3 Check the date that's displayed in the field named Show Sales Tax Due Through. It must match the end date of your current reporting period.

N O T E :   QuickBooks doesn't ask for a start date because it uses the period duration defined in your Sales Tax Preferences.

4 Click in the Pay column to insert a check mark next to those taxing authorities you want to pay.

5 If you're going to print the check, select the To Be Printed check box. If you write the check manually, or if you remit sales tax online using an electronic transfer from your bank, remove the check mark from the To Be Printed check box. (For electronic payment, open the bank account register and change the check number QuickBooks inserts automatically to ACH or another code indicating an electronic transfer.)

6 Click OK. The next time you print or write checks, the sales tax check appears in the Select Checks to Print dialog box.

Adjusting Sales Tax Amounts

You may need to adjust the amount of sales tax due. For example, most states offer a discount for timely payment. Or, you may owe a penalty if you're late remitting the sales tax.

To adjust a sales tax amount, select the appropriate sales tax item and click the Adjust button to open the Sales Tax Adjustment dialog box.

Sales Tax Adjustment

Adjustment Date 12/07/2007

Entry No. 12

Sales Tax Vendor City of East Bayshore

Adjustment Account 4000 · Income:4700 · Sales Tax Allo...

Adjustment
- Increase Sales Tax By
- Reduce Sales Tax By   Amount 2.00

Memo   Sales Tax collection allowance

OK   Cancel   Help

Specify the amount by which to reduce or increase the tax amount. Specify an Adjustment Account, and click OK to return to the Pay Sales Tax window, where QuickBooks has changed the amount to reflect your adjustment.

Running Payroll

In *this chapter:*

- Choosing a payroll service

- Setting up payroll

- Checking tax status, deductions, and other employee information

- Entering historical data

- Writing payroll checks

If you plan to do your own payroll rather than employ a payroll service, the information you need to set up and run payroll is covered in this chapter.

QuickBooks Payroll Services

QuickBooks offers a variety of payroll services. If you want to do your payroll in-house, here's a brief overview of the offerings.

- Standard Payroll, which provides updated tax tables, automatic calculations of paycheck deductions and employer expenses, and automatic creation of federal forms (941, W-2, and so on)
- Enhanced Payroll, which adds state forms, workers' compensation tracking, net-to-gross calculations
- Assisted Payroll, which provides all the features of enhanced payroll, but turns the job of government filings and deposits over to Intuit.
- Enhanced Payroll For Accountants, which lets you prepare payroll for up to 50 companies and supports After-the-Fact data entry.

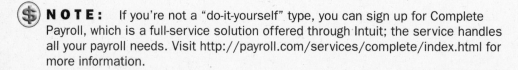

NOTE: If you're not a "do-it-yourself" type, you can sign up for Complete Payroll, which is a full-service solution offered through Intuit; the service handles all your payroll needs. Visit http://payroll.com/services/complete/index.html for more information.

QuickBooks does not make any calculations against the gross amount of the paycheck unless you've signed up for QuickBooks payroll services. No withholding appears, QuickBooks doesn't post amounts to employee and employer liability accounts, and no net amount appears on the check. You can, if you wish, use the printed tax tables in the Employer's Circular E from the IRS, calculate the deductions manually, and then issue a paycheck for the net amount to each employee. If you don't want to face that, you must sign up for payroll services.

NOTE: To process state tax forms, you must have an Enhanced Payroll subscription.

With any of the payroll services, you can purchase direct deposit services for your employees. Employees must sign a form giving permission for direct deposit, and you can print those forms directly from QuickBooks. Employees can opt to deposit their entire paychecks into one bank account or split the amount between two bank accounts.

To learn about or sign up for QuickBooks payroll offerings, choose Employees | Payroll | Learn About Payroll Options. QuickBooks opens its internal browser and takes you to the Payroll Services web site (see Figure 8-1). QuickBooks also checks for an Internet connection.

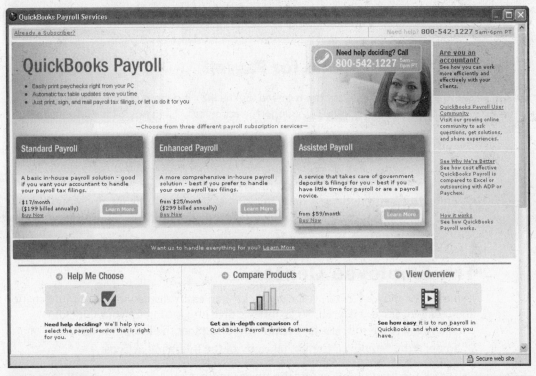

FIGURE 8-1   Select the payroll service you want to use

After you've used the links on the Payroll Services web site to learn about all the payroll offerings, click the Buy Now link for the Payroll Service you want.

A wizard walks you through the enrollment process. You must enter information about your company and provide a credit card number. If you want to sign up for direct deposit, you also need your bank's routing number and your bank account number. Follow the prompts in the ensuing windows, filling in information as required.

When you complete the sign-up process, QuickBooks downloads and automatically installs the files you need to run payroll, including the most current tax table, onto the computer you used to sign up for payroll. After QuickBooks completes the process of installing payroll, your Employees menu has all the commands you need to run payroll.

NOTE: During the process of installing the payroll files, Intuit e-mails a service key that you enter into your company file to confirm the fact that you've enrolled in one of the payroll services.

➡ FYI

Special Considerations for Payroll

Users with more than 250 employees are required, by the IRS, to deposit payroll liabilities and file W-2's electronically. QuickBooks 2007 supports electronically filing payroll tax liabilities or W-2's.

If you need to run payroll on another computer, sit down at that computer and download a payroll update so that QuickBooks can install the tax updates needed for payroll onto that computer. To download a payroll update, choose Help | Update QuickBooks.

The Employee Center

Using the Employee Center, you can quickly and easily display important information about employees and payroll. So, before we dive into setting up your QuickBooks company to use payroll, let's take a moment to explore the Employee Center.

To open the Employee Center, take any of the following actions:

- Click the Employee Center icon on the toolbar.
- Click the Employees icon on the left side of the Home page.
- Choose Employees | Employee Center from the menu bar.

As you can see in Figure 8-2, the layout of the Employee Center window is easy to understand and navigate.

 SECURITY NOTE: Users who do not have access permissions for Employee information do not see financial information when they open the Employee Center window.

The left pane of the Employee Center has three tabs: Employees, Transactions, and Payroll. The Employees tab replaces the Employee list used in earlier versions of QuickBooks. As you click any Employee on the Employees tab, QuickBooks displays transactions for that Employee on the right side of the screen. You can limit the transactions to a specific type to make the search easier, and you can filter the transactions by date range.

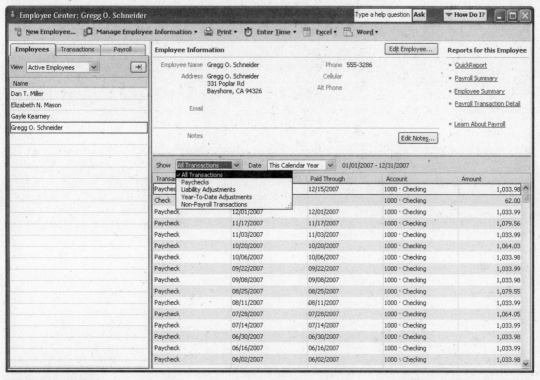

FIGURE 8-2   The Employees tab provides a robust way to find employee and transaction information about a specific employee

 TIP: Click the Show Full List Only button (it appears beside the View list box on the Employees tab) to make the Employee list fill up the entire Employee Center window.

The Transactions tab (see Figure 8-3) lists all employee-related transactions. You can use this tab to find a particular transaction or transactions that meet certain criteria. On the left side of the screen, select the transaction type for which you are searching. Then use the Date list box to narrow the search.

If you are a Payroll subscriber, then you can click the Payroll tab to see the Payroll Center (see Figure 8-4). On the left side of the Payroll Center, you see the status of your payroll subscription and a two-month calendar. On the right side of the Payroll tab, you can produce paychecks, view details about the last set of paychecks you produced, view and pay payroll tax liabilities, and prepare payroll tax forms. And, when you click the Learning Resources button, you see commands that you can use to get payroll news and updates, visit payroll message boards, access tax tools and resources, contact Intuit Customer Service, or visit the IRS web site.

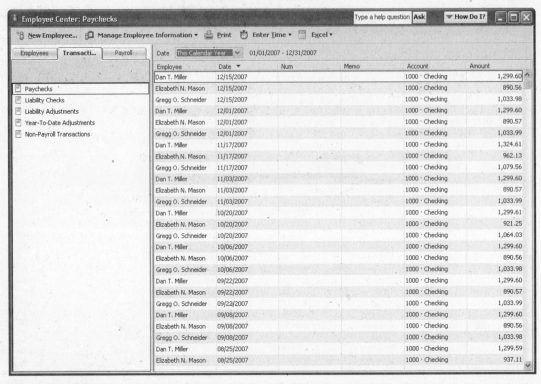

FIGURE 8-3   Use the Transactions tab to easily filter and find transactions

You can use the toolbar buttons in the Employee Center window and the links in the right pane of the Employees tab to open transaction windows and produce reports.

You can customize the Employee Center by resizing any of its panes. To resize a pane, move the mouse pointer over the edge of any pane; the mouse pointer changes to a vertical (or horizontal) bar with pointing arrows attached. Drag the pane left or right (up or down) to change its size. The other pane(s) will adjust to fill the space. In addition, you can choose the columns that QuickBooks displays in the Employees List by right clicking on the list. QuickBooks displays a context menu; choose Customize Columns.

Configuring Payroll Elements

To produce accurate paychecks, you need to complete setup tasks, including identifying the payroll taxes you have to withhold, the payroll taxes you have to pay as an employer, and the deductions you include on paychecks for benefits, garnishes, union dues, or any other reason. You also need to set up dependents and deductions for each employee.

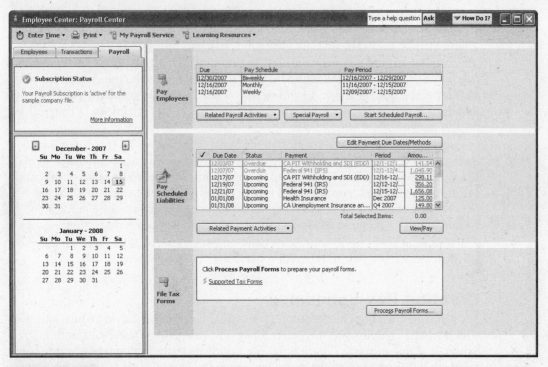

FIGURE 8-4   The Payroll tab is a one-stop shop for payroll activities

In the following sections, I'll go over all the elements and components involved in setting up payroll. You can perform all the tasks by either moving through the Payroll Setup wizard (covered later) or performing each task manually, using the QuickBooks menus. I'll go over both methods throughout this chapter.

Vendors

The payroll process creates liabilities for payroll taxes and deductions that your company must pay. To be able to send the money you owe to the appropriate vendors, set up those vendors before you set up payroll items (discussed in the next section) so that you can assign the payroll items to the proper vendors.

For withholding of federal income taxes, Medicare, FICA, and the matching employer Medicare and FICA payments, the vendor you use depends on the way you transmit the funds. If you use electronic transfer of funds, the vendor is the U.S. Treasury Department. If you use coupons, the vendor is your bank.

For local and state income tax, unemployment, disability, workers comp, and deductions for benefits, such as health insurance, set up a vendor for each agency to which you send checks. Read Chapter 2 to learn how to add vendors to your company file.

Payroll Items

A QuickBooks *payroll item* is any element that is part of a payroll check: the salary, wages, bonuses, and commissions that go into determining the gross amount of the payroll check, as well as the withheld taxes and deductions that determine the net amount of the payroll check. In addition, you need to set up company-paid benefits that don't deduct amounts from employee paychecks that are attached to payroll as payroll items.

QuickBooks creates some payroll items during your EasyStep Interview, if you indicate you'll be using payroll, but you'll probably have to create additional items. Each item you create has to be linked to an account in your chart of accounts. And because all the money you withhold or pay out as a company expense is turned over to somebody else—the government, an insurance company, or a pension administrator—you must set up vendors to associate with each deduction.

If you want to set up payroll items manually, see Chapter 2. Or, you can use the QuickBooks Payroll Setup wizard described later in this chapter.

Creating Pay Schedules

Pay schedules, new to QuickBooks 2007, enable you to establish schedules on which you pay employees. You create a pay schedule using the New Payroll Schedule dialog box (see Figure 8-5). You can display this dialog box working from the Payroll Center or from the menu bar. From the Payroll Center, select the Setup Payroll Schedules link within the Pay Employee's component area. From the menu

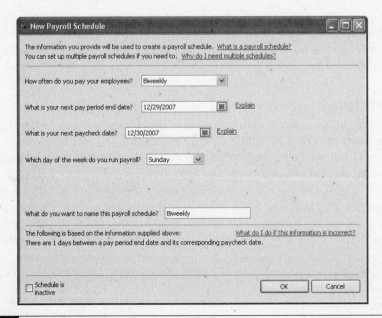

FIGURE 8-5   Use this window to define a pay schedule

bar, choose Employees | Pay Employees | Add or Edit Payroll Schedules to display the Pay Schedule List. Then, press CTRL+N.

The appearance of the New Payroll Schedule window changes, depending on the pay frequency you select. For example, when you select the Weekly pay frequency, you see the Day Of The Week For Payroll field, but you won't see this field if you select the Monthly pay frequency. For each pay schedule, you establish, at a minimum, the pay frequency, the pay period end date, and the next pay date.

Create one pay schedule for each group of employees you need to pay. You can create multiple pay schedules that use the same pay frequency. Suppose, for example, that your company pays everybody biweekly but runs payroll every Friday, splitting payroll so that one group of employees gets paid on one Friday and the other group gets paid the following Friday. In this case, you should create two biweekly pay schedules.

The first time you create a payroll schedule, QuickBooks asks if you want to assign that payroll schedule to all of your employees that use the same pay frequency. By answering "yes," QuickBooks will assign that schedule to the affected employees automatically. By answering "no," you will need to assign the payroll schedule as described earlier.

 N O T E :   If you have more than one payroll schedule with the same frequency, for example, Weekly 1, Weekly 2, QuickBooks cannot automatically assign the schedules to the affected employees. You will need to do this as described earlier.

QuickBooks displays each pay schedule that you create on the Payroll tab of the Employee Center to remind you when payroll is due, but the value of the pay schedule goes beyond serving as a reminder. In addition to creating the pay schedule, you also assign one pay schedule to each employee. Then, when you pay employees, you select a pay schedule and QuickBooks creates paychecks only for the employees assigned to that schedule. You assign a pay schedule to an employee when you enter or edit the employee's information, described in detail in Chapter 2. To assign a pay schedule to an employee, select the employee on the Employees tab of the Employee Center and double-click to open the Edit Employee dialog box. Then, in the Change Tabs list, select Payroll and Compensation Info. On the Payroll Info tab that QuickBooks displays, open the Pay Schedule list, select a pay schedule, and click OK to save your changes.

Employee Information

The information your store in QuickBooks about your employees contributes to the accuracy of the payroll checks you produce. Chapter 2 contains information on adding employees to your company records manually, or you can use the QuickBooks Payroll Setup wizard.

Chart Of Accounts

To support payroll processing, you'll need, at a minimum, the following accounts in your chart of accounts:

- A bank account for writing payroll checks or transferring direct deposit funds. Many businesses maintain a separate payroll account.
- A payroll liabilities account to track the money you withhold from paychecks.
- A payroll expense account to track employer-related payroll expenses such as the employer's share of Social Security and Medicare.

QuickBooks automatically adds the payroll liabilities and employer-related payroll expense accounts when you enable payroll in your company file (either during the EasyStep Interview or in the Preferences dialog box).

You can use one liability account and one expense account for all payroll entries, or create separate accounts for each type of liability/expense. I prefer the former approach and use one liability account and one expense account to keep my Balance Sheet and Profit & Loss report clean. To identify my current outstanding balance for any payroll liability, I view my vendor balances on the A/P Aging reports or on the Payroll tab of the Employee Center.

Entering Historical Data

If you're not starting to use QuickBooks at the very beginning of the year, you must enter all the historical information about paychecks. This is the only way to perform the payroll tasks required at the end of the year.

Payroll operates on a calendar year for all businesses, regardless of your fiscal year. Even though you can start using payroll for the current period before you enter the historical data, remember that the absence of historical data may affect some tax calculations. For example, your state may require that you deduct state unemployment insurance for the first $7,000.00 of gross wages. If you start using payroll in QuickBooks after employees have earned that $7,000.00 but before you enter historical information, you'll have to adjust the deductions on the current paychecks manually. If you enter the historical data before creating paychecks, QuickBooks can calculate the maximum deduction properly.

 TIP: To avoid a lot of historical data entry, aim to start using payroll at the beginning of a calendar quarter or year.

Understanding How QuickBooks Handles Historical Data

You probably prepared payroll before you started using QuickBooks. If you start using QuickBooks at any time other than January 1, then you need to enter historical payroll information to make your payroll data complete for reporting purposes. Here are some guidelines you can use when entering historical data.

- QuickBooks summarizes payroll records quarterly, because your 941 reports are due quarterly.
- You can't enter summarized data for the current quarter. Instead, for the current quarter, you must enter data for each individual weekly, biweekly, semimonthly, or monthly pay period. For prior quarters, you can enter quarterly totals.
- If you start using payroll on any date in the first quarter, you have to enter historical data for each pay period prior to your first payroll in QuickBooks, because you don't have a full quarter to summarize.
- If you start using payroll in the second quarter, enter a quarterly total for the first quarter and then enter the individual pay period numbers for the second quarter up to the date you first process payroll in QuickBooks.
- If you start using payroll in the third quarter, enter quarterly totals for the first two quarters and then enter each pay period up to the date you first process payroll in QuickBooks.
- If you start using payroll in the fourth quarter, you can follow the same pattern, but it might be just as easy to wait until January 1 to begin using QuickBooks payroll.

Entering the History

The Payroll Setup wizard makes it easy to enter payroll history in batches, and it walks you through the process. Read about the QuickBooks Payroll Setup wizard next. When you enter history, make sure that you enter the information exactly as it occurred before you started using QuickBooks. Remember the old adage: "History is history, and you can't change it." If you wrote payroll checks outside of QuickBooks that were wrong and they were cashed, you must enter them into the program exactly as they were—wrong. If you paid too much tax or too little tax, file an amended 941 report with the IRS.

Using the QuickBooks Payroll Setup Wizard

You can use the QuickBooks Payroll Setup wizard to set up all the components required for payroll. If you prefer, you can set up your payroll items and employees manually and then use the wizard to enter your historical data.

Regardless of whether you use the QuickBooks Payroll Setup wizard to set up all your components or to enter historical data only, set up all the vendors you need to remit payroll withholding and employer payroll expenses before using the wizard.

To use the wizard, choose Employees | Payroll Setup from the QuickBooks menu bar. The wizard window opens with all the tasks listed in the left pane (see Figure 8-6).

Setting up payroll is a lengthy process, but the wizard has a Finish Later button that you can click if you have to do other work or get tired. When you open the wizard again, you pick up where you left off.

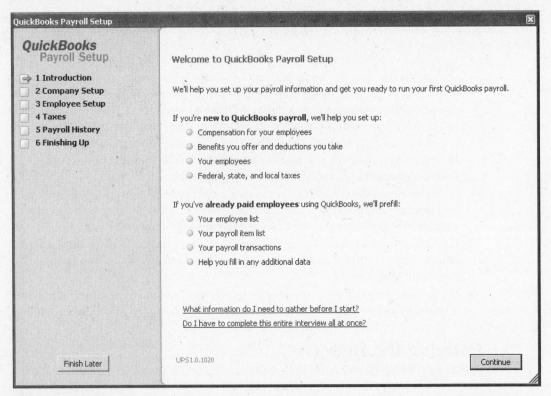

FIGURE 8-6   The QuickBooks Payroll Setup wizard walks you through the process of setting up payroll

The first few screens are informational, explaining the information you need to complete the wizard (the same information about employees, payroll items, deductions, and so forth, discussed earlier in this chapter). The real work starts in the Company Setup section, where the wizard asks you to describe the kind of compensation and benefits your company offers. The wizard then helps you set up your employees, describe the Federal and state taxes you pay, and schedule those tax payments so that QuickBooks can remind you when you need to pay them. Finally, you can enter payroll history information; you use this portion of the wizard if you start using payroll in QuickBooks on any date other than January 1.

Setting Up Payroll Items in the Wizard

In the Company Setup section, the wizard walks you through setting up payroll items for compensation and employee benefits. The instructions are easy to follow and include assigning the accounts and, if appropriate, the vendor associated with the payroll item. As I indicated earlier, it's easier to use the wizard if you've already added the accounts and vendors you need for payroll to your chart of accounts and Vendor List.

You'll set up payroll items for:

- Types of compensation, such as salary, hourly wages, overtime, bonuses, commissions, tips, and so on.

TIP: If your business is a C corporation or a Subchapter S corporation, you need to separate compensation for corporate officers from the compensation for other employees for tax-reporting purposes. To handle this need in QuickBooks, create a separate Earnings item called Officer Compensation and assign it to its own expense account. Then assign this Earnings item to each company officer.

- Benefits, such as insurance, pension, and so on. For each benefit you select, you configure the employee/employer contribution rates.
- Paid time off, such as sick leave and vacations. You can configure your formulas for calculating vacation time and sick time, if you let employees accrue time according to time worked.
- Other additions and deductions, such as workers comp, auto expense reimbursement, garnishments, union dues, charitable contributions, and so on.

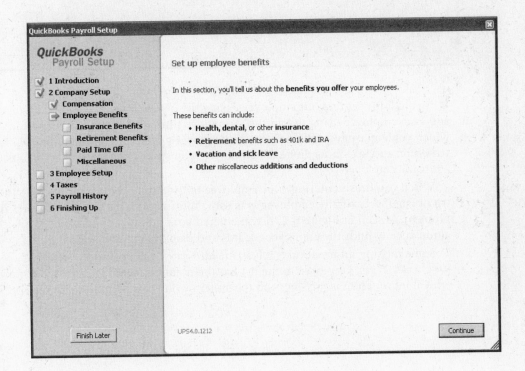

Setting Up Employees in the Wizard

In Section 3 of the Payroll Setup wizard, the wizard helps you set up employees.

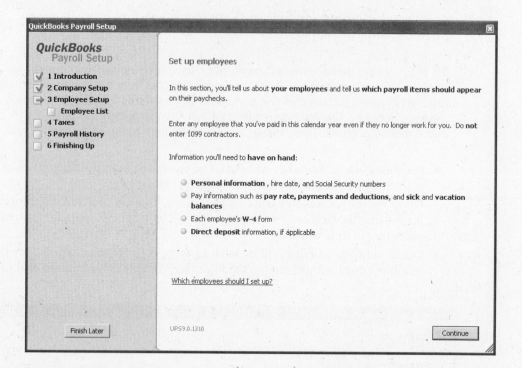

If you didn't set up your employees using the instructions in Chapter 2, you can add each employee using the wizard. You move through a series of windows in which you enter information about the employee's personal information, pay structure, and tax status. For each employee, you specify the taxes and benefits that affect the employee.

When you finish entering your employee information, the wizard displays the list of employees. If any employee is missing information, the wizard indicates the problem, as seen in Figure 8-7. If you entered your employees manually, the wizard automatically finds the employee records and displays the same list.

Some missing information, such as the hire date, isn't critical to issuing paychecks. If any employee in the list has the notation Fix This Error Now, it means critical information is missing, and the system won't be able to issue either a

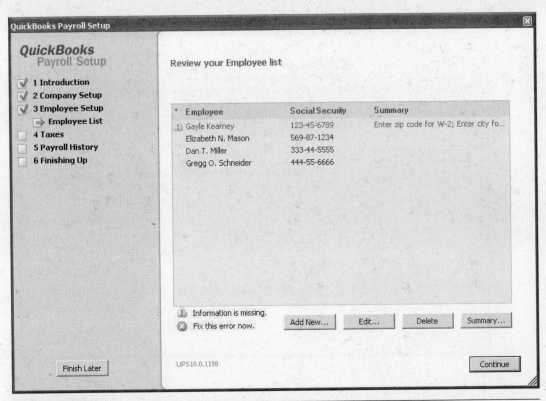

FIGURE 8-7 The wizard identifies employees with missing information so that you can correct the situation

paycheck or a W-2 form at the end of the year. Regardless of whether the missing information is critical, select the employee and click Edit to fix the problem.

You can also select an employee and click Summary to see all the information in the employee's record.

Setting Up Payroll Taxes in the Wizard

In the Taxes section, you tell the wizard about the federal, state, and local taxes you collect. If you set up your taxes as payroll items as described in Chapter 2, the wizard displays those entries, which are stored in the Payroll Item list.

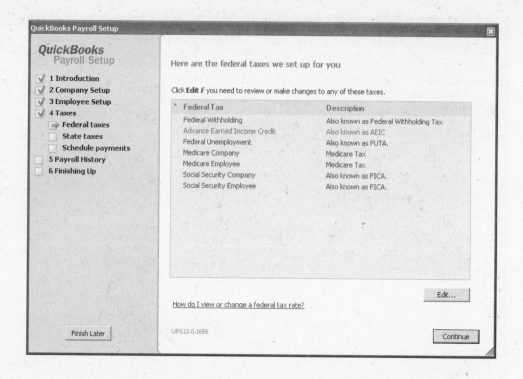

As you finish each category of tax, the wizard displays a list of all the taxes for that category. If the wizard finds anything amiss in your setup, a message appears in the Description column.

The wizard also helps you schedule your tax payments—an added benefit of being a QuickBooks payroll customer. When you schedule payments, QuickBooks tracks the amounts you owe and reminds you when you need to pay your taxes. QuickBooks schedules payments for Federal Form 940, Federal Form 941, state withholding and disability insurance, state unemployment insurance, and state training tax.

Scheduling Tax Payments

After you set up Federal and state taxes, QuickBooks prompts you to schedule the tax payments you make so that QuickBooks can remind you to pay your taxes when they're due. The Payroll Setup wizard displays a series of screens on which you identify the frequency with which you must remit withholding and employer taxes for federal, state, and, if appropriate, local taxing authorities. When you complete the set of screens, the Payroll Setup wizard displays a summary of your remittance dates.

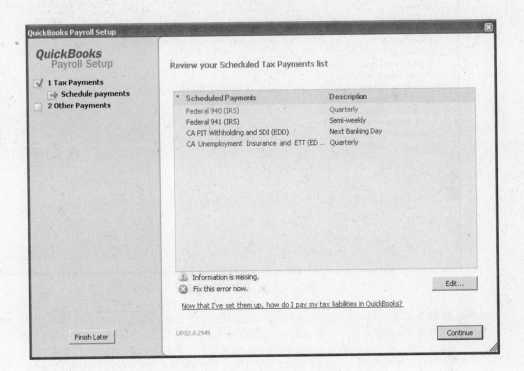

Entering Payroll History in the Wizard

When you walk through the Payroll History section, the wizard initially helps determine whether you need to enter historical data by asking if you've issued paychecks during the current year. When you indicate that you have issued paychecks during the current year, the wizard asks questions, initially focusing on the first quarter, to determine what historical information you need to provide for the quarter.

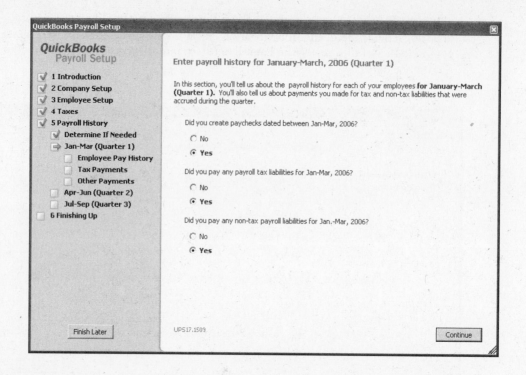

$ **NOTE:**   The information you enter through the Payroll Setup wizard does not affect general ledger accounts, an important fact to consider when setting up your company's opening account balances. For details on entering opening account balances, see Chapter 14. Then the wizard displays the employees you set up previously, and you select one and click Edit to enter historical information about that employee. If you paid an employee during the quarter, the wizard asks about the last paycheck you issued outside of QuickBooks.

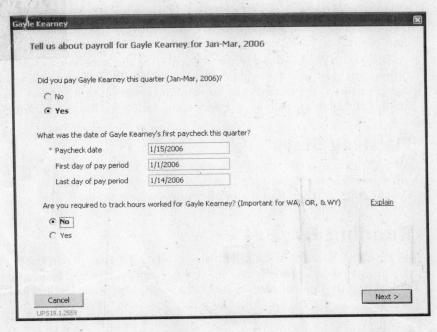

Using the information you provide, the wizard prompts you to enter the quarterly total for all earnings, withholding, company contribution, and company tax payroll items assigned to the employee.

When you finish entering employee information, the wizard walks you through the process of entering payments you made for employer withholding remittances, employer taxes, payments to pension and benefit plans, and so on.

The wizard then walks you through entering the same information for subsequent quarters. If you are performing this task in the second month of the current quarter, the wizard asks for batch information for the first month of the quarter and then individual paycheck information for the current month.

Finishing Steps

After QuickBooks verifies all your payroll data, the Payroll Setup wizard displays a series of Finishing Up screens that provide you with information on where, in QuickBooks, you can find the information you just set up.

Running Payroll

It's payday. You've entered all the historical data. It's time to run the payroll. If you're using direct deposit services, you need a two-day lead before the actual payday. If only some of your employees use direct deposit, you have two choices.

- Create paychecks two days before payday and hold the printed checks until payday.
- Run through the payroll procedure twice, selecting the appropriate employees each time.

 NOTE: The Payroll Center notifies customers who use Direct Deposit to process payroll two days before payday by displaying the correct Process Payroll Due Date in the Pay Employees area. QuickBooks will automatically adjust the date to accommodate bank holidays to ensure that you process your payroll on time.

Reviewing Employees to Pay

Open the Employee Center, click the Payroll tab, select a Pay Schedule, and then click Pay Employees. QuickBooks displays the Enter Hours window, shown in Figure 8-8, where you verify the hours QuickBooks enters for each employee paid by the hour in the selected Pay Schedule; you can change hours if necessary.

To make other types of changes to an employee's paycheck, you can click the link representing the employee's name in the Employee column; QuickBooks displays the Review Or Change Paycheck window, where you can make changes

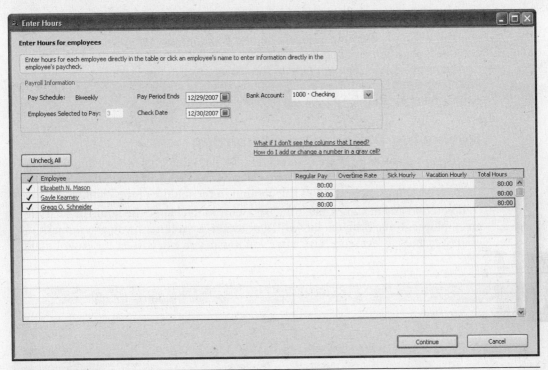

FIGURE 8-8   Enter hours as needed for employees paid by the hour

like assigning or changing the assignment of the employee's wages to a customer: job, changing the worker's compensation code, or, if appropriate, adding bonus pay. Once you finish working in this window, click Next to view the details of the next employee's check or click OK to redisplay the Enter Hours window.

No hours appear for salaried employees because their paychecks don't depend on the hours they work. You can, however, enter a salary amount; if you don't, QuickBooks uses the amount you entered when you set up the employee.

QuickBooks groups together employees who are paid at the same time for the same period of time. Select the employees you want to pay by clicking next to their names in the check-mark column. If you intend to include all employees, click the Mark All button, which then changes to the Unmark All button.

Verify the check date and the payroll period end date and make sure that you select the correct bank account. Click Continue.

TIP: If you have a separate payroll account, you can set it as the default account when you create paychecks so that you don't accidentally use the wrong bank account when creating paychecks. Choose Edit | Preferences and click the Checking category on the left side of the dialog box. On the Company Preferences tab, select the default bank account for creating paychecks and the default bank account for paying payroll liabilities.

Reviewing Paycheck Information

The Review and Create Paychecks window appears (see Figure 8-9). QuickBooks displays the totals in each payroll item category for each employee; the amount of the paycheck appears in the Net Pay column in the middle of the window.

If you find any mistakes, click the Back button to change the hours or salary for an employee. If the problem lies with a nonwage payroll item, you can unmark the employee and pay everyone else; after you finish, you can correct the payroll item

Review and Create Paychecks

Review and Create Paychecks

Payroll Information

Special Payroll

Pay Period Ends: 12/01/2007
Check Date: 12/15/2007

Employees Selected to Pay: 4
Bank Account: 1000 · Checking

Paycheck Options
○ To be printed
○ To be handwritten or direct deposited
Preferences

First Check Number
302

Unmark All

Review the payroll information below. Click on an employee name to preview check detail and enter additional information. When you're done, click Create Paychecks to complete the payroll run.

✓	Employee	Gross Pay	Taxes	Deductions	Net Pay	Employer Taxes	Contributions	Total Hours
✓	Dan T. Miller	1,596.15	-246.00	-25.00	1,325.15	122.11	266.11	
✓	Elizabeth N. Mason	1,180.00	-247.08	-25.00	907.92	90.27	121.18	80:00
✓	Gayle Kearney	2,884.62	-992.27	0.00	1,892.35	398.08	0.00	
✓	Gregg O. Schneider	1,380.00	-305.38	-12.50	1,062.12	105.57	13.11	80:00
		7,040.77	-1,790.73		5,187.54	716.03		

<-Back   Create Paychecks   Cancel

FIGURE 8-9 In the Review and Create Paychecks window, you can verify that paycheck amounts will be correct

as needed and then go through this process again to pay just one employee. If you see many mistakes, click Cancel to leave and double-check your payroll setup.

Select the To Be Printed option if you intend to print paychecks; otherwise, select the To Be Handwritten or Direct Deposited option.

 TIP: You can click the Preferences link to open the Preferences dialog box, where you can set pay stub and voucher check printing options.

Click Create Paychecks. QuickBooks creates and saves the paychecks in your company data file and then offers you printing options described in the next section.

Printing the Paychecks

After QuickBooks creates paychecks, you see a window like this one, where you can choose to print paychecks or pay stubs—or both!

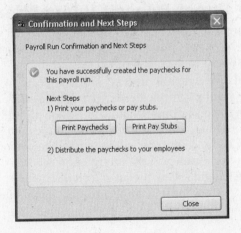

To print checks, follow these steps:

1. Click the Print Paychecks button. QuickBooks displays the Select Paychecks To Print window.
2. Select the bank account and make sure the First Check Number field matches the number of the first check loaded in your printer.
3. If you have both paychecks and direct deposit stubs to print, select the appropriate option at the bottom of the dialog box to display only those items.

④ Remove the check beside any paycheck you don't want to print by clicking in the check-mark column.

⑤ Click OK.

The Print Checks window opens, where you can select a printer and a check style. For details on this window, see Chapter 7.

Click Print to print the paychecks. QuickBooks displays a window in which you must confirm that everything printed properly or reprint any checks that had a problem. If everything is fine, click OK. If there's a problem, enter the number of the first check that had a problem and QuickBooks will reprint as necessary, starting with the next available check number.

QuickBooks redisplays the Confirmation and Next Steps window; if you need to print pay stubs, click the Print Pay Stubs button. The procedure for printing pay stubs is exactly the same as the procedure for printing paychecks; only the end result differs.

When you finish printing, click Close.

Sending Direct Deposit Information

If you use direct deposit services, you still go through the payroll process for the employees who opted for this service. You just don't print the checks. Instead, you notify QuickBooks to deposit the checks.

At the end of the payroll process, you will receive a confirmation and you will be instructed to print paycheck stubs. After you finish printing paycheck stubs, the confirmation screen reappears, and you will be prompted to Send Payroll Data to Intuit for processing. Selecting the button on the confirmation screen will takes you to the Send Center, where you can view the data you're about to upload, and you must confirm its accuracy. If the information is correct, click Go Online to begin the data transfer and follow the on-screen instructions. If something in the window isn't accurate, cancel the procedure and edit the paycheck to correct the information.

Editing a Paycheck

While you can edit a paycheck, it's really not wise. If you make a change that affects net pay, you will also change the wage base on the check and the tax amounts, and those changes affect your payroll liabilities, which could then mean filing amended payroll tax returns. There's a domino effect here that you want to avoid.

QuickBooks helps you avoid the problem with the Lock Net Pay option; as long as this option is selected, you can review paychecks and make changes that *don't* affect net pay, such as changing a worker's compensation code. To edit a paycheck, find it in the Employee Center and double-click it; when QuickBooks displays the check, click the Paycheck Detail button to display the Review Paycheck window shown in Figure 8-10.

Review Paycheck

Type a help question [Ask]   ▼ How Do I?   [X]

Dan T. Miller

Pay Period [12/16/2007] 🔲 - [12/29/2007] 🔲

☐ Use Direct Deposit

Earnings

Item Name	Rate	Hours	WC Code	Customer:Job
Salary	1,596.15		5553	

Sick Available   20:00
Vacation Avail.   248:45
Sick Accrued
Vac. Accrued   6:45

☐ Do not accrue sick/vac

Total Hours: 0:00

Other Payroll Items

Item Name	Rate	Quantity
Health Insurance	-25.00	

Employee Summary

Item Name	Amount	YTD
Salary	1,596.15	39,903.75
Health Insurance	-25.00	-600.00
Federal Withholding	-108.00	-2,796.00
Advance Earned Income Credit	0.00	0.00
Social Security Employee	-98.96	-2,474.03
Medicare Employee	-23.15	-578.61
CA - Withholding	-15.89	-462.53
CA - Disability Employee	0.00	-452.02

Company Summary

Item Name	Amount	YTD
CA - Employee Training Tax	0.00	7.00
Social Security Company	98.96	2,474.03
Medicare Company	23.15	578.61
Federal Unemployment	0.00	56.00
CA - Unemployment Company	0.00	367.50

Check Amount: 1,325.15

[OK]   [Cancel]   [Help]

◉ Lock Net Pay   ○ Unlock Net Pay   ☐ Enter net/Calculate gross

FIGURE 8-10   Use this window to make changes to a paycheck

Although you can unlock a paycheck and edit anything on it, you should check with your accountant before you take this action; your accountant may prefer that you void and reissue a paycheck. To void a paycheck, double-click it to display it in the Paycheck window. Then choose Edit | Void Paycheck.

➤➤ **FYI**

Making Changes to Social Security and Medicare

QuickBooks automatically adjusts flat percentage payroll liabilities such as Medicare and Social Security. If you make a change to one or both of these payroll liabilities on a paycheck, QuickBooks will attempt to compensate for the change on the next check. Therefore, don't manually change the Social Security or Medicare amount on a paycheck if the amounts are wrong.

Social Security and Medicare are calculated on gross wages. When Social Security and Medicare amounts aren't what you expect them to be, the culprit is likely to be another payroll item that affects the calculation of gross wages. So, instead of adjusting Social Security or Medicare on a paycheck, check the setup of other payroll items that affect the calculation of gross wages.

N O T E :   You should void a paycheck *only if* you have the paycheck so that you can destroy it.

Additional Features for Enterprise Solutions Users

If you're running QuickBooks Enterprise Solutions, you have some additional features available beyond the features covered in this chapter.

Employee Organizer

Sold separately for other versions of QuickBooks, the Employee Organizer comes with Enterprise Solutions and takes the worry out of even the most complex human resources and compliance tasks. You can use Employee Organizer to streamline the management of employee information, and employment laws and regulations. This software tool integrates employee information with payroll information in QuickBooks, making it easy to access, update, and generate reports about employee information.

Stay on Top of Employment Regulations

Employee Organizer includes an Employment Regulations Update Service, which gives you access to current federal and state employment laws and regulations.

Employment-related Processes Are Easier

Employee Organizer provides guidance as you wend your way through employment-related processes. Make sure your processes are always consistent by using the Employee Organizer's step-by-step guidelines for the following processes:

- Recruiting
- Interviewing
- Hiring
- Raises
- Promotions
- Termination
- Leaves of absence

Forms and Templates with a Click of a Mouse

Employee Organizer includes federal and state government forms, as well as a selection of templates for letters, other employment-related documents, and employee management forms, including the following:

- INS Form I-9
- COBRA notification

- Federal Form W-4
- Independent Contractor Agreement
- Job Descriptions Form
- Reference Check Form
- Driving Record Check Form

Expert Help and Advice

Send specific employment questions by e-mail. You'll receive answers including the text of relevant government policies, laws, and regulations on average within two business days. Answers are provided by CCH Incorporated, a leading provider of tax and business law information since 1913.

Government Payroll Reporting

In this chapter:

- Making tax deposits
- Preparing quarterly and annual returns
- Printing W-2 forms

Preparing payroll in-house involves printing reports, filling out forms, and writing checks. In this chapter, we'll review the tasks involved in making tax deposits and preparing payroll reports and forms.

If you have an active subscription for QuickBooks Assisted Payroll services, you don't have to worry about the sections in this chapter that are concerned with remitting federal and state withholdings; you'll be able to enter these transactions as journal entries. You do, however, have to remit any local payroll tax withholding.

Making Payroll Tax Deposits

The federal government requires you to deposit the withholding amounts, along with the matching employer contributions, at a specified time that is determined by the size of the total withholding amount you've accumulated. You may be required to deposit monthly, semimonthly, weekly, or within three days of the payroll. Check the current limits with the IRS or your accountant.

In addition, you probably also have state-related payroll liabilities that you must pay at times dictated by your state. Regardless of when you're required to deposit payroll taxes, most accountants advise you to make your tax deposits at the same time you create your paychecks to avoid penalties, and QuickBooks 2007 makes this task truly easy. You pay all payroll liabilities using the same technique in QuickBooks, and QuickBooks keeps track of how much you owe and reminds you when your payments are due. Read on.

 N O T E :   If you have an active Enhanced Payroll subscription, you can take advantage of E-File & Pay, a feature that allows you to pay federal and certain state payroll taxes electronically directly from QuickBooks. See the QuickBooks Help topic E-File & Pay for more information.

Setting up Tax Liability Payment Schedules

For Payroll subscribers, QuickBooks 2007 has a very cool new feature that enables you to set up scheduled tax payments to pay your payroll liabilities. Once you set up these schedules to pay your liabilities, QuickBooks tracks how much you owe and reminds you, on the Payroll tab of the Employee Center, exactly when your tax payments are due.

 N O T E :   You also can set up schedules for benefits and other payments set up as liabilities.

If you didn't set up scheduled tax payments when you set up Payroll in Chapter 8, you can set up the schedules now. To create your scheduled tax payments, open the Employee Center, and click the Payroll tab to display the Payroll Center. Click the Related Payment Activities drop-down arrow, and then click the Edit Payment Due

Dates/Methods button. The QuickBooks Payroll Setup Interview wizard starts, explaining on the first screen that you can add new scheduled tax payments or change existing ones. Click Continue.

The QuickBooks Payroll Setup Interview wizard then displays an informational screen, explaining that setting up a scheduled tax payment involves identifying who receives your tax payments and how often you pay them. Click Next.

The QuickBooks Payroll Setup Interview wizard displays the Set Up Payments For Federal 940 (IRS) screen (see Figure 9-1).

In the Payee list, select the vendor to whom you pay your 940 tax liability. The vendor may be an agency or a financial institution and must appear in the Vendor List. From the Deposit Frequency list, select the frequency with which you make the payment. Then click Next.

 NOTE: QuickBooks helps you select the frequency by telling you the usual frequency for this tax payment.

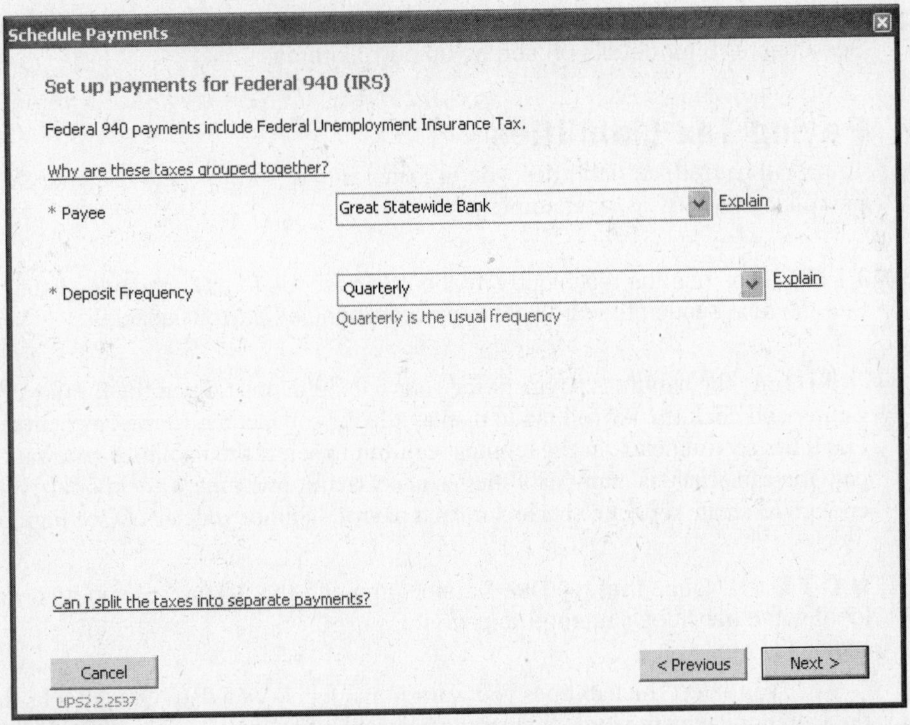

Schedule Payments ☒

Set up payments for Federal 940 (IRS)

Federal 940 payments include Federal Unemployment Insurance Tax.

Why are these taxes grouped together?

* Payee | Great Statewide Bank ▾ | Explain

* Deposit Frequency | Quarterly ▾ | Explain
Quarterly is the usual frequency

Can I split the taxes into separate payments?

| Cancel | | < Previous | Next > |

UPS2.2.2537

FIGURE 9-1 Use this screen to identify the vendor to whom you pay your 940 tax liability and the frequency with which you make the payment

After you finish setting up the 940 scheduled tax payment, the QuickBooks Payroll Setup Interview wizard displays screens just like the one shown in Figure 9-1 so that you can set up scheduled tax payments for the Federal 941 tax liability and state liabilities. When you finish creating these payroll tax liability payment schedules, the QuickBooks Payroll Setup Interview wizard offers you the opportunity to set up other scheduled tax payments for payroll items that are set up as liabilities, such as

- Payroll benefits like 401(k) contributions, health and dental insurance premiums
- Garnishments
- Charitable donations

If you need to set up scheduled payments for any of these other payroll-related payments, click Continue. The process is the same as the one I just described for creating payroll tax liability payment schedules, and QuickBooks will remind you when these payments are due.

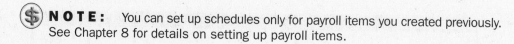 **NOTE:**   You can set up schedules only for payroll items you created previously. See Chapter 8 for details on setting up payroll items.

Paying Tax Liabilities

To pay all payroll tax liabilities, you use the same technique; let's use your 941 payroll tax liability as an example.

TIP: You use the technique I'm about to describe to pay scheduled liabilities. See the next section to learn how to pay unscheduled payroll liabilities.

To create the liabilities payment for your federal deposit, open the Employee Center and click the Payroll tab to display the Payroll Center. In the Pay Scheduled Liabilities section, click in the leftmost column to select the liabilities you want to pay. You can select as many liabilities as necessary at one time; QuickBooks is smart enough to create separate checks for each payroll liability you select (see Figure 9-2).

NOTE: Notice that the Due Date column and the Status column help you identify the liabilities you need to pay.

After you select the liabilities you want to pay, click View/Pay. QuickBooks displays the Liability Payment window, showing a check in the amount of the total liabilities due to the selected payroll tax vendor. If you selected more than one liability to pay

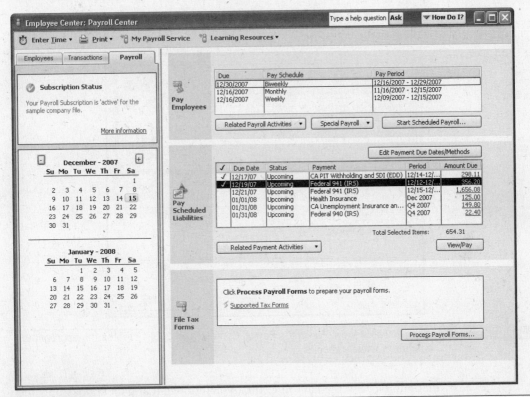

FIGURE 9-2 Select the payroll liabilities you want to pay

and your liabilities go to different vendors, QuickBooks automatically generates separate checks for each vendor—in Figure 9-3, QuickBooks created two payments for the liabilities I selected, as Payment 1 of 2 in the upper left corner of the window indicates.

If you are generating multiple liability checks, click Save & Next to save the first check and view the next one. If you are generating only one liability check, click Save & Close. When you finish reviewing liability checks, QuickBooks displays the Payment Summary window (see Figure 9-4).

Click Print Checks to produce the checks; QuickBooks displays the Select Checks to Print window, where you can select your liability checks and print them. See Chapter 7 for details on printing checks. After you print checks, QuickBooks redisplays the Payroll Summary window, where you can click the Print Summary button. When you click the Print Summary button, QuickBooks prints a copy of the summary window. When QuickBooks finishes and redisplays the Payment Summary window, you can click Close.

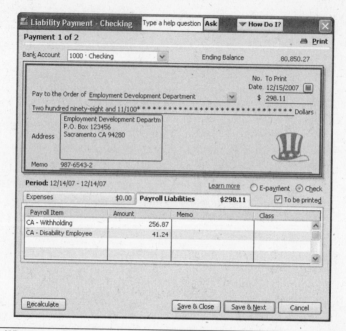

FIGURE 9-3   When you click View/Pay in the Payroll Center, QuickBooks creates the appropriate number of liability checks

If you double-check the Payroll Center, you'll notice that QuickBooks updated the Pay Scheduled Liabilities portion of the window, and the liabilities for the period you paid no longer appear.

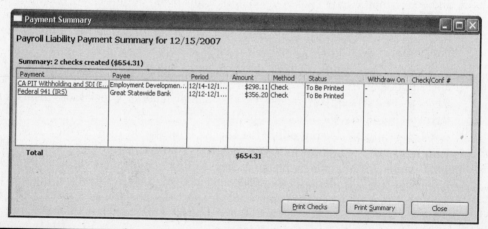

FIGURE 9-4   After you review the liability checks, QuickBooks displays the Payment Summary window

Paying Unscheduled Payroll Liabilities

Not all payroll liabilities have schedules and appear in the Pay Scheduled Liabilities section of the Payroll Center.

To pay an unscheduled liability, follow these steps:

1. In the Pay Scheduled Liabilities section of the Payroll Center, click the Related Payment Activities button. If you process your payroll manually, you won't be able to access the Payroll Center. Choose Employees ⊦ Pay Taxes and Liabilities ⊦ Pay Unscheduled Liabilities.

2. From the drop-down menu that appears, click Pay Unscheduled Liabilities. The Select Date Range For Liabilities dialog box appears.

3. Select the date range for the payroll liabilities you want to pay and click OK. The Pay Liabilities window appears (see Figure 9-5).

4. If necessary, remove the check from the To Be Printed option.

5. Select the bank account you use to pay payroll liabilities and enter the check date.

6. Specify whether you want to create the check without reviewing it, or review the check before finalizing it.

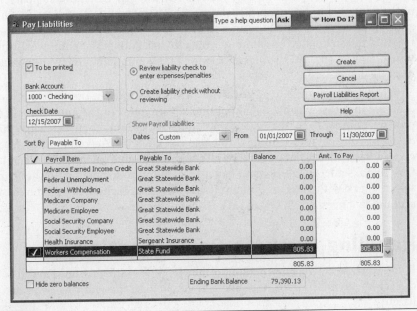

FIGURE 9-5   Use this window to pay unscheduled payroll liabilities

❼ Click in the leftmost column beside the liabilities you want to pay.

❽ Click Create. If you opted to review the check, it appears in the Write Checks window; click Save & Close. If you opted not to review the check, QuickBooks creates the check.

If you print checks, follow the steps in Chapter 7 to print checks.

Adjusting Payroll Liabilities

Occasionally, you need to adjust a payroll liability amount. For example, the amount you accrue for workers compensation may not match the insurance company's bill when it arrives.

To adjust payroll liabilities, open the Employee Center and click the Payroll tab to display the Payroll Center. Then, choose Related Payment Activities | Adjust Payroll Liabilities to display the Liability Adjustment window. If you process your payroll manually, choose Employees | Pay Taxes and Liabilities | Adjust Payroll Liabilities.

In the Date box, select a date for the liability adjustment.

In the Effective Date box, select the date that you want the liability adjustment to affect account balances.

Choose Company or Employee to identify the way QuickBooks posts the effects of the adjustment. For example, choose Company when you adjust a liability amount discrepancy due to rounding or because the workers compensation bill you received doesn't match the amount you accrued. Adjust the employee's amount if, for example, you used the higher rate for FUTA and then realize you should have used the lower rate.

Select a payroll item to adjust, type an amount, and, in the Memo column, describe the reason you are making the adjustment. For the amount, enter a positive number to increase your payroll liabilities, and enter a negative number to decrease your payroll liabilities. You also can click the Accounts Affected button to choose whether to affect your payroll liability account balances. By default, QuickBooks affects liability and expense accounts associated with the item you select; check with your accountant if you aren't sure whether you should affect account balances. Click OK to save the adjustment.

Handling Workers Compensation

If you have an active subscription to the QuickBooks Enhanced Payroll Service, you can set up payroll so that QuickBooks tracks and accrues your workers compensation liability.

Companies make workers compensation payments, typically to insurance companies, to provide benefits to workers who are injured on the job. When workers are injured and the injury is deemed work related, the insurance company pays workers compensation benefits that usually include medical expenses and possibly wages.

Each state establishes workers compensation categories and corresponding rates based on the danger level of the work performed by employees in the category. The insurance company calculates your premium based on:

- The amount of gross pay each employee receives,
- The workers compensation category of the employee, and
- The number of accidents that have occurred at your place of business.

The workers compensation rate for office workers is lower than the rate for construction workers because construction workers are more likely to be injured on the job than office workers. And, as the number of accidents increases, the premiums increase.

Workers compensation premiums accrue as you pay employees, so you need to set up workers compensation before writing paychecks; otherwise, the workers compensation reports and liability amount will not be accurate. So, plan to start using workers compensation in QuickBooks on January 1. If you start using the Workers Compensation feature in QuickBooks mid-year, you'll need to combine the information QuickBooks tracks with the information you tracked outside of QuickBooks.

To set up workers compensation, check with your insurance company to get the codes your insurance company uses and the rates charged for each code, your state's regulations for workers compensation and overtime, and your experience modification factor, if assigned by the insurance company. The experience modification factor is based on the number of prior workers compensation claims your company has in your state, and it increases or reduces your workers compensation premium.

Most companies pay an overtime premium, such as time-and-a-half, when an employee works more than the specified number of hours in a pay period. Time-and-a-half consists of the employee's regular hourly rate plus half of the regular hourly rate for the hours that exceed 40 hours per week. The extra half of the regular hourly rate—the amount that exceeds the regular rate of pay—is considered overtime premium. In many states, you calculate your workers compensation liability only on regular wages and you therefore pay less. If you pay overtime, check with your insurance company or your accountant to see if you can calculate overtime amounts as regular pay. If necessary, set up overtime payroll items for all types of wages prior to setting up workers compensation.

Setting Up Workers Compensation Tracking

To enable workers compensation tracking, choose Edit | Preferences and click the Payroll & Employees category. On the Company Preferences tab, click Set

Preferences in the Workers Comp area. QuickBooks displays the Workers Comp Preferences dialog box. Check the Track Workers Comp box.

You also can choose to see reminder messages to assign workers compensation codes when you create paychecks or timesheets. In addition, you can, if appropriate, select the option to exclude an overtime premium from the workers compensation calculation.

To set up the Workers Comp calculations, choose Employees | Workers Compensation | Set Up Workers Comp. The Workers Compensation Setup wizard starts; on the opening screen, you see a list of the things you'll need to complete the setup. When you have everything you need, click Next.

On the Who Is Your Workers Compensation Insurance Carrier screen, select the vendor to whom you pay your workers compensation insurance premium and optionally supply any account number by which that vendor recognizes you. Click Next.

On the Set Employee Default Classification Codes screen, click in the Workers Comp code column and choose <Add New>. The New Workers Compensation code dialog box appears.

Supply the workers compensation code number and description. In the Rate box, type the rate per $100.00 of gross wages. Click the Calendar icon to select a starting date for the rate and click OK. QuickBooks redisplays the Set Employee Default Classification Codes wizard screen; repeat this process to add the workers compensation codes you need to use. Then, assign a default workers compensation code to each employee (see Figure 9-6) and click Next.

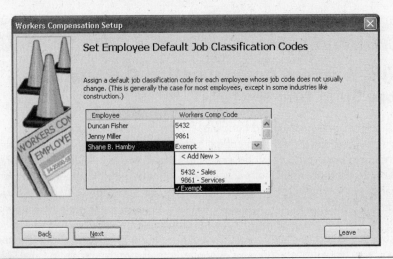

FIGURE 9-6 Assign a workers compensation code to each employee

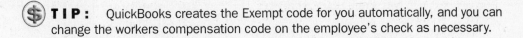

💲 **TIP:** QuickBooks creates the Exempt code for you automatically, and you can change the workers compensation code on the employee's check as necessary.

QuickBooks displays the Enter Your Experience Modification Factor (If Applicable) screen. If you use an experience modification factor, enter it and supply its effective date. Otherwise, click No, I Don't Use An Experience Modification Factor and click Next.

The Overtime Payments screen appears; asking if you pay overtime wages. Click Yes or No as appropriate and click Next. If you click Yes, the Overtime Premiums and Workers Compensation Calculations screen appears, where you specify whether you include or exclude overtime premiums from your workers compensation calculations. Click the appropriate response and click Next.

The Name Your Workers Compensation Payroll Item screen appears; this screen also appears if you click No on the Overtime Payments screen. Type a name for your workers compensation payroll item and click Next. The Workers Compensation wizard displays a summary screen for your workers compensation setup; click Finish.

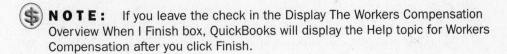

💲 **NOTE:** If you leave the check in the Display The Workers Compensation Overview When I Finish box, QuickBooks will display the Help topic for Workers Compensation after you click Finish.

The workers compensation codes you created appear in the Workers Comp List, which you can display from the Lists menu or by choosing Employees | Workers Compensation | Workers Comp List.

➡ **FYI**

Handling Workers Compensation Calculations for More Than One State

Although QuickBooks doesn't support handling workers compensation calculations for more than one state directly, you can use a portion of the feature. Set up separate workers compensation codes for the same job in different states, enabling QuickBooks to calculate basic workers compensation amounts accurately for each employee. The Workers Compensation feature supports only one experience factor at a time, however, so if you have different experience factors in different states, set your experience factor to 100 percent. When the experience factor is 100 percent, QuickBooks does not increase or reduce your workers compensation liability, and you can accurately calculate your liability manually. Filter the Workers Comp Summary report by selecting workers compensation codes for only one state. Export the report to Excel, where you can set up a column for your experience factor and multiply the Total WC Premium values by the factor to calculate the amount due.

Payroll and Workers Compensation

Once you set up the Workers Compensation feature, QuickBooks automatically accrues your workers compensation liability each time you pay an employee; you do not need to take any additional actions as long as you assigned a workers compensation code to each employee during setup. You can view the amount accrued on each paycheck as you preview paychecks. QuickBooks calculates the workers compensation amount by dividing gross wages by \$100 and then multiplying the result by the rate you set for each workers compensation code. If you set an experience modification factor, QuickBooks adjusts the workers compensation amount by multiplying it by your experience modification factor.

 TIP: If your experience modification factor changes, open the Workers Comp List, click the Experience Modification button, and click Edit. QuickBooks displays the Edit Experience Modification Factor dialog box, where you can set a new experience modification factor and its effective date.

You pay the workers compensation insurance bill from the Pay Liabilities window; follow the steps in "Paying Unscheduled Payroll Liabilities" earlier in this chapter. If the bill does not match the accrued liability amount, you may need to adjust the liability amount.

Reporting on and Paying Workers Compensation

You also can print a series of reports that provide information about workers compensation by choosing Reports | Employees & Payroll and then selecting the appropriate report. The Workers Comp Summary organizes information by workers compensation code and shows gross wages, any overtime premium, workers compensation wages and hours, the workers compensation rate, the workers compensation premium, the experience modification factor, and the adjusted workers compensation premium.

The Workers Compensation by Code and Employee report shows the same information as the Workers Comp Summary report, but breaks the information down further by listing employees that fall into each workers compensation code category.

If you assign an employee's hours to jobs, you can use the Workers Comp by Job Summary report to view a breakdown of overtime premium, workers compensation wages, hours, workers compensation premium, and adjusted workers compensation premium by job for each workers compensation code category.

The Workers Comp Detail report provides information for each paycheck within a workers compensation code category. On the report, you see the payee's name, the payroll items that appear on the paycheck, the gross wages, overtime premium, workers compensation wages, hours, workers compensation code rate, workers compensation premium, experience modification factor, and adjusted workers compensation premium. At the bottom of the report, totals appear for the report period.

The Workers Compensation Listing report shows you the same information that appears in the Workers Comp code List window—the workers compensation code, description, rate, and effective date. You can right-click in the column heading area of the Workers Comp code List window, select Customize Columns, and add the Next Rate column and Next Rate Effective Date column to the window that already appear on the report.

Preparing Your Quarterly 941 Form

Every quarter you must file a 941 form that reports the total amount you owe the federal government for withheld taxes and employer expenses. Many people fill out the preprinted 941 form they receive in the mail. You can have QuickBooks print the 941 form for you and then either send in the QuickBooks copy, which is accepted by the IRS, or copy the information onto the preprinted form.

To prepare the report, follow these steps:

1. Click the Employee Center icon and then click the Payroll tab to display the Payroll Center.

2. Click Process Payroll Forms in the File Tax Forms section. The Select Form Type dialog box appears.

③ Choose Federal Form and click OK. The Select Payroll Form dialog box appears.

④ Choose Quarterly Form 941/Schedule B—Interview For Your Form 941/ Schedule B.

⑤ In the Select Filing Period area, select a quarter and the quarter ending date and click OK.

A wizard asks you some questions and displays Form 941 and, if appropriate, Schedule B on-screen. The form contains information from your QuickBooks company data file. After you click Next to view all the pages, you see a page of filing and printing instructions.

Preparing Annual Payroll Documents

At the end of the year, most taxing authorities require that you prepare annual returns. In addition to using QuickBooks tools and reports, visit the online Year-End Center by going to http://www.quickbooks.com/support and clicking the link to the year-end center. There you'll find lots of good resources for preparing your year-end forms.

Preparing State and Local Annual Returns

To complete many state reports, you can use QuickBooks payroll reports and change the date range in the QuickBooks payroll reports. In addition, subscribers to the Enhanced Payroll Service can take advantage of the state forms that service supports.

Prepare your State Unemployment annual report before you complete the Federal Unemployment Report (FUTA) Form 940, because the payments you make to the state are relevant to the Federal Unemployment report (Form 940).

Preparing the 940 Report

The Federal Form 940 report (FUTA) is filed annually. To create your Form 940, open the Employee Center and click the Payroll tab. Then, click Process Payroll Forms. In the Select Form Type dialog box, choose Federal form and click OK. In the Select Payroll Form dialog box, select Annual Form 940/940-EZ—Interview For Your Form 940/Form 940-EZ, select a filing period, and click OK. Answer the question in the interview and review the form QuickBooks displays. When you finish, QuickBooks displays filing and printing instructions for you to follow.

Printing W-2 Forms

At the beginning of each year, you must print W-2 forms for the previous calendar year for your employees, government agencies, and your own files. To produce W-2 forms in QuickBooks, open the Employee Center and click the Payroll tab.

Then click Process Payroll Forms. In the Select Form Type dialog box, choose Federal form and click OK. In the Select Payroll Form dialog box, select Annual Form W-2/W-3—Wage And Tax Statement/Transmittal, select a filing period, and click OK.

 N O T E :   If you file 250 or more W-2 forms, the IRS requires that you file electronically.

In the Select Employees For Form W-2/W-3, QuickBooks selects all employees by default. Choose Review/Edit and the Welcome To The W-2 And W-3 Interview window appears. Click Next to answer the review questions; when you finish, click Next to begin reviewing each employee's W-2 form and the W-3 transmittal form. When you finish reviewing, QuickBooks displays filing and printing instructions.

As with Form 940 and Form 941, QuickBooks has a very clever troubleshooting tool for Form W-2 to help you see the calculations that make up any line of the W-2 by clicking that line of the form. Visit http://www.quickbooks.com/support and search for "Form W-2 instructions" without the quotation marks. On the page that appears, click the Form W-2 Instructions link.

Configuring and Tracking Inventory

n this chapter:

- Creating inventory items
- Creating assemblies
- Counting inventory
- Adjusting inventory
- Running inventory reports

Inventory is the Lifeblood of a business that sells products. You need to track and manage inventory items every bit as carefully as you track and manage customer receivables. Managing inventory well helps ensure that you never miss a sale because, if you don't have the item immediately in inventory, you know exactly when it will arrive. Managing inventory well helps ensure that you don't overstock items, tying up cash you need for other purposes.

 NOTE: You'll find information on managing backorders using sales order in Chapter 3.

Creating Inventory Items

The Item List in QuickBooks contains all the elements that might ever appear on a customer invoice, or a purchase order, including inventory items, services, and noninventory products you sell along with other miscellaneous items for discounts, sales tax, and so on.

Setting Inventory Preferences

Although the Item List appears in QuickBooks, you can't create inventory items or assemblies unless you enable inventory. Choose Edit | Preferences and click the Items & Inventory category. On the Company Preferences tab, place a check in the Inventory And Purchase Orders Are Active check box (see Figure 10-1).

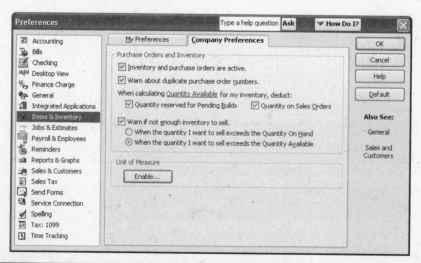

FIGURE 10-1   Enable inventory and set other inventory preferences

Once you enable inventory, you can set a variety of preferences.

- You can have QuickBooks warn you if you use a purchase order number more than once. If your company file is large, checking this box could slow down processing.
- When calculating quantity available, you can specify that QuickBooks exclude items because they make up an assembly you plan to build or because they appear on sales orders.
- You can determine how QuickBooks calculates how much inventory is available to sell before it warns you of insufficient quantities. When you choose When The Quantity I Want To Sell Exceeds The Quantity On Hand, QuickBooks looks at the number you have in stock. When you choose When The Quantity I Want To Sell Exceeds The Quantity Available, QuickBooks also considers quantities reserved for assemblies and sales orders.
- You can enable the Unit Of Measure feature, which is new to QuickBooks 2007. Read the next section for details on the Unit Of Measure feature.

Setting Up Units of Measure

When you enable the Unit Of Measure feature, QuickBooks adds the Unit of Measure field (U/M) to most list and transaction reports and some summary reports, and most windows in which you enter or edit items.

The QuickBooks U/M feature enables you to define the way in which you buy and sell items. QuickBooks supports two variations of the U/M field: Single U/M Per Item and Multiple U/M Per Item. You use Single U/M Per Item if you buy and sell the item in the same unit of measure; for example, you buy and sell lumber in feet. You use Multiple U/M Per Item if you buy the item in one unit of measure and sell it in another; for example, you buy lumber by the foot but sell it by the inch.

Not all versions of QuickBooks support both variations of the U/M feature; Table 10-1 lists the type of units of measure available by version of QuickBooks.

You can assign a unit of measure to the following types of items:

- Inventory Part
- Inventory Assembly
- Noninventory Part
- Service
- Group

To set up the Unit of Measure feature, follow these steps:

1. Choose Edit | Preferences to display the Preferences dialog box.
2. Click Items & Inventory.
3. Click the Company tab.

Enterprise Versions	U/M	Premier Versions	U/M
Accountant	Multiple	Accountant	Multiple
Contractor	Multiple	Contractor	Multiple
Mfg/Wholesale	Multiple	Mfg/Wholesale	Multiple
Nonprofit	Multiple	Nonprofit	Single
Professional	Multiple	Professional	Single
Nonindustry (plain)	Multiple	Nonindustry (plain)	Single
Retail	None	Retail	None

Note: "Multiple" lets you choose between Single or Multiple

TABLE 10-1   Types of Units of Measure Available by QuickBooks Version

④ Click the Enable button in the Unit Of Measure section. QuickBooks displays the Unit of Measure dialog box (see Figure 10-2). Choose Single U/M Per Item if you buy and sell the item using the same unit of measure; for example, you buy and sell by the yard. Choose Multiple U/M Per Item if you buy the item in one unit of measure but sell the item in another; for example, you buy by the yard but sell by the foot.

⑤ Click Finish; QuickBooks redisplays the Preferences dialog box, where you can change your mind about your choice if necessary.

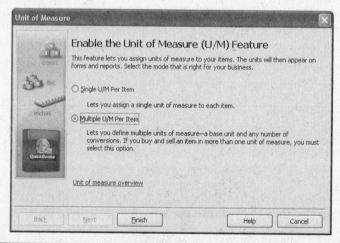

FIGURE 10-2   You can enable the unit of measure feature in QuickBooks to track single or multiple units of measure per item

If you select Multiple U/M Per Item when you enable the Unit Of Measure feature in the Preferences dialog box, you'll need to set up related units of measure that you can assign to inventory items.

Follow these steps to set up a related unit of measure when you enabled Multiple U/M Per Item:

NOTE: If you enabled Single U/M Per Item, you'll use these steps with some slight changes; see the note after the step for details.

① Choose Lists | U/M Set List. The U/M Set List window appears.

② Press CTRL-N. The Unit of Measure wizard starts.

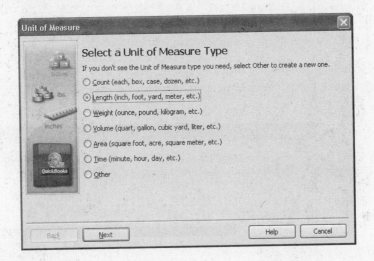

③ Select the unit of measure you want to set up.

TIP: If you don't see the unit of measure you need, click Other. The wizard lets you define the unit of measure.

④ Click Next. The Select A Base Unit Of Measure screen appears.

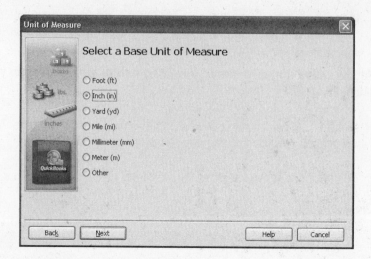

5 Select the smallest unit you sell or buy.

6 Click Next. The Add Related Units screen appears.

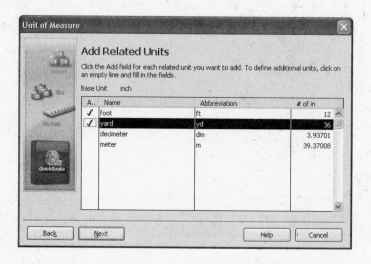

7 Check the other units of measure you sell or buy.

8 Click Next. The Select Default Units Of Measure screen appears.

9 Select the default unit of measure that QuickBooks should display when you buy items, sell items, and ship items. If you select a unit for shipping, the unit you select will override the unit of measure that appears on sales orders when you print a pick list.

⑩ Click Next. The Name Of The Unit Of Measure Set screen appears.

⑪ In the Set Name box, accept the name QuickBooks supplies or type a new name and click Finish.

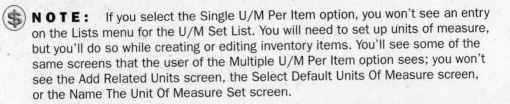

N O T E :   If you select the Single U/M Per Item option, you won't see an entry on the Lists menu for the U/M Set List. You will need to set up units of measure, but you'll do so while creating or editing inventory items. You'll see some of the same screens that the user of the Multiple U/M Per Item option sees; you won't see the Add Related Units screen, the Select Default Units Of Measure screen, or the Name The Unit Of Measure Set screen.

Creating New Items

You'll find instructions for adding items to the Item List in Chapter 2, but it's worth taking a moment here to go over the steps for creating inventory items.

Click the Items & Services icon on the Home page, or choose Lists | Item List from the menu bar, to display the Item List window (see Figure 10-3), where you can view a wide variety of information about the items you've set up in QuickBooks.

N O T E :   QuickBooks Premier users won't see the search fields at the top of the Item List window.

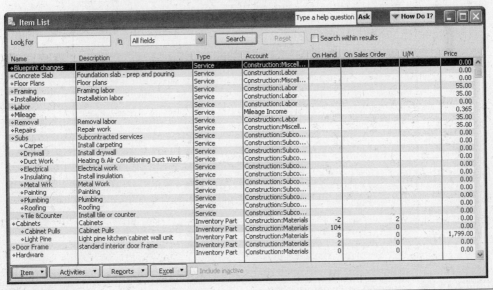

FIGURE 10-3   The Item List window displays a wide variety of information about established items

To add a new item to your inventory items list, press CTRL-N. When the New Item window opens, select Inventory Part for the item type, and fill in the information (see Figure 10-4):

- The Item Name/Number is your code for the item. This field must be unique in your Items List.
- You can create an accurate purchase order much more easily if you fill in the Manufacturer's Part Number field when you create an item. If you purchase from a distributor instead of a manufacturer, enter the distributor's part number.
- If you enabled the unit of measure feature, assign a U/M. If you enabled Multiple U/M Per Item, assign a U/M set, and QuickBooks will assign the default unit in the set definition in transaction windows. If you enable Single U/M Per Item, assign a specific unit of measure that QuickBooks will use in transaction windows.
- The text you enter in the Description On Purchase Transactions field automatically appears when you create a purchase order or a bill. The text you enter in the Description On Sales Transactions field automatically appears on invoices, estimates, sales receipts, and sales orders. You can change the information as you create transactions.

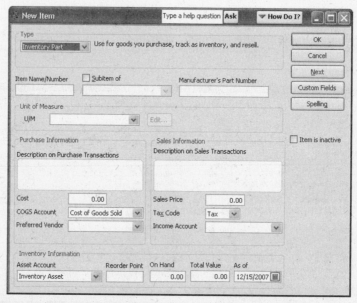

FIGURE 10-4   Setting up an inventory item

NOTE: If you change a description and then switch to a different item while creating a transaction, QuickBooks asks you if you want to use the new description or the default description for the new item. You can control this behavior in the Preferences dialog box. Choose Edit | Preference and click the General category. On the My Preferences tab, choose Ask, Always, or Never in the Keep Custom Item Information When Changing Item In Transactions section.

- The financial information (sales price and cost) that you enter can be changed on an individual transaction. The value in the Sales Price field appears by default when you sell the item, and the value in the Cost field appears by default when you purchase the item.

 NOTE: Don't confuse the Cost field with the inventory costing method Avg. Cost, which displays the value of the item in your inventory asset account. In case your accountant asks, QuickBooks uses the Average Costing inventory method and does not support FIFO or LIFO.

- Select the appropriate accounts for Cost of Goods Sold and Income.
- Enter a number in the Reorder Point field that reflects the minimum quantity you want to have in stock. If you turn on the QuickBooks Reminders feature, then QuickBooks will remind you to reorder the item when this quantity is reached. To turn on the Reminder feature, choose Edit | Preferences and click the Reminders category. On the My Preferences tab, check Show Reminders List When Opening A Company File check box. On the Company Preferences tab, choose either Show Summary or Show List for the Inventory To Reorder option.
- Instead of entering values in the On Hand or Total Value field, use the inventory adjustment transaction to set up opening balances for items. This approach provides the financial trail your accountant will prefer instead of using the boxes in the New Item dialog box. You can read more about the inventory adjustment transaction later in this chapter in the section "Making Inventory Adjustments."

If you created any custom fields for items, discussed in Chapter 2, click Custom Fields and enter data in any custom field that's appropriate for this item. If you want to add additional custom fields, click Define Fields. You can define up to five custom fields.

If you disabled automatic spell checks in the Preferences dialog box, click Spelling to make sure you have no spelling errors, letting the QuickBooks spelling checker add the words connected to this item to its dictionary and eliminating the need to check spelling when you use the item in a transaction. If you didn't disable the spelling checker, it will start when you click OK to save the item.

Creating Subitems

Subitems are useful when there are choices for items and you want all the choices to be part of a larger hierarchy so you can track them efficiently. For instance, if you sell interior and exterior doors you may want to create an item for "door" and subitems "interior" and "exterior."

To create a subitem, you must assign it to a parent item. When you create a parent item, use these guidelines.

- Use a generic name for the item; the details are in the subitem names.
- Enter the COGS Account because it's a required field for all inventory items.
- Enter the Income Account because it's a required field for all inventory items.

Don't fill in any of the other fields for the parent item; instead, store that information with the subitem.

Having created the parent item, subitems are easy to create. Create a new item and assign the item name. Then check the Subitem Of box and select the parent item from the drop-down list that appears when you click the arrow to the right of the field. Then fill in the rest of the New Item dialog box as described earlier in this chapter.

Making Items Inactive

Sometimes you have inventory items that you aren't buying or selling at the moment. Perhaps they're seasonal, or the cost is too high and you want to delay purchasing and reselling the item until you can get a better price. Or, you may have inventory items that you no longer buy or sell. Perhaps you have sold all the items or have disposed of the items.

As long as you're not using the item, you can make it inactive so that it won't appear on the Item List when you're entering transactions. To make an item inactive, open the Item List window and right-click the item. Then choose Make Item Inactive from the shortcut menu.

When you make an item inactive, it doesn't appear when you open the item list while recording a transaction and it doesn't appear in the Item List window. However, you can change the appearance of the Item List window to display inactive items. When you have made items inactive, QuickBooks makes the Include Inactive check box available; click it, and QuickBooks displays inactive items with an X to the left of the item.

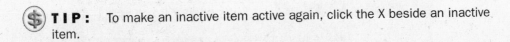 **TIP:**   To make an inactive item active again, click the X beside an inactive item.

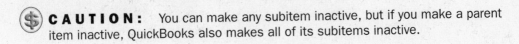 **CAUTION:**   You can make any subitem inactive, but if you make a parent item inactive, QuickBooks also makes all of its subitems inactive.

Inactive items don't appear on any of the inventory reports. If the inactive items have a quantity and dollar amount, you should activate all inventory items before running any inventory reports. This will ensure the dollar amounts on the inventory reports agree with the financial statements.

Creating Assemblies

The Inventory Assembly item type helps you use raw inventory parts to build finished goods items, and so it is particularly useful to companies for which manufacturing is a light to moderate portion of their business.

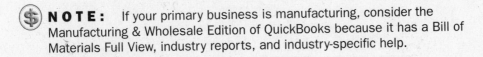 **NOTE:**   If your primary business is manufacturing, consider the Manufacturing & Wholesale Edition of QuickBooks because it has a Bill of Materials Full View, industry reports, and industry-specific help.

Creating an Assembly Item

To create an inventory assembly, make sure that you have previously set up the components of the assembly in the Item List; you can include Service, Non-Inventory, and Other Charge items as well as Inventory Part and Inventory Assembly items in an assembly. Choose Lists | Item List to display the Item List window. Then, press CTRL-N and select Inventory Assembly in the Type list.

TIP: You can create an inventory assembly item from an existing inventory part item. Just edit the item and change the Type to Inventory Assembly. However, once you make the switch, you can't change your mind.

When you create an inventory assembly item, you define the components of the assembly, which exist as raw parts in your inventory, as you can see in Figure 10-5. Simply click in the Item column of the Bill Of Materials section and select a component of the assembly; QuickBooks fills in the description, type, and cost of the item. You then supply the quantity and QuickBooks calculates the total.

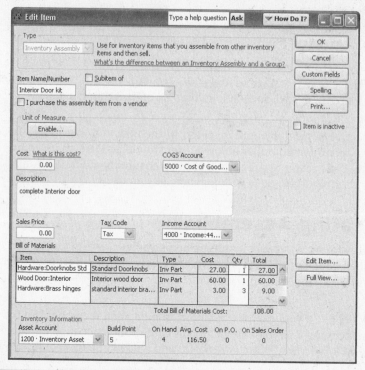

FIGURE 10-5   A typical inventory assembly item

➡ FYI

Assembly Cost

You might be tempted to think that the cost of your assembly will be the Total Bill Of Materials cost that appears when you create or edit the item. In fact, the Total Bill Of Materials cost that you see when you create or edit the item is the sum of the costs you supplied when you created each component of the assembly. QuickBooks will determine the actual cost of your assembly at the time that you build the assembly, and that cost will be the sum of the average costs of the components at the time of the build, which might be different from the Total Bill Of Materials Cost.

N O T E : Once you've created an inventory assembly item and used it in a transaction, you cannot change the component parts in the assembly transaction. You can edit the assembly item and change the Bill Of Materials, which will be used in a new transaction.

You assign a cost of goods sold account as well as an income account and tax code. You also assign an inventory asset account. You can supply a build point to identify the minimum quantity you want to have in stock. If you are setting up QuickBooks for the first time, don't enter values into the On Hand or Total Value columns to record existing assemblies in QuickBooks; instead, use inventory adjustment transactions. See the section "Making Inventory Adjustments" later in this chapter.

To enter new assemblies into inventory, you'll build them; read on.

Assembling Finished Goods

The assembly item you just created serves as the bill of materials for the assembly. Once you've created an assembly item, you build the assembly to place it in inventory. When you build assemblies, you use the components you specified in the bill of materials; building an assembly reduces the number of the component parts stored in your company data, while simultaneously increasing the number of the assembled item—the net effect on your inventory value is $0. QuickBooks tells you the number of complete assemblies you can build at the time you attempt to build assemblies, based on current inventory quantities of the component parts.

Follow these steps to build an assembly:

1. Choose Vendors | Inventory Activities | Build Assemblies. QuickBooks displays the Build Assemblies window (see Figure 10-6).
2. Open the Assembly Item list and select the assembly you want to build.
3. In the Quantity To Build box, type the number of assemblies you want to build. QuickBooks updates the Qty Needed box.
4. Click Build & Close.

 N O T E : When you build an assembly item that includes service, noninventory part, and other charge items, QuickBooks capitalizes the built item into the finished goods inventory asset account.

Pending Builds

Even if you don't have enough component parts, QuickBooks permits you to build more assemblies than the number listed as the Maximum Number You Can Build From Quantity On Hand. If you choose to build more than the maximum number, QuickBooks displays the warning box you see in Figure 10-7.

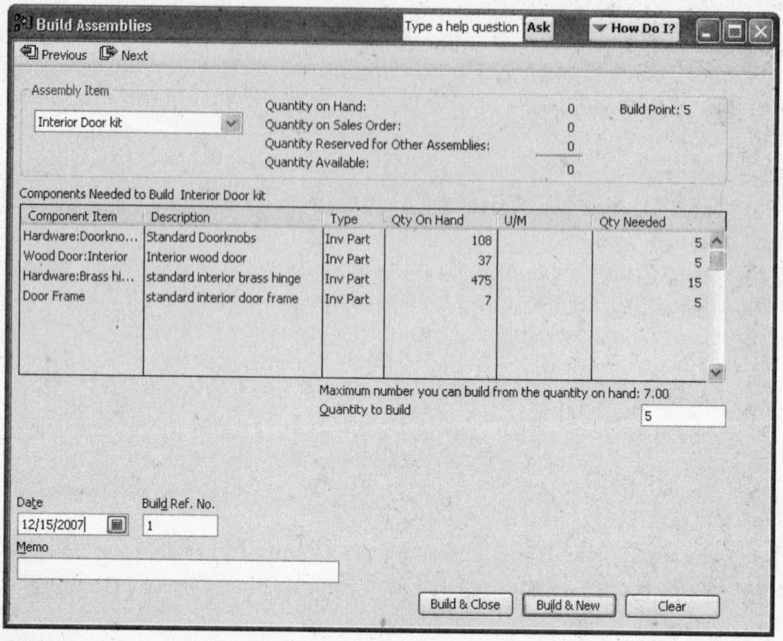

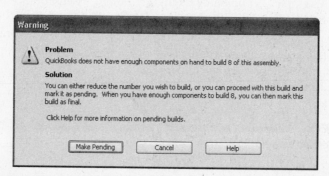

FIGURE 10-6 Assemble finished goods in this window

If you click Make Pending, QuickBooks marks the build as pending and doesn't update your inventory counts, so your finished goods are not yet available. When parts become available, you can finish the build.

FIGURE 10-7 By building more than your current inventory allows, you can create a pending build

Use the Pending Builds report to find pending builds to complete. Choose Reports | Inventory | Pending Builds to view the Pending Builds report. Drill down on any line on the report to display it in the Build Assemblies window.

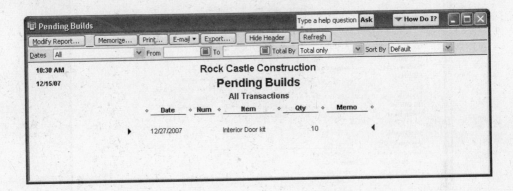

You can manually mark a build as pending. Create the build as described earlier. Then, while redisplaying it in the Build Assemblies window, choose Edit | Mark Build as Pending.

 CAUTION: Be aware that if you make inventory adjustments or modify transactions that include assemblies, builds that were previously final could become pending.

Disassembling Assemblies

"So, what if I accidentally build more assemblies than I really want? Am I stuck with them?" The answer is no. You can disassemble assemblies in any of the following ways:

- On an existing build transaction in the Build Assemblies window, reduce the quantity to build.
- Delete a build transaction completely.
- Use the Adjust Quantity/Value On Hand window to reduce the quantity of finished goods.

Printing the Components of Assemblies

"Is there an easy way to find out what components comprise an assembly item?" Open the Item List window, right-click the assembly, and click Print Assembly Item. If you don't want a paper report, you can preview the Bill Of Materials report on-screen.

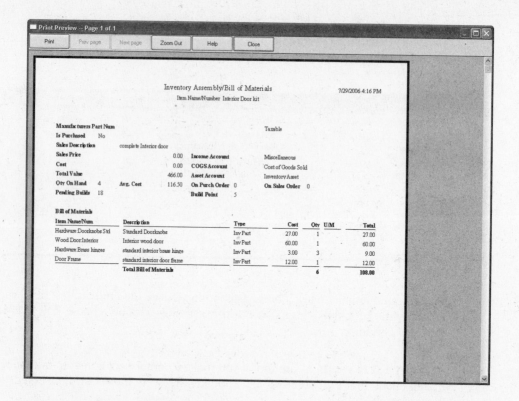

Counting Inventory

Although everyone makes a concerted effort to account for everything that comes and goes, you need to perform a physical inventory at least once each year—and twice in some industries—to make sure that your QuickBooks records match your physical inventory. While taking physical inventory isn't fun, it is important; remember, inventory is the lifeblood of businesses that sell products.

Printing the Physical Inventory Worksheet

Start by printing a Physical Inventory Worksheet (see Figure 10-8); choose Reports | Inventory | Physical Inventory Worksheet. This report lists your inventory items in alphabetical order, the item description, preferred vendor, and the current quantity on hand based on your QuickBooks transactions. In addition, there's a column that's set up to record the actual count as you walk around your warehouse with this printout (and a pen) in hand.

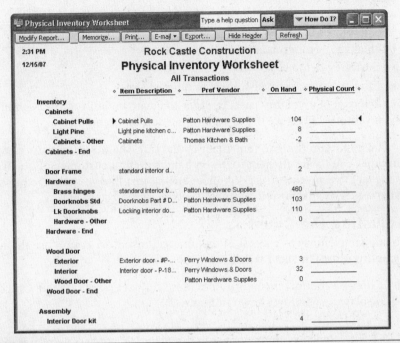

FIGURE 10-8 Use the column containing the blank lines to record physical inventory counts

Some businesses need the preferred vendor to help employees taking inventory to distinguish similar items that come from different vendors. If you have no use for the Pref Vendor column, you can remove it from the report if you drag the diamond on the right side of the column all the way to the diamond on the left side of the column.

The items appear on the report in alphabetical order, but you may want to reorganize the information to better support taking a physical inventory. For example, you may want to arrange the items to match the way that you've laid out your warehouse. Or, you may want to add bin numbers or row numbers to each item on the sheet. Click the Export button to export the Physical Inventory Worksheet report to Excel, where you can add warehouse location information and then sort the report using that location information.

Making Inventory Adjustments

After you've finished counting the inventory, you may find that the numbers on the worksheet don't match the physical count. In fact, it's almost a sure bet that the numbers won't match. Most of the time, the physical count values are lower than the values in QuickBooks. Typically, the discrepancy can be traced to breakage or to employee theft.

You can make adjustments to inventory at any time and for a variety of reasons:

- Breakage or other damage.
- Customer demo units.
- Gifts or bonuses for customers or employees.
- Removal of inventory parts in order to create prebuilt or preassembled inventory items (see the upcoming section on prebuilds).

The important thing to remember is that tracking inventory isn't just to make sure that you have sufficient items on hand to sell to customers. Equally important is the fact that inventory is a significant asset, just like your cash, equipment, and other assets. It affects your company's worth in a substantial way.

Adjusting the Count

To adjust inventory as a result of the physical inventory count, use the Adjust Quantity/Value On Hand window.

1 Choose Vendors | Inventory Activities | Adjust Quantity/Value On Hand to display the window shown in Figure 10-9.

$ NOTE: Inactive items appear in the Adjust Quantity/Value On Hand window.

2 In the Adjustment Date, enter the date.

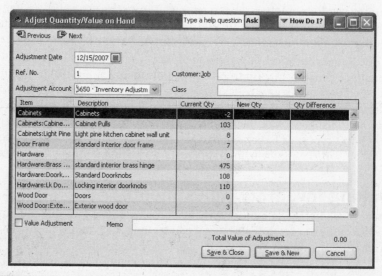

FIGURE 10-9   Correct the quantity and value of inventory to match the physical count

③ Use an optional reference number to track the adjustment. The next time you enter an adjustment, QuickBooks will increment the reference number by one.

④ In the Adjustment Account, choose the account to which you post inventory adjustments. If you don't have an inventory adjustment account, you can create one—typically, it's an expense account.

⑤ Select the item to adjust.

⑥ Use either the New Qty column or the Qty Difference column to enter the count. Whichever column you use, QuickBooks fills in the other column automatically.

⑦ Anything you enter in the Memo field appears on your Profit & Loss Detail report, which eliminates the question "What's this figure?" from your accountant.

Adjusting the Value

When you complete the entries, the total value of the adjustment you made appears in the lower right corner of the window. QuickBooks calculates that value using the average cost of your inventory. For example, if you received 10 widgets into inventory at a cost of $10.00 each and later received 10 more at a cost of $12.00 each, your average cost for widgets is $11.00 each. If your adjustment reduces the number of widgets by one, QuickBooks decreases the value of your inventory asset by $11.00.

You may need to change your inventory valuation. For example, an inventory item's market value may have declined. Your accountant wants you to change from the cost value to the market value for that item.

Click the Value Adjustment check box at the bottom of the window. QuickBooks adds the New Value column to the window (see Figure 10-10) and displays the

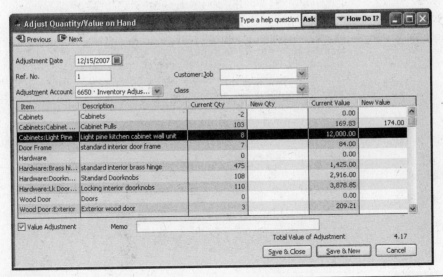

FIGURE 10-10 You can change the current value of any item

value of the total adjusted count for each item. If your inventory adjustment lowers the value of your inventory, QuickBooks debits the inventory adjustment account and credits the inventory asset account for the same amount. If your adjustment raises the value of your inventory, QuickBooks posts the debit to the inventory asset account and the credit to the inventory adjustment account.

Running Inventory Reports

You'll probably find that you run reports on your inventory status quite often. For most businesses, tracking the state of the inventory is the second most important set of reports (right behind reports about the current accounts receivable balances).

QuickBooks provides several useful, significant inventory reports, which you can access by choosing Reports | Inventory. A description of the available reports appears in Table 10-2.

Report	Description
Inventory Valuation Summary Report	This report gives you a quick assessment of the value of your inventory. By default, the date range is the current month to date. For each item, the report shows the item description, the quantity on hand, the U/M if enabled, the average cost, the asset value, the percent of total assets, the sales price, the retail value, and the percent of total retail value.
Inventory Valuation Detail Report	This report lists each transaction that involved each inventory item. The report shows no financial information about the price charged to customers, because your inventory value is based on cost. You can double-click any sales transaction line to see the details (and the amount you charged for the item). The report also includes assemblies and inventory adjustments in which the item was involved.
Inventory Stock Status	Among other things, this report shows the preferred vendor, the item reorder point, the number currently on hand, for sales orders, for assemblies, the U/M if enabled, a check mark to remind you to order items that are below the reorder point, the number currently on purchase orders, the next delivery date based on purchase order information, and the average number of units sold per week. Two versions of the report exist so that you can sort the information by item or by vendor.
Physical Inventory Worksheet	This is the report you print when it's time to take an inventory count. See the section "Counting Inventory" for more information.
Pending Builds	This report details the current state of assemblies you create from existing items (called *builds*, or *prebuilds*).
Inventory QuickReports	QuickReports provide valuable information about an individual inventory item or all inventory items. In the Item List window, select an item and press CTRL-Q to display a QuickReport.

TABLE 10-2   Inventory Reports

Some notes on the Inventory Valuation Summary Report:

- Because QuickBooks permits you to sell items you don't have in stock (let's hope you really do have them but you haven't used a QuickBooks transaction to bring them into stock), it's possible to have a negative number in this column.
- QuickBooks calculates asset value by multiplying the number on hand by the average cost.
- QuickBooks displays the sales price listed when you create the item; changes you make to prices as you sell aren't reflected in this report.
- QuickBooks calculates the retail value by multiplying the number on hand by the retail price.

Managing Bank and Credit Card Accounts

n this chapter:

- Making deposits
- Transfering funds between accounts
- Dealing with bounced checks
- Voiding disbursements
- Managing cash
- Balancing credit card statements

Working with a bank account involves more than writing checks; in this chapter, we'll walk through the wide variety of bank account–related activities, including making deposits, transferring funds between bank accounts, handling bounced checks, and voiding disbursements. Then we'll look at the ways you can use QuickBooks to handle tracking your credit card activity.

Making a Deposit

In Chapter 4, you saw how QuickBooks takes care of depositing money into your bank account when you receive money from customers. But there are times when you receive money that's unconnected to a customer payment. For example, you might receive a cash refund from a vendor or a rebate on a purchase you made.

Entering a deposit that isn't a customer payment into your QuickBooks check register isn't much different from entering a deposit into a manual checkbook register. Actually, it's easier because you don't have to make any calculations— QuickBooks takes care of that.

The window you choose to record these deposits depends on whether you plan to record the deposit as a single, separate deposit or whether you want to include the money in a deposit with other funds—even customer payments. If you plan to record the deposit as a single, separate deposit, you can enter it directly in the bank account register. If you intend to include the money in a deposit with other money, you can use the Make Deposit window.

To record the deposit directly in the register, click Check Register on the Home page or press CTRL-R and then select the bank account into which you intend to deposit the money. Fill in the date and then click in the deposit column to enter the amount. Assign the deposit to an account, and use the Memo field for an explanation of the deposit so that you'll remember where you got the money when your accountant asks you. Then click the Record button.

To enter the money as part of a deposit containing other checks or cash, use the Make Deposits window. I covered the Make Deposits window in detail in Chapter 4, so I'll summarize briefly here. Click Record Deposits on the Home page; in the

---

➡ FYI

Selecting an Account for a Deposit

If you're depositing your own money into the business, that's capital; you should post the deposit to a capital account (it's an equity account). If you're depositing the proceeds of a loan (from yourself or from a bank), post the deposit to the liability account for the loan (you may have to create the liability account). If you're making a deposit that's a refund from a vendor, you can post the amount to the expense account that was used for the original expense. When in doubt, ask your accountant.

Payments to Deposit dialog box, check the other transactions you want to include in this deposit and click OK. In the Make Deposits window that appears, click in the From Account box on a blank line and select the account that you want to assign to the deposit, and use the Memo field for an explanation of the deposit so that you'll remember where you got the money when your accountant asks you. In the Amount column, type the amount and click Save & Close.

Transferring Funds between Accounts

Moving money between bank accounts is a common procedure in business. If you have a bank account for payroll, you move money out of your operating account into your payroll account every payday. Some people deposit all the customer payments into a money market account (which pays interest) and then transfer the necessary funds to an operating account when it's time to pay bills. Others do it the other way around, moving money not immediately needed from the business operating account to a money market account. Lawyers, agents, real estate brokers, and other professionals have to maintain escrow accounts and move money between these accounts and the operating account.

QuickBooks makes it easy to transfer funds between accounts.

To make a transfer, follow these steps:

1. Choose Banking | Transfer Funds from the menu bar to open the Transfer Funds Between Accounts dialog box (see Figure 11-1).
2. Select the account containing the funds you want to transfer.
3. Select the account to which you want to transfer the funds.
4. Type the amount you want to transfer.
5. Click Save & Close.

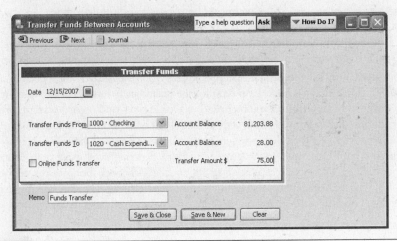

FIGURE 11-1   Transferring funds is easy

QuickBooks posts the transaction; you'll see it marked as TRANSFR in both bank accounts if you open their registers.

Handling Bounced Checks

Sometimes, a customer's check doesn't clear the bank because the customer didn't have sufficient funds in his or her account when you tried to deposit the check you received. The bank refers to this check as an NSF check—a nonsufficient funds check. You need to record the occurrence of the NSF check in QuickBooks so that you can maintain an accurate audit trail that describes the events as they happen. For example, if you deposit an NSF check, your bank will charge you a fee for processing the check and reduce the balance in your bank account. In QuickBooks, you need to account for the extra bank charge as well as for the reduction to your bank account caused by the NSF check. You also must decide if you are going to attempt to collect the debt. In addition, you might want to charge the customer the fees you incurred at your bank because of the bounced check. You may want to collect a service charge from the customer.

To record the transactions you need in QuickBooks to account for an NSF check, you do a little setup work and then you adjust your bank balance to reflect the NSF check. Then you decide whether you're going to redeposit the NSF check, and, if necessary, you reinvoice the customer for the money owed, for any bank charges you incurred, and for any service charges you impose for processing an NSF check.

➡ FYI

Why You Shouldn't Delete the NSF Payment

You may be tempted to simply delete the original payment to adjust the balance in your bank account. But deleting the transaction will not provide you with the correct audit trail of events. Your bank statement will show the deposit, and, if you delete the deposit, you will have trouble reconciling your bank statement; for more on reconciling your bank statement, see Chapter 12.

In addition, you may still expect the customer to pay; in this case, you may decide to redeposit the check or you may hold the check and wait for the customer to issue a new check. You may be tempted to delete the first payment you recorded in QuickBooks and record a second receipt when you redeposit the check. This approach also will not help you maintain an accurate audit trail that describes the events as they happen, and you won't have all the transactions you'll need to reconcile your bank statement. In this case, your bank statement will show both deposit attempts, as well as a transaction representing the uncollected check that reduces your cash balance. And, your bank statement will also show the bank's processing fee. Simply deleting the original payment and entering a new one will not address any of these issues.

Setting Up to Handle NSF Checks

To account for the bad check, you'll need an expense account—I call mine "Returned Checks." To create the account, click the Chart Of Accounts icon on the Home page. In the Chart of Accounts window, press CTRL-N. On the Select Account Type screen, select Expense and click Continue. In the Add New Account window that appears, type a name and click Save & Close.

You'll also need to set up a vendor—I call mine Returned Check Vendor. By using the same vendor for each NSF check, you can easily find NSF checks. Click the Vendor Center icon to display the Vendor Center. Then click the Vendors tab and press CTRL-N. Type the name of the new vendor and click OK.

Adjusting Your Accounts for the Bad Check

You need to reduce your bank balance by the amount of the NSF check. Most banks will allow you to try to redeposit an NSF check one additional time after your initial deposit. If the check comes back NSF the second time, the bank will not permit you to redeposit it again.

You use the technique I'm about to describe to adjust your bank balance twice—once before you attempt to redeposit, and once more if the check still doesn't clear the bank—with one slight difference. After you attempt to redeposit the check, record the following transaction *without* creating reimbursable expenses. The way you record the transaction the second time depends on whether the check cleared the bank after you redeposit it.

- If the check still doesn't clear after you try to redeposit it, record the transaction again and create reimbursable expenses.
- If the check *does* clear the second time, record the transaction again and create a reimbursable expense for *only* the amount of the bank service charge.

To adjust your bank balance, follow these steps:

1. Press CTRL-W to open the Write Checks window.
2. Select the bank account affected by the NSF check.
3. In the Pay To The Order of field, select the Returned Check Vendor.
4. In the Check Number field, type a number such as "RetChk." You can (and should) reuse an alphabetic entry in the Check Number field for the same vendor.
5. On the Expenses tab, select the Returned Checks expense account, enter the amount of the check, and select the customer who wrote the check in the Customer: Job column.
6. On a second line, select your Bank Service Charges account, supply the amount the bank charged you, and again, select the customer who wrote the check in the Customer: Job column (see Figure 11-2).

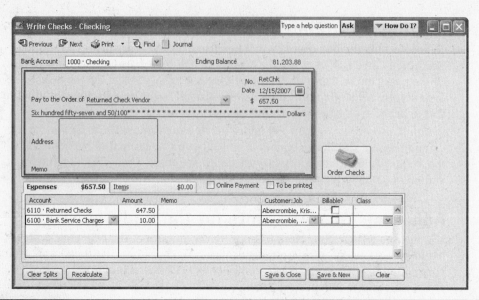

FIGURE 11-2   Record a check to adjust your bank account for the NSF check

NOTE: If you have not yet redeposited the bounced check, then don't create reimbursable expenses by removing the check marks from the Billable column. If the bounced check failed to clear after redepositing it, leave the check marks in the Billable column. If the bounced check cleared after you redeposited it, create a reimbursable expense for only the bank service charge.

⑦ Click Save & Close.

Attempting to Redeposit the NSF Check

If you intend to attempt to redeposit the NSF check, enter a deposit using the Make Deposits window. Enter the customer in the Received From field. Use the Returned Checks expense account in the From Account field. In the Memo field, note that this is a redeposit and enter the rest of the check information (see Figure 11-3).

If the check comes back marked NSF a second time and the bank will not permit you to redeposit it, perform the preceding steps and create reimbursable expenses. Then read on.

Recollecting the Debt

To account for recollecting an NSF check, you should send an invoice to your customer. The invoice should include the original amount of the NSF check and the service charge you incurred for processing the check. At your discretion, you

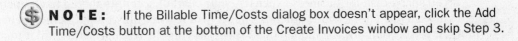

FIGURE 11-3 Recording an attempt to redeposit an NSF check

may add a penalty charge to the service charge amount to discourage customers from issuing NSF checks. Follow these steps:

1. Press CTRL-I to open the Create Invoices window.

2. Select the customer who issued the bad check. The Billable Time/Costs dialog box appears.

NOTE: If the Billable Time/Costs dialog box doesn't appear, click the Add Time/Costs button at the bottom of the Create Invoices window and skip Step 3.

3. Click Select The Outstanding Billable Time And Costs To Add To This Invoice? and click OK. The Choose Billable Time and Costs dialog box appears.

4. Click the Expenses tab. Two entries appear that represent the amount of the NSF check and the amount of your bank's service charge.

5. Check both entries.

6. Optionally, you can add your own fee in the Markup Amount or % box. If you do, select the Bank Service Charges account for the Markup Account.

7. Click OK. The charges appear on the invoice; you can edit the descriptions on the invoice to make them more meaningful.

8. Print the invoice.

Voiding Disbursements

Sometimes you have to void a check that you've written. Perhaps you decided not to send it for some reason, or perhaps it was lost in the mail. Whatever the reason, if a check isn't going to clear your bank, you should void it.

The process of voiding a check is quite easy, and the only trouble you can cause yourself is *deleting* the check instead of *voiding* it. Deleting a check removes all history of the transaction, interrupting the audit trail. Voiding a check keeps the record of the check number but sets the amount to zero.

To void a check, press CTRL-R and select the account containing the check you want to void; QuickBooks opens the bank account register. Right-click anywhere on the check's transaction line; QuickBooks opens a shortcut menu. Choose Void Check. QuickBooks automatically adjusts the expense accounts to which the check was posted. Click Record to save the transaction.

Tracking Cash

Although most of your transactions don't deal with cash directly, some do. Using an ATM machine makes it easy to take cash out of your bank account. Many businesses maintain a petty cash box to dispense cash to employees or owners who need cash as a reimbursement for money they've spent for the company or as an advance against future expenditures.

When you use cash, you have to account for both the portion you spend and the portion that remains in your pocket because the cash belongs to the business.

Creating a Petty Cash Account

If you spend cash for business expenses, your chart of accounts should have a petty cash account. This account functions like a cash register till: you put money in it, then you account for the money that's spent, leaving the rest in the till until it too is spent. Then you put more money into the till. The petty cash account doesn't represent a real bank account; it just represents that portion of the money in the real bank account that moved into the till. In QuickBooks, you use a bank account to track petty cash.

If you don't have a petty cash account in your chart of accounts, use these steps to create one:

1. Click the Chart Of Accounts icon on the Home page, or press CTRL-A to display the Chart Of Accounts window.
2. Press CTRL-N. The Select Account Type window appears.
3. Select Bank and click Continue. The New Account window appears, with the Account Type already selected.

④ If you number your accounts, use a number that places your new petty cash account near the other bank accounts in your chart of accounts.

⑤ Leave the opening balance at zero.

⑥ Click Save & Close.

Putting Money into Petty Cash

You have to put money into your petty cash till and account for it. Most of the time, you'll write a check for petty cash. To write the check, create a name in the Other Names list for the payee; I call mine "Cash." Then, use the Write Checks window or the register to write the check. Use the "Cash" name as the payee, and, on the Expenses tab, select the petty cash account.

 TIP: If you're going to obtain the petty cash account money using an ATM, you can account for it the same way you record an ATM Withdrawal, as described in the next section.

Recording ATM Withdrawals

When you withdraw money from your bank account with your ATM card, it's not an expense; it's petty cash. When you spend the cash, you'll incur an expense.

Using the ATM receipt and receipts for any stuff you purchased with the ATM cash back to the office, you need to record some transactions in QuickBooks.

First, take the cash out of your QuickBooks bank account and put it into your petty cash account using the Transferring Funds Between Accounts window; for details, see "Transferring Funds between Accounts" earlier in this chapter. Read on to record petty cash expenses.

Recording Petty Cash Disbursements

As you spend the money you withdraw via an ATM transaction, or by taking cash out of the petty cash box in the office, you must record those expenditures in the petty cash register.

 TIP: Don't let anyone take money out of the petty cash till without a receipt. If the money is an advance against a purchase instead of payment for a receipt, use an IOU. Later, replace the IOU with the purchase receipt.

Open the petty cash account register and use the receipts you've collected to assign expense accounts to the transaction. You can enter one transaction, splitting each receipt among all the affected expense accounts, or enter individual transactions. You can delete the check number that QuickBooks automatically inserts in the Number field, or you can leave the number there. You don't typically

►► FYI

Vendor or Other Name?

You may be wondering if you should enter a real payee, set up in the Vendor List, for each petty cash transaction. Typically, you set up vendors when you want to track information about a payee. In most cases, you don't really have any interest in tracking information about payees for petty cash transactions.

I suggest that you set up vendors for those payees from whom you receive bills, or to whom you disburse checks, and for whom you want to track activity.

reconcile the petty cash account, so it doesn't matter. You can either skip the Payee field or use a payee you set up in the Other Names list named Petty Cash.

If you spent less than the amount of cash you withdrew, the balance stays in the petty cash account in QuickBooks while the cash is in your pocket. When you spend it later, repeat this process to account for that spending.

Managing Your Credit Cards

When you use a business credit card, you have a couple of choices for tracking and paying the credit card bill. You can pay either the entire bill every month or part of the bill, and keep a running credit card balance. For either approach, you can choose between two methods of handling credit card purchases in QuickBooks.

- Treat the credit card bill as an ordinary vendor and enter the bill when it arrives.
- Treat the credit card bill as a liability and enter each transaction as it's made.

Treating Credit Cards as Vendors

You can set up your credit card as an ordinary vendor instead of a liability account and enter the bill into QuickBooks when it arrives. Most of the time, you post the expenses to multiple accounts, so the credit card bill transaction is a split transaction that credits Accounts Payable and debits each expense account you list (see Figure 11-4).

If you don't pay off the card balance each month, subsequent credit bills will contain interest charges in addition to your purchases. Post the interest charges to an interest expense account.

If you enter the bill in the Enter Bills window, and then use the Pay Bills window to write the check, select the oldest bill and make a partial payment or full payment. You can select additional bills and pay part or all of them, but always pay the oldest bill first.

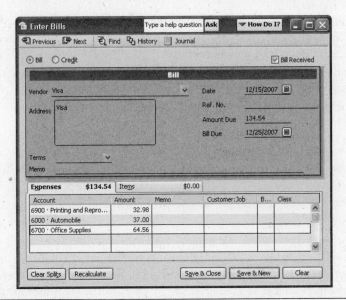

FIGURE 11-4   You usually post credit card bills to multiple accounts

Treating Credit Cards as Liability Accounts

You also can set up a credit card liability account and track each transaction against the account as it occurs. Then when the bill arrives, you match the transactions against the bill and decide how much to pay. Using this approach, the credit card liability account acts like an Accounts Payable account, but for only one vendor. QuickBooks maintains all of the transactions for your credit card separately from the rest of your Accounts Payable balance.

Creating a Credit Card Account

To create a credit card account, click the Chart Of Accounts icon on the Home page or press CTRL-A to display the Chart Of Accounts window. Then press CTRL-N to display the Select Account Type window. Select Credit Card and click Continue. In the New Account window, type a name for the credit card account, and, if you use account numbers, assign a number in the range of your liability accounts. Don't enter an opening balance and click Save & Close.

Entering Credit Card Charges

If you intend to enter each credit card charge when you incur it, you can

- Set up your credit card account for online banking and download the transactions (covered in Chapter 16).
- Enter transactions manually.

If you enable your credit card for online banking, there is no need to enter the transactions manually; downloading the transactions is faster, easier, and less error prone. See Chapter 16 for instructions.

To enter credit card charges manually, choose Banking | Enter Credit Card Charges to open the Enter Credit Card Charges window (see Figure 11-5).

Select the appropriate credit card account and then use the store receipt as a reference document to fill in the transaction.

- You can skip the Purchased From field.
- If the transaction is a return, be sure to select the Refund/Credit option at the top of the window.
- You can enter the receipt number in the Ref No. field.
- Enter the date of the purchase.
- Use the Expenses tab for general expenses; use the Items tab if you used the credit card to buy inventory items for resale.
- If you use the credit card to purchase an item or incur an expense for a customer, select the customer so you can bill the customer for reimbursement (see Chapter 6 for details about entering reimbursable expenses).

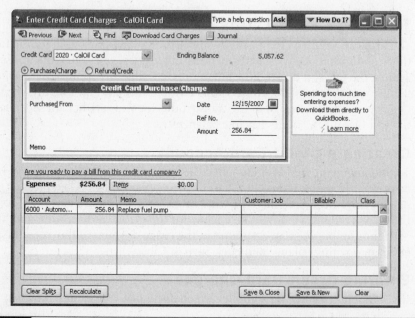

FIGURE 11-5   You can manually enter credit card transactions using this window

Click Save & New to save the record and record another credit card transaction, or click Save & Close if you're finished entering credit card charges.

 TIP: You can also enter these charges directly in the register of your credit card account.

Reconciling the Credit Card Bill

Eventually, the credit card bill arrives, and you have to perform the following chores:

- Reconcile the bill against the entries you recorded.
- Decide whether to pay the entire bill or just a portion of it.
- Write a check.

You can read about reconciling bank and credit card accounts in detail in Chapter 12. Before you can reconcile a bank or credit card account the first time, you need to set up the account's beginning balance; you'll find information about setting up the beginning balance for a bank or credit card account in Chapter 14. In the following section, I'll briefly describe the reconciliation process, which, for a credit card, ends with the option of paying the credit card bill.

Choose Banking | Reconcile from the QuickBooks menu bar to open the Begin Reconciliation window. In the Account field, select the credit card from the drop-down list. In the Begin Reconciliation dialog box enter the following data:

- The ending balance from the credit card bill.
- Any finance charges on the bill in the Finance Charge box, along with the date on which the charges were assessed.
- The account you use to post finance charges.

Click Continue to open the Reconcile Credit Card window, which displays the credit card purchases and payments you entered into QuickBooks. Click the check mark column for each transaction on your window that has a matching transaction on the credit card bill.

 NOTE: You can add any transactions you forgot to enter by opening the credit card register and entering the transactions. Right-click and choose Use Register. Or, select a transaction and click the Go To button to open the Enter Credit Card Charges window.

When the Difference is $0.00, click Reconcile Now. If the difference is not $0.00, read Chapter 12 to learn how to troubleshoot reconciliations.

Paying the Credit Card Bill

When you finish working in the reconciliation window, QuickBooks asks you whether you want to write a check now or create a vendor bill that you'll pay the next time you pay your bills.

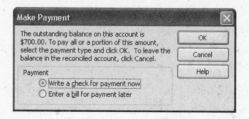

If you choose to enter a bill, QuickBooks debits your credit card liability account and credits your Accounts Payable account, moving the liability from one liability account to another. When you subsequently pay the bill using the Pay Bills window, QuickBooks will debit Accounts Payable and credit Cash (your bank account). If you choose to write a check, QuickBooks skips the step that moves the liability from one liability account to another; instead, QuickBooks debits the credit card liability account and credits Cash.

Select the appropriate response and click OK. QuickBooks opens either the Enter Bills or Write Checks window in the background; in the foreground, QuickBooks asks you to print a reconciliation report; see Chapter 12 to learn about printing reconciliation reports.

After you print your reconciliation report, you can click Save & Close in the Enter Bills window or the Write Checks window; QuickBooks has already filled in the window with all the necessary information.

Reconciling Bank Accounts

In this chapter:

- Reconciling an existing bank account the first time

- Using the Begin Reconciliation window

- Entering interest income and service charges

- Reconciling transactions

- Finishing reconciliation

- Printing reconciliation reports

- Troubleshooting reconciliation issues

Reconciling bank accounts is one of the most dreaded tasks connected with financial record keeping, but reconciling a bank account in QuickBooks can make the task much easier than reconciling on paper. In this chapter I'll go over the steps required to reconcile your bank accounts.

 NOTE: The information in this chapter also applies to credit card accounts that you reconcile.

Establishing the Bank Account's Opening Balance

When most people start using QuickBooks, they already have a bank account that they must set up in QuickBooks. Setting up the correct opening information is essential to successfully reconciling the account, both the first time and in the future. Before you try to reconcile your bank account or credit card account for the first time, see Chapter 14 to set the proper opening balance.

Using the Begin Reconciliation Window

After your bank statement arrives, you must find some uninterrupted moments to compare it to the information in the corresponding QuickBooks account.

If your bank sends your canceled checks in the envelope along with the statement, you can arrange the checks in numerical order before you start this task. However, instead of sorting and collating the physical checks, try using the list of check numbers on your statement, which appear in numerical order. An asterisk or some other mark usually appears to indicate a missing number; missing numbers can occur for any of these reasons:

- The bank hasn't yet processed a check.
- The bank processed the check in a previous period.
- You voided the check and didn't issue it, so the bank won't ever process it.

The process of reconciling makes sure that all transactions that appear on the bank statement also appear in the corresponding QuickBooks account. If the reconciliation process identifies transactions that appear on the bank statement but not in QuickBooks, you add them to QuickBooks using the same procedures you used to enter the transactions that appear both on the bank statement and in QuickBooks. Refer to Chapter 4 for details on making deposits and Chapter 7 for details on paying vendor bills and writing direct disbursement checks.

Reconciling your bank account starts with the Begin Reconciliation window, which you open by clicking the Reconcile icon on the Home page or by choosing Banking | Reconcile. If you have more than one bank account, select the account you want to reconcile from the drop-down list in the Account field.

NOTE: You also can reconcile credit card accounts; see Chapter 11 for details.

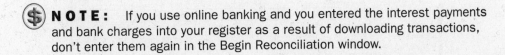

Compare the Beginning Balance field in the window against the beginning balance on the bank statement. If the beginning balances match, enter the ending balance from your statement in the Ending Balance field, enter the statement date, and continue reading.

If the beginning balances do *not* match, skip to the section "Troubleshooting Reconciliation Issues" later in this chapter. After you resolve the beginning balance issue, return to the next section "Enter Interest Income and Service Charges" and keep reading from there.

Entering Interest Income and Service Charges

If interest and bank service charges appear on your statement, enter those numbers in the Begin Reconciliation window and choose the appropriate account for these entries.

NOTE: If you use online banking and you entered the interest payments and bank charges into your register as a result of downloading transactions, don't enter them again in the Begin Reconciliation window.

By "bank charges," I mean the standard charges that banks assess, such as monthly charges that may be assessed for failure to maintain a minimum balance. Bank charges do not include special charges for bounced checks (yours or your customers') or any purchases you made that are charged to your account (such as the purchase of checks or deposit slips). You should enter those types of transactions as discrete transactions, using the Memo field to explain the transaction, to create an audit trail, and to make them easier to find in case you have to talk to the bank about your account.

Reconciling the Transactions

After you've filled out the information in the Begin Reconciliation dialog box, click
Continue to open the Reconcile window shown in Figure 12-1.

Setting Up the Reconcile Window

You can change the way that QuickBooks displays transactions to make it easier to
work in the window.

Eliminate Future Transactions

If the list is long, you can shorten it by selecting the option Show Only Transactions
On Or Before The Statement Ending Date. Theoretically, transactions that weren't
created before the ending date couldn't have cleared the bank. Removing them from
the window leaves only those transactions likely to have cleared. If you select this
option and your reconciliation doesn't balance, remove the check from the box so
you can clear the transactions in case one of the following scenarios applies:

- You issued a postdated check and the recipient cashed it early. Since it's rare for
  a bank to enforce the date, this is a real possibility.
- You made a mistake when you entered the date of the original transaction. You
  may have entered a wrong month or even a wrong year, which resulted in
  moving the transaction date into the future.

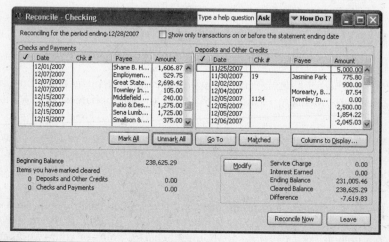

FIGURE 12-1   Uncleared transactions appear in the Reconcile window

Customize the Column Display

You can change the columns that display on each pane of the Reconcile window by clicking Columns To Display. Add or remove columns, depending on their usefulness to you as you clear transactions.

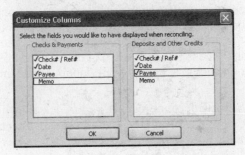

Clearing Transactions

To reconcile the bank statement with your QuickBooks bank account, you need to mark the transactions that appear on the bank statement as cleared transactions in QuickBooks.

In the Reconcile window, click each transaction that appears on the bank statement. A check mark appears in the leftmost column to indicate that the transaction has cleared the bank. If you clear a transaction in error, click again to remove the check mark—it's a toggle.

Use the following shortcuts to speed your work:

- If all, or almost all, of the transactions have cleared, click Mark All. Then click the transactions that didn't clear to unmark them.
- Mark (or unmark) multiple, contiguous transactions by dragging down the Cleared column.
- If the account you're reconciling is enabled for online access, click Matched to automatically clear all transactions that were matched in the QuickStatements you've downloaded over the month. QuickBooks asks for the ending date on the statement and clears each matched transaction up to that date.

As you check each cleared transaction, the Difference amount in the lower-right corner of the Reconcile window changes. The goal is to get that figure to $0.00.

Adding Transactions during Reconciliation

While you're working in the Reconcile window, if you find a transaction on the statement that you haven't entered into QuickBooks, such as one of those ATM withdrawals you forgot to enter, you don't have to shut down the reconciliation process to remedy the situation. You can just enter the transaction into the bank account register.

NOTE: Deposits that appear on the bank statement but not in QuickBooks can be the result of not having moved the money you collected for cash sales or customer receipts from Undeposited Funds to your bank account. If you find a deposit on the bank statement that doesn't appear in the Reconcile window, don't enter it in the bank account register. Instead, see the section "Pausing the Reconciliation Process" so that you can check the Make Deposits window for deposits you should have moved from Undeposited Funds to your bank account.

To open the bank account register, right-click anywhere in the Reconcile window and choose Use Register from the shortcut menu. When the account register opens, record the transaction. Return to the Reconcile window, where you'll see that transaction. Pretty nifty! Check it off as cleared, of course, because it was on the statement.

You can switch between the Reconcile window and the register for the account you're reconciling all through this process. Just click anywhere on the window you want to use to make it active.

Editing Transactions during Reconciliation

Sometimes you'll want to change some of the information in a transaction. For example, when you see the real check, you realize the amount you entered in QuickBooks is wrong. You might even have the wrong date on a check.

Whatever the problem, you can correct it by editing the transaction. Double-click the transaction in the Reconcile window to display it in the transaction window where you created it. Enter the necessary changes and close the window; answer Yes when QuickBooks asks if you want to record the changes. QuickBooks then redisplays the Reconcile window, where you see the changed transaction.

Deleting Transactions during Reconciliation

Sometimes you find that a transaction in the Reconcile window that shouldn't be there, such as an ATM withdrawal that you entered twice.

Because I'm not a fan of deleting transactions, I suggest that you void the transaction. Double-click the transaction; when it appears in the window where you created it, right-click it and choose "Void" or choose Edit | Void. Close the window and save your changes; when QuickBooks redisplays the Reconcile window, the transaction is gone.

Resolving Missing Check Numbers

Most bank statements list your checks in order and indicate a missing number with an asterisk. For instance, you may see check number 1234 followed by check number *1236 or 1236*. When a check number is missing, it means one of three things.

- The check cleared in a previous reconciliation.
- The check is still outstanding.
- The check number is unused and is probably literally missing.

If a missing check number on your bank statement is puzzling, you can check its status. To see if the check cleared in the last reconciliation, open the Previous Reconciliation report (discussed later in this chapter) by choosing Reports | Banking | Previous Reconciliation.

To investigate further, right-click anywhere in the Reconcile window and choose Missing Checks Report from the shortcut menu. When the Missing Checks Report dialog box appears, select the appropriate account and click OK. QuickBooks displays the Missing Checks report (see Figure 12-2).

If the Missing Checks report indicates that check numbers are missing, they truly are missing; they don't exist in the account register. Investigate the following possible causes:

- You deleted the check.
- The check is physically missing.
- While you were printing checks, your printer jammed, and you restarted check printing with the number of the first available check. In this case, QuickBooks doesn't mark checks as void; it just omits the numbers in the register.

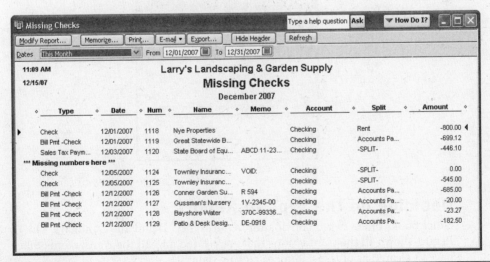

FIGURE 12-2 This report clearly identifies gaps in the check numbering sequence

Pausing the Reconciliation Process

If you find a deposit on the bank statement that doesn't appear in the Reconcile window or if the account doesn't reconcile (the Difference figure isn't $0.00), and you don't have the time, energy, or emotional fortitude to tackle the problem at the moment, you can stop the reconciliation process without losing the work you've done so far.

Click the Leave button in the Reconcile window and do something else for a while. QuickBooks saves the information you've recorded up to this point—the numbers on the Begin Reconciliation window and the entries you've cleared in the Reconcile window. When you restart the reconciliation process, you start at the point you left, with all your work in place.

Finishing the Reconciliation

If the Difference figure at the bottom of the Reconcile window displays $0.00, you've finished this part of the reconciliation. Click Reconcile Now and read the following section to print your reconciliation report. If the Difference amount is an amount other than $0.00, read the section "Troubleshooting Reconciliation Issues" later in this chapter.

Printing the Reconciliation Report

After you click Reconcile Now, QuickBooks offers to print a reconciliation report. The window has a Close button so that you can skip the report, but you should print the report; it can help you resolve reconciliation errors that may crop up in the future. And, it provides an audit trail of your work.

Deciding on the Type of Report

QuickBooks offers two reconciliation report types: Detail and Summary. The Detail Report shows all the transactions that are cleared and all the transactions that haven't cleared as of the statement closing date.

The Summary Report breaks down your transactions in the same way, but it doesn't list the individual transactions; it shows only the totals for each category: Cleared and Uncleared, breaking down the total for uncleared transactions into two categories and listing the number of transactions in each category.

- Checks and Payments
- Deposits and Credits

Selecting the Detail Report makes it easier to resolve problems in the future. You have a list of every check and deposit and when it cleared.

Printing the Reports

You also have to decide whether to print or to display the report. I suggest that you print both versions of the reconciliation report and attach them to your bank statement. Then, file both the bank statement and the report. Having these documents can make the difference between being able to fix the problem or having to undo the reconciliation and start from scratch, which can take hours.

Troubleshooting Reconciliation Issues

The number of things that can go wrong when you reconcile a bank account is the primary reason most people dread reconciling bank accounts. In this section, I'll present some common techniques you can use to resolve discrepancies.

When the Ending Balance and the Cleared Balance Differ...

When you're ready to investigate the cause of a difference between the ending balance and the cleared balance, follow the guidelines I present here to find the problem.

Count the number of transactions on the bank statement. Then look in the lower-left corner of the Reconcile window, where QuickBooks displays the number of items you have cleared. Mentally add another item to that number for each of the following:

- A service charge you entered in the Begin Reconciliation box
- An interest amount you entered in the Begin Reconciliation box

If the numbers differ, the problem lies in your QuickBooks company; there's a transaction you should have cleared but didn't, or a transaction you cleared that you shouldn't have.

If you're sure you didn't make any mistakes clearing transactions, do the following:

- Check for transposed figures by adding the digits of the amount QuickBooks displays as the Difference. If the digits sum to 9, or a multiple of 9, you're working with a transposed number. It's possible that you recorded a transaction for say $549.00 and the bank cleared the same transaction for $594.00.
- Check the amount of each transaction against the amount in the bank statement.
- Check your transactions and make sure a deposit wasn't inadvertently entered as a payment (or vice versa). A clue for this is a transaction that's half the difference. If the difference is $220.00, find a transaction that has an amount of $110.00 and make sure it's a deduction if it's supposed to be a deduction (or the other way around).

 TIP: You might want to let somebody else check over the statement and the register, because sometimes you can't see your own mistakes.

Resolving Unexpected Differences in the Beginning Balance

If this isn't the first time you've reconciled the bank, the beginning balance that's displayed on the Begin Reconciliation window should match the beginning balance on the bank statement. That beginning balance is the ending balance from the last reconciliation, and nothing should change its amount.

If the beginning balance doesn't match the statement, you probably performed one of the following actions:

- You changed the amount on a transaction that you had cleared previously.
- You voided a transaction that you had cleared previously.
- You deleted a transaction that you had cleared previously.
- You removed the cleared check mark from a transaction that you had cleared previously.

QuickBooks has a tool to help you figure out which one of those actions you took after you last reconciled the account. If you're viewing the Begin Reconciliation window, click the Locate Discrepancies button to open the Locate Discrepancies window and then click Discrepancy Report. If you've paused the reconciliation process and aren't viewing any of the reconciliation windows, you can choose Reports | Banking | Reconciliation Discrepancy to view the report.

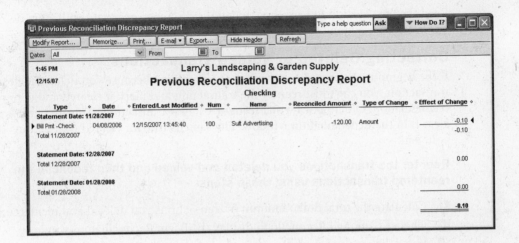

Understanding the Discrepancy Report

This report shows you the details of the transactions that cleared during a previous reconciliation and the transactions changed since that reconciliation. If the Reconciled Amount column shows a positive number, the original cleared transaction was a deposit; a negative number indicates a disbursement.

The Type Of Change column provides a clue about the action you must take to correct the unmatched beginning balances.

- **Uncleared** Means you removed the check mark in the Cleared column of the register even though QuickBooks warned you about the dangers of taking this action.
- **Amount** Means you changed the amount of the transaction by the amount in the Effect Of Change column.
- **Deleted** Means you deleted the transaction.

If you void a previously reconciled transaction, QuickBooks marks it as changed, and the Type Of Change is Amount. A transaction with a changed amount equal to and opposite of the original amount was almost certainly a transaction you voided after it cleared.

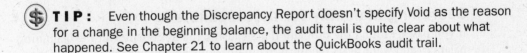

TIP: Even though the Discrepancy Report doesn't specify Void as the reason for a change in the beginning balance, the audit trail is quite clear about what happened. See Chapter 21 to learn about the QuickBooks audit trail.

For transactions where the Type Of Change is either Uncleared or Amount, open the register and correct the transaction—either check the Cleared column or change the transaction amount back to its original amount to undo your mistake.

Read the next section to learn how to handle discrepancies that result from deleted or voided transactions that you previously cleared.

Correcting Deleted or Voided Transactions

If the beginning balance doesn't match the statement because you deleted a cleared transaction, you can't just reenter the transaction and mark it cleared and continue reconciliation. QuickBooks won't recognize a new transaction as cleared unless you clear it in the Reconciliation window. The same is true for cleared transactions that you void.

Reenter the transactions you deleted and voided and then reconcile the reentered transactions using these steps:

1. Calculate the total dollar amount of transactions you deleted and reentered.
2. Choose Banking | Reconcile to display the Begin Reconciliation window.
3. Enter the result of the following calculation in the Ending Balance box:
   a) Subtract the amount of reentered checks or charges from the Beginning Balance amount.
   b) Add the amount of reentered deposits or credits to the amount you calculated in the preceding step.
4. In the Statement Date field, select the date of the statement you received from your financial institution that cleared these transactions. If you don't know this date, refer to reports you may have printed, or estimate a date just previous to your last reconciliation.

($) **IMPORTANT:** The date you enter can affect the accuracy of past reconciliation reports; try to keep the date within the timeframe covered by the statement on which these transactions cleared.

5. Click Continue to display the Reconcile window.
6. Mark each of the transactions you reentered as cleared. After you have selected all reentered transactions, the Difference amount in the lower right of the window should be zero.
7. Click Reconcile Now.
8. Print the reconciliation report.

Searching Manually for Discrepancies

If you haven't found the problem that's causing the discrepancy in the beginning balances and want to search for it manually, you can compare the reconciliation report and the account register. Any transaction that appears on the reconciliation report should also appear in the register.

- Check the amounts on the printed reconciliation report against the data in the register for amounts that changed after the account was reconciled. If you find any, restore the original amount.
- If a transaction appears in the register but is marked VOID, reenter it and reconcile it using the steps in the preceding section "Correcting Deleted or Voided Transactions." That transaction wasn't void when you performed the last reconciliation; it had cleared and shouldn't be marked void.
- If a transaction appears on the reconciliation report but not in the register, it was deleted. Reenter it and reconcile it using the steps in the preceding section "Correcting Deleted or Voided Transactions."

Viewing the Last Reconciliation Report

Even if you don't display or print a reconciliation report after you reconcile an account, QuickBooks saves the report. If you're trying to track down a discrepancy in the beginning balance, viewing the last reconciliation report may be helpful. QuickBooks Premier and QuickBooks Enterprise save multiple reconciliation reports.

To display a reconciliation report for a previous reconciliation, choose Reports | Banking | Previous Reconciliation. QuickBooks displays the Select Previous Reconciliation Report dialog box.

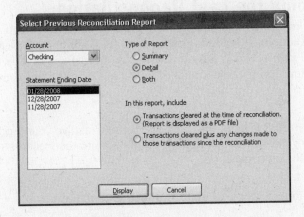

Select the type of reconciliation report you want to view; see "Deciding on the Type of Report" earlier in this chapter.

Then, select the transactions you want to include in the report. Choose Transactions Cleared At The Time Of Reconciliation (Report Is Displayed As A PDF File) to view an accurate account of your last reconciliation. If you printed a reconciliation report the last time you reconciled the account, the PDF file matches your printout.

➡ **FYI**

About PDF Files

PDF stands for Portable Document Format file; to view a PDF file, you must have Adobe Reader (or another PDF reader program) installed on your computer. If you don't, when you select this report QuickBooks opens a dialog box with a link to the Adobe web site, where you can download Acrobat Reader (it's free!). You cannot drill down on the PDF file to see transaction details because this report is not directly linked to your QuickBooks data.

Transactions Cleared Plus Any Changes Made To Those Transactions Since The Reconciliation is a report on the current state of the account register, sorted in a way to display the account's transactions according to cleared/uncleared/new categories. You can compare this report to the PDF version to help determine what has changed since a prior reconciliation, if you suspect cleared transactions were altered.

But you'll be best equipped to track down discrepancies if you print and file a reconciliation report every time you reconcile a bank account.

Undoing the Last Reconciliation

QuickBooks lets you undo the last reconciliation; when you undo the last reconciliation, QuickBooks unclears all transactions that cleared during that reconciliation. This is a good way to start over if you're mired in difficulties and confusion during the current reconciliation, and the problems seem to stem from the previous reconciliation.

 TIP: Just in case this process doesn't resolve your problem, back up your company file so you can restore the data in its reconciled state. See Chapter 21 for details on backing up.

Follow these steps to undo the last reconciliation:

1. Choose Banking | Reconcile the Begin Reconciliation dialog box.
2. Click the Locate Discrepancies button.
3. In the Locate Discrepancies window (see Figure 12-3), select the appropriate account.
4. Click Undo Last Reconciliation.
5. Click Continue.

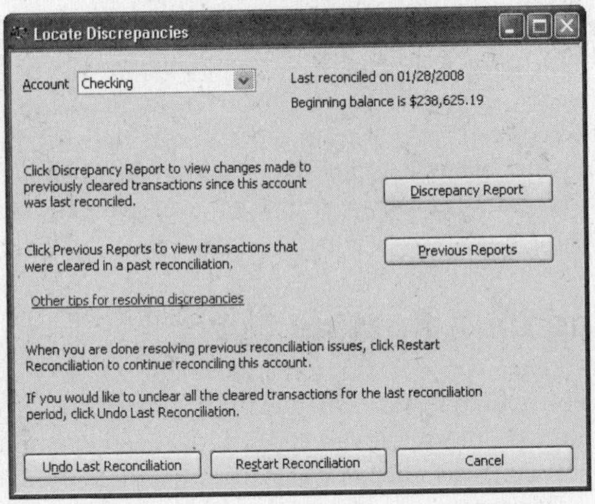

FIGURE 12-3   You can undo the last reconciliation from this window

QuickBooks performs the following actions:

- Removes the cleared status of all transactions you cleared during the last reconciliation
- Leaves the amounts you entered for interest and bank charges

When the process completes, QuickBooks displays a message that tells you the actions I just described were performed. Click OK to redisplay the Locate Discrepancies window.

If you let QuickBooks make an adjustment entry during the last reconciliation, which is often the catalyst for undoing and redoing reconciliation, click Cancel to close the window. Open the account's register and delete the adjustment entry—it's the entry posted to the Opening Bal Equity account.

Start the reconciliation process again. When the Begin Reconciliation window opens, the data that appears is the same data that appeared when you started the last reconciliation—the last reconciliation date, the statement date, and the beginning balance are back.

Enter the ending balance from the bank statement. Do *not* enter the interest and bank charges again; they weren't removed when QuickBooks undid the last reconciliation.

Good luck!

Giving Up the Search for a Reason

You may not be able to determine why an account won't reconcile. Sometimes, you just can't find the mistake. And, there's a point at which it isn't worth your time to keep looking for the error. You have to ask yourself, "Is it worth a bookkeeper's time at $20/hour to track down a $10 discrepancy?"

When you reach the point where you are ready to let the error go, give up and click the Reconcile Now button in the Reconcile window, even though the reconciliation won't balance. QuickBooks will make an adjusting transaction at the end of the reconciliation process, and if you ever learn the reason, you can remove that transaction.

Permitting an Adjusting Entry

When the Difference is not $0.00 in the Reconcile window and you click Reconcile Now, QuickBooks offers to make an adjusting entry. When you click Enter Adjustment, QuickBooks makes an entry in the bank account register. One side of the entry adjusts your cash balance and the other side of the entry posts to a Reconciliation Discrepancies account that QuickBooks automatically creates when you make an adjustment. If you ever figure out what the problem is, you can make the proper adjustment transaction and delete the adjusting entry.

Using Budgets and Planning Tools

In this chapter:

- Understanding budgets and QuickBooks

- Creating a budget

- Reporting on budgets versus actual figures

- Exporting budgets

- Projecting cash flow

- Using QuickBooks decision tools

A *budget* is a tool you use to help you track your progress against your plans. A well-prepared budget can also help you draw money out of your business wisely because knowing what you plan to spend on staff, overhead, or other expenses in the future prevents you from carelessly withdrawing profits when you have a good month.

Budgets and QuickBooks

Before you begin creating a budget, let's take a look at some information I think you'll find useful when you create a budget.

Types of Budgets

QuickBooks offers several types of budgets, and you can create one of each for a particular time period:

- Budgets based on your Balance Sheet accounts
- Profit & Loss budgets based on your income and expense accounts
- Profit & Loss budgets based on income and expense accounts and a customer or job
- Profit & Loss budgets based on income and expense accounts and a class (if you've enabled class tracking)

You can create Profit & Loss budgets from scratch or by using the actual figures from the previous year; you create Balance Sheet budgets from scratch.

Once you begin creating a budget, the data you record in the Set Up Budgets window reappears whenever you open the window. You create and edit a budget by choosing Company | Planning & Budgeting | Set Up Budgets; you'll learn more about the details of creating a budget later in this chapter in the section "Creating a Budget."

You can create only one of each type of budget for a particular time period. If you want to redo, for example, a Profit & Loss budget that you created, you edit the existing budget, which appears when you choose Company | Planning & Budgeting | Set Up Budgets. Your changes replace the original figures.

Deleting a Budget

Although you can't create two budgets of the same type for the same time period, you can delete an existing budget. Once you delete a budget, you can create a new budget of that type for that time period.

TIP: If you really want two budgets of the same type for the same time period, export the budget to Excel before you delete it and then create your new budget. See the section "Exporting Budgets" later in this chapter.

To delete a budget, choose Edit | Delete Budget from the QuickBooks menu bar while viewing the budget in the Set Up Budgets window.

Understanding the Budget Window

Let's review the purpose of the buttons you'll see in the Set Up Budgets window.

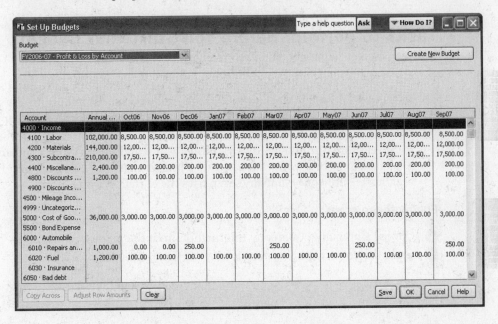

- **Clear**   Deletes all figures in the budget window—you cannot use this button to clear a row or column.
- **Save**   Records the current figures and leaves the window open so you can continue to work.
- **OK**   Records the current figures and closes the window.
- **Cancel**   Closes the window without saving any changes.
- **Create New Budget**   Opens the Create New Budget wizard. If you've entered any data, QuickBooks asks if you want to record your budget before closing the window. If you record your data (or have previously recorded your data with the Save button), the next time you open the Set Up Budgets window and view this budget, it will contain the data you recorded.

- **Show Next 6 Months**   Exists only if the display resolution of your computer is set lower than 1024 × 768; in this case, QuickBooks displays only 6 months of the budget in the window and adds buttons to the window to move the display to the next 6-month period, simultaneously changing the button name to Show Prev 6 Months. If your display resolution is equal to or higher than 1024 × 768, all 12 months of the year appear in the Set Up Budgets window, and you won't see these buttons.

You use the other buttons in the Set Up Budgets window when you're entering data, and I go over them later in this chapter in the section "Enter Budget Amounts."

Tasks to Perform Before You Start Your Budget

Before you create a budget, you need to check the following details:

- The accounts you need must appear in your chart of accounts; you cannot add accounts while you're working in a budget, and you cannot budget for any account you marked "inactive." For details on adding an account, see Chapter 2.
- The first month of the budget should be the same as the first month of your fiscal year for your budget to work properly. If you don't run your company on a calendar year or if you want to create a budget that's not based on your fiscal year, make sure your company setup uses the correct starting month.

Follow these steps:

1. Choose Company | Company Information from the menu bar.
2. Enter the correct starting month for your fiscal year and click OK.

 N O T E :   The tax year doesn't affect budgeting.

Creating a Budget

Because you can't predict the amounts for most Balance Sheet accounts, most companies budget only for a few Balance Sheet accounts; for example, most companies will have a budget to purchase and replace equipment and other fixed assets. Since budgeting for Profit & Loss accounts is more multifaceted than Budgeting for Balance Sheet accounts, I'm going to focus on creating Profit & Loss budgets.

To create a Profit & Loss budget, follow these steps:

1. Choose Company | Planning & Budgeting | Set Up Budgets. If this is the first budget you're creating, the Create New Budget wizard opens automatically. If you've already created a budget, the Set Up Budgets window displays with your existing budget; click Create New Budget to start the wizard.

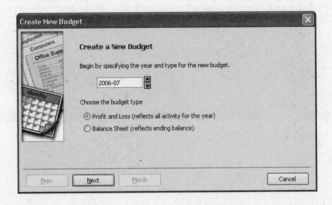

② Enter the year for which you're creating the budget.

NOTE: If you're not operating on a calendar year, the budget year field spans two calendar years, for instance, 2007–08 to accommodate your fiscal year.

③ Select Profit & Loss and click Next.

④ Select any additional criteria for this budget and click Next. You can include customers and jobs or classes in your budget. For this example, I'll create a Profit & Loss budget unconnected to customers or classes. I'll explain later in this chapter how to budget for customers and jobs, and for classes.

⑤ Choose between creating a budget from scratch or from the figures from last year's activities. I'll start by creating a budget from scratch; you can read about using last year's data to create a budget later in this chapter in the section "Create a Budget from Last Year's Data."

⑥ Click Finish to display all your income and expense accounts in the Set Up Budgets window (see Figure 13-1).

NOTE: Use Steps 1 to 3 to create a Balance Sheet budget, but, in Step 3, select Balance Sheet instead of Profit & Loss. Then, skip to Step 6.

Enter Budget Amounts

To create budget figures for an account, select the account and then click in the column of the first month for which you want to budget. Enter the budget number, press TAB and enter the appropriate amount for the next month. Repeat until you've entered budget values for all the months for this account. As you enter each monthly amount and press TAB, QuickBooks automatically calculates and displays the annual total for the account (see Figure 13-2).

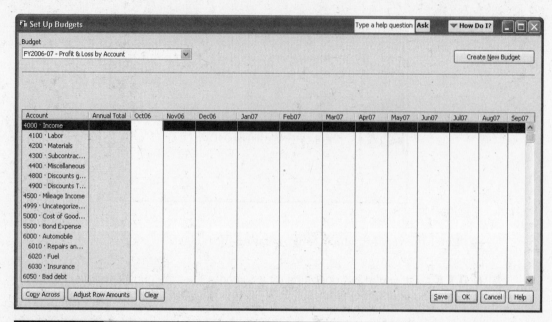

FIGURE 13-1 All active income and expense accounts appear in the Set Up Budgets window

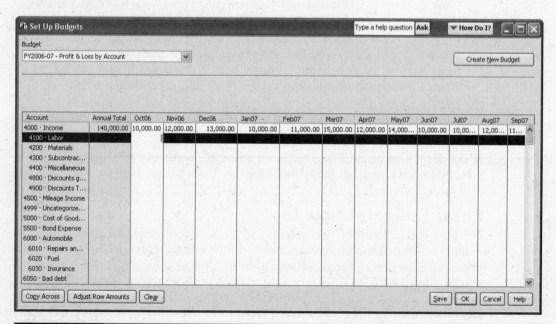

FIGURE 13-2 QuickBooks takes care of tracking the running total of your budget entries

NOTE: If you see the Show Next 6 Months button, when you enter the amount for the sixth month, click it to continue entering budget values for the rest of the months. When you finish entering the figures for the twelfth month, click Show Prev 6 Months to redisplay the first half of the year and the next row.

Copy Numbers Across the Months

You can copy a monthly figure from the month containing the insertion point to all succeeding months. Click in a month, enter the figure, and click Copy Across instead of pressing TAB. QuickBooks copies the numbers to all the rest of the months of the year.

If you enter your rent in the first month and choose Copy Across, you've saved a lot of manual data entry. If your landlord sends you a notice that your rent is increasing beginning in July, you can easily adjust the July–December budget figures. Just place the insertion point in July, enter the new rate, and click Copy Across.

You can also use the Copy Across button to clear a row. Delete the figure in the first month and click Copy Across. QuickBooks removes any entries from all months in the row.

Create a Budget from Last Year's Data

If you used QuickBooks last year, you can create a budget based on last year's actual figures. Use the steps that appeared in the section "Creating a Budget" with one exception: in Step 5, select the option to create the budget from the previous year's actual figures.

The Set Up Budgets window appears, displaying last year's actual data (see Figure 13-3). For each account that had activity, the ending monthly balances appear in the appropriate month.

When you build a budget using last year's figures, you can use some techniques that are effective once numbers appear in the Set Up Budgets window.

Automatically Increase or Decrease Monthly Figures

Once figures appear in all the months on an account's row, you can raise or lower monthly figures automatically. For example, you may want to raise an income account by an amount or a percentage starting in a certain month because you expect to sign a new customer or a new contract.

Select the first month that you want to adjust and click Adjust Row Amounts to open the Adjust Row Amounts dialog box.

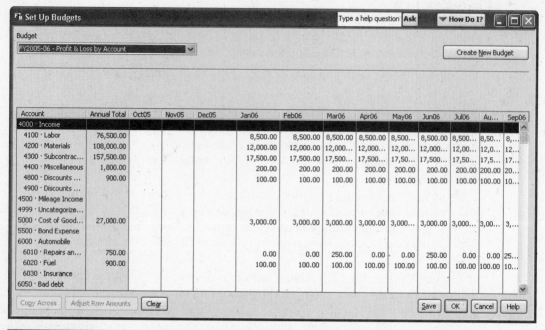

FIGURE 13-3 Build a budget using last year's figures as a starting point

$ TIP: If you intend to adjust all amounts starting from the first month, it doesn't matter where the insertion point appears on the account's row.

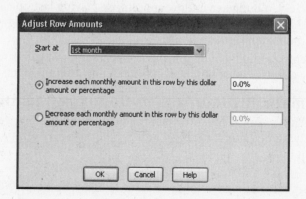

Choose 1st Month or Currently Selected Month as the starting point for the calculations; for this example, I chose Currently Selected Month.

To increase the existing amount by a specified amount, click the first option and enter the amount. You also can increase the existing amount by a percentage: enter the percentage rate and the percentage sign.

To decrease the existing amount by a specified amount, click the second option and enter the amount. You also can decrease the existing amount by a percentage: enter the percentage rate and the percentage sign.

Compound the Changes

If you select Currently Selected Month in the Adjust Row Amounts dialog box, QuickBooks adds an additional option to the dialog box: the Enable Compounding check box.

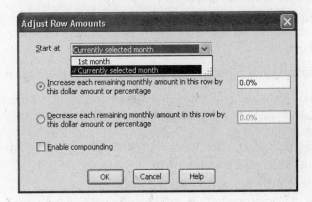

$ TIP: Although the Enable Compounding option appears only when you select Currently Selected Month, if you place the insertion point in the first month and select the Currently Selected Month option, you can use compounding for the entire year.

When you enable compounding, QuickBooks increases or decreases the calculations for each month based on a formula starting with the currently selected month and taking into consideration the resulting change in the previous month.

Use Table 13-1 to compare the results of using compounding versus not using compounding. For this example, assume the following conditions:

- Initially all months for the row are empty.
- You enter $1,000.00 in the first month.
- You choose Currently Selected Month in the Start At box of the Adjust Row Amounts dialog box.
- You choose to increase by $100.00.

Compounding Enabled?	Current Month Original Figure	Current Month New Figure	Next Month	Next Month	Next Month	Next Month
Yes	1,000.00	1,000.00	1,100.00	1,200.00	1,300.00	1,400.00
No	1,000.00	1,100.00	100.00	100.00	100.00	100.00

TABLE 13-1   Compounding versus Not Compounding

Customer:Job Budgets

You can create a Profit & Loss budget for a customer or job. Usually, you only do this for a project that involves a substantial amount of money and/or covers a long period of time.

To create you're a budget for a customer or a job, follow these steps:

1. Choose Company | Planning & Budgeting | Set Up Budgets. If this is the first budget you're creating, the Create New Budget wizard opens automatically. If you've already created a budget, the Set Up Budgets window displays with your existing budget; click Create New Budget to start the wizard.
2. Enter the year for which you're creating the budget.
3. Select Profit & Loss and click Next.
4. On the Additional Profit and Loss Budget Criteria screen of the wizard, select Customer: Job and click Next.
5. Choose to create a budget from scratch and click Finish. QuickBooks displays your income and expense accounts in the Set Up Budgets window.

The Set Up Budgets window contains a new field—the Current Customer: Job drop-down list box; select the Customer: Job for this budget from the drop-down list.

You can enter a monthly budget figure for each account as you did for a regular Profit & Loss budget. Or, you can enter a total budget figure in the first month. The latter option lets you compare accumulated data for expenses against the total budgeted figure by creating modified reports, where you change the report date to reflect the elapsed time for the project and filter the report for this job only.

If the project is lengthy, you may budget some accounts for some months and other accounts for other months. For example, if you have a project that involves purchases of goods, followed by installation of those goods, or training for the customer's employees, you might choose to budget the purchases for the first few months and then the cost of the installation or training for the months in which those activities occur. Don't forget to click the Save button to save your work.

CAUTION: Customer:Job budgets don't work unless you're faithful about assigning transactions to the customer or job. If you've only been filling in the Customer:Job fields when the customer is billable, you won't be able to produce accurate budget versus actual reports.

After you've created one budget based on a customer or job, creating a budget for a different customer or job is simple. After you save the first customer: job budget, display it in the Set Up Budgets window by opening the Budget drop-down list and selecting it. Then, select a different customer:job customer from the drop-down list and begin entering data; when you finish, click the Save button to save the budget for the second customer: job.

Class Budgets

If you're using class tracking, you can link your budget to any class you've created. If you're using classes to track income and expenses for branch offices, company divisions, or company departments, you can create useful budgets.

Look at your class-based reports, and if you find yourself asking, "Aren't those expenses higher than they should be?" or "Why is one class less profitable than the other classes?," you might want to budget for that class to get a handle on where and when expenses got out of hand. If you find yourself asking, "Is this department contributing the income I expected?," include income accounts in your budget. You can use income accounts in class budgets to provide incentives to your employees— perhaps a bonus to a manager if the reality is better than the budget.

To create a class-based budget, use the steps described earlier to create a budget and choose Class on the Additional Profit And Loss Budget Criteria wizard screen. When QuickBooks displays the Set Up Budgets window, a Current Class field appears. Select the class for which you want to create a budget from the drop-down list and begin entering data.

To create class budgets for other classes, use the first budget for a class as a foundation.

Budget Reports

QuickBooks provides a number of budget reports you can use to see how you're doing. To print these reports, choose Reports | Budgets & Forecasts from the menu bar and then select one of the following reports:

- Budget Overview
- Budget vs. Actual
- Profit & Loss Budget Performance
- Budget vs. Actual Graph

Budget Overview

QuickBooks supplies a wizard to help you produce an overview of a Profit & Loss budget, a Balance Sheet budget, a Customer:Job budget, and, if you use classes, a Class budget. Regardless of the type of budget you choose, the report shows the accounts you budgeted and the amounts you budgeted for each month. The report doesn't include accounts that you didn't include in the budget.

Profit & Loss Budget Overview

If you created a Profit & Loss budget, select Profit & Loss By Account on the first Budget Report wizard screen and click Next. On the next screen, select the Account by Month layout. Click Next, and then click Finish. The report opens and looks like the Profit & Loss Budget Overview report in Figure 13-4. Essentially, the Overview report type produces the display you'd see if the window you use to create a budget had a button labeled Print The Budget.

If you use subaccounts in your budget, you can click the Collapse button at the top of the report window to see only the parent account totals. The button name changes to Expand, and clicking it makes the subaccount lines reappear on the report.

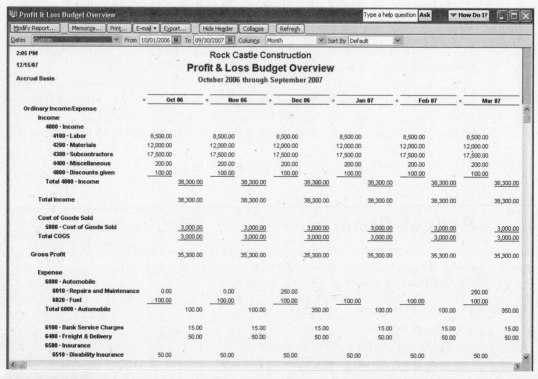

FIGURE 13-4   The Profit & Loss Budget Overview displays your budget in an easy-to-read format

Use the Columns drop-down list to select a different interval. The default is Month, but you can choose another interval, and QuickBooks will calculate the appropriate figures. For example, you might want to select Quarter to see four columns of three-month subtotals.

If you want to tweak the budget, or play "what if" games by experimenting with different numbers, click the Export button to send the report to Microsoft Excel. See "Exporting Reports" later in this chapter for more information on exporting budget reports to Excel.

Balance Sheet Budget Overview

You print the Balance Sheet version of the Budget Overview using the technique described in the preceding section, selecting Balance Sheet By Account on the first Budget Report wizard screen, and then clicking Next. QuickBooks displays a graphical representation of the report's monthly layout. Click Finish to see the report.

Customer:Job Budget Overview

To print a Budget Overview report for a customer: job, select Profit & Loss By Account And Customer:Job on the first Budget Report wizard screen and click Next. Select a report layout from the drop-down list and click Finish:

- **Account By Month**   Lists each account you used in the budget and displays the total budget amounts (for all customer budgets you created) for each month that has data. No budget information for individual customers appears.
- **Account By Customer: Job**   Lists each account you used in the budget as a row on the report and each customer appears in a column. This report also includes a column that displays the annual total for each account.
- **Customer: Job By Month**   Displays a row for each customer that has a budget and a column for each month. The report includes budget totals for each month and each customer: job; no individual accounts appear on this report. Each job that has a budget appears as a row under the appropriate customer's row.

Class Budget Overview

If you created a Class budget, select Profit & Loss By Account And Class on the first Budget Report wizard screen and click Next. Select a report layout from the drop-down list and click Finish.

- **Account By Month**   Lists each account you used in the budget and displays the total budget amounts for each month that has data. No budget information for individual classes appears.
- **Account By Class**   Lists each account you used in the budget as a row and each class as a column. This report also includes a column that displays the annual total for each account.

- **Class By Month**   Displays a row for each class that has a budget and a column for each month. The report includes totals for each month and each class; no individual accounts appear on this report.

Budget vs. Actual

This report's name says it all—you can see how your real numbers compare to your budget figures. For a straight Profit & Loss budget, the report displays the following data for each month of your budget, for each account:

- Amount posted
- Amount budgeted
- Difference in dollars
- Difference in percentage

Like the Budget Overview report, you produce this report using the Budget Report wizard, and the choices for the budget type are the same as the Budget Overview.

This report lists all of the accounts in your general ledger, even if you didn't include them in your budget. However, only the accounts you used in your budget show budget figures. You can remove accounts that don't show budget figures by customizing the report. Click the Modify Report button at the top of the report window. In the Modify Report dialog box, click the Advanced button to open the Advanced Options dialog box. Click the Show Only Rows And Columns With Budgets option. Click OK twice to redisplay the Budget Vs. Actual Report window, which now displays only data connected to your budgeted accounts.

 TIP: You can memorize the report settings so you don't have to make these modifications the next time you want to view the report. Click the Memorize button at the top of the report window and then give the report a meaningful name. To view the memorized report, choose Reports | Memorized Reports.

Profit & Loss Budget Performance

This report, similar to the Budget vs. Actual report, displays your actual income and expenses compared to what you budgeted for the current month and the year to date.

By default, the date range is the current month, but you can change that to see last month's figures or the figures for any previous month. You use the Budget Report wizard to create this report, and you make the same choices you made to produce the other reports described in this chapter. For details on the report choices, see the section "Budget Overview" earlier in this chapter.

Budget vs. Actual Graph

To produce the Budget vs. Actual Graph report, choose Reports | Budgets & Forecasts | Budget vs. Actual Graph; all the choices you can make that determine the appearance of the graph appear as buttons across the top of the report. Click the type of report you want to see.

Exporting Budgets

If you need to manipulate your budgets and you have Excel installed, you can export your budgets to Excel.

Use the following steps:

1. Prepare the report you want to export using the steps outlined in the preceding sections.
2. When the report appears on-screen, click Export. The Export Report dialog box appears.
3. On the Basic tab, select A New Excel Workbook.
4. On the Advanced tab, check the Auto Outline and Auto Filtering boxes, leaving the rest of the options as they appear by default.

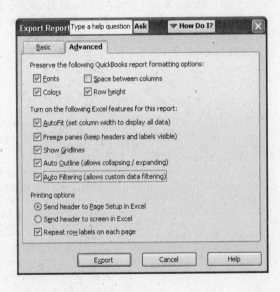

5. Click Export. Excel opens, containing your report. You can use the Auto Outline and Auto Filtering features of Excel to hide and display data.

Analyzing Your Business

QuickBooks includes a number of tools you can use to analyze your fiscal condition and make decisions about the way you manage your business. You can see the list of tools on the submenu displayed when you choose Company | Planning & Budgeting | Decision Tools. Table 13-2 provides a brief description of each tool; you can get more information on each tool from QuickBooks Help (choose Help | QuickBooks Help), or by clicking the Help button you'll find as you use the tool.

Tool	Menu Command	Purpose
Forecasts	Company | Planning & Budget | Set Up Forecast	This tool creates a forecast for revenue and cash flow. The process, the user interface, and the linked reports for the forecast feature all closely resemble the QuickBooks budget feature.
Cash Flow Projector	Company | Planning & Budget | Cash Flow Projector	Expanding on the cash flow reports available in QuickBooks, this tool builds a report that projects your cash flows using your own criteria while letting you remove and add accounts and adjust figures.
Measure Profitability	Company | Planning & Budget | Decision Tools | Measure Profitability	A tool that looks at your profit margin and offers advice based on that data.
Analyze Financial Strength	Company | Planning & Budget | Decision Tools | Analyze Financial Strength	This tool calculates your Current Ratio, which compares your current assets to your current liabilities, and helps you determine whether the amount of cash and assets your business has available is sufficient to manage emergencies and continue operation in spite of slow accounts receivable collections.
Compare Debt And Ownership	Company | Planning & Budget | Decision Tools | Compare Debt And Ownership	This tool examines your data and calculates the debt-to-equity ratio, which analyzes the amount of assets in your business that is controlled by debt. The more equity-owned assets, the easier it is to use your company's assets as collateral.
Depreciate Your Assets	Company | Planning & Budget | Decision Tools | Depreciate Your Assets	Although this tool doesn't read data from your QuickBooks company, it enables you to enter information about each asset you own and then calculate depreciation using one of three depreciation methods: Straight Line, Sum Of The Years' Digits, or Double Declining Balance. The Fixed Asset Manager (see Appendix A) is a more powerful tool.

TABLE 13-2   QuickBooks Tools to Analyze Your Business

Tool	Menu Command	Purpose
Manage Your Receivables	Company | Planning & Budget | Decision Tools | Manage Your Receivables	This tool helps you improve credit management by creating and implementing a credit policy.
Employee, Contractor or Temp?	Company | Planning & Budget | Decision Tools | Employee, Contractor or Temp?	This tool provides a brief overview of the differences between employees and independent contractors, along with some explanation of the risks involved in choosing to treat workers as independent contractors when IRS rules don't support your decision. For details, visit www.irs.gov/govt/fslg/article/0,,id=110344,00.html.
Improve Your Cash Flow	Company | Planning & Budget | Decision Tools | Improve Your Cash Flow	This tool offers suggestions for improving your cash flow and provides information about QuickBooks features that can help you collect receivables.
Periodic Tasks	Company | Planning & Budget | Decision Tools | Periodic Tasks	This tool provides general advice about QuickBooks tasks that you should perform on a periodic basis.

TABLE 13-2   QuickBooks Tools to Analyze Your Business (*continued*)

Using Journal Entries

I *n this chapter:*

- Understanding the QuickBooks journal entry window

- Entering the opening trial balance

- Making adjustments to the general ledger

- Depreciating fixed assets

- Journalizing outside payroll services

Chapter 14

As you work in the transaction windows in QuickBooks, QuickBooks transfers the amounts involved in the financial transactions to your general ledger. In addition to updating the general ledger using transaction windows, you can enter numbers directly into the general ledger using a journal entry transaction.

You should use journal entries, also called general journal entries, only when you can't find a standard transaction window to accomplish the task of updating the general ledger.

The QuickBooks Journal Entry Window

You record journal entries using the Make General Journal Entries window (see Figure 14-1). The format of the transaction window matches the standard approach to viewing the general ledger: columns for account numbers, debit amounts, and credit amounts (called a *T-Account* format). In addition, QuickBooks provides a memo column and columns you can use to link the journal entry information to customers and classes. A list of existing journal entries appears at the bottom of the window; you can hide the list by clicking the Hide List of Entries button.

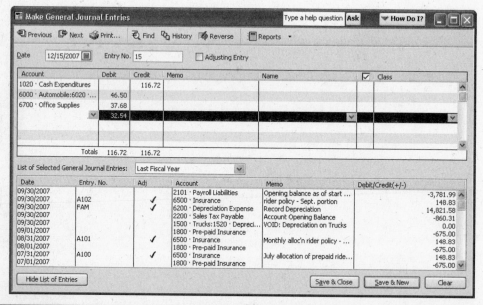

FIGURE 14-1   As you enter a journal entry, QuickBooks displays the remaining balance of the entry on the last line so you don't have to recalculate

To create a journal entry, follow these steps:

1 Choose Company | Make General Journal Entries. A message telling you that QuickBooks automatically assigns numbers to journal entries. You can enable and disable the automatic numbering feature in the Accounting category of the Preferences dialog box.

2 Check the Do Not Display This Message In The Future box and then click OK.

3 Click in the Account column, and then click the arrow to see a drop-down list of your chart of accounts. Choose the account you need.

4 Press TAB to either the Debit or Credit column, whichever is appropriate for this line of the entry, and enter the amount for the selected account.

5 Repeat Steps 3–4 for all the lines of the journal entry.

As you enter each amount, QuickBooks displays the offsetting total in the next line. For example, if the lines you've entered so far have a higher total for the debit side than the credit side, then the next line presents the balancing offset.

Use the columns QuickBooks adds to a traditional journal entry window in the following ways:

- Use the Memo column to describe the purpose of the journal entry, which will appear in account registers and on reports.

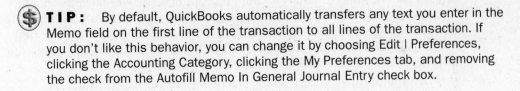

TIP: By default, QuickBooks automatically transfers any text you enter in the Memo field on the first line of the transaction to all lines of the transaction. If you don't like this behavior, you can change it by choosing Edit | Preferences, clicking the Accounting Category, clicking the My Preferences tab, and removing the check from the Autofill Memo In General Journal Entry check box.

- Use the Name column to link the selected line of the journal entry to a customer, vendor, employee, or other name. You must supply a name if you assign a journal entry line to an A/R or A/P account.

- If you select an expense account and assign a customer name to it, you can make the expense reimbursable if you click in the column beside the Name column.

- If you enabled classes, you can use the Class column to assign the line to a class. See Chapter 21 for information about classes.

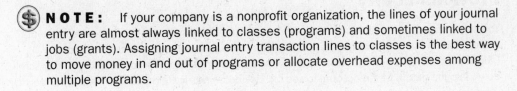

NOTE: If your company is a nonprofit organization, the lines of your journal entry are almost always linked to classes (programs) and sometimes linked to jobs (grants). Assigning journal entry transaction lines to classes is the best way to move money in and out of programs or allocate overhead expenses among multiple programs.

Entering the Opening Balances

If you opted to skip entering opening balances during your EasyStep Interview, or when you created new accounts, you need to enter the opening balances for your accounts. If you start using QuickBooks at or near the beginning of your fiscal year, you only need to establish opening balances for the balance sheet accounts; you can add any transactions that took place since the beginning of the year to update income and expense accounts and create a thorough history of transactions.

Consult your accountant to determine each account's opening balance. You can ask your accountant to provide you with a Trial Balance as of the day before you start using QuickBooks. Then, to establish the opening balances of your Balance Sheet accounts, enter a journal entry that does *not* include bank accounts and credit card accounts for which you record every transaction, Accounts Receivable, Accounts Payable, or Inventory; the next sections explain how to handle the details for these accounts. Post the amount needed to balance the entry to the Opening Bal Equity account. After you enter *all* opening balances, including the ones described in subsequent sections of this chapter, the balance in the Opening Bal Equity account should be $0.

The technique that I describe here lets you use the Opening Bal Equity account to check your work, record details that provide a good audit trail, and have the transactions you need to track outstanding balances. The total amount that you enter in the Opening Bal Equity account on your opening journal entry should equal the sum of the amounts you will enter using the techniques I describe in the next few sections to update bank and credit card accounts, Accounts Receivable, Accounts Payable, Inventory, and payroll liability accounts. The transactions you will enter will offset the amount in the Opening Bal Equity account.

When you finish entering opening balances—the journal entry and the transactions I'm about to describe—print your Balance Sheet report; if the Opening Bal Equity account equals $0, it won't appear on the report and you've successfully entered your opening balances. If the Opening Bal Equity account appears on the report, it does *not* equal $0; you've probably missed an individual transaction that you should have entered.

➡ FYI

Previous Equity

You can create a separate equity account for your previous equity; using a separate account makes it easier to maneuver numbers at the end of the year when you're closing books. QuickBooks will post profit (or loss) to the Retained Earnings equity account, and you can scroll down into the details of the account to see the closing entries to Retained Earnings separately by year, making it less necessary to set up a separate equity account for previous equity.

If you start QuickBooks so late in the year that you don't want to enter individual transactions since the beginning of the year, you can create a separate journal entry for the opening balances of income and expense accounts and post the amount needed to balance the entry to the Opening Bal Equity account.

Entering Opening Balances for Bank Accounts and Credit Card Accounts

NOTE: Everything I say in this section about bank accounts also applies to credit card accounts. To keep things simple, I'll talk in terms of bank accounts; if you're working with a credit card account, change the words "bank account" to "credit card account."

When most people start using QuickBooks, they already have a bank account that they must set up in QuickBooks. And, establishing the correct opening information for an existing bank account that you set up in QuickBooks includes two kinds of information:

- Setting the correct opening balance.
- Recording transactions that occurred but did not clear your bank before you started using QuickBooks.

Setting up the correct opening information is essential to successfully reconciling the account, both the first time and in the future, so establish your bank and credit card account opening balances before you try to reconcile these accounts.

Setting the Opening Balance

The opening balance for your bank account is a number that reflects transactions that took place before you started using QuickBooks. It will include checks and deposits that have cleared the bank as well as checks and deposits that have *not* cleared the bank. In Chapter 2, when we talked about creating accounts, I suggested that you not supply an opening balance for your bank accounts. Assuming that you have followed that advice, let's establish the opening balance for your account now, so that your first reconciliation is successful.

The opening balance that you use should be the ending balance that appears on your last bank statement before beginning to use QuickBooks. For example, if you start using QuickBooks on February 1, use the ending balance on your bank statement as of January 31. If you didn't reconcile your last bank statement, you need to do so before you can reconcile in QuickBooks; the longer you postpone, the uglier the task gets. But, if you take the time now, future reconciliations will be easy.

Use the following steps to set the beginning balance for checking your account:

1. Open the bank account register (press CTRL-R and select the appropriate account).
2. Add a transaction dated earlier than the beginning date on your bank statement. Set the amount of the transaction to the beginning balance on your bank statement and don't enter anything in the Number column.

($) NOTE: If you originally set up this account with an amount other than $0 for the opening balance, you'll see an opening balance entry. It's probably the earliest entry in the register and uses the Opening Bal Equity account in the Account field. Instead of adding a transaction in Step 2, edit the existing transaction to change its amount to match the beginning balance on your bank statement. When you save the transaction, QuickBooks issues a warning message about changing this transaction and asks if you really want to record your changes; click Yes.

3. Click Record to save the transaction.

Recording Missing Transactions

After you adjust the opening balance of the bank account to match the ending balance on your last bank statement, you need to bring the account up to date with transactions that occurred but did not clear the bank before you started using QuickBooks.

You can record checks you wrote that did not clear the bank before you started to use QuickBooks using the register or using the Write Checks window. When you select an account, use the Opening Bal Equity account. You can record the purpose of the check in the Memo field.

You can record deposits you made that did not clear the bank before you started to use QuickBooks using the register. Make sure that you enter the deposit amount, not individual checks, and again, record the deposits to the Opening Bal Equity account.

($) NOTE: Because the effects of these transactions are already reflected in regular account balances you recorded in the journal entry described earlier in this chapter, you don't want to post these transactions to regular accounts.

If you prefer, you can use the Make Deposits window; when you choose Banking | Make Deposits and the Payments to Deposit window appears, click Cancel. Then, in the Make Deposits window, record one deposit for each date that you made a deposit at the bank; click Save & New as you complete an individual deposit. Recording the transactions that occurred but did not clear the bank before you started using QuickBooks in this way creates an audit trail and makes reconciliation easy.

Entering Opening Customer and Vendor Balances

Although you may be tempted to supply an outstanding balance number as you set up a customer or vendor, this approach doesn't let you track the details of an outstanding balance, which can be important if the balance includes more than one outstanding invoice or bill. You'll need those details to:

- Deal with disputes over specific invoices or bills,
- Easily apply payments to associated invoices or bills, and
- Easily track amounts for reimbursed expenses.

So, I suggest that you enter individual transactions for outstanding invoices and bills, using the original dates you created those transactions when you enter those invoices and bills. By using the original date, you retain aging for the outstanding transactions. You need to post these transactions to the Opening Balance Equity account; set up a special item—you might call it OBE (for Opening Bal Equity) and use it on each invoice and bill you create. To avoid creating lots of items that you'll only use once while setting up QuickBooks, use the Description field to describe the detail that appeared on these invoices and bills created before you started using QuickBooks.

NOTE: Because the effects of these transactions are already reflected in regular account balances you recorded in the journal entry described earlier in this chapter, you don't want to post these transactions to regular accounts.

When you complete this process along with the other opening balance entries described previously and subsequently in this chapter, the balance in the Opening Bal Equity account should be $0.

CAUTION: QuickBooks offsets any opening balance you enter for a customer as you create the customer to Uncategorized Income, not to Opening Bal Equity. If you entered opening balances for customers as you set up the customers, create a journal entry that debits Uncategorized Income and credits Opening Bal Equity. Then, use the approach I describe here.

Entering Opening Balances for Inventory Items

To create an opening balance for your inventory account, use the Inventory Adjustment transaction, described in Chapter 10, and set the Adjustment account for each transaction to the Opening Bal Equity account. After you enter these transactions and complete the other opening balance entries described previously in this chapter, the balance in the Opening Bal Equity account should be $0.

Entering Opening Balances for Payroll Liabilities

You *should* include both Payroll Liabilities and Payroll Expenses when you record your opening journal entries. When you use the Payroll Setup Wizard to enter historical balances for employees, one section of the wizard also prompts you to enter payroll liability payments you have made. The employee history you enter through the Payroll Setup Wizard *does not* affect payroll liability or expense accounts.

Making Adjusting Entries

In some circumstances, such as changing accounts and tracking depreciation, you'll need to record journal entries to adjust your general ledger. Some journal entries are easy to figure out later, but you may find it difficult to remember the reason you made other entries, and the text you entered in the Memo field isn't jogging your memory.

You can specifically mark a journal entry as an adjusting entry by checking the Adjusting Entry check box at the top of the Make General Journal Entries window. Because the majority of journal entries are created to make an adjustment, the Adjusting Entry check box has a check mark in it by default.

 N O T E :   The Adjusting Entry check box appears in all editions of QuickBooks Enterprise and in the Accountant's Edition of QuickBooks Premier.

You also can print the Adjusting Journal Entries report to display adjusting journal entries you made. Click the arrow beside the Reports button in the Make General Journal Entries window and choose Adjusting Journal Entries.

Making Journal Entries for Changed Accounts

Suppose that, after you've been using QuickBooks for a while, you decide that you want to track income differently. Instead of one income account, you want to use separate income accounts that are more specific to make business analysis easier.

To make this adjustment, create the new account(s) and then take the appropriate amount of funds out of the original account and put it into the new account(s). In this example, you would debit the original account for the amount that belongs in the new account(s) and credit each new account for its share of the amount you debited.

To complete the change in the way you plan to do business, open the Items List and change the necessary items to use a different income account.

You may make the same decision about expenses, deciding to break down an expense to better manage it. For example, you may want to separate your insurance account into several subaccounts for car insurance, equipment insurance, building insurance, malpractice insurance, and so on.

For this example, you would credit the original expense account for the amount you're taking out of it and then debit each new subaccount(s) for the appropriate amount(s).

You can apply this logic to a fixed-asset account named Vehicles that you want to divide into more specific accounts to track a truck separately from a car, especially if you purchase them in different years. You can also separate out any accumulated depreciation to assign it to the correct asset.

Making Depreciation Entries

You depreciate a fixed asset that loses value as it ages to track the asset's current value. The basis of an asset's depreciation from an accounting point of view is determined by a complicated set of rules. In addition, the IRS makes rules, and those rules change frequently.

You record depreciation using a journal entry. Most small businesses enter the depreciation of their assets at the end of the year, but some companies perform depreciation tasks monthly or quarterly. The two accounts involved in a depreciation journal entry are a fixed asset and a depreciation expense account.

I find using families of accounts for fixed assets and depreciation the most effective way to quickly and easily get information I might need. I create a parent account and subaccounts for each type of fixed asset. For example, the fixed-asset section of my chart of accounts looks like this:

Parent Accounts	Subaccounts
Computers	
	Computers-Original Cost
	Computers-Depreciation
Furniture	
	Furniture-Original Cost
	Furniture-Depreciation
Trucks	
	Trucks-Original Cost
	Trucks-Depreciation

I never use the parent account. I post asset purchases to a subaccount and I post my journal entry for depreciation to a subaccount for the following reasons:

- I can look at either the asset subaccount or the depreciation subaccount to see a running total instead of a calculated net total.
- Tracing the year-to-year depreciation is easy. Each line in the depreciation subaccount register represents a year.

- It's quick and easy to open the depreciation subaccount if I'm asked about the depreciation total—handy if you sell the asset and have to add back the depreciation.
- The net value of my fixed assets is easily visible on my Balance Sheet report (see Figure 14-2).

To depreciate fixed assets, you record a journal entry that uses a depreciation account in the Expense section of your chart of accounts.

Follow these steps:

1. Choose Company | Make General Journal Entries from the menu bar.
2. Choose the first asset accumulated depreciation subaccount.
3. Enter the depreciation amount in the Credit column.
4. Repeat Steps 2 and 3 for each asset you need to depreciate. QuickBooks automatically tracks the offsetting amount in the Debit column as you work.

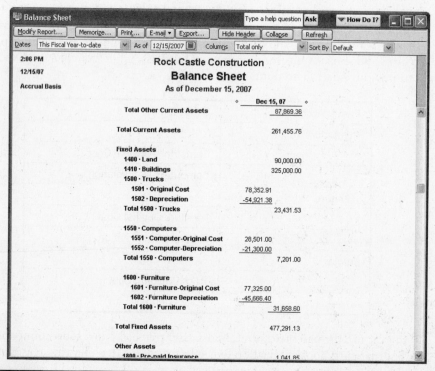

FIGURE 14-2   Using subaccounts provides a detailed view of depreciation activity

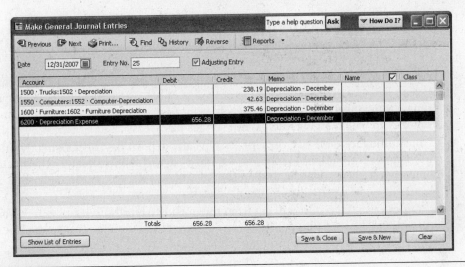

Account	Debit	Credit	Memo	Name	✓	Class
1500 · Trucks:1502 · Depreciation		238.19	Depreciation - December			
1550 · Computers:1552 · Computer-Depreciation		42.63	Depreciation - December			
1600 · Furniture:1602 · Furniture Depreciation		375.46	Depreciation - December			
6200 · Depreciation Expense	656.28		Depreciation - December			
Totals	656.28	656.28				

FIGURE 14-3   A typical depreciation journal entry

⑤ Choose the Depreciation Expense account. The total amount of the credits appears automatically in the Debit column (see Figure 14-3).

⑥ Click Save & Close.

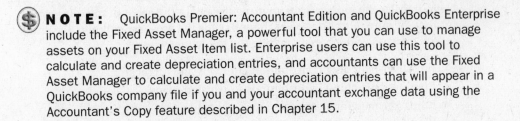

N O T E :   QuickBooks Premier: Accountant Edition and QuickBooks Enterprise include the Fixed Asset Manager, a powerful tool that you can use to manage assets on your Fixed Asset Item list. Enterprise users can use this tool to calculate and create depreciation entries, and accountants can use the Fixed Asset Manager to calculate and create depreciation entries that will appear in a QuickBooks company file if you and your accountant exchange data using the Accountant's Copy feature described in Chapter 15.

Reversing Entries

Reversing entries are general journal entries that you enter on one date and then reverse on another (later) date. For example, you may need to accrue wages and salaries for amounts earned in one year but paid in the next year. You can use a reversing journal entry to handle this situation. When QuickBooks reverses the journal entry at the first of the new year, the net expense for each year will be just what was earned in that year.

To enter a reversing journal entry, click the Reverse icon at the top of the Make General Journal Entries window after you save the journal entry. By default, QuickBooks creates the new, reversed journal entry and dates it the first day of the following month.

Recording Payroll from Outside Payroll Services

If you use an outside payroll service, typically, you should have a separate bank account for payroll, because outside payroll services automatically deduct payroll money from your bank account and you want to maintain control over the amount of money to which an outside payroll service has access.

In addition, outside payroll services typically deposit paychecks directly into your employees' bank accounts. In fact, most payroll services require that your company use direct deposit, and most companies prefer to use direct deposit because it is cheaper than printing paychecks.

You can use the report you get from the outside payroll service to enter a journal entry in QuickBooks that accounts for the payroll transactions that took place. There are three parts to recording payroll:

- Transferring money to the payroll account
- Entering the payroll figures
- Entering the employer expense figures

Transferring Money to the Payroll Account

To transfer the money you need for any payroll, choose Banking | Transfer Funds. Then, transfer the money from your regular operating account to your payroll account. Be sure to transfer enough money for the gross payroll plus the employer payroll expenses, which may include the following:

- Employer-matching contributions to FICA and Medicare
- Employer-matching contributions to pension plans
- Employer-matching contributions to benefits
- Employer state unemployment assessments
- Employer FUTA
- Any other government or benefit payments paid by the employer

Recording the Payroll

The debits and credits associated with paychecks are fairly complicated. Many businesses record a journal entry for the paychecks, then a separate journal entry for the employer expenses when they're transmitted.

If your payroll service takes care of making employer payments, you can record a journal entry for those payments. However, if you prepare the employer reports and send the checks directly, the checks you write in QuickBooks will create the debits and credits, so you don't need a journal entry.

Account	Debit	Credit
Salaries and Wages expense	Gross Payroll	
FIT liability		Total Federal Income Tax Withheld
FICA liability		Total FICA withheld
Medicare liability		Total Medicare withheld
State Income Tax liability		Total State Tax withheld
Local Income Tax liability		Total Local Tax withheld
State SDI liability		Total State SDI withheld
State SUI liability		Total State SUI withheld
Benefits contribution liability		Total Benefits withheld
401(k) contribution liability		Total 401(k) withheld
Other deductions liability		Total Other deductions withheld

TABLE 14-1   Typical Journal Entry to Record Payroll Created by an Outside Service

Table 14-1 shows a typical template for recording the payroll run as a journal entry.

Recording Employer Payments

Table 14-2 is a sample journal entry for recording payments the employer makes for payroll liabilities and expenses; record a journal entry like this one if your outside payroll service makes these payments for you. If you write checks for these payments, don't enter a journal entry; the checks you write in QuickBooks will update the general ledger for you.

In this journal entry, you post withholdings to the same account you used when you withheld the amounts, effectively "washing" the liability accounts; you're not really spending money, you're remitting money you've withheld from employees.

You can have as many individual employer expense accounts as you think you need, or you can post all the employer expenses to one account named "payroll expenses."

 N O T E :   Don't have your payroll service take their fee from the payroll account. Instead, write them a check from your operating account. The fee for the service is not a payroll expense; it's an operating expense.

Account	Debit	Credit
Federal Payroll Tax expense	Employer FICA and Medicare	
Federal Withholdings liability	All federal withholding	
State And Local Withholdings liability	All local withholding	
SUTA expense	Employer SUTA	
FUTA expense	Employer FUTA	
Employer Contributions expense	All employer benefit, pension, etc.	
Payroll Bank Account		Total of checks written

TABLE 14-2   Typical Journal Entry for Employer-Side Transactions

Create Your Own Boilerplate

You can save a lot of time and effort by creating a template for the payroll journal entries that you memorize. Open a Make General Journal Entries window and fill out the Account column only. Enter the first account, then press the Down arrow and enter the next account, and keep going until all accounts are listed. QuickBooks automatically inserts 0.00 as you skip the Debit and Credit columns.

When you have listed all the accounts, press CTRL-M to open the Memorize Transaction dialog box. Name the memorized transaction and select the option Don't Remind Me; the reports from the payroll company are your reminder.

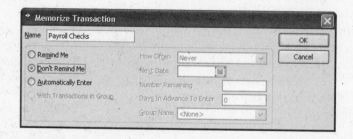

Close the Make General Journal Entries window. QuickBooks displays a message asking if you want to save the transaction you just created. Click No and then repeat this process for the journal entry you create to record employer payments.

When you're ready to record payroll, open the memorized transactions, fill in the correct figures, and save them.

Reconciling the Payroll Account

The process for reconciling a payroll bank account is no different than the process for reconciling an operating bank account; see Chapter 12 for details. Because most payroll services directly deposit paychecks into employees' bank accounts, the transactions that appear on your payroll bank account statement are "lump sum" transactions that will match the journal entries we just described. And, the number of transactions on the payroll bank account statement will match the number of times you pay your employees each month. So, reconciling your payroll bank account should be a fairly simple process, even though you won't see any check numbers.

Reporting on Journal Entries

You can produce reports on journal entries from the Make General Journal Entries window. You can control the list of selected journal entries that appears at the bottom of the window to display entries for a timeframe you choose. Or you can click the down arrow beside the Reports button to print the Adjusting Journal Entries report or reports of journal entries entered today, last month, last fiscal quarter, this fiscal year to date, or all journal entries.

Running Financial Reports

n this chapter:

- Reporting a trial balance

- Generating a balance sheet

- Generating a profit & loss statement

- Creating an accountant's copy

- Understanding cash flow statements

After you spend a considerable amount of time entering information about the state of your business, you'll want to produce reports that show you that information in a variety of ways. QuickBooks contains a wide variety of reports that show you the information you enter from a variety of perspectives. In addition to the standard reports available in QuickBooks, you can customize any QuickBooks report.

In this chapter, I focus on the financial reports available in QuickBooks.

Reporting the Trial Balance

A *trial balance* is a list of all your general ledger accounts and their current balances. It's a quick way to see what's what on an account-by-account basis. The bottom of the report has a total for debits and a total for credits, and they're equal. Most accountants ask to see a trial balance when they're preparing your taxes or analyzing the health of your business.

To see a trial balance, choose Reports | Accountant and Taxes | Trial Balance. Your company's trial balance appears on-screen. It looks similar in form to Figure 15-1. You can scroll through it to see all the account balances. Click the Print button on the report's button bar to print the report.

Changing the Appearance of the Trial Balance Report

You can change the way the trial balance report displays information using options available for this report. Click the Modify Report button on the report's button bar to display the Modify Report window shown in Figure 15-2. If you make changes that don't work as you thought they would, click the Revert button that appears on each tab of the Modify Report window to reset all options to their default state.

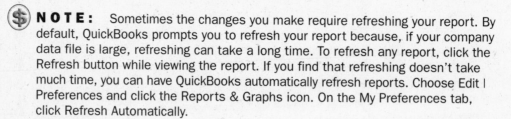 **NOTE:** Sometimes the changes you make require refreshing your report. By default, QuickBooks prompts you to refresh your report because, if your company data file is large, refreshing can take a long time. To refresh any report, click the Refresh button while viewing the report. If you find that refreshing doesn't take much time, you can have QuickBooks automatically refresh reports. Choose Edit | Preferences and click the Reports & Graphs icon. On the My Preferences tab, click Refresh Automatically.

Accrual vs. Cash Trial Balance

QuickBooks can show you account balances on an accrual basis or on a cash basis using the Report Basis options on the Display tab of the Modify Report dialog box.

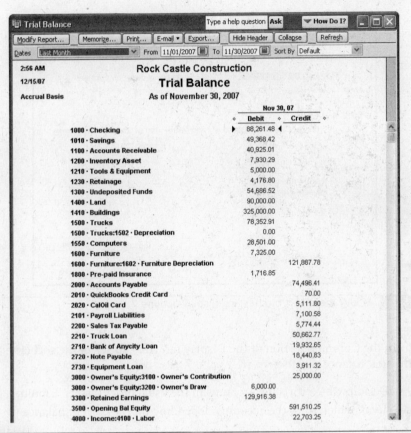

FIGURE 15-1 A trial balance reports the current balance of every account

Accrual numbers are based on your transaction activity. QuickBooks records revenue when you invoice a customer; similarly, QuickBooks records an expense when you enter a vendor bill.

Cash numbers are based on the flow of cash. QuickBooks doesn't account for revenue until the customer pays the bill, and QuickBooks doesn't account for expenses until you write the checks to pay your vendor bills.

By default, QuickBooks, like most accounting software, displays accrual reports. Accrual reports are generally more useful for analyzing your business. However, if you pay taxes on a cash basis, your accountant will want to see a cash basis trial balance.

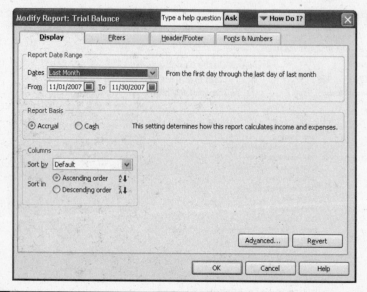

FIGURE 15-2   Modify the report by changing display options

In the Columns section of the Display tab you can select the sort criterion. For the trial balance the choices are:

- Default, which sorts the accounts in the usual order (assets, liabilities, and so on)
- Total, which sorts the accounts depending on the current balance

 NOTE: The report window itself has a field labeled Sort By, which you can use to change the sorting scheme.

Setting Advanced Options

Click the Advanced button on the Display tab to see the Advanced Options window, where you have two choices for changing the criteria for displaying information and a choice for determining the calendar basis of the report.

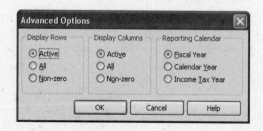

The two display choices (Rows and Columns) change the criteria for displaying information.

- Select Active to display only those accounts in which financial activity occurred. This includes accounts that have amounts of $0.00 as a result of financial activity.
- Select All to see all accounts, regardless of whether they had activity or have a balance of $0.00.
- Select Non-Zero to see only those accounts that had activity and have a balance other than $0.00.

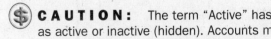 **CAUTION:** The term "Active" has nothing to do with the account's status as active or inactive (hidden). Accounts marked Inactive appear on the report because their balances are part of your trial balance.

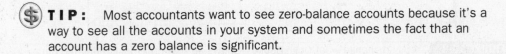 **TIP:** Most accountants want to see zero-balance accounts because it's a way to see all the accounts in your system and sometimes the fact that an account has a zero balance is significant.

The Reporting Calendar option determines the calendar basis of the report. You can change the option if your company's preferences use a fiscal year and a tax year that don't coincide with the calendar year.

- Fiscal Year sets the reporting calendar to start at the first month of your company's fiscal year.
- Calendar Year sets the reporting calendar to start on January 1.
- Income Tax Year sets the reporting calendar to start on the first day of the first month of your company's tax year.

Click OK to return to the Modify Report window.

Filtering the Data

Click the Filters tab in the Modify Report window to filter the contents of the report (see Figure 15-3). Select a filter from the list in the Choose Filter section and decide how it should be displayed. Different categories have different filtering criteria. For instance, you can filter amounts that are less than, equal to, or greater than a certain amount.

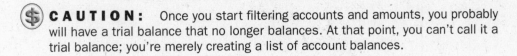 **CAUTION:** Once you start filtering accounts and amounts, you probably will have a trial balance that no longer balances. At that point, you can't call it a trial balance; you're merely creating a list of account balances.

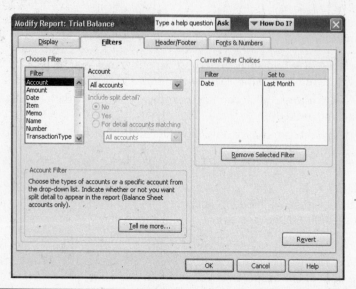

FIGURE 15-3   You can change what QuickBooks displays on the report by filtering the data

Changing the Header and Footer

You can customize what appears on the header and footer of your report by changing the options on the Header/Footer tab shown in Figure 15-4.

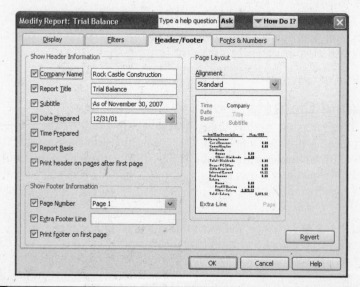

FIGURE 15-4   Set up the information in the top and bottom of the report page using the Header/Footer tab

The options you set here have no bearing on the figures in the report; this is just the informational stuff. Most of the fields are self-explanatory, but the Date Prepared field is worth mentioning. The date you see in this tab has nothing to do with the current date; it's just a sample format. Click the arrow to the right of the field to see other formats for displaying the date.

Changing the Fonts and Numbers Display

The Fonts & Numbers tab, shown in Figure 15-5, lets you change the font you use for the various elements in the report. Select any part of the report from the list on the left side of the dialog box and click Change Font. Then select a font, a style (bold, italic, etc.), a size, and special effects such as underline.

On the right side of the dialog box, you can change the way QuickBooks displays numbers on your report. Select a method for showing negative numbers. If you wish, you can also select a method for displaying all the numbers on the report:

- Divided By 1000 reduces the size of the numbers by showing them as multiples of 1000. This is useful for companies that report seven- and eight-digit numbers.
- Except Zero Amounts removes all instances of $0.00 and leaves the entry blank.
- Without Cents eliminates the decimal point and the two digits to the right of the decimal point from every amount. Only the dollars show, not the cents. QuickBooks rounds the cents to the nearest dollar.

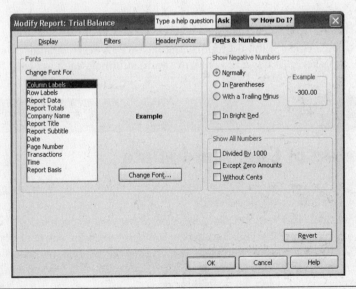

FIGURE 15-5   Change the appearance of information in the report

Memorizing a Customized Report

If you find that you often make the same customization changes to a report, then you can save yourself some time if you memorize the report. Click the Memorize button at the top of the report window, and the Memorize Report window appears; supply a name for your customized version of the report and, if you want, save the report in a Memorized Report Group. Then click OK.

Display a memorized report by choosing Reports | Memorized Reports from the QuickBooks menu bar and selecting the report name from the submenu.

Generating a Balance Sheet

A Balance Sheet report is specifically designed to show only the totals of the Balance Sheet accounts (assets, liabilities, and equity) from your chart of accounts. It's really a report on your financial health. The Balance Sheet is based on the following formula:

Assets = Liabilities + Equity

QuickBooks offers several Balance Sheet reports; select the one you want to see by choosing Reports | Company & Financial and then choosing the report. As with the Trial Balance report shown previously, you can customize any Balance Sheet report using all of the options covered earlier in this chapter. If appropriate, you can memorize the report by clicking the Memorize button in the report window.

Balance Sheet Standard Report

The Balance Sheet Standard reports the balance in every Balance Sheet account (unless the account has a zero balance) and subtotals each account type: asset,

▶▶ FYI

The Meaning of Last Year-to-Date

While I'm going to use Last Year-to-Date as my example, the following explanation is true for any period ... think "Last X-to-Date" as you read.

You might think that "Last Year-To-Date" means all of last year through today. It actually means from the beginning of last year through the same day as today one year ago. If today is July 26, 2007 and I run a report using Last Year-To-Date for the date, my report will show information from January 1, 2006 to July 26, 2006, not July 26, 2007. If you really want a "last year through today" report, select the dates by hand.

liability, and equity. QuickBooks automatically displays year-to-date figures on the report, using your fiscal year and the current date.

Balance Sheet Detail Report

This report displays every transaction in every Balance Sheet account. By default, the report displays transactions in the current month-to-date. Even early in the month, this report is lengthy.

Balance Sheet Summary Report

This report, shown in Figure 15-6, displays totals by account type and gives you a quick way to view totals. For example, you won't see individual bank accounts on this report, but you'll see one line for Checking/Savings accounts. This report easily answers the question, "How am I doing?" To print this report, choose Reports | Company & Financial | Balance Sheet Summary.

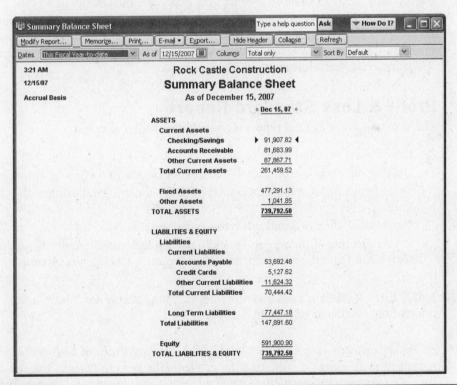

FIGURE 15-6   Check your financial health with the Balance Sheet Summary Report

Balance Sheet Prev Year Comparison Report

The comparison Balance Sheet is designed to show you what your financial situation is compared to a year ago. The report contains four columns:

- The year-to-date balance for each Balance Sheet account.
- The year-to-date balance for each Balance Sheet account for last year.
- The amount of change between last year and this year.
- The percentage of change between last year and this year.

Generating a Profit & Loss Report

You'll probably run your Profit & Loss report more often than any other report—it's natural to want to know if you're making any money. The Profit & Loss report shows all your income accounts and displays their total, all your expense accounts and displays their total, and then displays the difference between the two totals on the last line. If you have more income than expenses, the last line is a profit.

All of the Profit & Loss reports are available by choosing Reports | Company & Financial. And, you can use the QuickBooks Modify Report features discussed earlier in this chapter to tailor Profit & Loss reports so they print exactly the way you want to see the information and memorize it.

Profit & Loss Standard Report

The standard Profit & Loss report is a straightforward document:

- QuickBooks lists and totals income.
- QuickBooks then lists and totals the Cost of Goods Sold (COGS) accounts.
- QuickBooks deducts the COGS total from the income total to show the Gross Profit.
- QuickBooks then lists and totals the expenses.
- On the last line of the report, QuickBooks displays the difference between the Gross Profit and the total expenses; the amount is labeled Net Income.

 N O T E :   If you don't sell inventory items, you probably don't have a Cost of Goods Sold section in your Profit & Loss.

The default date range for the QuickBooks standard Profit & Loss is the current month-to-date, using only the transactions from the current month. You can change the date range to view a variety of different scenarios—the current month, the current quarter, the current year, just to name a view.

Profit & Loss Detail Report

The Profit & Loss Detail report lists every transaction for every account in the Profit & Loss format. This lengthy report is good to have if you notice some numbers that seem "not quite right" in the standard Profit & Loss report.

Profit & Loss YTD Comparison Report

The YTD (year-to-date) comparison report compares the current month's income and expense totals with the year-to-date totals.

Profit & Loss Prev Year Comparison Report

If you've been using QuickBooks for more than a year, this is a great report! If you recently started with QuickBooks, next year you'll say, "This is a great report!"

This version of the Profit & Loss report shows income and expenses for the current year-to-date, with a column that shows last year's figure for the same period, giving you an instant appraisal of your business growth or ebb. The report contains two additional columns: the difference between the years in dollars and in percentage.

Profit & Loss By Job Report

This report presents a year-to-date summary of income and expenses posted to customers and jobs. In effect, it's a customer Profit & Loss. Each customer or job gets its own column, and the bottom row of each column is the net income or loss for each customer or job.

Profit & Loss By Class Report

If you've enabled class tracking, this report appears on the Reports menu and presents a column showing the Profit & Loss for the class. If you use classes for branch offices or company divisions, this is the way to get a separate Profit & Loss for each.

Profit & Loss Unclassified Report

If you've enabled class tracking, you should run the Profit & Loss Unclassified report, which displays a Profit & Loss generated from transactions to which you didn't assign a class. Even if you think you don't care about assigning classes to these transactions, you should examine the report and double-click each entry to view the individual transactions. You can then assign a class to a transaction if appropriate and click Yes when QuickBooks asks if you want to save the changes you made to the transaction.

TIP: Because this report uses filtered accounts and transactions, instead of all the transactions in your system, it isn't really a Profit & Loss, and you can ignore the bottom line profit/loss figure.

Creating an Accountant's Copy

Many accountants support QuickBooks directly and have a copy of QuickBooks on their own computer systems. At various times during the year, your accountant might want to look at your QuickBooks company data. There might be quarterly reports and adjustments, a physical inventory that resulted in serious changes to your Balance Sheet, expenses that should be posted to different accounts, or any of a hundred other reasons to examine your transactions. Your accountant could visit, sit in front of your computer, and make the necessary changes. If your accountant doesn't want to visit, he or she may request reports and then write notes on the reports that describe things you need to do.

Some accountants ask for a backup of your company file or a portable company file. The accountant then uses your company file to make necessary changes. When your accountant finishes working in your company file, he or she sends the file back, and you need to start work in that version of the file, because it includes the changes your accountant made.

Meanwhile, during the period your accountant has the file and is making changes, you can't record any transactions in QuickBooks. If you continue to work, the transactions you enter won't appear in the company file when your accountant returns it to you.

QuickBooks has a better solution. You can give your accountant a specially designed review copy of your company file that lets your accountant do the work back at his or her office, while you continue to work in your copy. When your accountant returns the file to you, with changes, QuickBooks merges the changes into your copy of the company file, and both your work and your accountant's work will appear in the file.

 NOTE: To work with your QuickBooks 2007 files, your accountant must have installed the Accountant Edition of QuickBooks Premier 2007 or QuickBooks Enterprise 2007.

You can give the accountant's copy file that you create to your accountant on a CD, on a flash drive, or via e-mail.

 NOTE: Be aware that e-mail may not be a truly viable option for two reasons: first, many e-mail systems won't handle attachments above 10 MB and the accountant's copy of your data may well exceed that limitation. Second, e-mail is not secure, so you are sending your financial information over an unsecured channel.

To create an accountant's copy, follow these steps:

1 Choose File | Accountant's Copy | Create Accountant's Copy from the QuickBooks menu bar. You may see a message indicating you must be in single-user mode to create an Accountant's Copy. Then the Accountant's Copy: Overview dialog box appears, providing you with an overview of the Accountant's Copy.

2 Click Next. The Dividing Date screen of the wizard appears (see Figure 15-7). Supply a dividing date; your accountant can work on transactions dated before this date, and you can work on transactions dated after this date. The date you supply should be a date in the past that represents the ending date of the period you want your accountant to review.

3 Click Next. If you see a message telling you that QuickBooks must close all open windows, click OK. QuickBooks displays the Save Accountant's Copy To dialog box.

4 Select a drive and folder for the file you're about to save. If you're going to burn the file to a CD or send it via e-mail, make sure you note the folder in which you place the file.

N O T E :   QuickBooks automatically appends .qbx, to the filename; it's a good idea to use the filename that QuickBooks suggests, which is based on your company name.

5 Click Save to create the accountant's copy.

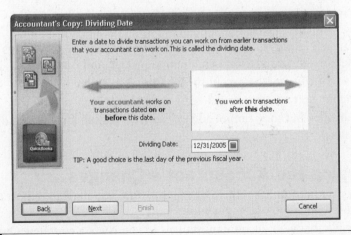

FIGURE 15-7   Supply a dividing date

QuickBooks displays a message when the process completes; the message displays your dividing date and instructions to send the file to your accountant. In addition, the title bar of the program changes to display your company name followed by Accountant's Changes Pending in parentheses.

 CAUTION: If you've password-protected your QuickBooks data file, you must give your accountant the admin password so that your accountant can open the file.

Working during the Accountant's Copy

When you create the accountant's copy, QuickBooks locks transactions in your company file dated prior to the dividing date so you can't make changes that will be incompatible with the data that your accountant returns. You can add or edit items on every list in QuickBooks with one exception: you cannot edit the Chart Of Accounts List. You also can change list entries to make them inactive, and you can sort lists. You cannot delete or merge in any list, and you cannot reconcile. You can create budgets and forecasts, and you can memorize reports.

Table 15-1 identifies what you can and can't do with transactions based on the dividing date. To summarize the information you see in Table 15-1, you can add transactions dated prior to the dividing date, but you cannot edit or delete any transactions dated on or before the dividing date.

Your accountant has restrictions as well. Table 15-2 describes what an accountant can and cannot do with the accountant's copy file.

With respect to lists, accountants

- Can add and edit accounts and make accounts inactive on the Chart of Accounts
- Can add entries to all lists *except* the Payroll Item List, Worker's Comp List, Memorized Transaction List, Reminders List, and Alerts List
- Cannot edit any list except the Chart of Accounts
- Cannot sort any lists or delete or merge list entries on any list
- Can view but they cannot add or change budgets, forecasts, and memorized reports

Merging the Accountant's Changes

When your accountant returns changes to you, you need to import those changes into your QuickBooks company file.

The file that your accountant returns to you is *not* a complete QuickBooks company file. It contains only the changes your accountant made, so expect a fairly small file with a .qby extension. This file is encrypted and cannot be opened by any company file other than the one into which the changes should be imported.

| | Client Transactions | | | | | |
| | Prior Period | | | Current Period | | |
	Add	Edit	Delete	Add	Edit	Delete
Banking						
Journal Entries	N	N	N	Y	Y	Y
Write Checks	N	N	N	Y	Y	Y
Make Deposit	N	N	N	Y	Y	Y
Transfers	N	N	N	Y	Y	Y
Credit Card Charge & Credit	N	N	N	Y	Y	Y
Reconciliations	N	N	N	N	N	N
Sales and Customers						
Sales Orders	N	N	N	Y	Y	Y
Estimates	N	N	N	Y	Y	Y
Sales Receipts	N	N	N	Y	Y	Y
Invoices & Credit Memos	N	N	N	Y	Y	Y
Statement Charges	N	N	N	Y	Y	Y
Receive Payment	N	N	N	Y	Y	Y
Purchases and Vendors						
Purchase Orders	N	N	N	Y	Y	Y
Enter Bills	N	N	N	Y	Y	Y
Vendor Credit	N	N	N	Y	Y	Y
Item Receipt	N	N	N	Y	Y	Y
Pay Bills	N	N	N	Y	Y	Y
Pay Sales Tax	N	N	N	Y	Y	Y
Adjust quantity/value on hand	N	N	N	Y	Y	Y
Build Assemblies	N	N	N	Y	Y	Y
Payroll						
Paychecks	N	N	N	Y	Y	Y
Pay Payroll Liabilities	N	N	N	Y	Y	Y
Payroll Adjustments	N	N	N	Y	Y	Y

TABLE 15-1   What You Can and Cannot Do In Relation to the Dividing Date While an Accountant's Copy Exists

Function	Historical Period			Current Period		
	Add	Edit	Delete	Add	Edit	Delete
Banking						
Journal Entries	Y	Y	Y	Y	N	N
Write Checks	Y	Y	Y	Y	N	N
Make Deposit	Y	N	Y	Y	N	N
Transfers	Y	Y	Y	Y	N	N
Credit Card Charge	Y	Y	Y	Y	N	N
Credit Card Credit	Y	Y	Y	Y	N	N
Sales and Customers						
Sales Orders	Y	N	N	Y	N	N
Estimates	Y	N	N	Y	N	N
Sales Receipts	Y	Y	Y	Y	N	N
Invoices	Y	Y	Y	Y	N	N
Credit Memo	Y	Y	Y	Y	N	N
Statement Charges	Y	Y	Y	Y	N	N
Receive Payment	Y	Y	Y	Y	N	N
Purchases and Vendors						
Purchase Orders	Y	N	N	Y	N	N
Enter Bills	Y	Y	Y	Y	N	N
Vendor Credit	Y	N	Y	Y	N	N
Item Receipt	Y	N	Y	Y	N	N
Pay Bills	Y	Y	Y	Y	N	N
Pay Bills (credit card)	Y	N	Y	Y	N	N
Pay Sales Tax	N	N	Y	Y	N	N
Adjust quantity/value on hand	Y	N	Y	Y	N	N
Build Assemblies	Y	N	Y	Y	N	N

TABLE 15-2   What an Accountant Can and Cannot Do with a Review Copy

Function	Historical Period			Current Period		
	Add	Edit	Delete	Add	Edit	Delete
Payroll						
Enter Time	N	N	N	Y	N	N
Pay Employees	N	N	N	Y	N	N
Pay Payroll Liabilities	N	N	N	Y	N	N
YTD Adjustment	N	N	N	Y	N	N
Adjust Payroll Liabilities	N	N	N	Y	N	N
Non Transactions						
Reconciliation	N	N	N	N	N	N
Print 1099/1096	Y	N/A	N/A	N/A	N/A	N/A
Process Payroll Forms	Y	N/A	N/A	N/A	N/A	N/A

TABLE 15-2 What an Accountant Can and Cannot Do with a Review Copy *(continued)*

 NOTE: In earlier versions of QuickBooks, the extension of the file your accountant returned to you was aif, and the extension changed in QuickBooks 2007 to qby.

Follow these steps to make changes:

1 Make the file you received from your accountant available. If your accountant gave you the file on a CD or flash drive, insert it. If you received the file via e-mail, note the folder you used to place it on your hard drive.

2 Choose File | Accountant's Copy | Import Accountant's Changes. If you see a message telling you that QuickBooks must close all open windows, click OK. The Import Accountant's Changes dialog box appears.

3 Select the .qby file to import and click Open. QuickBooks displays the Import Accountant's Changes window, which allows you to preview the changes that will be merged into your company data file. You also can print the changes or save them to a pdf file, particularly helpful if something you see concerns you and you want to discuss it with your accountant before you import the changes. You may also see a note from your accountant in this window.

④ Click Import. QuickBooks backs up your current file before importing and then merges the changes into your company data file. The Import Accountant's Changes window appears, letting you know that the changes were merged successfully. Once again, you have the opportunity to print the changes or save them to a pdf file.

⑤ Click Close.

QuickBooks opens your company file, and it contains the changes your accountant made. QuickBooks displays the Closing Date dialog box, offering you the opportunity to update the closing date and password to prevent changes to the period on which your accountant just worked. You now can work with your file using all features available in QuickBooks.

Unlocking Your Files without Receiving a Review

If you make an accountant's copy in error, or if your accountant tells you there are no changes to be made, you can unlock your files to put everything back as if you'd never created an accountant's copy. Choose File | Accountant's copy | Cancel Accountant's Changes. QuickBooks asks you to confirm your decision.

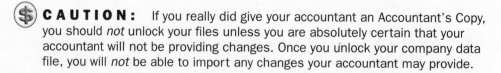 **CAUTION:** If you really did give your accountant an Accountant's Copy, you should *not* unlock your files unless you are absolutely certain that your accountant will not be providing changes. Once you unlock your company data file, you will *not* be able to import any changes your accountant may provide.

Because you cannot import changes from your accountant if you cancel the Accountant's Copy, QuickBooks asks you to confirm the cancellation; type Yes if you're sure you want to cancel.

Voided and Deleted Transactions Reports

QuickBooks contains three reports that you can use to track voided and deleted transactions. You can print all three reports by choosing Reports | Accountant & Taxes and then selecting any of these reports: Voided/Deleted Transactions, Voided/Deleted Transactions Detail, or Audit Trail.

Voided/Deleted Transactions Summary Report

This report displays a summary of all voided and deleted transactions in the selected period (the default period is Today). The report shows the current state (void or deleted) and the original state (including the amount) of each affected transaction.

NOTE: The Voided/Deleted Transaction Report and the Voided/Deleted Transactions History Report were added to QuickBooks 2005, so they report only on transactions voided or deleted using QuickBooks 2005 or later. That is, if you deleted a transaction using QuickBooks 2004, it will not appear on this report. If you deleted a transaction *dated* in 2004 using QuickBooks 2005, that transaction will appear on the report.

Voided/Deleted Transactions Detail Report

In addition to the information provided by the Voided/Deleted Transactions report, this report displays the credit and debit amounts and the posting accounts. If the transactions included items or payroll items, the items appear in the Memo column.

Audit Trail Report

Audit trail is the term used to describe the sequence of events for actions you take. An audit trail includes not only correct transactions but also incorrect transactions—and the actions you took to correct them. Accountants use an audit trail to follow the entry of transactions from financial statements back to ledgers, journals, and, finally, original source documents. Auditors can attest to the accuracy of a company's financial statements by following the audit trail to be sure transactions are posted correctly. Before making a loan, a banker wants to know that neither income nor assets are overstated on a company's books. The company's owners want accurate books to help deter embezzlement and to help them make sound financial decisions.

The Audit Trail feature in QuickBooks is useful because it doesn't interfere with the way QuickBooks works; it just functions in the background while you work. When you edit a transaction, QuickBooks doesn't replace the existing transaction with the edited version. Instead, QuickBooks negates the effects of the first transaction but preserves it in the data files; at the same time, QuickBooks adds your corrected version of the transaction. Similarly, if you delete a transaction, QuickBooks doesn't remove the transaction; instead, it negates the transaction but leaves it in the data file. You won't see the transaction in either the register or a forms window, but you can print the Audit Trail report. The Audit Trail report closely resembles the Voided/Deleted Transactions Detail report, except that the Audit Trail report includes modified transactions as well as deleted and voided transactions. The Audit Trail report also identifies who modified or deleted the transaction (see Figure 15-8).

 NOTE: The Audit Trail is most useful if you set up roles in QuickBooks and assign passwords so that each user logs in using his or her own name. Don't let everyone log in as Admin; you'll find it very difficult to track down honest mistakes, not to mention embezzlement. When everyone signs in using his or her own name, the Audit Trail report shows exactly who made what changes and when.

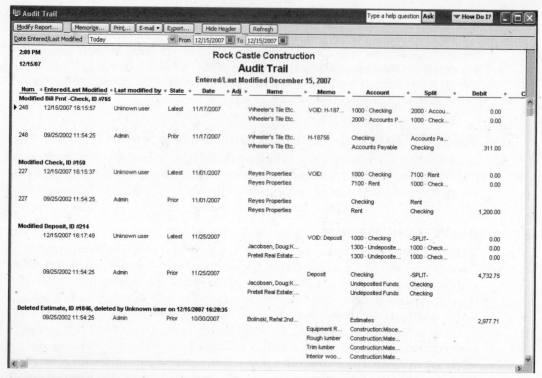

FIGURE 15-8   The Audit Trail report

Cash Flow Reports

QuickBooks offers two cash flow reports on the Company & Financial Reports menu: Statement of Cash Flows and Cash Flow Forecast. Essentially, the Statement of Cash Flows differs from the Cash Flow Forecast because the Statement of Cash Flows looks back and the Cash Flow Forecast looks ahead. Both of these reports can be useful for analyzing the current health of your business.

Cash flow reports are complicated documents and are accurate to the degree that the accounts included in the reports contain transaction figures that should actually be included. Your accountant can look at the activity in any account to determine whether it's appropriate to include or exclude that account's activities in the calculation of cash flow reports.

 N O T E :   It's beyond the scope of this book to provide detailed instructions about verifying and modifying cash flow reports because that's a complicated accounting topic, not a software subject.

Statement of Cash Flows

The Statement of Cash Flows report displays information about your cash position over a period of time (by default, year-to-date). You can see where your cash came from and where it went, categorized as follows:

- **Operating Activities**   The transactions involved with maintaining the business.
- **Investing Activities**   The transactions involved with the acquisition of fixed assets.
- **Financing Activities**   The transactions involved with long-term liabilities and owners' activities (such as investments and draws).

Accounts Used for the Statement of Cash Flows

QuickBooks predetermines the accounts used in the Statement of Cash Flows report, and you can view the account list by choosing Edit | Preferences and selecting the Reports & Graphs icon in the left pane. On the Company Preferences tab, click Classify Cash to open the Classify Cash dialog box seen in Figure 15-9.

You can add and remove accounts and move selected accounts to a different category, but that's dangerous unless your accountant recommends such a step. The default settings that QuickBooks established work quite well. If your accountant knows you're using an account that's not selected for transactions that should be included in the report, or vice versa, it's okay to make changes.

$ CAUTION: Make sure your accountant knows that QuickBooks doesn't permit Balance Sheet accounts to be removed from the list, although they can be moved to a different category.

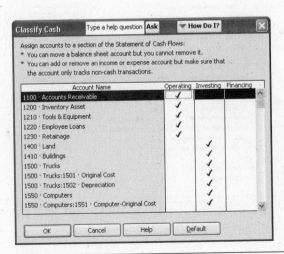

FIGURE 15-9   Check with your accountant before you make any changes here

Creating a Statement of Cash Flows

To create the Statement of Cash Flows report, choose Reports | Company & Financial | Statement Of Cash Flows. The report opens, showing your cash flow from the first day of your fiscal year to the current date, as seen in Figure 15-10.

This report is generated on an accrual basis, and unlike most QuickBooks reports, you can't specify accrual or cash-based calculations. Because cash flow is a cash-based figure, QuickBooks adjusts amounts to turn this accrual-based report into a cash-based report. The bottom line is cash-based, but instead of just displaying cash-based figures, QuickBooks takes an accrual-based report and shows you the adjustments that had to be made. If you don't owe money to anyone and nobody owes you money, you won't see any adjustments.

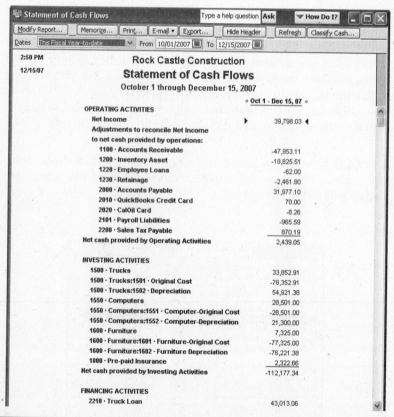

FIGURE 15-10   See how your cash position changed during the period you specified in the date fields

| Cash Flow Forecast | | | Type a help question | Ask | How Do I? | | |

Modify Report... | Memorize... | Print... | E-mail ▼ | Export... | Hide Header | Refresh

Dates | Next 4 Weeks ▼ | From 12/09/2007 | To 01/05/2008 | Periods Week ▼ | Delay Receipts 0

2:52 PM
12/15/07

Rock Castle Construction
Cash Flow Forecast
December 9, 2007 through January 5, 2008

	Accnts Receivable	Accnts Payable	Bank Accnts	Net Inflows	Proj Balance
Beginning Balance	4,143.16	33,232.30	160,363.87		131,274.73
Week of Dec 9, 07	▶ 14,671.79	◀ 0.00	-11,329.53	3,342.26	134,616.99
Week of Dec 16, 07	0.00	550.00	-2,824.55	-3,374.55	131,242.44
Week of Dec 23, 07	11,609.99	2,680.00	0.00	8,929.99	140,172.43
Week of Dec 30, 07	18,879.98	13,098.18	7,633.28	13,415.08	153,587.51
Dec 9, '07 - Jan 5, 08	45,161.76	16,328.18	-6,520.80	22,312.78	
Ending Balance	49,304.92	49,560.48	153,843.07		153,587.51

FIGURE 15-11 This report predicts cash inflow and outflow

Cash Flow Forecast

The Cash Flow Forecast report does what its name implies—forecasts your cash flow as of a given future date. The forecast includes cash in, cash out, and the resulting cash balances. To create the report, choose Reports | Company & Financial | Cash Flow Forecast (see Figure 15-11).

QuickBooks produces this forecast using the assumption that all accounts receivable will arrive when due, and all accounts payable will be paid when due, and that assumption may not be realistic for your business. To enhance the reality of the report, you can use the Delay Receipts field to tell QuickBooks to assume that your customers will pay late by the amount of days you specify in that field. This is useful if you know that your customers pay late by an average of x number of days.

Net Worth Graph

You can display a graph of your net worth by choosing Reports | Company & Financial | Net Worth Graph (see Figure 15-12). Each graphical element represents a specific month. Because it's reporting net worth, it's based on balance sheet accounts, as follows:

- Your total assets, which are represented by the bars above the $0 line.
- Your total liabilities, which appear below the $0 line.
- Your equity (net worth), which is the calculated difference between assets and liabilities. This figure appears as a small yellow box, and if it's a positive figure, it's above the line.

If you double-click an asset bar, liability bar, or equity box, QuickBooks displays a pie chart graph representing the percentage that each account balance contributed to the total.

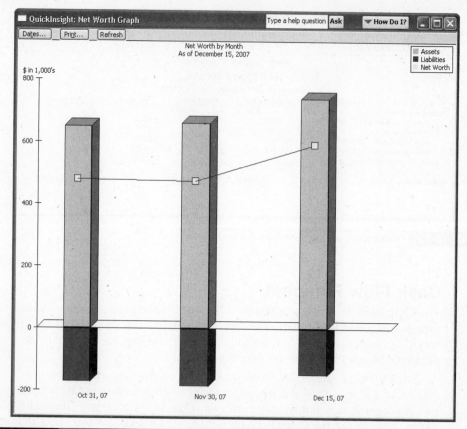

FIGURE 15-12   This graph provides an at-a-glance view of your financial position

Export and Import Memorized Reports

If you customize a report that has absolutely everything you need, arranged in a beautifully logical order, you can memorize it. Then it's available every time you need exactly that information in exactly that format.

To add more power to this already potent feature, you also can export a memorized report. If you're an accountant, you can create and memorize a report that has exactly what you need, laid out exactly the way you need it, and then send the memorized report to your client. You can run the report when you visit the client or have your client run the report, export the contents to Excel, and then send it to you.

 N O T E :   To import a report, you must be using a version of QuickBooks that is compatible with the version that exported the report—typically, all versions from the same year are compatible. For example, a QuickBooks Premier 2007 user can import a report exported from QuickBooks Enterprise 2007.

When you export a memorized report, the exported document is called a template, and the template can be imported into any edition of QuickBooks.

 C A U T I O N :   Don't include custom fields that you added to the company file you're using when you memorize the report. Those fields won't exist in other QuickBooks company files.

To export a memorized report template, follow these steps:

1 Choose Reports | Memorized Reports | Memorized Report List.

2 Click the report you want to export.

3 Click the Memorized Report button at the bottom of the window and select Export Template. QuickBooks displays the Specify Filename For Export dialog box.

4 Navigate to the drive and folder where you want to save the report.

5 Click Save. QuickBooks saves the report template.

You can now send the report template to a QuickBooks user via e-mail or disk.

If you receive an exported report template, the process of importing it converts the template into a memorized report that's added to the currently open company file.

To import a template, follow these steps:

1 Choose Reports | Memorized Reports | Memorized Report List.

2 Click the Memorized Report button at the bottom of the window, and select Import Template. QuickBooks displays the Select File To Import dialog box.

3 Navigate to the drive and folder that contains the template file you received, and double-click it. QuickBooks displays the Memorize Report dialog box.

4 Enter a name for the report or accept the displayed name, which is the name used by the person who exported the template.

5 You can place the report in an existing memorized report group; check the Save In Memorized Report Group box and use the drop-down arrow to select the group.

6 Click OK. The report now appears in the Memorized Report List.

Process Multiple Reports

Using the Process Multiple Reports feature, you can print several memorized reports simultaneously. QuickBooks displays all the reports using their default settings even if you have set preferences to display the Modify Reports dialog box before producing a report. To take advantage of this feature, choose Reports | Process Multiple Reports. QuickBooks displays the Process Multiple Reports window. You can use the Select Memorized Reports From list to limit the list of memorized reports that QuickBooks displays, or you can view all memorized reports. Place checks beside the reports you want to view and then click Display to view them on-screen or Print to send them all to the printer. If you choose Print, QuickBooks gives you the opportunity to select a printer and specify the number of copies to print.

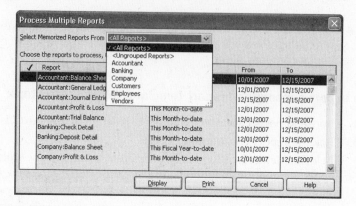

Consolidated Reports for Multiple Companies

 NOTE: This feature is only available in QuickBooks Enterprise Solutions editions, and you must have Microsoft Excel to use it.

If you have separate QuickBooks company files for multiple companies, or for multiple locations, divisions, and so forth, you can use the Combine Reports feature to get a consolidated view of all the data files. You can create the following reports as consolidated reports:

- Balance Sheet Standard
- Balance Sheet Summary
- Profit & Loss Standard
- Statement of Cash Flows
- Trial Balance

You set up the consolidated reports in QuickBooks, selecting the companies and the report types. Then QuickBooks sends the data to Microsoft Excel for consolidation, so you must have Excel installed on your computer to use this feature.

If you have permission to create consolidated company reports, follow these steps to create a combined report:

1 Open one of the companies you want to include in the report(s).

2 Choose Reports | Combine Reports From Multiple Companies. The Combine Reports From Multiple Companies window appears (see Figure 15-13). The open company appears in the window by default.

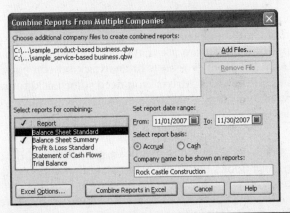

FIGURE 15-13   Use this window to select companies to combine and combined reports to produce

③ Click the Add Files button to navigate to the locations of other companies you want to include in the combined reports. You can include any QuickBooks Enterprise company with a company filename extension of .qbw or .qba.

④ Click beside each report you want to combine to select the report.

⑤ If necessary, change the report date range.

⑥ Select Cash or Accrual for the report basis.

⑦ If you want, change the name in the Company Name To Be Shown On Reports box.

⑧ You can click the Excel Options button to turn on Excel features such as Auto Outline and Auto Filtering.

⑨ Click Combine Reports in Excel. QuickBooks opens each company you included in the Combine Reports From Multiple Companies window in multiuser mode and collects the data it needs to send to Excel.

⑩ Excel opens and displays your combined report.

ODBC Reporting

QuickBooks Enterprise ships with an ODBC driver specifically for QuickBooks that allows QuickBooks Enterprise users to easily connect their QuickBooks company data files with ODBC-compliant programs like Excel, Access, Crystal Reports, or FoxFire Report Writer. ODBC stands for Open Data Base Connectivity. ODBC, an open standard developed by Microsoft and widely adopted by other software vendors, attempts to make it possible for any ODBC-compliant application to communicate with any other ODBC-compliant application. A wide variety of report writing tools rely on the ODBC standard so that they can connect to backend database systems and allow end users to generate reports based on the data contained within these databases.

QuickBooks Enterprise users can use the ODBC driver as a conduit used to get your data from QuickBooks to another application; once the QuickBooks data is in the other application, you can use that other application to manipulate your QuickBooks data to produce reports or analyze your company data. To effectively take advantage of the ODBC driver, you need some background in database connectivity, and you need to know how to use the program you intend to connect to your QuickBooks data.

$ TIP: A single-user access read-only version of the ODBC driver is included in the box with QuickBooks Enterprise. Users of other versions can purchase the driver; there are versions available for all current versions of the QuickBooks product line. See the Upgrade tab of the Configure ODBC Driver For QuickBooks dialog box for more information.

$ NOTE: While ODBC allows ODBC compliant access to QuickBooks .qbw files, it does not provide direct access to the QuickBooks data tables.

To install the ODBC driver, insert your QuickBooks Enterprise Solutions 7.0 installation CD in your CD drive; if setup starts, cancel it. Using My Computer, navigate to X:\QBooks\ODBC (where X is your CD drive) and double-click ODBC.exe. The welcome screen of an installation wizard appears; click Next and the ODBC driver is installed. Click Finish to close the setup wizard.

$ NOTE: The ODBC driver is always being improved, so you may need to download an update at some point. Open a browser window and visit http://www.quickbooksenterprise.com/odbc.

Once you complete the installation, you can configure the ODBC driver. For the most part, you want to accept the default options you'll see while configuring.

To configure the driver, choose File | Utilities | Configure ODBC. The Configure ODBC Driver For QuickBooks dialog box appears. The dialog box contains five tabs: General, Messages, Optimizer, Upgrade, and About. From the General tab, you can

- Select the company data file to which the ODBC driver will connect/communicate.
- Assign a unique DSN name for the connection.
- Test the connection to make sure that the driver is communicating properly with the QuickBooks company data (QBW) file.

You should use the default settings for these options.

From the Messages tab, you can

- Check and clear the ODBC Message Log.
- Check the SDK Message Log.
- Review and clear the optional Trace Log.
- Turn the ODBC Status Panels on and off.

You use the three logs listed above for troubleshooting purposes. Status Panels notify you when the ODBC driver is accessing QuickBooks data; you'll want to enable the Display Optimizer Status Panel option and the Display Driver Status Panel option.

From the Optimizer tab, you can turn the Optimizer on and off, and you can specify the frequency with which you optimize your data. The ODBC Optimization routine takes the information from the QuickBooks company file, optimizes it, and stores it in an encrypted file outside the QuickBooks company file. The Optimizer stores the optimized file on a local drive on your network even if your QuickBooks company file resides on your server. You want to use the Optimizer because it speeds up the rate at which third party applications are able to pull information from QuickBooks company files. However, you should consider changing the default frequency to The Last Time I Pressed One Of The Load Data Buttons. Intuit feels this option offers you the best trade-off between up-to-date data and performance.

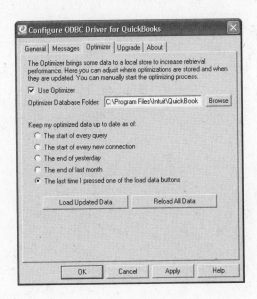

The first time you optimize any QuickBooks company file, you'll need to fill out a security certificate that allows the ODBC driver to access that QuickBooks company file. You'll also need to fill out a security certificate to allow third party applications to access your QuickBooks company file.

The last two tabs are informational: from the Upgrade tab, you can purchase the version of the ODBC driver that permits you to write data back to your QuickBooks file as well as read data from your QuickBooks data file. From the About tab, you can identify your version of the ODBC driver.

Using Online Banking Services

n this chapter:

- Understanding online banking

- Setting up a connection to QuickBooks on the Web

- Setting up online bank accounts

- Performing online transactions

- Receiving online payments from your customers

If you have an Internet connection, you can use the wide range of online services offered by QuickBooks, including Internet-based banking, which is the subject of this chapter. You'll discover that QuickBooks and most banks have taken advantage of the Internet to make banking a snap. Using QuickBooks, you can sign up for the following online features:

- Online banking, which enables you to view the status of your bank accounts, see which transactions have cleared, and generally maintain your accounts via your Internet connection.
- Online payments, which enables you to send money to vendors via the Internet instead of writing checks. If your vendor accepts electronic deposits, the bank deposits the money directly into your vendor's bank account; otherwise, the bank generates and mails a check for the vendor.
- Online receipts, which enables you to accept payments from your customers electronically.

Online services are also available for your credit card accounts, so you can view credit card transactions online and download them to enter them in your credit card account register. To take advantage of online credit card tracking, you must set up your credit cards as liability accounts in QuickBooks, which is discussed in Chapter 11.

Understanding Online Banking

Online banking lets you use the Internet to view information stored on your bank's computer about your accounts. The bank's computer is a server, configured for the secure exchange of data. QuickBooks provides two methods for using the online banking services your bank offers:

- **Web Connect**   Use this method when your bank doesn't provide a way to connect QuickBooks directly to the bank's server. Instead, the bank maintains a page on its web site that lets you view and download your bank statement; you then import the downloaded file into QuickBooks, and the import process is quick and easy.
- **Direct Connection**   Use this method when your bank exchanges data interactively with QuickBooks. This method allows you to download transactions, transfer money between bank accounts, e-mail messages to the bank, and pay bills online from within QuickBooks instead of working from your bank's web site.

Instructions for using the Web Connect and Direct Connection features appear later in this chapter in the section "Getting Bank Account Data Online."

Setting Up a Connection

Before you can use online services with QuickBooks, you have to tell QuickBooks about your Internet connection. After this simple step, QuickBooks does its online work on autopilot.

Choose Help | Internet Connection Setup from the menu bar. This launches the Internet Connection Setup wizard (see Figure 16-1).

 N O T E : No matter which selection you choose, when you click Next, the last wizard window appears (it's a small, efficient wizard). Click Done when you've read the information in the second window.

Dial-up Connections

The option Use The Following Connection refers to a dial-up connection, using a modem. Any dial-up connections you've configured appear in the Internet Connection Setup window. If no connection appears and you know you've configured a dial-up connection, QuickBooks had a problem finding it or identifying it. Close the window but leave QuickBooks open. Connect to the Internet and, while still connected, choose Help | Internet Connection Setup again; QuickBooks should find your Internet connection.

Highlight the connection, click Next, and click Done on the next window and you're ready to work online with QuickBooks.

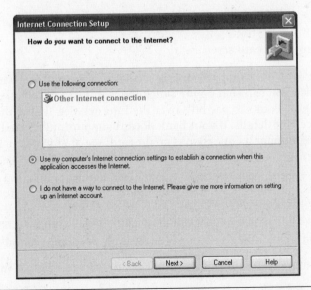

FIGURE 16-1 Tell QuickBooks how your computer connects to the Internet

CAUTION: If QuickBooks doesn't detect your connection and you had to connect to the Internet before configuring this wizard, you'll probably have to connect manually every time you want to use Internet services in QuickBooks.

Network or Always-on Connections

If you connect to the Internet via a DSL/cable modem or through another computer on your network using Internet connection sharing, select the option Use My Computer's Internet Connection Settings.... Then click Next to see an explanation of the connection QuickBooks found; then, click Done.

No Internet Connection

If you don't have an Internet connection and you click the third option and then click Next, you'll see a message that explains that you must sign up for Internet service before using the Internet Connection Setup wizard. The window has an option to launch the Windows Internet Connection wizard, which walks you through the process of setting up a new connection. After you sign up with an Internet Service Provider (ISP), return to this window and set up your QuickBooks online connection.

Setting Up Online Banking

You can sign up for three types of online banking services:

- Online account access.
- Online bill paying.
- Online credit card services.

If your bank only supports online account access, and you want to pay bills over the Internet, you can sign up for QuickBooks Bill Pay, a fee-based service that lets you use QuickBooks to pay bills over the Internet. See "Using the QuickBooks Bill Pay Service" for details. If your bank doesn't support online credit card services, you can sign up for a QuickBooks credit card; see "Using a QuickBooks Credit Card" later in this chapter.

You take three steps to enable online banking:

1. Apply for online services with your bank.
2. Receive a personal identification number (PIN) from your bank.
3. Enable a QuickBooks account (or multiple accounts) for online services.

To get started, choose Banking | Online Banking from the menu bar.

Finding Your Bank Online

If you haven't signed up for (or discussed) online services with your bank, choose Available Financial Institutions to see if your bank participates. QuickBooks displays a dialog box telling you it has to open a browser to travel to the Internet. Click OK, and when you're connected to the Internet, you see the Financial Institutions Directory web site (see Figure 16-2).

The four buttons in the upper left corner of the left pane determine the contents of the Financial Institution Directory list below the buttons. The window displays the results of selecting Any Services, and all the listed banks provide some type of online service.

If you're interested in a particular online service, select that option, and the list of banks changes to those banks that offer the selected service.

Scroll through the list to find your bank and click its listing. The right pane of the Financial Institutions Directory window displays information about the bank's online services (see Figure 16-3) and a telephone number you can call for more information or to apply for online services. You may also see an Apply Now button, if your bank supports online signup.

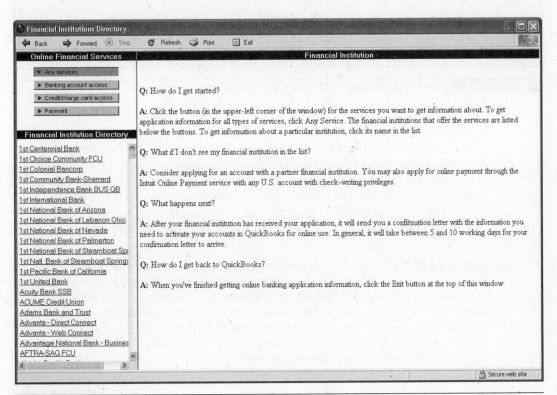

FIGURE 16-2   Select the type of online service you want to use and then look for your bank in the list

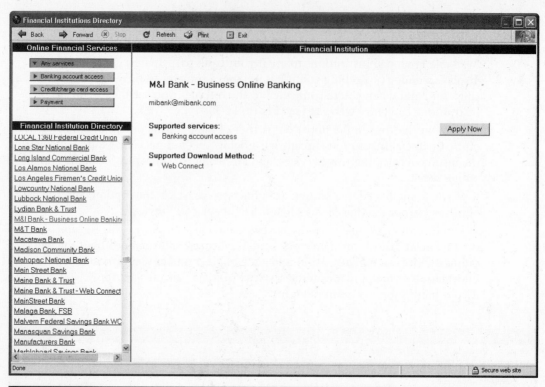

FIGURE 16-3   Check to see if your bank offers the services you want to use

Click the Apply Now button if you want to start the application process here and now. If no Apply Now button appears, follow the instructions for setting up online services at the bank—usually the bank displays a phone number. If you can apply online, fill out the form and submit the information. Your bank will send you information about using its online service, along with a PIN. All banks provide a method of changing the PIN to one of your own choosing. In fact, many banks insist that you change the PIN the first time you access online services.

CAUTION: You may see a warning that you are about to send information to an Internet zone in which it might be possible for other people to see the data you send. Select Yes to continue (you might want to select the option not to be warned in the future). The information you send is encrypted with the same kind of technology used on secure web sites such as amazon.com, so, if you're comfortable buying products online with a personal credit card, then you should be comfortable with online banking services.

Using the QuickBooks Bill Pay Service

Here's the situation: You want to pay bills electronically using QuickBooks. Your bank either:

- Doesn't offer online bill-paying services, or;
- Your bank uses Web Connect, which doesn't permit you to pay bills electronically from within QuickBooks.

You can pay bills electronically from within QuickBooks if you sign up for the QuickBooks Bill Pay service.

From the Online Banking submenu, choose Available Financial Institutions. When the Financial Institutions list appears, scroll through the list to find QuickBooks Bill Pay Service in the left pane. You'll see two listings:

- QuickBooks Bill Pay—New!, which is the listing you should select.
- QuickBooks Bill Pay—TM, which is the listing for existing customers who use older versions of QuickBooks; you can't sign up for this service anymore.

When you select QuickBooks Bill Pay—New!, the right pane displays information about this service (see Figure 16-4).

To sign up, click Apply Now. After you answer a couple of questions about your business, click the Continue button. An application form appears on your screen. Follow the prompts and instructions to complete the enrollment process.

Using a QuickBooks Credit Card

If you want to download credit card transactions into QuickBooks and your credit card provider doesn't support that feature, you can sign up for a QuickBooks credit card. In the Financial Institutions list, select QuickBooks Platinum Plus and follow the instructions for signing up.

Setting Up Online Access

 NOTE: If you've already applied for online services at your bank and received your PIN, you can skip this part.

The Setup Account For Online Access command under the Online Banking menu launches the Online Banking Setup Interview wizard that walks you through either of the following functions, depending on your selections in the wizard windows:

- The wizard searches for your bank on the Internet so you can apply online or get information about applying by telephone or in person. You accomplish the same thing if you choose the Available Financial Institutions command, find your bank, and click Apply Now.

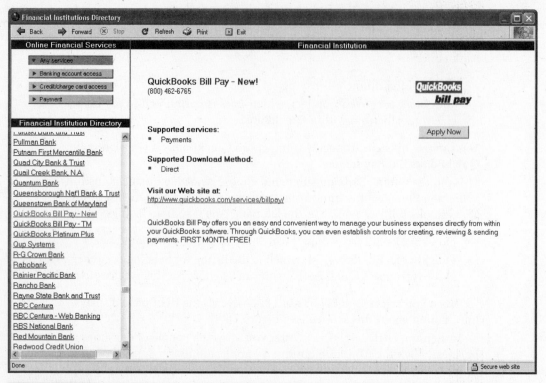

FIGURE 16-4 If your bank doesn't offer online bill paying, you can sign up for the QuickBooks Bill Pay service

- After you've completed the paperwork at your bank and received a PIN, the Online Banking Setup Interview wizard walks you through the process of enabling your bank account for online banking in QuickBooks. These functions are discussed in the following sections.

Enabling Direct Connect Online Bank Accounts

You use different techniques to enable bank accounts for online access, depending on whether your bank uses Direct Connect or Web Connect.

If your bank uses Direct Connect, choose Banking | Online Banking | Setup Account For Online Access. QuickBooks displays a message telling you that it must close any open windows to complete this task. Click Yes to continue.

The Online Banking Setup Interview wizard appears. Click the Enable Accounts tab, and step through the instructions the wizard presents, answering the questions the wizard poses. As you go through the steps in the wizard, you're configuring a bank account as an online account. You'll be asked to select the online services you'll use with this account. Choose online account access, online payments, or both, depending on the services you intend to use through your bank.

TIP: You can create online bank accounts in QuickBooks for as many accounts and different financial institutions as you need (and have signed up for).

Enabling Web Connect Online Bank Accounts

If your bank uses Web Connect, the first time you download transactions also enables your bank account for online access.

Follow these steps:

1 You can leave QuickBooks open, but open your browser and navigate to your bank's web site and sign in.

2 Click the Download to QuickBooks button. QuickBooks displays a window, asking you to identify the QuickBooks account that is associated with the information you intend to download from your financial institution.

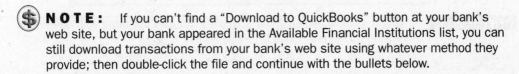 **NOTE:** If you can't find a "Download to QuickBooks" button at your bank's web site, but your bank appeared in the Available Financial Institutions list, you can still download transactions from your bank's web site using whatever method they provide; then double-click the file and continue with the bullets below.

- If you already have established a bank account in QuickBooks, click Use Existing QuickBooks account and select the account from the drop-down list.
- If you haven't set up an account in QuickBooks, click Create A New QuickBooks Account to create the account as part of the process of enabling it for online access. Give it an appropriate name.

3 Click Continue. Your web site downloads recent transaction information into the selected bank account.

In the future, you'll work inside QuickBooks when you want to download transaction information from your bank to QuickBooks; see "Exchanging Data with Web Connect" later in this chapter.

Getting Bank Account Data Online

After you've set up your online banking permissions with your financial institutions and established your online bank account(s) in QuickBooks, you're ready to use the online services your bank offers. The way you interact with your bank from QuickBooks depends on whether your account is a Web Connect account or a Direct Connect account.

Exchanging Data with Web Connect

To connect to your bank, choose Banking | Online Banking | Online Banking Center. In the Online Banking Center window, seen in Figure 16-5, select your bank from the

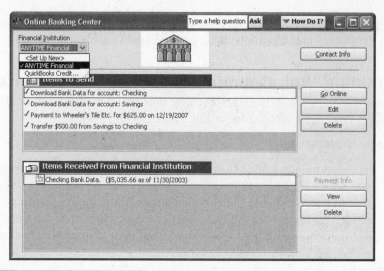

FIGURE 16-5   You'll see multiple entries in the Financial Institution list only if you've set up multiple financial institutions for online access

Financial Institution drop-down list at the top of the window. The drop-down list offers multiple entries only if you've set up more than one financial institution for online access. Click Go Online, and QuickBooks opens the bank's web site.

Log in and view your bank statements. You can print the statement from your browser and then enter transactions manually, but that defeats the purpose of having online access. Instead, download a file that you can import into QuickBooks. When you click the Download File button on the web site, the standard Windows Download dialog box appears. Choose Open or Save. If you choose Open, you don't need to take any additional action. When you open or switch to QuickBooks and view the Online Banking Center, you'll see your downloaded transactions.

If you choose Save, select a location for the file. Make sure you download the right file type; QuickBooks should appear in the list of files types you can download. Once the file finishes downloading, you can import the data into QuickBooks.

To import a downloaded QuickBooks transaction file, follow these steps:

1 Choose File | Utilities | Import | Web Connect Files from the QuickBooks menu bar. The Open Online Data File dialog box appears.

2 Select the file you downloaded (the file extension is .QBO) and click Open. The Select Bank Account dialog box opens.

3 Select Use An Existing Online Account and click Continue to begin the import process.

④ When QuickBooks finishes importing the file, a message appears to inform you of that fact.

⑤ Click OK.

Exchanging Data with Direct Connection

If your bank uses the Direct Connection method of online banking, you can perform the following online tasks from within QuickBooks:

- Exchange e-mail messages with your bank.
- Transfer funds between accounts at the bank.
- Receive a list of transactions that have cleared your account.
- Pay bills.

Some banks won't let you pay bills interactively through QuickBooks, although they may have a bill-paying service available outside of QuickBooks, which you can access on the bank's web site. If that's the case, and you prefer to pay your bills online through QuickBooks, see the section earlier in this chapter on using the QuickBooks Bill Pay Service.

Creating Messages to Send to Your Bank

Banks that support Direct Connection have a two-way message feature: you can both send and receive messages while working in QuickBooks. To send a message to your bank, choose Banking | Create Online Banking Message. Enter the message text in the Online Banking Message dialog box, and click OK. You send the message when you connect to your bank; read on.

Connecting to Your Bank

To connect to your bank, choose Banking | Online Banking | Online Banking Center to open the Online Banking Center window shown previously in Figure 16-5.

If you use online services at more than one financial institution, select the appropriate bank from the drop-down list in the Financial Institution field at the top of the window. The window has two sections: Items To Send and Items Received From Financial Institution. Any items in the Items Received From Financial Institution section that *do not* have check marks beside them are items you haven't yet reviewed.

Sending Data to Your Bank

The Items To Send section of the Online Banking Center window contains the data you send to your bank. By default, all items have a check mark, and they'll be sent to the bank when you click the Go Online button.

- If you don't want to send an item, click its check mark to remove it.

- You can edit any item except a request to receive bank data. To edit an item, select it, click the Edit button, make the necessary changes, and click OK.
- You can remove any item except a request for bank data. Select the item you want to remove and click the Delete button.

Click the Go Online button to contact your bank over the Internet. A dialog box opens to accept your PIN or password. Click OK to begin transmitting information. You'll see progress messages as QuickBooks contacts the bank's server, sends any messages you created, and downloads any new transactions that cleared the bank since the last time you went online.

If your bank account hasn't cleared any new transactions since the last time you went online, you'll see a message with that information. If QuickBooks downloads new transactions, the Online Transmission Summary window displays a report. You can print the new transactions if you want; click Close to return to the Online Banking Center window.

Viewing the Received Data

The Items Received From Financial Institution section of the Online Banking Center window displays all the items QuickBooks downloaded from your bank during the online session. Select an item and click View to see it.

When you view bank data, QuickBooks opens the Match Transactions window, which displays the account register at the top and the list of new transactions at the bottom.

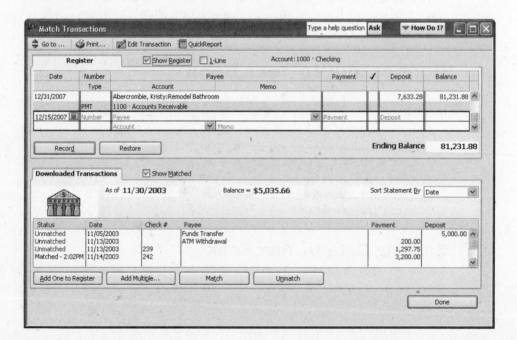

Matching Transactions

QuickBooks automatically tries to match downloaded transactions to the transactions in your register and marks each downloaded transaction as either matched or unmatched.

If all the downloaded transactions are matched, you have nothing else to do. QuickBooks clears every matched transaction by inserting a lightning bolt in the Cleared column of your register. To handle unmatched transactions, read on.

 TIP: A check mark in the Cleared column indicates a transaction has cleared and has also been through reconciliation. Chapter 12 covers bank reconciliation.

Matching Unmatched Transactions

If any transactions are marked unmatched, you have to correct the register. QuickBooks may not match a transaction for several reasons.

Differing Check Numbers and Amounts

If a downloaded transaction's check number and amount differ from the transaction in the register, QuickBooks won't match the transactions. For example, you may have entered check 2034 in the amount of $100.00 in your register, but the only downloaded $100.00 check is listed as check 2035.

Correct the transaction in the register. If the problem is a check number, change the check number in the register; it's unlikely the downloaded transaction's check number is wrong because banks read check numbers electronically, using the metallic ink at the bottom of your check.

If the problem is a difference in the amount for a specific check number, it could be either your error or the bank's error. However, for the time being, change the register to match the downloaded transaction. Then contact your bank to find out what happened. If the bank made a mistake in the amount, it will adjust your account for the appropriate amount and that transaction will show up in the future when you download transactions, matching the adjusting entry you make in the register when you finish talking to the person at the bank.

Unmatched Bank Charges

Often, the transactions you download don't appear in your register. Bank charges download when they're assessed. Add the bank charges to the register by selecting the transaction in the Downloaded Transactions section and clicking the Add One To Register button. In the Add Unmatched Transaction dialog box, select the method you want to use to add the transaction; the choices differ depending on whether you're working with a bank account or a credit card account. Follow the prompts and enter the information. You don't have to enter a payee for a bank charge, you just have to enter the account to which you post bank charges.

If you have a merchant account (you accept credit cards for customer payments), you're assessed a monthly charge that appears as an unmatched transaction just like a bank charge. Add this charge the same way you add a bank charge, posting the merchant card fee/charge to the appropriate account.

Unmatched Checks and Withdrawals

A check that has no matching transaction means you wrote and sent a check but didn't enter it in the register. Click Add One To Register, then select Add To Register or Add In Write Checks from the Add Unmatched Transaction dialog box, and click OK. When you save the transaction in the appropriate window, QuickBooks automatically matches the downloaded transaction to the transaction in your register.

If you print checks, or you know you entered every manual check you wrote in your QuickBooks register, you may have a more serious problem—someone may have stolen a check. Call your bank immediately.

If you use an ATM card to withdraw cash from your bank account, any withdrawals you didn't enter in the register appear as unmatched in the Match Transactions window. Click Add One To Register, enter the transactions, and QuickBooks matches them as soon as you record them.

Unmatched Deposits

If QuickBooks downloads a deposit that doesn't match any transaction in the register, check to see whether income you recorded in a Sales Receipt or Received Payment transaction is still in the Undeposited Funds account. If so, open the Make Deposits window, select the appropriate transaction(s), and walk through the steps to make the deposit. As soon as you finish, QuickBooks automatically matches the deposit to the downloaded deposit.

If a deposit doesn't exist in QuickBooks, you need to create the transaction. Use either a Sales Receipt for a direct sale, or a Received Payment for a customer's invoice payment. When you finish recording the transaction, QuickBooks automatically matches it to the downloaded transaction.

Matching Merchant Card Deposits

Most of the time, your merchant card deposits appear as unmatched transactions when you download because you keep the merchant card funds in the Undeposited Funds account until your merchant card provider deposits the money. Merchant card deposits work in one of the following ways:

- Your financial institution deposits the entire amount of the sale and removes all fees incurred during the month from your account once a month.
- Your financial institution deducts the fee before depositing the proceeds of the sale but your Undeposited Funds account lists the total amount of the sale.

If your merchant card provider deposits the gross sale proceeds, match the transaction by selecting the transaction in the Make Deposits window and following the steps for depositing the funds.

If your merchant card provider deposits the net after deducting the fee and you didn't deduct the fee when you entered the sales transaction, you need to deduct the fee to match the deposit.

Click the Record Deposits icon on the Home page (or choose Banking | Make Deposits from the menu bar), and select the credit card transaction in the Payments To Deposit dialog box. Click OK to open the Make Deposits dialog box, where you create an additional line for this transaction.

- In the From Account column, enter the account to which you post merchant card fees.
- In the Amount column, enter the fee as a minus figure; you have to calculate the amount—it's the difference between your sale amount and the amount of the downloaded transaction.

The net deposit, displayed at the bottom of the dialog box, matches the downloaded transaction. When you click Save & Close, QuickBooks automatically matches the downloaded transaction to the deposit.

Using Aliases to Match Online Bill Payments

If you use your bank's online bill-paying service on the bank's web site and download the transactions into QuickBooks, the downloaded file lists the name of the payee for online bill payments. For regular checks, the downloaded file lists the check number, not the name of the payee.

You may see transactions marked as "unmatched," even though you entered the transaction in your bank register; this occurs because the payee name on the online transaction doesn't match the payee name on your register entry.

In addition, if you didn't enter the transaction in your bank register, you won't have much luck because QuickBooks won't be able to find a vendor name to match the name on the downloaded transaction.

To resolve theses issues, you can create an alias for each online payee whose names don't match the names of vendors in your QuickBooks company file.

Follow these steps:

1. Select a transaction and click Add One To Register.
2. Select the way to add the transaction (Add To Register, Write Checks, or Pay Bills). Because the Payee in the downloaded transaction doesn't match an existing vendor, a Name Not Found dialog box appears.
3. Choose Create Alias to open the Create Alias dialog box.
4. Select an existing vendor name from the drop-down list.
5. Click OK and confirm the addition of this alias for this vendor.

The next time you download transactions with this payee name, QuickBooks recognizes the alias and matches the transaction if it exists in the register. If the transaction doesn't exist in the register, select the downloaded transaction and click Add One To Register. QuickBooks automatically adds it to the register, replacing the alias with the vendor name. If necessary, you can add multiple aliases to the same vendor name.

Transferring Money Between Accounts Online

If you have multiple accounts at your financial institution, you can transfer money between those accounts. To transfer money online, you must have applied at your financial institution for online banking for both accounts. In addition, you must have enabled both accounts for online access within QuickBooks.

There are two methods you can use to transfer funds between online accounts: the transfer funds function or direct data entry in the register for either account.

Using the Transfer Funds Function

The simplest way to move money between your online accounts is to use the QuickBooks Transfer Funds Between Accounts window; choose Banking | Transfer Funds from the menu bar. Specify the sending and receiving accounts and enter the amount you want to transfer. Check the Online Funds Transfer box and click Save & Close.

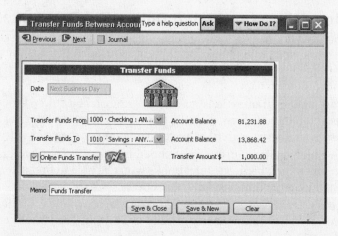

Then choose Banking | Online Banking Center, make sure the transaction has a check mark, and click Go Online.

Using the Bank Register to Transfer Funds

You can enter a transfer directly into the account register of the bank account from which you are sending the money. The significant data entry is the one in the Check Number column; instead of a check number, type the word **Send**. Don't enter a payee; enter the amount, and enter the receiving account in the Account field. Then choose Banking | Online Banking | Online Banking Center, make sure the transaction has a check mark, and click Go Online.

Paying Bills Online

You can pay your bills in QuickBooks, then go online to send the payments to the payees. You can either use your own bank (if it's capable of working with QuickBooks

---

▶▶ FYI

Web Connect and Paying Bills

Many banks that use Web Connect with QuickBooks also offer online bill paying, but you can't pay bills online from QuickBooks when your bank uses Web Connect. If you want to pay bills online, you have two choices: you can use QuickBooks Bill Pay, discussed later in this chapter, or you can use your bank's bill-paying service through your bank's web site. If you choose this latter option, your challenge then becomes keeping your QuickBooks data accurate and up-to-date.

Bill paying involves writing checks; using the Web Connect service, you'll download the checks you write online when you download transactions. You can handle check writing in QuickBooks in either of the following ways:

- You can skip entering and paying bills in QuickBooks, and just download transactions from your bank's web site. This approach doesn't provide you with the tools available in QuickBooks to manage payables effectively.
- You can enter and pay bills in QuickBooks without printing checks; you'll match downloaded transactions to existing QuickBooks transactions when you download; see "Matching Transactions" earlier in this chapter. Although this approach involves duplicating data entry, you do maintain control over your payables and sometimes online bill paying is cheaper than writing and mailing checks.

You'll need to decide if using an online bill-paying service that doesn't connect directly with QuickBooks is worth the time and effort. If your bank uses Web Connect and offers online bill paying, you may want to stick to downloading transactions only and not use online bill paying unless you determine that you'll save more money using online bill paying than writing and printing checks.

to pay bills online), or use the QuickBooks bill-paying service. In this section, when I say "bank," you can mentally substitute the QuickBooks service if that's what you're using.

When you make an online payment, the bank transmits the following information to your vendor in addition to money:

- The date and number of the vendor's bill(s).
- Information about any discounts or credits you've applied.
- Anything you inserted as a memo or note when you prepared the payment.

If the vendor is set up to receive electronic payments, the bank transfers the money from your bank account directly to the vendor's bank account. If the vendor's account is not accessible for online payments, your bank writes a check and mails it, along with all the necessary payment information.

($) **N O T E :**   Being set up to receive electronic payments does not mean your vendor must be using QuickBooks; there are many and varied methods for receiving electronic payments and many companies have these arrangements with their banks.

You can use the Write Checks window, the Pay Bills window, or the bank account register to create the transaction in QuickBooks; in each case, you need to indicate that you're paying electronically. In the Write Checks window, check the Online Payment box. In the Pay Bills window, select the Online Bank Pmt option from the Payment Method list box. In the register, type **Send** as the check number.

($) **C A U T I O N :**   If you add a memo, your text can be delivered only as a voucher or stub. This means that your bank won't make the payment electronically even if the vendor is able to accept electronic payments. Instead, the bank will send a paper check, which delays the payment.

Choose Banking | Online Banking | Online Banking Center, open the Online Banking Center window; then, click Go Online. QuickBooks sends your electronic payments to the big bill-paying machine on the Net.

Creating Online Transaction Reports

You can track your online activities using reports available in QuickBooks. The quickest way to see your online transactions is to modify a Transaction Detail By Account report.

Follow these steps:

1. Choose Reports | Accountant & Taxes | Transaction Detail By Account.
2. In the report window, click the Modify Report button to display the Modify Report dialog box.
3. Click the Filters tab.
4. In the Filter list box, select Online Status.
5. Click the arrow to the right of the Online Status box and select the online status option you need:

- **Online To Send** Reports the online transactions you've created but not yet sent online.
- **Online Sent** Reports only the online transactions you've sent.
- **Any Online** Reports on all the online transactions you've created, both sent and waiting.
- **Not Online** Excludes the online transactions from the report. (Obviously, you don't want to choose this option.)

After you've set the filter options, click OK to redisplay the report window.

Receiving Customer Payments Online

Besides the online activities that permit you to track your own bank account activity, transfer money, and pay your own bills, you can use QuickBooks Billing Solutions to let your customers pay you online. At the QuickBooks Billing Solutions web site, the customer can enter a credit card number to pay the bills or use an online payment service.

You can notify the customer about this online service by e-mailing the invoice with the online service URL in the cover note, or by snail-mailing the invoice and sending an e-mail message with the online service URL. The customer clicks the URL link to visit the QuickBooks web site and arrange to pay your invoice.

QuickBooks notifies you that the customer has paid the invoice, and you can download the payment information into your bank register, using the standard online banking procedures.

To learn more about this service or to sign up, visit the web site http://www.quickbooksmerchantservice.com/services/billing_solutions/features.php.

Year-End Procedures

In this chapter:

- Running reports on your financial condition

- Printing 1099 forms

- Making year-end journal entries

- Getting ready for tax time

- Closing the books

The end of the year is a madhouse for bookkeepers, and that's true for major corporations as well as for small businesses. There is so much to do: so many reports to examine, corrections to make, entries to create, adjustments to apply—whew!

You can relax a bit. You don't have to show up at the office on January 1. You don't have to have everything done on the first day of your new fiscal year. QuickBooks is date-sensitive so you can continue to work on finishing up the old year while you work in the new year. As long as you date new transactions after the last day of your fiscal year, QuickBooks will correctly assign the transactions to the new year.

Understanding Year-End Tasks

The end of the year means more than just closing the books in QuickBooks. You'll want to make sure that the books are accurate before you close them. The government also has a variety of year-end reporting requirements that you must meet. Typically, at the end of the year, you:

- Reconcile bank, credit card, and petty cash accounts for the year you plan to close.
- Review fringe benefits and complete payroll tax forms.
- Verify and print 1099 forms for eligible vendors.
- Review the records for assets you purchased during the year to make sure that the records are complete for future depreciation calculations.
- Review financial reports.
- Enter journal entries to record adjustments, asset depreciation, and other year-end accruals.
- Perform a physical inventory, if appropriate, and reconcile the results with your QuickBooks inventory.
- Review tax reports to verify tax tracking.
- Export tax data and prepare for the new year.
- Set a closing date in QuickBooks.
- Back up your data.

In this chapter, you'll read about most of these tasks; some of the tasks, such as reconciling bank and other accounts, preparing payroll tax forms, and performing a physical inventory, appear in appropriate chapters throughout the book.

In addition to the information you find in this chapter, the web site http://www.quickbooks.com/yearend/ contains a wealth of information about year end; be sure to check it out.

Running Year-End Financial Reports

The standard financial reports you run at year-end provide a couple of services for you:

- You can see the economic health of your business.
- You can examine the report to make sure everything is posted correctly before you organize information for paying taxes.

To run financial reports, click the Reports menu. For year-end reports, you'll need several types of reports; see Chapter 15 for information about modifying and customizing the standard financial reports.

Don't forget that reports have date ranges like "current year" and "last fiscal year." If you perform these tasks before the end of your fiscal year, you're still in the current year. However, if you're working after the last date of your fiscal year, you want to make sure that you report on the last fiscal year.

Year-End Profit & Loss Report

The Profit & Loss report, also called an *income statement*, shows you revenue and expenses over a specified period of time. To print a Profit & Loss Standard report, choose Reports | Company & Financial | Profit & Loss Standard. When QuickBooks displays the report, be sure that the date range is the entire fiscal year; by default, the date range is the current month to date.

The report displays the year-end balances for all the income and expense accounts in your general ledger that had any activity during the reporting period. Examine the report, and if anything seems out of whack, double-click the line to see the transactions that QuickBooks posted to that account. If you question any of the information you see, double-click any line to see the original transaction in the window where you created it.

If there's a transaction that seems to be in error, you can take corrective action. You cannot delete or void a bill you paid or a customer invoice for which you received payment. However, you might be able to talk to a customer or vendor for whom you've found a problem and work out a satisfactory arrangement for credits. Or you may find that you posted an expense or income transaction to the wrong general ledger account. If so, make a journal entry to correct it (see Chapter 14 for information on journal entries). Then run the year-end Profit & Loss report again.

Year-End Balance Sheet

Often described as a "snapshot" of the company's financial condition on a particular date, the Balance Sheet is a statement of the book value of a business on a specified date. To print your company's Balance Sheet, choose Reports | Company & Financial | Balance Sheet Standard.

Issuing 1099 Forms

If any of your vendors qualify to receive 1099 forms, they must be in the vendor's hands by January 31. So, sometime in January of the new year, you'll need to issue 1099 forms to vendors who qualify to receive 1099 forms. Before you print the forms, you should check your 1099 setup and then print a report that shows you what you can expect to see on 1099 forms when you print them. You can perform these tasks before you print the forms or as part of the form printing process. I prefer to perform the tasks as part of the form printing process.

To print the 1099 forms, choose File | Print Forms | 1099s/1096. QuickBooks opens a wizard that will walk you through the process to make sure every step is covered and every amount is correct (see Figure 17-1).

This isn't a standard wizard because you don't walk through a series of windows. Instead, as you click each button, QuickBooks opens the appropriate window so you can check and, if necessary, change information. When you close the window, QuickBooks redisplays the wizard window.

Checking 1099 Vendor Information

Click the first Run Report button, and QuickBooks prints the Vendor 1099 Review report shown in Figure 17-2. Using this report, you can make sure that you have correctly identified all vendors who are eligible for 1099 forms and that you have

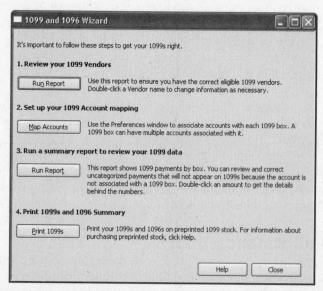

FIGURE 17-1   The 1099 and 1096 Wizard makes it easy to issue 1099 forms to vendors

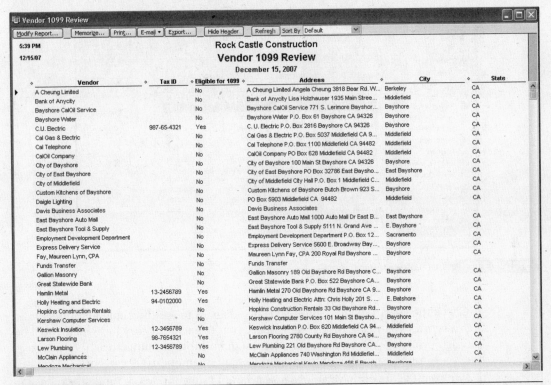

Vendor	Tax ID	Eligible for 1099	Address	City	State
A Cheung Limited		No	A Cheung Limited Angela Cheung 3818 Bear Rd. W...	Berkeley	CA
Bank of Anycity		No	Bank of Anycity Lisa Holzhauser 1935 Main Stree...	Middlefield	CA
Bayshore CalOil Service		No	Bayshore CalOil Service 771 S. Lerimore Bayshor...	Bayshore	CA
Bayshore Water		No	Bayshore Water P.O. Box 61 Bayshore CA 94326	Bayshore	CA
C.U. Electric	987-65-4321	Yes	C. U. Electric P.O. Box 2816 Bayshore CA 94326	Bayshore	CA
Cal Gas & Electric		No	Cal Gas & Electric P.O. Box 5037 Middlefield CA 9...	Middlefield	CA
Cal Telephone		No	Cal Telephone P.O. Box 1100 Middlefield CA 94482	Middlefield	CA
CalOil Company		No	CalOil Company PO Box 628 Middlefield CA 94482	Middlefield	CA
City of Bayshore		No	City of Bayshore 100 Main St Bayshore CA 94326	Bayshore	CA
City of East Bayshore		No	City of East Bayshore PO Box 32786 East Baysho...	East Bayshore	CA
City of Middlefield		No	City of Middlefield City Hall P.O. Box 1 Middlefield C...	Middlefield	CA
Custom Kitchens of Bayshore		No	Custom Kitchens of Bayshore Butch Brown 923 S...	Bayshore	CA
Daigle Lighting		No	PO Box 5903 Middlefield CA 94482	Middlefield	CA
Davis Business Associates		No	Davis Business Associates		
East Bayshore Auto Mall		No	East Bayshore Auto Mall 1000 Auto Mall Dr East B...	East Bayshore	CA
East Bayshore Tool & Supply		No	East Bayshore Tool & Supply 5111 N. Grand Ave ...	E. Bayshore	CA
Employment Development Department		No	Employment Development Department P.O. Box 12...	Sacramento	CA
Express Delivery Service		No	Express Delivery Service 5600 E. Broadway Bay...	Bayshore	CA
Fay, Maureen Lynn, CPA		No	Maureen Lynn Fay, CPA 200 Royal Rd Bayshore ...	Bayshore	CA
Funds Transfer		No	Funds Transfer		
Gallion Masonry		No	Gallion Masonry 189 Old Bayshore Rd Bayshore C...	Bayshore	CA
Great Statewide Bank		No	Great Statewide Bank P.O. Box 522 Bayshore CA...	Bayshore	CA
Hamlin Metal	13-2456789	Yes	Hamlin Metal 270 Old Bayshore Rd Bayshore CA 9...	Bayshore	CA
Holly Heating and Electric	94-0102000	Yes	Holly Heating and Electric Attn: Chris Holly 201 S. ...	E. Batshore	CA
Hopkins Construction Rentals		No	Hopkins Construction Rentals 33 Old Bayshore Rd...	Bayshore	CA
Kershaw Computer Services		No	Kershaw Computer Services 101 Main St Baysho...	Bayshore	CA
Keswick Insulation	12-3456789	Yes	Keswick Insulation P.O. Box 620 Middlefield CA 94...	Middlefield	CA
Larson Flooring	98-7654321	Yes	Larson Flooring 2780 County Rd Bayshore CA 94...	Bayshore	CA
Lew Plumbing	12-3456789	Yes	Lew Plumbing 221 Old Bayshore Rd Bayshore CA...	Bayshore	CA
McClain Appliances		No	McClain Appliances 740 Washington Rd Middlefiel...	Middlefield	CA
Mendoza Mechanical		No	Mendoza Mechanical Kevin Mendoza 456 E Baysh...	Bayshore	CA

FIGURE 17-2 Use this report to confirm that you have Tax ID and address information for all vendors who will receive 1099 forms

completed the Tax ID and address for each 1099-eligible vendor; you'll need this information to produce the form.

($) NOTE: Businesses organized as LLCs can opt to be proprietorships, partnerships, or corporations for the purpose of filing tax returns. If you have a vendor that is organized as an LLC, ask whether the vendor is reporting as a corporation because you don't need to print 1099 forms for corporations.

When you close the report, the 1099 and 1096 Wizard window reappears.

Checking 1099 Setup

Click the Map Accounts button to display the Company Preferences tab of the Tax: 1099 category in the Preferences dialog box (see Figure 17-3).

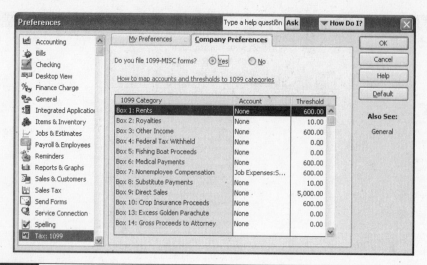

FIGURE 17-3   Set 1099 Preferences

Check the latest IRS rules and make any changes to the threshold amounts for the categories you need. Also assign an account to each category for which you'll be issuing Form 1099 to vendors. You can assign multiple accounts to a 1099 category, but you cannot assign the same account to more than one 1099 category.

For example, if you have an expense account "subcontractors" and an expense account "outside consultants," you can assign both of the accounts to the same 1099 category (Nonemployee Compensation). However, once you assign those accounts to that category, you cannot assign those same accounts to any other 1099 category.

To assign a single account to a category, click the text in the account column to select it. Then click the arrow to select the account for this category.

To assign multiple accounts to a category, instead of selecting an account after you click the arrow, choose the Multiple Accounts option at the top of the list. In the Select Account dialog box, click each account to check it. Click OK to assign all the accounts you checked. Then click OK to close the Preferences dialog box. The 1099 and 1096 Wizard window reappears.

Verifying Vendor 1099 Balances

Click the Run Report button just below 1. Review Your 1099 Vendors to preview the information that will appear on the 1099 forms. QuickBooks displays the 1099 Summary Report, which lists each vendor eligible for a 1099 with the total amount paid to the vendor.

➤➤ **FYI**

Using 1099 Options to Troubleshoot

1099 Options appear at the top of both the 1099 Summary report and the 1099 Detail report; as you would expect, the defaults deliberately set up the report to focus on 1099 information. You can also use these options cleverly to help you troubleshoot. For example, on the 1099 Summary report, you can verify that you have correctly identified all 1099 vendors by opening the 1099 Options box and changing Only 1099 Vendors to All Vendors. Then compare the new version of the report with the default version. If additional vendors appear on the new version of the report, you have posted payments against a 1099 account for a vendor that you didn't set up as a 1099 vendor.

Or suppose that a 1099 vendor's reported amount looks low. On the 1099 Detail report, change the 1099 Options to display all accounts instead of only 1099 accounts; you may find that you erroneously posted 1099-eligible transactions to an account not designated as a 1099 account.

If an entry on this report looks suspicious, double-click the suspicious amount; QuickBooks displays the 1099 Detail report for the vendor of the transaction you double-clicked, showing you a list of the transactions that make up the total reported for the vendor. You can print this report for all 1099-eligible vendors by choosing Reports | Vendors & Payables | 1099 Detail.

When all the 1099 information is correct, close the reports to redisplay the 1099 and 1096 Wizard.

Print 1099 Forms

Click Print 1099s in the wizard window. The wizard asks you to confirm the year for which you're printing.

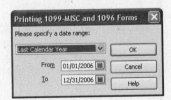

Click OK to display the Select 1099s To Print dialog box. QuickBooks displays the vendors for whom it will print 1099s.

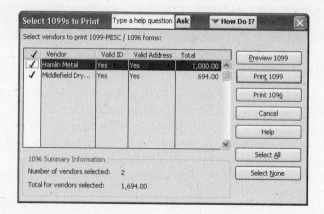

Click Preview 1099 to see what the form will look like when it prints. You can click Zoom In to make sure your company name, address, and EIN number are correct, and also check the vendor's information. Click Close on the Print Preview window to return to the Select 1099s window.

Then load the 1099 forms into your printer and click Print 1099. If you're using a laser or inkjet printer, set the number of copies to three: one for the vendor, one for your files, and one to submit to the government.

After the forms print, click Print 1096 in the Select 1099s To Print dialog box. Enter the name of the contact person in your company who can answer questions about these forms; QuickBooks prints the name on the 1096 Form. Print two copies of the 1096, so you have one for your files.

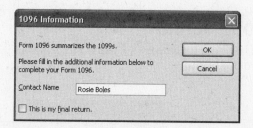

Send each vendor a copy of his or her 1099 by January 31. Send the government a copy of each 1099, along with a 1096 Transmittal Form.

Making Year-End Journal Entries

Your accountant may want you to make some journal entries before you close your books for the year.

- Depreciation entries.
- Prior retained earnings moved to a different account or retained earnings moved to owner or partner equity accounts.

- Any adjustments needed for cash versus accrual reporting; these are usually reversed on the first day of the next fiscal year. For example, you may need to accrue wages and salaries for amounts earned in one year but paid in the next year. You can use a reversing journal entry to handle this situation. When QuickBooks reverses the journal entry at the first of the new year, the net expense for each year will be just what was earned in that year.

- Adjustment of prepaid expenses from asset accounts to expense accounts.

 N O T E : See Chapter 14 for detailed information about creating journal entries.

You can send the Profit & Loss report and the Balance Sheet report to your accountant by e-mailing the reports as PDF files: click the E-Mail button at the top of the report window and then click Send Report As PDF. Ask your accountant for journal entry instructions.

You can also send your accountant an Accountant's Copy of your company data and let your accountant make the journal entries. You import the changes when the review copy is returned. See Chapter 15 to learn how to use the Accountant's Copy feature.

Running Tax Reports

Most small businesses turn over the tax preparation chores to their accountants, but some business owners prepare their own taxes manually or by using a tax software program like TurboTax.

No matter which method you choose for tax preparation, you should run the reports that tell you whether your QuickBooks company file is ready for tax preparation. Is all the necessary information entered? Do the bottom-line numbers call for some special tax planning or special tax considerations? Even if your accountant prepares your taxes, the more organized your records are, the less time the accountant spends on your return, making your bill from the accountant smaller.

Checking Tax Line Information

If you're going to do your own taxes, you need to assign every account in your chart of accounts that is tax related to the correct tax form in the account's tax line assignment. To see if any tax line assignments are missing, choose Reports | Accountant & Taxes | Income Tax Preparation. The report lists all of your accounts, along with the tax form assigned to each account. If you created your own chart of accounts, instead of accepting a chart of accounts during company setup, the number of accounts that lack a tax form assignment is likely to be quite large.

Before you can use your QuickBooks data to prepare your own taxes, you must edit each account to add the tax information. Open the chart of accounts and select an account. Press CTRL-E to edit the account and select a tax form from the Tax Line Mapping drop-down list.

Your selections vary depending upon whether your company is organized as a proprietorship, partnership, S corp, C corp, and so on.

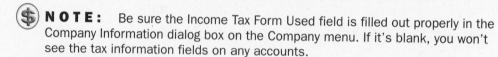 **N O T E :**   Be sure the Income Tax Form Used field is filled out properly in the Company Information dialog box on the Company menu. If it's blank, you won't see the tax information fields on any accounts.

If you don't know which form and category to assign to an account, here's an easy trick for getting that information:

1. Choose File | New Company to open the EasyStep Interview wizard.
2. Click Skip Interview.
3. On the Enter Your Company Information screen, enter a name in the Company Name field. It doesn't matter what name you use; you're not really creating a company file. Click Next.
4. On the How Is Your Company Organized? screen, select the option for the correct organizational type and click Next.
5. Select the month in which your fiscal year starts and click Next.
6. On the Select Your Industry screen, select the type of company that best describes your business. If nothing comes close to matching your business, select General Product-Based Business.
7. Click Next and then click Finish. QuickBooks displays the Filename For New Company dialog box.
8. Click Save to save the new company file.

When the new company opens in QuickBooks, open the chart of accounts list and press CTRL-P to print the list, which has the tax form information you need. Reopen your real company, open the chart of accounts, and use the information on the printed document to enter tax form information.

Calculating Officer Compensation

If your business is a C corporation, you file tax form 1120, while a Subchapter S corporation files tax form 1120S. Both of these forms require you to separate compensation for corporate officers from the other employee compensation. You will have to add those totals from payroll reports (either QuickBooks payroll or an outside payroll service).

You can avoid the need to make this calculation by creating a separate Payroll item called Officer Compensation and assigning it to its own expense account.

Then open the Employee dialog box for each officer and change the Earnings item to the new item. You may have read the tips in Chapters 2 and 8 concerning this special Earnings item; if you didn't, do this for next year because it's too late for this year's end-of-year process.

Using TurboTax

If you purchase TurboTax to do your taxes, you don't have to do anything special in QuickBooks to transfer the information. Open TurboTax and tell it to import your QuickBooks company file.

Almost everything you need transfers to TurboTax. There are some details you'll have to enter directly into TurboTax, such as home-office expenses for a Schedule C form. You can learn more about TurboTax at www.turbotax.com.

Closing Your Books

After you have printed all the year-end reports, entered any necessary journal entries, and filed your taxes, it's traditional to go through the exercise of closing the books. Typically, closing the books occurs some time after the end of the fiscal year, usually within the first couple of months of the next fiscal year, as soon as you have filed your business tax forms.

The exercise of closing the books is performed to lock the books, so no user can add, remove, or change any transactions. After you have filed taxes based on the information in the system, you should never change anything.

Understanding Closing in QuickBooks

QuickBooks doesn't use the procedures traditionally used by other accounting software packages. In most other accounting software packages, closing the year means you cannot post transactions to any date in that year, nor can you manipulate any transactions in the closed year. Closing the books in QuickBooks does not set the information in cement; users with the appropriate permissions can change and/ or delete the information.

QuickBooks does not require you to close the books in order to keep working. You can work forever, year after year, without performing a closing process. However, many QuickBooks users prefer to lock the transactions for a year as a way to prevent any changes to the data except by users with the appropriate permissions. Some users set the closing date even more frequently—after they have filed their sales tax returns or payroll returns.

Closing the Year

In QuickBooks, you close the year by entering a closing date to lock transactions from changes by unauthorized users.

To set a closing date, follow these steps:

1. Choose Edit | Preferences to open the Preferences dialog box.
2. Click the Accounting icon.
3. Select the Company Preferences tab.
4. Click the Set Date/Password button at the bottom of the tab. The Set Closing Date And Password dialog box appears (see Figure 17-4).
5. Enter the closing date.
6. Fill in the Closing Date Password and Confirm Password boxes to prevent users from changing transactions in the closed year and to permit certain users to access those transactions when needed.
7. Click OK twice to save your changes.

Closing Date Exception Report

Even with password protection in place, it is possible to make changes to a closed year. And, those changes can make this year's opening balances not be exactly the same as last year's closing balances. If your accountant or you discover that this year's opening balances are not equal to last year's closing balances, you can use this report to identify the cause of mismatched opening and closing balances.

You can print the Closing Date Exception Report, which lists all transactions that were added or changed after the closing date established for the company. A transaction that was changed shows the date and amount of the modification, as well as the date and amount of the original transaction. If you set up users for your QuickBooks company file, the report shows the name of the user who changed the transaction.

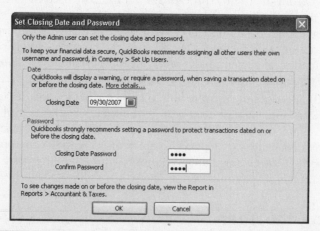

FIGURE 17-4   Entering a closing date is the first step toward preventing changes to the previous year's transactions

To view the Closing Date Exception Report, choose Reports | Accountant & Taxes | Closing Date Exception Report. Any transactions that changed after the closing date appear in the report.

Creating a Year-End Backup

Once you have completed all your year-end tasks and entered a closing date as described in the previous section, do a separate backup in addition to your normal daily backup. Don't put this backup on one of the disks or flash drives that you're using for your normal backups—use a fresh disk or a separate flash drive. When you make the backup, name it "Year-End Backup 2007" and put it in a safe place. See Chapter 21 to learn about backing up your QuickBooks files.

Tracking Time and Billing

Most service businesses charge for their services by charging for the time they spend performing a service. Product-based businesses also might need to track time for employees or outside consultants.

Tracking mileage is a universal need for any business in which vehicles are used to deliver services or products. Vehicle expense deductions on your tax return need to be able to pass an audit, and many companies insist that every employee keep a travel log. In addition, many service businesses bill clients for mileage when employees work at the client site or travel on the client's behalf.

Part Three of this book covers all the steps you need to take to set your system up for tracking time and mileage with maximum efficiency and accuracy.

Using Time Tracking

In this chapter:

- Setting up time tracking
- Filling out timesheets
- Editing timesheets
- Billing for time

Chapter 18

411

QuickBooks includes a time-tracking feature that lets you record the amount of time you and your staff spend completing a project, working for a customer, or working for your company (administrative tasks). You can use that information to invoice customers for time.

In addition to tracking billable time, you can also use this information to analyze your business. For example, if you charge retainer fees for your services, time tracking is a terrific way to figure out which customers may need to have the retainer amount raised.

Setting Up Time Tracking

When you create a company in QuickBooks, you have the opportunity to enable time tracking in QuickBooks. If you opt not to enable time tracking, you can turn it on later if you change your mind.

To turn on time tracking, choose Edit | Preferences from the QuickBooks menu bar. Click the Time Tracking category and the Company Preferences tab. Make sure the Yes option is selected.

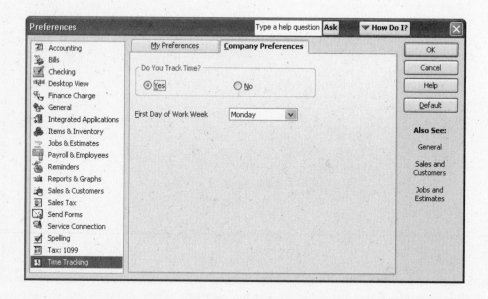

By default, QuickBooks assumes your workweek starts on Monday. However, if your business is open every day of the week, you might want to use a Sunday-to-Saturday pattern for tracking time.

Setting Up Workers

You need to set up each person for whom you will track time in QuickBooks:

Employees

Outside contractors

Other workers

Tracking Employee Time

If you're using the payroll feature in QuickBooks, you've already set up employees. You don't need to take any additional steps to track the time of any employee who fills out a timesheet. Employees can fill out timesheets even if you don't pay them based on the hours they report.

However, if you want to use the timesheet information to pay an employee, you need to set an option in the employee's record that tells QuickBooks to use hours recorded on timesheets when paying employees.

 N O T E : If your company does not use the Payroll feature in QuickBooks but does wish to track employee time for the purposes of billing customers, you need to set up employees.

To change the employee's record, follow these steps:

1. Open the Employee Center by clicking the Employees icon on the left side of the Home page, or by clicking the Employee Center icon on the toolbar.
2. Select the Employees tab to display the Employee list.
3. Double-click an employee.
4. In the Change Tabs drop-down list, choose Payroll And Compensation Info.
5. Check the Use Time Data To Create Paychecks box (see Figure 18-1).
6. Click OK to close the employee record and redisplay the Employee list.

If you *do* follow the steps above, QuickBooks may display a message while the employee is filling out timesheets, saying that the activity the employee is reporting is not linked to an hourly rate. QuickBooks will report the rate at $0.00/hour, which is fine, especially for employees on salary.

Tracking Vendor Time

You can track the time of any vendor in your company data file whom you pay for his or her time for the purpose of billing customers. Most of the time, these vendors are outside contractors or subcontractors. You don't have to do anything to the vendor record to track time for the vendor; you merely need to record the time as the vendor bills you for it.

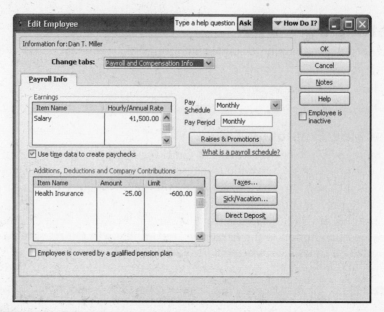

FIGURE 18-1   To pay an employee based on hours reported, check the Use Time Data To Create Paychecks box

NOTE: When you actually pay a subcontractor, you should post payments to an expense account that you designated as a 1099 account; see Chapter 17 for details on 1099 accounts.

Tracking Other Worker Time

You may need to track the time of people who are neither employees nor vendors. QuickBooks provides a system list called Other Names, and you can use this list to collect names that don't fit in the other QuickBooks lists. Following are some situations in which you'll need to use the Other Names list:

- You have employees and use QuickBooks payroll, but you are not an employee because you take a draw instead of a paycheck. In this case, you must add your name to the Other Names list to track your own time.
- You have no employees and your business is a proprietorship or a partnership. Owner or partner names must be entered into the Other Names list in order to track time.

NOTE: When you pay an owner or partner for work, you should post the payments to a draw account set up as an equity account.

Setting Up the Tasks

Most of the tasks you track already exist in your company data file as service items, and you use these items to invoice customers for services. However, because you can use time tracking to analyze the way people in your organization spend their time, you may want to add service items that are not related to customer tasks.

For example, you can track the time your employees spend performing administrative tasks for the business by adding a service item called Administration to your items list. If you want to be more specific, you can name the particular administrative tasks you want to track, such as bookkeeping, equipment repair, new sales calls, and public relations. If you decide to break down administrative items in this way, consider creating a parent item called Administration and creating subitems for the types of administrative activity.

To enter new items to track administrative work, follow these steps:

1. Click the Items & Services icon on the Home page or choose Lists | Item List from the menu bar.
2. Press CTRL-N to display the New Item dialog box.
3. Select Service for the item type because QuickBooks only tracks service items on timesheets; then name the new item.
4. Don't enter an amount in the Rate box because you won't charge a customer for this service. The time entries using administrative items will appear as $0.00 reimbursable expenses for customers.
5. So that you can assign an income account to the item, use <Add New> to create an income account called Time Tracking Revenue and assign the administrative service item to this account. Because you don't bill these items to customers, QuickBooks won't post any transactions to the account.

Although time tracking for billing purposes is connected to customers, you don't need to assign administrative time to a customer; as you record the entry, make sure that no check appears in the Billable box.

 NOTE: If you're using user and password features in QuickBooks, you must make sure each user who uses timesheets has permission to do so. See Chapter 21 for detailed information about performing this task.

Using Timesheets

You can record time using either the Single Activity window or the Weekly Timesheet window.

In the Single Activity window, you record one entry at a time, entering what you did, when did it, and how long you spent doing it. The Single Activity window also contains a stop watch that you can use to time work as you do it.

➡ **FYI**

Using Time Tracker

The QuickBooks Time Tracker is a Web-based tool that your vendors and employees can use to enter time spent on your projects. The information entered into Time Tracker downloads directly into QuickBooks, so there's no duplication of effort. To learn more about this fee-based service, choose Employees | Enter Time | Learn About Online Timesheets.

You use the Weekly Timesheet to record many single activities at the same time. You record the same information, but you have the opportunity to record more than one activity in the window. Because of the nature of the window, you won't find a timer in this window.

The window you choose to use is a matter of personal preference. Some people track time more accurately if they use the Single Activity window and the timer. Other people find the Weekly Timesheet window more efficient to use because they are recording time they already tracked.

 TIP: When you fill out a Single Activity window, QuickBooks automatically displays that activity in the Weekly Timesheet window in that week corresponding to the entry's date.

Tracking a Single Activity

To track one event or task with a Single Activity form (see Figure 18-2), click the Enter Time icon on the Home page, and choose Time/Enter Single Activity or choose Employees | Enter Time | Time / Enter Single Activity from the menu bar.

 NOTE: Everyone tracking time may not have access to QuickBooks, but you can use the Timer program to handle this situation. The Timer is an independent program that you can legally distribute to anyone whose time you need to track. You send a file containing your company's list entries to each Timer user, and the Timer user periodically sends you a file of time entries. The Timer program ships on your product CD. You can read more about using it in Chapter 20.

Follow these steps to fill in the window:

1 QuickBooks automatically fills in the Date field, but you can change the date if necessary.

2 Click the arrow to the right of the Name field and select the name of the person who performed the work from the list that appears. The list contains vendors, employees, and names from the Other Names list.

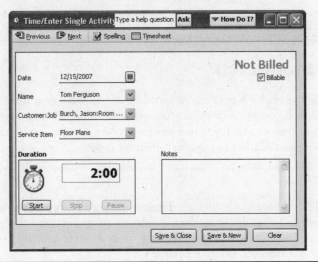

FIGURE 18-2 Fill out the details to describe how you spent your time

③ In the Customer: Job field, select the customer for whom the work was performed. You don't need to select a customer: job if you don't intend to invoice for the work.

④ In the Service Item field, select a task, and in the Duration box, enter the amount of time you're reporting, using the default format hh:mm or the stop watch to time your work; see "Using the Stopwatch" for details.

TIP: If you've changed the time format preference to decimal, QuickBooks automatically converts minutes to fractions of an hour.

⑤ QuickBooks checks the Billable check box by default. If you're not going to invoice for the time, click the box to remove the check mark.

⑥ If the Payroll Item field appears, select the appropriate wage payroll item. The Payroll Item field appears only if you selected an employee in the Name field that you set up to be paid for hours recorded using time tracking, as explained earlier in this chapter.

⑦ Use the Notes box to enter any comments or additional information you want to record about this activity. Be aware that the information you enter here may appear on customer invoices.

CAUTION: Don't enter anything in the Notes box that you wouldn't want anyone to see. You never know when somebody will accidentally include the contents of the Notes box.

⑧ When you've finished creating the activity, click Save & New to fill out another Single Activity form, or click Save & Close to finish.

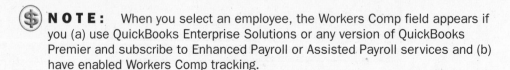

➡ FYI

Using the Stopwatch

You can let QuickBooks track the time you're spending as you work on a task. Click the Start button in the Duration box of the Activity window when you begin the task. QuickBooks tracks hours and minutes as they elapse. If you're interrupted while you work, you can pause the stop watch by clicking Pause. Click Start to resume timing the activity. When you finish, click Stop.

N O T E : When you select an employee, the Workers Comp field appears if you (a) use QuickBooks Enterprise Solutions or any version of QuickBooks Premier and subscribe to Enhanced Payroll or Assisted Payroll services and (b) have enabled Workers Comp tracking.

You can set the format for reporting time, both on the activity sheet and in the stopwatch window. Some companies prefer the hh:mm format; others prefer a decimal format (such as 1.5 hours). To establish a default based on your preference, choose Edit | Preferences and click the General category. Then select the Company Preferences tab and use the options in the Time Format section of the dialog box to select the format you want to use. By default, QuickBooks chooses Minutes.

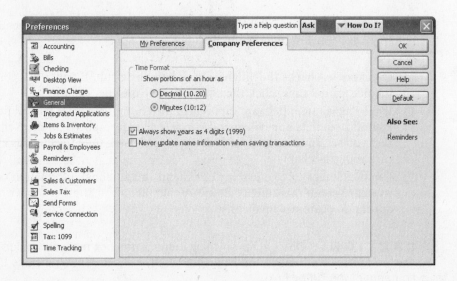

Using Weekly Timesheets

A Weekly Timesheet records the same information as the Single Activity form, except that you record the information in week-at-a-time blocks. To use this form, click the Enter Time icon on the Home page, and choose Use Weekly Timesheet or choose Employees | Enter Time | Weekly Timesheet from the menu bar. The Weekly Timesheet window appears (see Figure 18-3).

Use the following steps to fill out the timesheet:

1 In the Name field, select the name of the person for whom you are recording time from the list that appears when you click the arrow beside the Name field.

2 Click the Calendar icon beside the currently displayed date to select a week in which to enter time.

3 Click in the Customer: Job column to open the Customer List and select the customer connected to the activity you want to record. If you don't intend to bill for the time you are recording, you don't need to select a customer.

4 Enter the service item that describes the activity.

5 If you are recording time for an employee whose paycheck is linked to his or her timesheets, select the Payroll Item that fits the activity. The Payroll Item field doesn't appear if, in the Name field, you selected an employee who is not paid from the timesheets or a name from the Other Names list or the Vendor list.

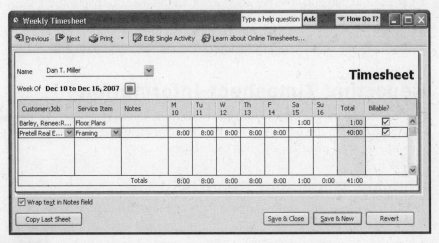

FIGURE 18-3 You may find it easier to enter time on a weekly basis

($)**NOTE:**   When you select an employee, the Workers Comp field appears if you (a) use QuickBooks Enterprise Solutions or any version of QuickBooks Premier and subscribe to Enhanced Payroll or Assisted Payroll services and (b) have enabled Workers Comp tracking.

⑥ In the Notes column, enter any comments you feel are necessary. Be aware that the information you enter here may appear on customer invoices.

($)**CAUTION:**   Don't enter anything in the Notes box that you wouldn't want anyone to see. You never know when somebody will accidentally include the contents of the Notes box.

⑦ In the column that represents the day for which you are entering this activity, enter the number of hours the person worked on this task. Repeat this step for each day that he or she performed this activity.

⑧ In the Billable column, indicate whether the time is billable. QuickBooks marks all time entries billable by default. If you don't select a customer in Step 3, remove the check from the Billable column.

⑨ Repeat Steps 3 to 8 for each activity that the person performed this week.

⑩ Click Save & Close.

($)**TIP:**   You can copy the previous week's timesheet by clicking the Copy Last Sheet button after you enter the current date in the timesheet window and select a name. Employees who have similar timesheet information every week, such as office staff, can make use of this feature.

Reporting Timesheet Information

Before you use the information on the timesheets to bill customers or pay workers, check the data on the timesheet reports. You can view and customize reports, edit information, and print the original timesheets.

Running Timesheet Reports

To run reports on timesheets, choose Reports | Jobs, Time & Mileage. You'll see the following time-tracking reports:

Report	Displays
Time By Job Summary	Reports the amount of time spent for each service on your customers and their jobs.
Time By Job Detail (see Figure 18-4)	Reports the details of the time spent for each customer and job, including dates and whether or not the time was marked as billable. A billing status of Unbilled indicates the time is billable but hasn't yet been transferred to a customer invoice.
Time By Name	Reports the amount of time each user tracked.
Time By Item	Provides a quick analysis of the amount of time spent performing services your company is providing and to whom.

If you've made it a practice to encourage people to enter comments in the Notes section of the timesheet, you should customize the report format so it includes those comments.

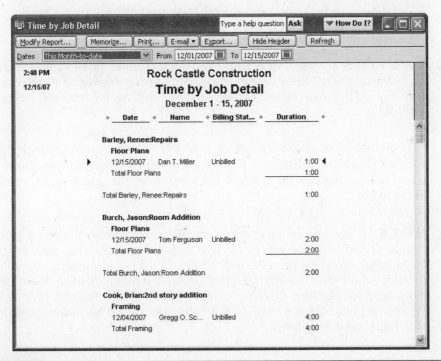

FIGURE 18-4 Create a report to check everything before billing customers or entering payroll information

You can customize the Time By Job Detail report to show this detail:

1 Open the Time By Job Detail report and click the Modify Report button on the button bar.

2 On the Display tab of the Modify Report dialog box, select Notes from the Columns list.

3 Click OK.

You can have QuickBooks memorize this report so that you don't need to set it up each time you want to view notes. Click the Memorize button on the report button bar to open the Memorize Report dialog box, and enter a name for the report. You can then view and print the report using the Memorized Reports list.

Editing Time Entries

While you're browsing the report, you can double-click an entry to view the original in the Time / Enter Single Activity window. You can make changes to the original entry, such as selecting or deselecting the billable option, changing the amount of time listed, or changing the note field.

($) **C A U T I O N :**   If you've already used the timesheet data to create an invoice for the customer or to pay the employee, don't bother making changes. Quite correctly, QuickBooks doesn't update existing customer invoices and payroll records.

If you make changes, when you click Save & Close to return to the report window, QuickBooks displays a message to ask whether you want to refresh the report to accommodate the changes. Click Yes to see the new, accurate information in the report.

($) **N O T E :**   Sometimes the changes you make require refreshing your report. By default, QuickBooks doesn't refresh your report because, if your company data file is large, refreshing can take a long time. To refresh any report, click the Refresh button while viewing the report. If you find that refreshing doesn't take much time, you can have QuickBooks automatically refresh reports. Choose Edit | Preferences and click the Reports & Graphs icon. On the My Preferences tab, click Refresh Automatically.

Printing the Weekly Timesheets

It's a common practice to have employees print their Weekly Timesheets and deliver them to the appropriate management people. To print timesheets, choose File |

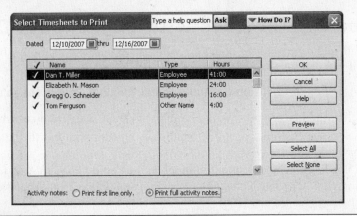

FIGURE 18-5   Print timesheets for anyone who tracks time

Print Forms | Timesheets from the QuickBooks menu bar to open the Select Timesheets To Print window shown in Figure 18-5.

- Change the date range to match the timesheets you want to print.
- By default, QuickBooks selects all timesheets. To remove a timesheet from the selection, click the checkmark beside it. You also can click Select None and then select one or more specific users.
- To see the complete text of notes on timesheets, select the Print Full Activity Notes option. QuickBooks selects the Print First Line Only option by default.

You can click the Preview button to display the selected timesheets on-screen. If you click the Print button in the Preview window, QuickBooks prints the timesheets immediately, giving you no opportunity to change the printer or any printing options. Click the Close button in the Preview window to redisplay the Select Timesheets To Print dialog box, where you can click OK to display the Print Timesheets dialog box, where you can change the printer or printing options.

 T I P :   Change the number of copies to print to match the number of people to whom you're distributing the timesheets.

The last column on the printed or previewed timesheet displays the billing status using codes.

- **B** Billable but not yet invoiced to the customer
- **N** Not billable
- **D** Billable and already invoiced to the customer

Creating Invoices with Timesheets Data

The billable time tracking data you collect is, essentially, reimbursable expenses for which you can invoice customers.

When you're ready to invoice customers for time, follow these steps:

1. Click the Invoice button on Home page. The Create Invoices window appears.

2. Select the customer or job. QuickBooks notifies you that the customer or job has billable time charges.

3. Click Select The Outstanding Billable Time And Costs To Add To This Invoice? and click OK. The Time tab of the Choose Billable Time And Costs window appears (see Figure 18-6).

4. Select the entries you want to include on this invoice. You can click Select All to use all the entries; otherwise click in the leftmost column to check the entries you want to include.

5. If you don't want to change any options, click OK to transfer the items to the invoice. See the following section if you want to make changes.

6. Click Save & New to continue to the next invoice or Save & Close if you are finished creating invoices.

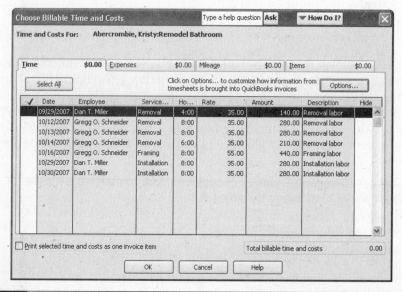

FIGURE 18-6   Select the timesheet entries you want to include on the invoice

Changing Invoicing Options for Time Charges

You can change the way the timesheet data appears on the invoice. You're not changing data or amounts; you're changing the way that data appears on the client's invoice. While viewing the Create Invoices window, if the Choose Billable Time and Costs window isn't open, click the Add Time/Costs button.

If you want to invoice for the total amount of the time charges instead of listing each activity on the invoice, click the check box next to the selection Print Selected Time And Costs As One Invoice Item.

When you click OK, QuickBooks redisplays the invoice, listing individual activities and individual totals. However, the on-screen invoice is not the same as the printed invoice. The Reimb Group item appears on the first line of the on-screen invoice, and no amount appears in the Amount column on this line. The description and amount for the Reimb Group item appear below the individual time charges. When you print the invoice, it will list only the description and the amount shown on-screen for the Reimb Group item; you can click the Template Print Preview button to see the printed invoice.

If you don't want to combine all the time charges into one line, you can still be selective about the way QuickBooks transfers information to the invoice. Click the Options button at the top of the Choose Billable Time And Costs dialog box to see your choices.

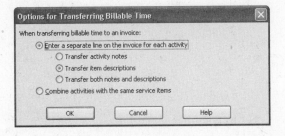

If you select the option to enter a separate line on the invoice for each time activity, you can choose to print the notes of each activity, the service item description, or both. The text for both the notes and the service item description appears in the Description column of the invoice.

 CAUTION: Don't transfer notes unless you have checked every timesheet as described earlier in this chapter to make sure an employee hasn't entered a note you'd prefer the customer didn't see.

You can select the option Combine Activities With The Same Service Items to enter a single line item for each activity type. For example, if you have Consulting and Training as separate services, and there are several activities for each of those services, selecting this option will list a line item for Consulting and another line item for Training on the invoice. Each line will have the total for that service.

Using Timesheets for Payroll Job Costing

In this chapter:

- Configuring payroll from timesheets
- Configuring services and reports for job costing

When you turn on time tracking (covered in Chapter 18), you can connect it to your QuickBooks payroll functions. You just move the information about each employee's time into the employee's paycheck. In addition to speeding up the process of creating paychecks, this means you can improve job costing by tracking your payroll expenses against jobs.

Linking Employee Time to Payroll or Job Costing

Linking employee time to payroll or job costing involves a few easy steps:

- Modify employee records to be able to use time data when you create paychecks.
- Set preferences to include job information from paychecks in payroll reports.
- Evaluate using class tracking in conjunction with payroll job costing information.

Modifying the Employee Record

To be able to use time data for an employee, when creating a paycheck, you need to modify the employee's record. When you make this change, you'll have the opportunity to include timesheet information on an employee's paychecks, but you won't be restricted in any way; you'll still have total control over the hours and pay rate for the paycheck:

- For hourly workers, if the employee's payroll information includes the hourly rate and the overtime hourly rate, QuickBooks automatically inserts that information in that employee's timesheet. If you haven't entered an hourly rate for the employee during the data entry process in the timesheet, QuickBooks displays a message indicating that it will use a rate of $0.00 because no hourly rate exists. You can enter a rate when you're creating paychecks, or you can go enter a rate in the Edit Employee dialog box and set a rate.
- For salaried workers, QuickBooks still displays the message about no hourly rate, but you don't need to worry about it for payroll purposes; you will still be paying a salary to your employee. If you want to track payroll expenses as part of job costing, enable time tracking for salaried employees.

To modify employees to use time data on paychecks, follow these steps:

1. Open the Employee Center by clicking the Employees icon on the left side of the Home page, or by clicking the Employee Center icon on the toolbar.
2. Select the Employees tab to display the Employee list.

③ Double-click an employee.
④ In the Change Tabs drop-down list, choose Payroll And Compensation Info.
⑤ Check the Use Time Data To Create Paychecks option.
⑥ Click OK to close the employee record and return to the Employee list.

Setting Payroll Preferences for Job Costing

If your time tracking is just as important for job costing analysis as it is for payroll, you can configure your payroll reporting to include job costing information.

Follow these steps:

① Choose Edit | Preferences from the menu bar. The Preferences dialog box appears.
② Click the Payroll & Employees category on the left side of the dialog box.
③ Click the Company Preferences tab.
④ Make sure a check appears in the Job Costing, Class And Item Tracking For Paycheck Expenses box (see Figure 19-1).
⑤ If you're using classes, specify the way to assign a class; see the next section, "Using Classes for Payroll Job Costing," for details.
⑥ Click OK to save your preferences.

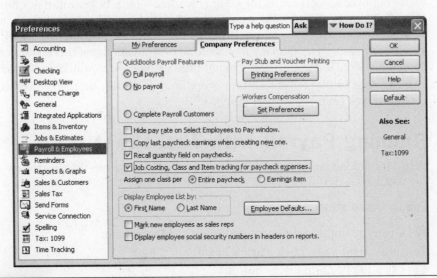

FIGURE 19-1 Setting up QuickBooks to include payroll costs in job costing

Using Classes for Payroll Job Costing

If you've established classes, you may be able to use those classes for the payroll expenses you're tracking as part of your job costing if you can easily assign an employee or an earnings item to a class, which are the two class-related payroll options available in the Payroll & Employees Preferences dialog box:

- **Entire Paycheck**   Means you assign all payroll expenses on a check, including company-paid taxes, to one class.
- **Earnings Item**   Means you can assign each payroll item that appears in the Earnings section of the paycheck to a class.

If your classes provide a tidy way to fit each employee into a class, the entire paycheck option will work. For example, if you have branch offices, each of which is a class, you can assign the paychecks according to the location of the employee. If your classes divide your company by the products or services you provide, then you should track classes by payroll item to produce useful reports. If your classes don't match the tracking options, you can just ignore the Class column when you're entering data or creating reports.

Using Timesheets Efficiently

To effectively use time information to pay employees, you need to make sure that each employee reports hours for all time worked—both billable and nonbillable time. To help your employees account for nonbillable time, you can create a payroll item for nonbillable time, calling it something like Administration or In-Office. Also set up your own company as a customer—you can name this customer something like "In House"—and assign this customer to nonbillable hours.

Make sure employees account for every hour of the day on their timesheets, including sick time or vacation time.

Running Payroll with Timesheet Data

When it's time to run the payroll, you can use the data from the timesheets to create the paychecks.

Follow these steps:

1. Open the Employee Center, and select the Payroll tab.
2. In the right pane, click a pay schedule.
3. Click the Pay Employees button.
4. When the Enter Hours window opens, the Total Hours column displays the number of hours employees accounted for on their timesheets (see Figure 19-2).

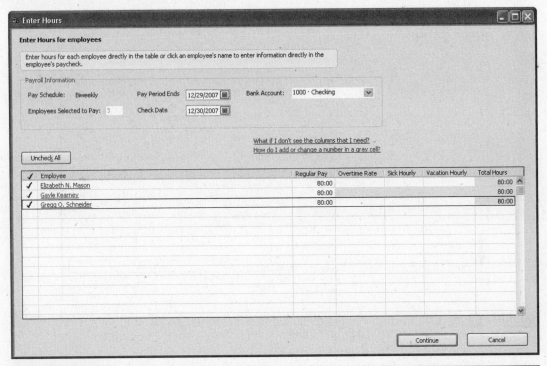

FIGURE 19-2 For the current pay period, employees accounted for the number of hours displayed in the Total Hours column

⑤ Select the employees to pay by placing a check in the leftmost column beside the employee's name; by default QuickBooks selects all employees for you.

⑥ To edit any employee's check, click the employee's name. The Review Or Change Paycheck window appears (see Figure 19-3). For employees whose paychecks are generated from timesheets, QuickBooks displays the timesheet information in the Earnings section. Make any changes and click OK to redisplay the Enter Hours window.

⑦ Click Continue. The Review And Create Paychecks window appears, letting you review payroll information and select options to produce paychecks by hand or by printing. You also have another opportunity to edit any paycheck by clicking the employee's name.

⑧ Click Create Paychecks.

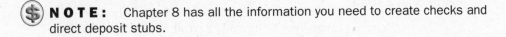

NOTE: Chapter 8 has all the information you need to create checks and direct deposit stubs.

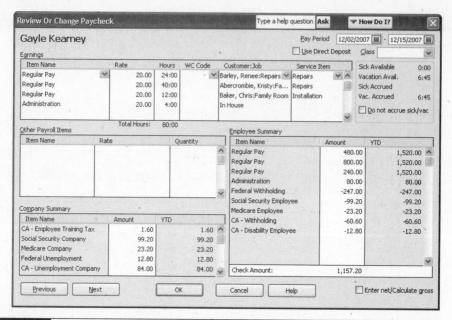

FIGURE 19-3   You can make changes to the paycheck before you print it

It's possible that the timesheet data that appears on the paycheck won't account for all of the employee's time. In this case, when you edit the paycheck, enter a nonbillable, administrative payroll item in the Earnings section and supply the employee's rate and the number of hours needed to account for the balance of the employee's time.

QuickBooks does not update the employee's timesheet with the changes you make to the employee's paycheck. If you want accurate historical timesheets, don't make the changes while creating a paycheck; instead, use the Weekly Timesheet window.

Running Payroll Reports for Cost Information

When you use time tracking, you can report on your payroll expenses as they relate to customers and jobs. You can use the Payroll Transaction Detail report to highlight job costing information.

Follow these steps:

1. Choose Reports | Employees & Payroll | Payroll Transaction Detail.
2. Enter the date range you want to examine.

③ Click the Modify Report button to open the Modify Report dialog box.

④ On the Display tab, make the following changes in the Columns section:

- In the Columns list, remove the check that appears beside Wage Base.
- Also in the Columns list, check Name. The Name field will display the customer name, and the Source Name (already checked) column will display the employee name.

⑤ Open the Sort By list and select either Source Name or Name; both present useful views.

⑥ Click the Filters tab.

⑦ In the Filter list, select Payroll Item. From the Payroll Item drop-down list, choose Multiple Payroll Items and select the payroll items you want to track for customers and jobs. I think you'll find Salary, Regular Pay, and Overtime Hourly Rate useful, since those three account for employee wages you charged to jobs.

⑧ Click OK twice to redisplay the report window with its new information (see Figure 19-4).

You can use the Sort By drop-down list on the report to change the Sort By selection to see totals by employee (Source Name) or totals by customer (Name).

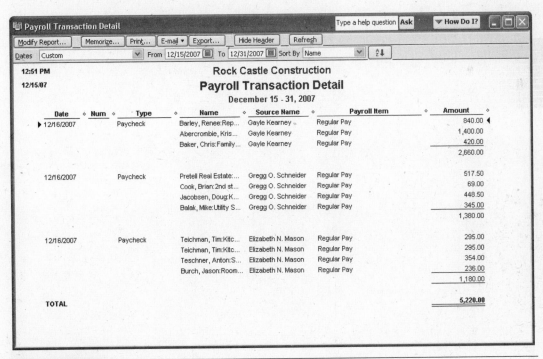

FIGURE 19-4   This customized report is a quick, accurate view of payroll job costs

You can save this report by clicking the Memorize button and giving it a meaningful name, such as Payroll Job Costing. If you decide to memorize the report, I suggest that you change the report name first. Click the Modify Report button and, in the Modify Report dialog box, click the Header/Footer tab. Change the contents of the Report Title box and click OK. Then, click the Memorize button to memorize the report.

Using QuickBooks Timer

I n this chapter:

- Installing the Timer

- Making copies for other users

- Using the Timer

- Exporting information to Timer users

- Importing files from Timer

QuickBooks includes QuickBooks Timer, a program that permits you and people who perform work for you to track time automatically and to import the time into QuickBooks, where you can report on it, pay employees based on it, or bill clients for it. The Timer works by providing an on-screen clock that ticks away as you perform tasks. Each time you start a task, you tell Timer what you're doing, and the program keeps track of the amount of time it takes to complete each task.

Distributing the Timer Software to Others

The Timer software is not part of the standard QuickBooks installation; you install it separately using original QuickBooks installation disk. Then you can give copies of the program to employees, subcontractors, or anyone else whose time you must track; the QuickBooks Timer software license legally permits you to distribute the program. A Timer user doesn't have to install and use QuickBooks; they are two independent applications that can work together.

In addition to distributing the Timer to others, you'll need to install it on your own computer. Put your QuickBooks software CD in the CD-ROM drive. If AutoRun launches the CD and asks if you want to install QuickBooks, click No. Choose Start | All Programs | QuickBooks | Install QuickBooks Timer. When the installation program launches, follow the prompts that appear on-screen. When the installation finishes, the QuickBooks Pro Timer program listing appears in the QuickBooks Timer program group on the All Programs menu.

($) N O T E :   Although the program name reads "QuickBooks Pro Timer," the Timer works with QuickBooks Premier and QuickBooks Enterprise.

Now you're ready to distribute the Timer to those who will be using it; you can distribute the program by placing it on a CD or by e-mailing it.

($) T I P :   You can use the QuickBooks software CD to install the program for someone who works in your office but doesn't have QuickBooks installed on his or her computer. At the computer where you want to install the Timer program, insert the QuickBooks CD, navigate to the QBTimer folder, and double-click the setup.exe file. Then follow the prompts on-screen.

To place the Timer program on a CD, copy the QBTimer folder from the QuickBooks 2007 CD and paste it to a location on your hard drive. Then, use your CD recording software or Windows XP to burn a CD of the files in the QBTimer folder.

TIP: When you burn the CD, select only the files in the QBTimer folder; don't select the folder. If you select the folder, recipients will have to drill down into the folder to find the installation file.

If you and your recipients have high-speed Internet connections and your ISP permits large attachments, you can e-mail the Timer software files instead of placing the files on a CD; the Timer files are about 5 MB in size. Start an e-mail message and attach all the files in QBTimer folder on the QuickBooks 2007 software CD to the message.

Installing the Timer on a Recipient Computer

On the receiving end, the installation of Timer is straightforward and easy (although you should provide specific directions to your recipients along with the files.

If you placed the program on a CD for a recipient, the installation program doesn't launch automatically when the recipient inserts the CD in the drive. The recipient should open My Computer, double-click the CD drive and double-click Setup.exe. Then follow the prompts to complete installation.

If you e-mailed the Timer to the recipient, he or she should create a folder to hold the software files, naming it something like TimerSoftware, and then save the files from the e-mail message into that folder. The recipient can then close e-mail, open the new folder containing the e-mailed files, double-click Setup.exe, and follow the prompts to install the software.

Exporting Data Lists to Timer Users

You export information from your QuickBooks company file that Timer users then import and use as they create time-related transactions in the Timer. The export file you create contains the information in your Employee, Customer: Job, Vendor lists along with service items and classes, if you're using classes in QuickBooks.

To export this information, choose File | Utilities | Export | Timer Lists from the QuickBooks menu bar to open the Export Lists For Timer window. Click OK to begin the export process.

 NOTE: Importing and exporting timer data can only be done in single user mode.

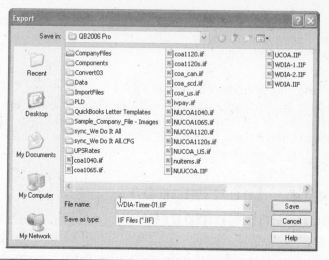

FIGURE 20-1   Save the Export file so you can send it to users

When the Export window opens (see Figure 20-1), choose a location for the file and give the file a name, using the following guidelines:

- If you are creating the export file for your own use, save it in a folder on your hard drive.

- If you are creating an export file that you're going to send on a floppy disk, click the arrow to the right of the Save In field and choose your floppy drive. Although the disk doesn't have to be blank, it's best to work with a blank, formatted floppy disk in the drive.

- If you are creating an export file that you're going to send via e-mail, you can save it to any folder on your hard drive, making sure that you remember where you saved it so that you can attach it to an e-mail.

- Give the file a name that will remind you of the company associated with the information. For instance, if the company name is A. J. Backstroke, Inc., you might want to name the export file AJB.iif. I also suggest you add a number to the filename (see the filename I used in Figure 20-1), because you may be sending replacement lists as you add customers, services, or other items to your QuickBooks company file. The increasing number in the filename clearly identifies the latest file.

QuickBooks adds an .iif file extension automatically. Click Save to save the export file, and QuickBooks displays a message indicating that the data has been exported successfully. Now you and other Timer users can use the file.

You need to go through the process of exporting lists each time you add items, names, or other important data to your company so that you can provide the new information to Timer users.

Using the Timer

You use Timer to track your work and report the time you spend on each task. Periodically, you send your Timer entries to the person who uses QuickBooks; that person then imports your Timer entries into the company file. The imported Timer entries appear in a timesheet and, if you get paid based on the time you work, those entries drive your paycheck. In addition, when you create your Timer entries and assign them to a customer, you can mark them as billable or not billable. If the entries are billable, the person who uses QuickBooks can include them on an invoice to the customer.

Opening the Timer for the First Time

The first time you use Timer, you have a little setup work to do, after which you can go on to autopilot. Start Timer by choosing Start | All Programs | QuickBooks Timer | QuickBooks Pro Timer.

When the software opens for the first time, you need to create a file to save the information you record in the Timer. Select the Create New Timer File option and click OK.

The Timer opens the New Timer File window; enter a location and a filename for the information you'll record while you use the Timer. By default, the Timer offers to save the file in the same folder in which the software exists; click Save to save the file.

The Timer displays a message telling you that you must import company information before you can use your new file, and it also offers to open a Help file that explains how to perform this task. You can click No to that offer, because the instructions are available right here.

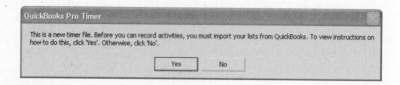

To import the file containing QuickBooks company list information, choose File | Import QuickBooks Lists from the menu bar to open the Import QuickBooks Lists introductory window.

 TIP: You can click the option to stop displaying this window in the future.

Click Continue to display the Open File For Import window. Select the folder or floppy drive that contains the file of list information you received, select the file, and click Open.

The Timer imports the file and then displays a message telling you that the file was imported successfully. Click OK to dismiss the message and start tracking your time as you work.

 NOTE: From time to time, the person who uses QuickBooks will send you a newer file of list information that you'll need to import. You can do this easily: choose File | Import QuickBooks Lists. This is a safe, normal operation, and it doesn't harm the Timer file.

Setting Up an Activity

All the menu items in the Timer software window are now accessible, and you're ready to record your first time-tracking. An *activity* is the work performed by a Timer user for one customer, during one day. An activity links three elements:

- The person using Timer
- The type of work that person is performing
- The customer for whom that work is performed

Each time you change one of these variables, you create a new activity.

Click the New Activity button to open the New Activity window and complete the form to set up an activity (see Figure 20-2).

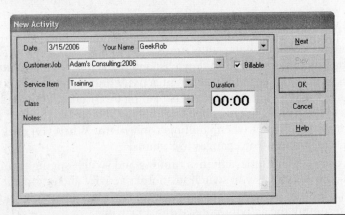

FIGURE 20-2 Configuring an activity means specifying who, what, and for whom

The Timer automatically fills in the current date, and you fill in the other fields by clicking the arrow to the right of each field. The list opens to display the information you imported earlier in this chapter. In the Notes field, type a description of the work associated with this activity; when your activities are imported into QuickBooks, the first 1000 characters from the Notes field appear—that's around 150 words. If the activity is billable to the customer, be sure to check the Billable box.

 C A U T I O N : You can't add new entries to any list; you can only work with the items stored in the company's imported file.

After you've filled in the window, click Next to set up another activity or click OK to return to the Timer window.

The Timer saves each activity you set up as a template, and you use the activity template as the foundation for creating a timed activity. Having the template available saves you the time of selecting the customer, the service, and your name (the user) each time you want to time an activity. All that's missing from the template is the amount of time.

Editing the Activity

Select the activity you want to edit from the Current Activity list and click the Edit Activity button to open the window you saw in Figure 20-2. Make the changes you need to make, like changing the service item or a changing whether the activity is billable.

Timing Your Work

The activity templates you create are always available. To go to work, select one from the Current Activity drop-down list and then click the Start button. "-Timing-" appears at the right edge of the current activity, and the elapsed minutes appear on the Timer window. The counter starts reading 00:01 after 30 seconds, because it rounds to the nearest minute. The Start button changes to the Stop button so that you can stop the Timer when you finish an activity. When you click the Stop button, the button name changes to Resume.

You can keep multiple activities running and switch among them. The Timer pauses each activity as you switch to another activity and automatically starts the clock for the new activity. As you switch from activity to activity in the same day, you're resuming the activity, not starting a new one.

The original template, sans the elapsed time, remains in the Current Activity list for later use. When you aren't timing an activity, the Timer window looks like the one shown in Figure 20-3. The title bar identifies your company, and you can click the button to the right of the Start button to reduce the size of the Timer window to display only the clock. To redisplay the full window, click the button again.

Setting Preferences in the Timer

After you've used the Timer for a while, you may want to set preferences so the software works the way you prefer. Choose File | Preferences from the Timer menu bar to display the submenu, and use the following submenu items to configure the Timer:

- **Default Name**   You can select a name that automatically appears in the Your Name field when you launch an activity. When you select this option, the Choose A Default Name window opens so you can select your name from the list. You also can choose to make your time billable or nonbillable by default.
- **Number Of Days To Remember Activities**   You can specify the number of days that the Timer keeps an activity template; the default is 30. When the number of days passes, the Timer removes the template.

FIGURE 20-3   Timing an activity

- **Turn On All One Time Messages**   You can bring back the message dialog boxes for which you selected the option Don't Show This Message Again.
- **Show Time When Minimized**   Specify whether you want to see the elapsed time counter in the taskbar button when you minimize the Timer window. Minimizing the Timer window does not have the same effect as clicking the icon beside the digitally displayed time in the Timer window.

Exporting Timer Files

When you've completed your tasks or stopped for the day, you can send the company the information about your working hours. Some companies may want daily or weekly reports; others may want you to wait until you've completed a project.

Before you send your files back to QuickBooks, you can review the information. Choose View | Time Activity Log from the Timer menu bar. When the Time Activity Log window opens, today's activities appear (see Figure 20-4).

If you wish, you can view a larger range of activities by changing the dates covered by this log. Click the arrow to the right of the Dates field and choose a different interval, or enter dates directly in the From and To fields.

You can change the information in any entry by double-clicking it (see Figure 20-5). You may want to change the time if you worked on this activity away from your computer without running a timer or to add a note. If you want to change the time, enter the new time in the Duration field.

NOTE: Template activities appear in the Time Activity Log along with activities for which you recorded time. While you can open a template activity from the Time Activity Log window, you can't make any changes.

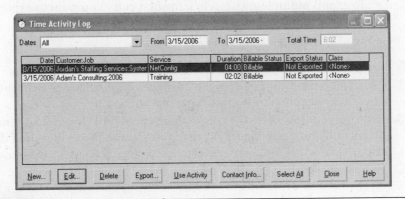

FIGURE 20-4   What did you do today?

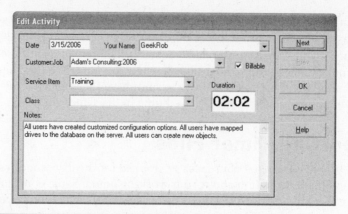

FIGURE 20-5   Make adjustments to the data, add a note, or do both

You can export specific entries or export all the information in your Timer file by following these steps:

1 Stop all Timer activities.

2 Choose View | Time Activity Log.

💲 TIP: If you know you want to export all your activities, you don't have to open the Time Activity Log. Instead, from the QuickBooks Pro Timer window, choose File | Export Time Activities. Follow the on-screen prompts, and the Timer exports all your unexported time activities.

3 Choose the entries to export, as follows:

- To export all entries, click the Select All button.
- To export multiple entries, click the first entry you want to export and hold down the CTRL key as you click any additional entries.
- To export a single entry, select it.

4 Click the Export button to start the Export Time Activities process.

5 Click Continue if the opening explanation window appears. Remember, you can select the option to stop showing this window.

6 In the Export Time Activities dialog box, choose All Unexported Time Activities Through and enter the date you want to use as the cutoff date for selecting activities; or choose Selected Activities, if you selected one or more activities to export.

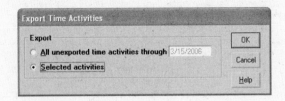

⑦ Click OK, and the Create Export File window opens.

⑧ Select a location to store the file and give it an appropriate name. It's a good idea to use your initials in the name so that the user at the QuickBooks computer who imports Timer files can distinguish your file from other Timer files.

⑨ Click Save. The Timer displays a message telling you that the file was exported successfully.

Send the file back to the person who's responsible for entering this data into QuickBooks. You can send a disk or use e-mail.

Importing Timer Files into QuickBooks

The QuickBooks user imports into QuickBooks the Timer files he or she receives from employees and subcontractors.

The process is simple; follow these steps:

① Choose File | Utilities | Import | Timer Activities from the QuickBooks menu bar. The Import window appears.

⑤ NOTE: The first time you perform this task, you see another one of those Timer explanatory windows; this one is welcoming you to the file-importing process. Select the option to skip this window in the future and click OK.

② Locate and select the file.

③ Click Open to import the file. QuickBooks notifies you when the file has been imported and displays a summary of the contents.

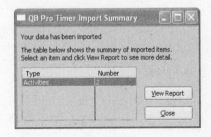

If you want to see details, click View Report; QuickBooks displays the Timer Import Detail report (see Figure 20-6).

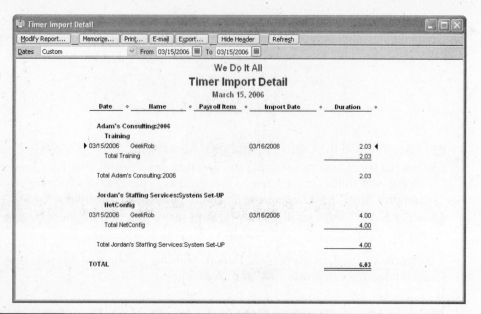

FIGURE 20-6   View the information contained in the Timer file

Double-click a line item in the report to view the details of the entry in the Time/Enter Single Activity window that QuickBooks created for the entry (see Figure 20-7). You can edit the entry if you wish; it's common to make the final decision at this point about whether you want to bill the activity to the client. You can also edit or remove any notes added by the user.

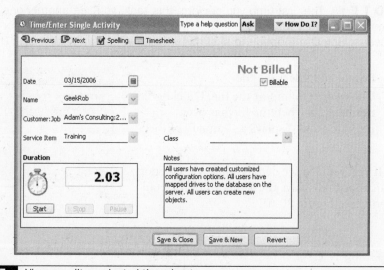

FIGURE 20-7   View or edit a selected timesheet

If you prefer, you can view the information in the Weekly Timesheets window (choose Employees | Enter Time | Weekly Timesheet) and edit the information there. You can use the information to create reports and paychecks.

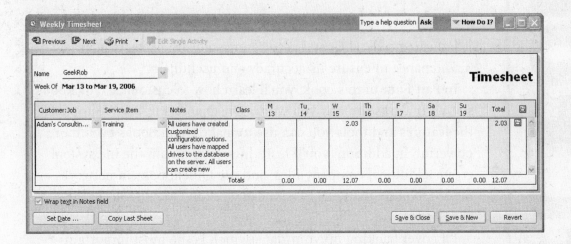

See Chapter 18 for more information about using timesheets; see Chapter 19 for information about integrating timesheets with payroll.

Part Four

Managing QuickBooks

All software needs TLC, and accounting software needs regular maintenance to ensure its accuracy and usefulness.

In Part Four of this book, you'll learn how to customize QuickBooks so that it works the way you work. The chapters in Part Four cover the features and tools you can use to make QuickBooks even more powerful. In addition, you'll learn how to maintain the file system, create additional company files, and use QuickBooks in network mode (so more than one person can work in QuickBooks at the same time).

I'll cover backing up your data, which is the most important maintenance task. Once you put your accounting data into QuickBooks, your business life depends on it. Hard drives die, motherboards freak out, power supplies go to la-la land, and all sorts of other calamities are just waiting to happen. Backing up saves your business life.

Customizing
QuickBooks

Chapter 21

In this chapter:

- Setting preferences
- Managing users and passwords
- Creating classes
- Customizing the QuickBooks window

QuickBooks "out of the box" is set to run efficiently, providing powerful bookkeeping tools that are easy to use. However, you may want to do things "a certain way," perhaps because of the way you run your company, the way your accountant likes things done, or the way you use your computer. If so, it's likely that QuickBooks can accommodate you.

Setting Preferences

The preferences you establish in QuickBooks have a great impact on the way QuickBooks stores and reports information. It's not uncommon for QuickBooks users to change or tweak these preferences periodically. In fact, the more you use QuickBooks and understand the way it works, the more comfortable you'll be about changing preferences.

All the preferences you set appear in the Preferences dialog box; choose Edit | Preferences from the QuickBooks menu bar. The first time that you open the Preferences dialog box, QuickBooks displays the General category (see Figure 21-1). If you've used the Preferences dialog box previously, it opens to the category you were using when you closed the window.

You can view the preferences for any category in the Preferences dialog box by clicking the appropriate category in the left pane. No matter which category you view, you see two tabs: My Preferences and Company Preferences.

• Use the My Preferences tab to set your preferences as a QuickBooks user. Each user you create in QuickBooks can set individual preferences. QuickBooks will apply the correct preferences as each user logs into the software. You won't always see options on the My Preferences tab.

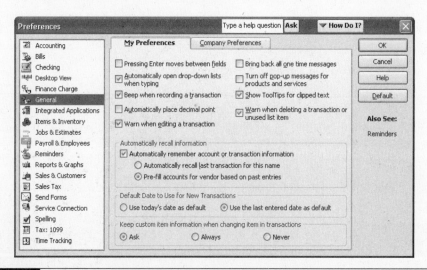

FIGURE 21-1   Configure QuickBooks to behave the way you prefer

- Use the Company Preferences tab to define the way the QuickBooks accounting features work for the current company, regardless of the user who is using the company.

As you set options and move from one category of the Preferences dialog box to another, QuickBooks asks whether you want to save the changes in the section you just left.

Setting My Preferences for the General Category

The My Preferences tab of the General category offers a number of options you can select. They're all designed to let you control the way QuickBooks behaves while you're working in transaction windows.

Pressing Enter Moves Between Fields

By default, QuickBooks prompts you to save your work when you press ENTER and moves from field to field when you press TAB. If you enable this setting, you can use both the Enter key and the Tab key to move from field to field.

Automatically Open Drop-Down Lists When Typing

By default, QuickBooks automatically opens drop-down lists in any field containing a drop-down list as soon as you type a character that matches an entry in the list. This feature helps you quickly find the list entry you want, because QuickBooks selects the item that most closely matches what you type. If you type enough characters, QuickBooks will select the entry you want.

Beep When Recording A Transaction

By default, QuickBooks makes your computer beep when recording a transaction. You also can control sound effects while working in QuickBooks by assigning sounds to actions. For more information on working with sounds in QuickBooks, see the section "Desktop View Preferences" later in this chapter.

Automatically Place Decimal Point

When you enable this feature and enter monetary characters in a field, QuickBooks inserts the decimal point automatically to the left of the last two digits. When you type 5421 and move to the next field, QuickBooks changes the number to 54.21. To type even dollar amounts, you can type 5400 or you can type a period after you enter 54; QuickBooks automatically adds two zeros to the right of the period.

Warn When Editing A Transaction

Selected by default, this option makes QuickBooks flash a warning message when you change a transaction and try to close the transaction window without explicitly saving the changed transaction, giving you a chance to abandon the edits. If you uncheck the option, QuickBooks saves the edited transaction with your changes, unless the changed transaction is linked to other transactions; in this case, QuickBooks displays a warning message explaining that problem.

Bring Back All One Time Messages

Onetime messages are those informational dialog boxes that include a Don't Show This Message Again option. If you've selected the Don't Show option, select this check box to see those messages again.

Turn Off Pop-Up Messages For Products And Services

Selecting this option stops pop-up messages from QuickBooks that are connected to products and services available from Intuit. For example, when creating checks, Intuit displays a pop-up message explaining that you can buy checks at the Intuit Marketplace.

Show ToolTips For Clipped Text

This very handy option is enabled by default; if a field contains more text than you can see, hover your mouse over the field, and QuickBooks will display the entire block of text.

Warn When Deleting A Transaction Or Unused List Item

When selected, this option produces a warning when you delete a transaction or a list entry that has not been used in a transaction—it's a standard message asking you to confirm your action. QuickBooks won't delete an item or a name that has been used in a transaction.

Automatically Recall Information

Use the options in this section to automatically fill in transactions as you create them. If you choose Automatically Recall Last Transaction For This Name, QuickBooks will prefill the data for a bill, check, or credit card charge when you select a vendor in the transaction window. This feature is useful for repeating transactions, even if one item (such as the amount) changes for the current transaction. If you choose Pre-Fill Accounts For Vendor Based On Past Entries, QuickBooks prefill accounts and amounts for a vendor transaction. QuickBooks reviews all recent transactions, looking for consistently used accounts or amounts. QuickBooks prefills the transaction if QuickBooks finds consistently used accounts or amounts. On the other hand, QuickBooks won't prefill the transaction if QuickBooks doesn't find consistently used accounts or amounts.

Default Date To Use For New Transactions

Use this option to tell QuickBooks to fill in the current date or the date of the last transaction you entered when you open a transaction window. If you frequently enter transactions for the same date over a period of several days (for example, you start preparing invoices on the 27th of the month, but the invoice date is the last day of the month), select the option to use the last entered date.

Keep Custom Item Information When Changing Item in Transactions

Your selection for this option determines what QuickBooks does when you change the description or price of an item on a transaction form and then select a different item on the same line as your customized description or price.

 N O T E :   Changes affect only the current transaction; QuickBooks makes no changes to item records.

If you select Always, QuickBooks always keeps the descriptive text you wrote on the transaction, even though you selected a different item.

If you select Never, QuickBooks always fills in the description that goes with the new item you selected.

If you select Ask, QuickBooks prompts you each time you change an item's description or price and then select a different item on the same line as the customized description or price.

Setting Company Preferences for the General Section

Click the Company Preferences tab in the General section to set the following options:

Time Format

You can select a format for entering time, choosing between decimal (for example, 11.5 hours) or minutes (11:30).

Always Show Years As 4 Digits

You can check this box if you prefer to display the year with four digits instead of two digits; that is, 01/01/2006 instead of 01/01/06.

Never Update Name Information When Saving Transactions

By default, QuickBooks asks if you want to update the original information for a name when you change it while entering a transaction. For example, if you're entering a vendor bill and you change the address, QuickBooks offers to make that change on the vendor record. If you don't want to be offered the opportunity to change name information permanently on name records as you record transactions, select this option.

Accounting Preferences

Click Accounting on the left pane of the Preferences dialog box; the My Preferences tab contains only one option—you can choose to let QuickBooks automatically fill the subsequent memo lines of a journal entry with the text entered on the first memo line. You can set the following Company Preferences for the Accounting category (see Figure 21-2).

Use Account Numbers

Choose this option if you want to use numbers for your chart of accounts in addition to names.

Show Lowest Subaccount Only

This option, available only if you use account numbers, means that when you view an account number in the drop-down list of a transaction window, QuickBooks displays only the subaccount. If you don't select this option, you see the parent account followed by the subaccount; in this case, I suggest that you select the Show ToolTips For Clipped Text option on the My Preferences tab in the General category.

Require Accounts

When enabled, QuickBooks will require you to assign every item and transaction you create to an account. If you disable this option, QuickBooks posts transaction amounts that you don't manually assign to an account to Uncategorized Income or Uncategorized Expense. If you don't post transactions to accounts, you won't be able to produce reports that analyze your business, and producing a tax return will be painful at best.

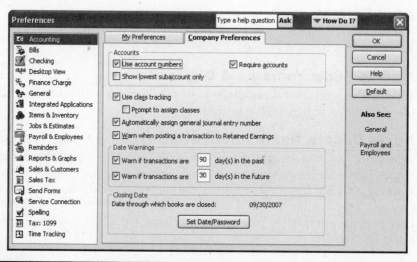

FIGURE 21-2   Select accounting-related options

Use Class Tracking

This option turns on the Class feature for your QuickBooks system, which is discussed later in this chapter in the section "Using Classes." Selecting the Prompt To Assign Classes suboption makes QuickBooks prompt you to fill in the Class field whenever you close a transaction window without doing so.

Automatically Assign General Journal Entry Number

By default, QuickBooks automatically assigns the next available number to each general journal entry transaction.

Warn When Posting A Transaction To Retained Earnings

By default, QuickBooks displays a warning if you use the Retained Earnings account in a general journal entry.

Date Warnings

By default, QuickBooks warns you if you set the date of a transaction 90 or more days in the past or 30 or more days in the future.

Closing Date

You can click the Set Date/Password button to set a password-protected closing date for your QuickBooks data file. Once you set the date and create a password, users can't manipulate any transactions that are dated on or before the closing date unless they know the password. See Chapter 17 to learn about closing your file.

Bills

The Company Preferences tab has two configuration options for entering and paying vendor bills:

Entering Bills

Use the options in this section to set default payment terms for vendors in general and to display a warning if you enter a vendor bill that has the number of a bill you already entered from this vendor. QuickBooks uses the default terms you enter here for all vendors until you actually set each individual vendor's terms.

Paying Bills

If you select the Automatically Use Discounts And Credits option, QuickBooks will apply any credits from the vendor to the open bills automatically and take any discount that the vendor's terms permit based on terms stored in the vendor's record. If you select this option, enter the account to which you want to post discounts taken. See Chapter 7 for detailed information about paying bills.

Checking Preferences

This category has options on both the My Preferences and Company Preferences tabs. On the My Preferences tab, you can select default bank accounts for different types of transactions. You can skip these options if you only have one bank account.

From the Company Preferences tab (see Figure 21-3), you can set several options concerned with check printing.

Print Account Names On Voucher

If you print your checks and your check forms have vouchers (stubs), you can select this option to print posting accounts on the stub.

Change Check Date When Check Is Printed

Select this option to assign the current date to checks when you print them. If you don't select this option, QuickBooks prints the check date you specified when you filled out the check window, even if that date has already passed.

Start With Payee Field On Check

By default, QuickBooks selects the Bank Account field as the first field when you open the Write Checks window. If you enable this option, QuickBooks places the insertion point in the Payee field when you open the Write Checks window. If you always write checks from one specific bank account, enable the option to save time.

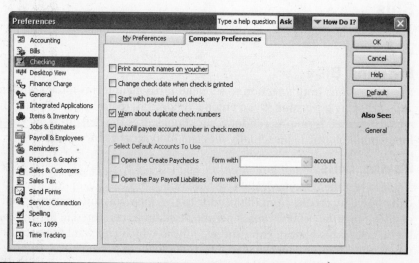

FIGURE 21-3   Set the options you need to make check writing more efficient

Warn About Duplicate Check Numbers

By default, QuickBooks will warn you if a check number you're filling in already exists.

Autofill Payee Account Number In Check Memo

Most vendors maintain an account number for their customers. If you store your account number on the Additional Information tab of the Edit Vendor window, QuickBooks will print your account number in the lower-left section of the check.

Select Default Accounts To Use

You can set the default bank accounts for different types of payroll transactions. Then, when you print these checks, you don't have to select the bank account from a drop-down list in the transaction window.

Desktop View Preferences

Using Desktop View preferences, you can control the way the QuickBooks window looks and acts. The My Preferences tab (see Figure 21-4) contains basic configuration options.

In the View section:

- Choose One Window to limit the QuickBooks screen to displaying one window at a time, even if you have multiple windows open. QuickBooks stacks the windows on top of each other, and only the top window is visible. In this mode, you cannot resize or minimize any windows other than the program window; to switch between multiple windows, use the Window menu.

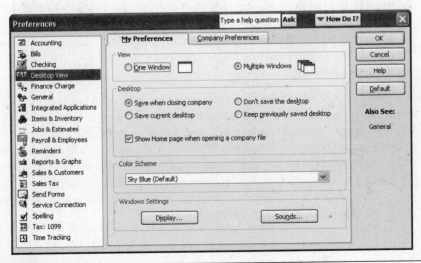

FIGURE 21-4   Set options to control the look and behavior of QuickBooks

- Choose Multiple Windows to view multiple windows on your screen at the same time. Often, you can switch from one window to another simply by clicking the window you want to use.

In the Desktop section, you can specify what QuickBooks should do with the current desktop view when you exit the software.

- **Save When Closing Company**   By default, QuickBooks saves the state of the desktop when you close the company or exit QuickBooks. Whatever QuickBooks windows were open when you left will reappear when you return so that you can pick up where you left off.

($) **N O T E :**   If you select the option Show Home Page When Opening A Company File, that option overrides any of the other options in the Desktop section; if you close the company file after closing the Home page, QuickBooks redisplays the Home page when you open the company file.

- **Save Current Desktop**   When you select this option, QuickBooks displays the desktop as it was when you selected this option every time you open QuickBooks. Select this option after you've opened only those QuickBooks windows you want to see each time you start the program.
- **Don't Save The Desktop**   When you select this option, QuickBooks displays only the menu bar, Icon Bar, the Home Page if you selected that option, and other navigation bars when you open this company file or when you start QuickBooks again after using this company file.
- **Keep Previously Saved Desktop**   When you select this option, QuickBooks displays the desktop as it was the last time you used the Save Current Desktop option. This option only appears after you've used the Save Current Desktop option, and QuickBooks automatically selects it.
- **Show Home Page When Opening A Company File**   Select this option to display the Home page when you open the company file. This option overrides the other desktop settings.

In the Color Scheme section, you can select a scheme from the drop-down list. In addition, you can click the Display or Sounds buttons to configure Windows settings for your monitor and sound card. Clicking either button opens the associated applet in your Windows Control Panel, and any changes you make to your display affect your computer and all your software, not just QuickBooks.

On the Company Preferences tab, you can customize the contents of the Home page; you can choose to include or exclude some of the default features that appear on the Home page if you enable those features.

Finance Charge Preferences

Choose the Finance Charge category to turn on, turn off, and configure finance charges. Finance charges can get complicated, so read the complete discussion about this topic in Chapter 5. QuickBooks contains no preferences for Finance Charges on the My Preferences tab.

Integrated Applications Preferences

You can let third-party software have access to the data in your QuickBooks files. Click the Integrated Applications icon and move to the Company Preferences tab to specify the way QuickBooks works with other software programs. You can give permission to access all data, no data, or some data.

Items & Inventory

Use the options on the Company Preferences tab to enable the inventory and purchase orders features and then define their behavior (see Figure 21-5). No preferences appear on the My Preferences tab.

Inventory And Purchase Orders Are Active

Select this option to tell QuickBooks that you want to enable the inventory and purchase orders features.

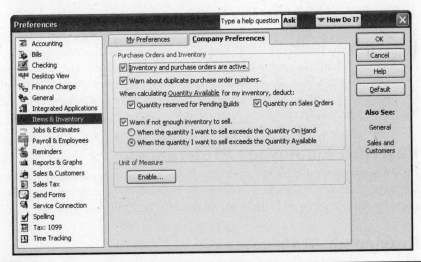

FIGURE 21-5 Set options for the behavior of inventory and purchase orders

Warn About Duplicate Purchase Order Numbers

By default, QuickBooks displays a warning if you attempt to save a purchase order using a purchase order (PO) number that already exists.

When Calculating Quantity Available For My Inventory, Deduct:

Use these options to control the way QuickBooks calculates Quantity Available. By default, QuickBooks excludes items that make up an assembly you plan to build and items that appear on sales orders.

Warn If Not Enough Inventory To Sell

Use these options to determine how QuickBooks calculates how much inventory is available to sell before it warns you of insufficient quantities. When you choose When The Quantity I Want To Sell Exceeds The Quantity On Hand, QuickBooks looks at the number you have in stock. When you choose When The Quantity I Want To Sell Exceeds The Quantity Available, QuickBooks also considers quantities reserved for assemblies and sales orders.

Unit Of Measure

Click the Enable button to make the Unit Of Measure feature available. This feature is new to QuickBooks 2007 and functions differently for QuickBooks Premier and QuickBooks Enterprise. See Chapter 10 for details.

Jobs & Estimates Preferences

No options appear on the My Preferences tab, but you can use the Company Preferences tab (see Figure 21-6) to establish job status description labels, enable the Estimates feature, enable the Progress Invoicing feature, specify whether QuickBooks warns you about duplicate estimate numbers, and specify whether QuickBooks prints items with zero amounts on progress invoices. Read Chapter 3 for more information about creating estimates and invoices.

Payroll & Employees Preferences

No options appear on the My Preferences tab for this category, and you use the Company Preferences tab of this category to set all the configuration options for payroll. Read Chapter 8 to understand the selections in this window.

Reminders Preferences

The Reminders category of the Preferences dialog box has options on both tabs. The My Preferences tab has one option, which turns on the Reminders feature. When you enable the Reminders feature, QuickBooks displays the Reminders List when you open a company file.

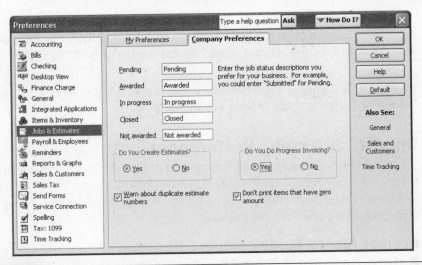

FIGURE 21-6 Enable and configure estimates and progress invoicing

The Company Preferences tab lists the available reminders, and you can select the ones you want to use (see Figure 21-7).

$ CAUTION: The Reminders List window is sometimes hidden behind the Home page. Click Window on the menu bar to switch to it, or minimize the Home page to reveal it.

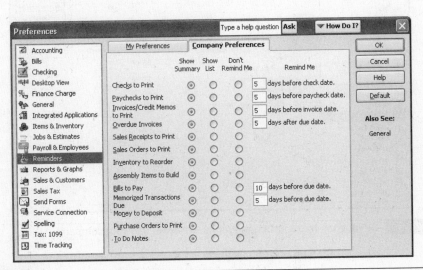

FIGURE 21-7 Select the tasks for which you want to view reminders

For each item, decide whether you want to see a summary that lists the task and the total amount of money involved, a complete detailed list, or nothing at all. You also can determine the amount of lead time you want for your reminders.

 TIP: If you choose Show Summary, the Reminders List window has an Expand All button you can click to see the details.

Reports & Graphs Preferences

This section has choices on both tabs, so you can set your own user preferences and then set those options that affect the current company.

The My Preferences tab (see Figure 21-8) controls the way QuickBooks produces reports and graphs for the current user.

Prompt Me To Modify Report Options Before Opening A Report

If you find that almost every time you select a report you have to customize it, check this box to tell QuickBooks to open the Modify Report dialog box whenever you select a report.

Reports and Graphs Settings

While you're viewing a report or a graph, if you make changes that affect the information on the report, QuickBooks needs to refresh the report. By default,

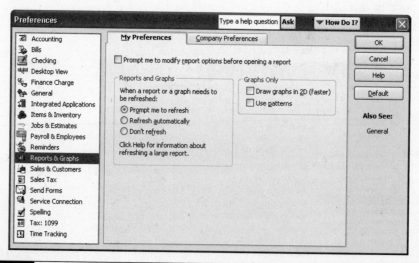

FIGURE 21-8   Set options for reports and graphs while you use your company

QuickBooks doesn't automatically refresh reports because your company file may be large and refreshing could take some time. You can control how QuickBooks refreshes reports and graphs:

- Choose Prompt Me To Refresh to have QuickBooks display a message asking you whether you want to refresh the report or the graph.
- Choose Refresh Automatically to have QuickBooks automatically update the report or graph with any changes you make. If you work with QuickBooks across a network, this could slow down your work a bit because QuickBooks will refresh the report whenever any user makes a change to data that's used in the report/graph.
- Choose Don't Refresh if you want to decide for yourself, without any reminder from QuickBooks, when to click the Refresh button on the report window.

Graphs Only

Give QuickBooks instructions about creating your graphs:

- Choose Draw Graphs In 2D (Faster) to display graphs in two dimensions instead of three. This doesn't impair your ability to see trends at a glance; it's just not as "high-tech."
- Choose Use Patterns to draw the various elements in your graphs with black and white patterns instead of colors. For example, one pie wedge may be striped, another speckled. This is handy if you print your graphs to a black and white printer.

On the Company Preferences tab of the Reports & Graphs category, you set company preferences for reports (see Figure 21-9).

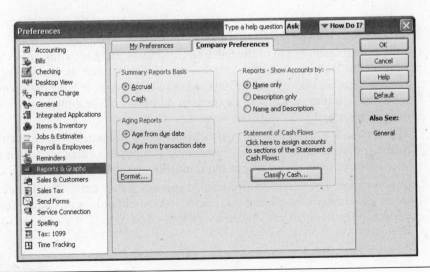

FIGURE 21-9 Set company-wide defaults for reports

Summary Reports Basis

Use these options to specify whether you want to see accrual-based or cash-based summary reports. You're only setting the default specification here, and you can always change the basis in the Modify Report dialog box when you actually display the report.

Aging Reports

Specify whether you want to generate A/R and A/P aging reports using the due date or the transaction date.

Reports—Show Accounts By

Specify whether you want reports to display account names, account descriptions, or both.

Setting Report Format Defaults

You can set the default formatting for reports by clicking the Format button and making changes to the default options for the Header/Footer area of the report and to the fonts and number formatting used in the report.

Configuring the Cash Flow Report

QuickBooks contains cash flow reports available in the list of Company & Financial reports. These reports use a specified list of accounts and categorize these accounts as either operating, investing, or financial.

You can view the way QuickBooks has categorized the accounts by clicking the Classify Cash button, but you shouldn't mess around with the selections in the window that appears until you check with your accountant. You can learn about cash flow reports in Chapter 15.

Sales & Customers Preferences

On the My Preferences tab of the Sales & Customers category, you can set your preference for the way QuickBooks behaves when you create an invoice for a customer for whom reimbursable expenses exist. You can set your preferences to let QuickBooks prompt you to select expenses, add none of the expenses, or offer you these choices when you create the invoice.

If you choose to be prompted, QuickBooks will automatically open the Choose Billable Time And Costs dialog box whenever you select a customer:job in the Create Invoices window for whom reimbursable expenses exist.

If you choose not to add reimbursable expenses if they exist, then QuickBooks won't notify if reimbursable expenses exist and QuickBooks won't add reimbursable expenses to the invoice; you'll need to click the Add Time/Costs button in the

Create Invoices window to check for reimbursable expenses and add them if appropriate.

If you choose to be offered choices, QuickBooks will display a message each time you select a customer:job for whom reimbursable expenses exist; you'll be able to choose between excluding the reimbursable costs or opening the Choose Billable Time And Costs dialog box.

On the Company Preferences tab, you'll find the following options (see Figure 21-10):

Sales Forms

In the Sales Forms section, you can set these options.

- **Usual Shipping Method**   Set the default shipping method if you use the same shipping method most of the time. This saves you the trouble of making a selection from the drop-down list unless you're changing the shipper for a particular invoice.
- **Usual FOB**   Set the FOB (Free On Board) language for invoices, which describes the location from which shipping is determined to be the customer's responsibility. You're limited to 13 characters, and the FOB has absolutely nothing to do with your finances.
- **Warn About Duplicate Invoice Numbers**   When enabled, QuickBooks warns you if you're creating an invoice with an invoice number that's already in use.

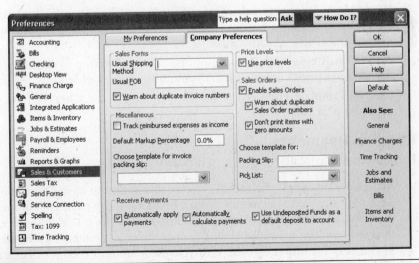

FIGURE 21-10   Set Company Preferences for the Sales & Customers Category

Miscellaneous

In the Miscellaneous section, you can set these options.

- **Track Reimbursed Expenses As Income**   Use this option to change the way your general ledger handles payments for reimbursements. When you enable the option, you can assign the reimbursement to an income account instead of posting back to the original expense account.

  If you enable the Track Reimbursed Expenses As Income feature, you can set a default markup percentage for expenses you're billing back to customers. See Chapter 6 to learn how to enter and invoice reimbursable expenses.

- **Choose Template For Invoice Packing Slip**   Select a default template to use when you print packing slips. If you've created customized packing slips, you can make one of them the default. Detailed information on using templates appears in Chapter 3.

Use Price Levels

This option turns on the Price Level feature; this feature has been discussed in detail in Chapter 2.

Sales Orders

In the Sales Orders section, you can set these options.

- **Enable Sales Orders**   Checking this box enables the sales order feature in QuickBooks.
- **Warn About Duplicate Sales Order Numbers**   Checking this box makes QuickBooks display a warning if you attempt to save a sales order using a sales order number that already exists.
- **Don't Print Items With Zero Amounts**   Use this option to control whether QuickBooks prints items with zero amounts on sales orders.
- **Choose Template For**   Select default templates to use when you print packing slips and pick lists.

Receive Payments

In the Receive Payments section, you can set these options.

- **Automatically Apply Payments**   Select this option to have QuickBooks automatically apply payments to open invoices. If the payment amount is an exact match for an open invoice, QuickBooks applies it to that invoice. If the payment amount is smaller than any open invoice, QuickBooks applies the payment to the oldest invoice. If the payment amount is larger than any open invoice, QuickBooks applies payments, starting with the oldest invoice, until the payment amount is used up. If you don't enable this option, you must manually apply each payment to an invoice. Read Chapter 4 to learn about receiving and applying customer payments.

- **Automatically Calculate Payments**   When you select this option, you can select invoices to pay in the Receive Payment window before you enter the amount of the customer's payment check. When you've finished selecting invoices, either paying them entirely or applying a partial payment, the amounts you've applied should equal the amount of the check you received.
- **Use Undeposited Funds As A Default Deposit To Account**   Selecting this option automates the process of depositing all cash received into the Undeposited Funds account. Enabling this option helps you match deposits you make at your bank to the ones that will appear on your bank statement.

Sales Tax Preferences

No options appear on the My Preferences tab for this category. If you collect sales tax, you should enable the sales tax feature in QuickBooks and then set options on the Company Preferences tab. The new Manage Sales Tax feature will help you set these options, which are easy to set because most of the selections are predefined by state tax laws and state tax report rules. Check with your accountant and read the information that came with your state sales tax license. For more information about managing sales taxes, see Chapter 7. To use the new Manage Sales Tax feature, choose Vendors | Sales Tax | Manage Sales Tax.

Send Forms Preferences

On the My Preferences tab, you can tell QuickBooks to automatically check the To Be E-Mailed box if you selected E-Mail for the customer's Preferred Send Method. If you send transactions to customers via e-mail, use the Company Preferences tab to design the message that accompanies the invoice. See Chapter 3 for more information.

Service Connection Preferences

If you use QuickBooks services on the Internet, use this category to specify the way you want to connect to the Internet for those services.

The My Preferences tab contains options related to online banking if your bank uses the Web Connect method of online access. Chapter 16 has detailed information about online banking services.

- **Give Me The Option Of Saving A File Whenever I Download Web Connect Data**   Select this option if you want QuickBooks to allow you to save Web Connect data to import whenever you choose instead of automatically importing downloaded transactions.
- **If QuickBooks Is Run By My Browser, Don't Close It After Web Connect Is Done**   Select this option so that QuickBooks remains open after you process Web Connect data in a browser window that opened QuickBooks.

From the Company Preferences tab, you can set the following connection options:

- **Automatically Connect Without Asking For A Password**   Select this option to let all users log into the QuickBooks Business Services network automatically.
- **Always Ask For A Password Before Connecting**   Select this option to force users to enter a login name and password to access QuickBooks Business Services.
- **Allow Background Downloading Of Service Messages**   Select this option to let QuickBooks check the Intuit web site periodically for updates and information when you're connected to the Internet.

Spelling Preferences

The Spelling category contains options only on the My Preferences tab. From this tab, you can control the way the QuickBooks spell checker works. You can instruct QuickBooks to check spelling automatically before saving or printing any form. In addition, you can specify those words you want the spelling checker to skip, such as Internet addresses, numbers, and capital letters that probably indicate an abbreviation.

Tax:1099 Preferences

No options appear on the My Preferences tab for this category. Use the Company Preferences tab of this category to establish 1099 form options. For each type of 1099 payment, you must assign an account from your chart of accounts. See Chapter 17 for more information about configuring and issuing 1099 forms.

Time Tracking Preferences

No options appear on the My Preferences tab for this category. Use the Company Preferences tab of this category to turn on Time Tracking and to tell QuickBooks the first day of your workweek, which becomes the first day listed on your timesheets. Read about tracking time in Chapter 18.

Using Classes

QuickBooks provides a feature called Class Tracking that permits you to group items and transactions in a way that matches the kind of reporting you want to perform. Think of this feature as a way to "classify" your business activities. To use classes, you must enable the feature, which appears in the Accounting section of the Preferences dialog box.

➡ FYI

A Note About Classes

Before you start using classes, you should understand two important points.

- You can assign classes to transactions but not to names; for example, you can assign a class to one line on an invoice or the entire invoice, but you cannot assign the class to the customer:job.
- You can report on Profit & Loss accounts by class, but you cannot report on Balance Sheet accounts by class.

People commonly use classes to:

- Report by location if you have more than one office.
- Report by division or department.
- Report by business type (perhaps you have both retail and wholesale businesses under your company umbrella.)

You should use classes for a single purpose. For example, you can use classes to separate your business into locations or by types of business, but don't try to do both. If you need to further define a class or narrow its definition, you can use subclasses.

When you enable classes, QuickBooks adds a Class field to transaction forms. For each transaction or each line of any transaction, you can assign one of the classes you create.

Creating a Class

To create a class, choose Lists | Class List from the QuickBooks menu bar to display the Class List window.

 NOTE: The Class List appears on the Lists menu only if you enable classes on the Company Preferences tab of the Accounting category in the Preferences dialog box.

Press CTRL-N to add a new class. Fill in the name of the class in the New Class window. Click Next to add another class, or click OK if you are finished.

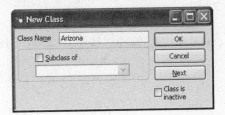

Creating a Subclass

You can use subclasses to further refine the definition of your classes. Subclasses work similarly to subaccounts in your chart of accounts. If you set up a subclass, you must post transactions only to the subclass, never to the parent class.

You create a subclass using the basically same steps required to create a class; when you create a subclass, check the Subclass Of box and then choose the appropriate parent class from the drop-down list.

Editing, Deleting, and Merging Classes

The Class List works like all other lists in QuickBooks; you use the same techniques to change, remove, and merge classes that you use to change, remove, or merge items in any other list. If you've used a class in transactions, you can't delete the class, and you can delete a parent class only if you delete all of its subclasses.

See Chapter 2 for details on editing, deleting, and merging list entries.

Using a Class in Transactions

When you're entering transactions, QuickBooks displays the Class field at the top of each transaction window so that you can assign the entire transaction to a class. However, you can instead assign a class to each line item of the transaction. In Figure 21-11, I assigned the entire invoice to one class by using the Class field at the top of the form, next to the Customer:Job field. Using the Class column at the bottom of the form, I could have assigned each line to an individual class. Remember, using the Class field at the top of the form assigns the transaction, not the name beside it, to a class.

Reporting by Class

There are two types of reports you can run for classes.

- Individual class reports
- Reports on all classes

Reporting on a Single Class

To report on a single class, open the Class list and select the class on which you want to report. Then press CTRL-Q to display a QuickReport on the class. When the Class QuickReport appears, you can change the date range or customize the report as needed.

Reporting on All Classes

If you want to see one report in which all classes are used, open the Class list and click the Reports button at the bottom of the list window. Choose Reports On All

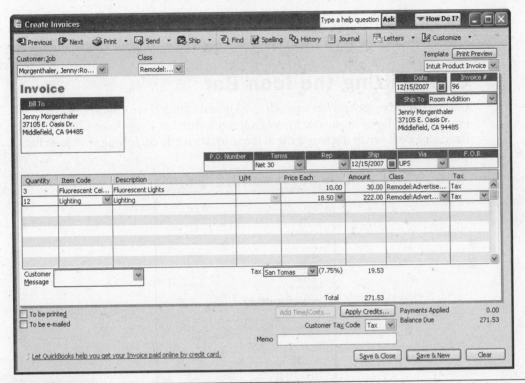

Classes and then select either Profit & Loss By Class, Profit & Loss Unclassified, or
Graphs. From the Graphs menu you can produce an Income & Expenses graph or a
Budget Versus Actual graph.

Profit & Loss By Class Report

The Profit & Loss By Class report is the same as a standard Profit & Loss report,
except that each class appears in a separate column. The Totals column provides
the usual Profit & Loss information for your company. This report is also available
on the submenu under Reports | Company & Financial.

Profit & Loss Unclassified Report

This report displays Profit & Loss totals for transactions on which you didn't assign
classes. You can drill down to the transactions and add the appropriate class to each
transaction. This is likely to be a rather lengthy report if you enabled class tracking
after you'd already begun using QuickBooks.

You can find detailed information about running and customizing Profit & Loss
reports in Chapter 15.

NOTE: You can customize many of the reports you run regularly to report class information. Use the Filters tab to configure the report for all, some, or one class.

Customizing the Icon Bar

Use the QuickBooks Icon Bar to work quickly and efficiently in QuickBooks. To customize the Icon Bar, choose View | Customize Icon Bar to open the Customize Icon Bar dialog box, which displays a list of the icons currently occupying your Icon Bar.

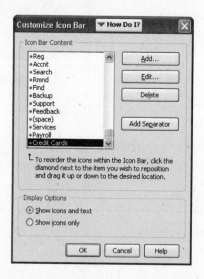

If you updated to QuickBooks 2007 from a previous version, the Icon Bar retains all the icons from the previous version. For new users or new companies, the default Icon Bar has a limited number of icons. The QuickBooks Centers icons are collectively called the Navigation Bar, so they don't appear in the Customize Icon Bar dialog box. If you want to hide the Navigation Bar, choose View | Navigation Bar; use the same process to redisplay the Navigation Bar.

 TIP: If your organization has set up user names, each user can customize the Icon Bar without affecting any other users.

Changing the Order of Icons

You can change the order in which icons appear on the Icon Bar. The list of icons in the Customize Icon Bar dialog reads top to bottom, representing the left-to-right display on the Icon Bar. Therefore, when you move an icon up in the Customize Icon Bar dialog box, QuickBooks moves the icon to the left on the Icon Bar.

To move an icon, drag the small diamond to the left of the icon to a new position.

Display Icons without Title Text

By default, QuickBooks displays both icons and text on the Icon Bar. At the far right edge of the Icon Bar, a button with two right-pointing carats appears; you can click that button to see additional buttons that QuickBooks can't fit on your screen.

To reduce the size of the icons on the bar, you can select Show Icons Only to remove the title text under the icons. As a result, you can see more icons on the Icon Bar without needing to click the button that appears at the far right edge of the Icon Bar. Positioning your mouse pointer over a small icon displays the icon's description as a ToolTip.

 N O T E :   The "Center" buttons are not part of the Icon Bar and so are unaffected by this option.

Change the Icon's Graphic, Text, or Description

To change an individual icon's appearance, select the icon and click Edit. Then choose a different graphic, change the Label, or change the Description, which appears as the ToolTip text.

Separate Icons

You can insert a separator between two icons, which is an effective way to create groups of icons. The separator is a gray vertical line. In the Customize Icon Bar dialog, select the icon that should appear to the left of the separator bar and click Add Separator. QuickBooks inserts the separator on the icon bar and "(space)" appears in the Icon Bar Content list to indicate the location of the separator.

Removing an Icon

If there are any icons you never use or use infrequently, you can remove them. Select the icon in the Customize Icon Bar dialog box and click Delete. When you click OK, QuickBooks displays the new Icon Bar minus the icons you removed.

 N O T E :   You're deleting the icon from the Icon Bar, not from QuickBooks. If you want to display the icon on the Icon Bar again, read on.

Adding an Icon

You can add an icon to the Icon Bar in either of two ways:

- Choose Add in the Customize Icon Bar dialog box.
- Automatically add an icon for a window, transaction, or report you're currently using.

Using the Customize Icon Bar Dialog Box to Add an Icon

Unless you select an icon before you click Add, QuickBooks places the new icon at the right end of the Icon Bar. To position your new icon at a specific place within the existing row of icons, select the existing icon that you want to appear to the left of your new icon. Then, click Add. The Add Icon Bar Item dialog box appears.

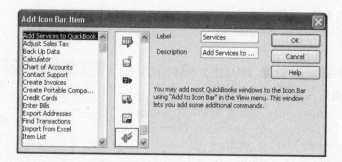

Scroll through the list to select the task you want to add to the Icon Bar; QuickBooks selects a default graphic for the icon. If you don't like the default icon, choose a different graphic to represent the new icon.

If you wish, you can change the Label, which is the title that appears below the icon or the Description, which is the text that appears in the ToolTip when you pause your mouse pointer over the icon.

Adding an Icon for the Current Window

If you're currently working in a QuickBooks window, you can add an icon to the Icon Bar for the window quickly and easily. Choose View | Add X To Icon Bar, where X is the name of the current window. A dialog box appears so you can choose a graphic, label, and description for the new icon.

 N O T E :   Using this method, QuickBooks always adds your icon to the end of the Icon Bar. If the Icon Bar is already full, click the button at the right edge of the Icon Bar that contains two right-pointing carats to see additional buttons that QuickBooks can't fit on your screen.

Managing Multiple Users in QuickBooks Premier

Many businesses using QuickBooks Premier have multiple users accessing their QuickBooks company files. You can have multiple users who share QuickBooks on a single computer, taking turns using QuickBooks, or in a multi-user network environment if you purchased a multi-user version of QuickBooks.

The new installation process for the QuickBooks Premier 2007 guides you through properly setting up the program to operate in a network environment. For details on this process, see the Startup and Quick Reference Guide that came in the box with your software.

In this section, we'll focus on effectively setting up your company data file so that multiple users can use it.

 N O T E : In a multi-user environment, all QuickBooks users must use the same version of QuickBooks.

Creating, Removing, and Changing User Information

When you want to create or modify users, choose Company | Set Up Users from the QuickBooks menu bar. If you are setting up multiple users for the first time, QuickBooks displays the Set Up QuickBooks Administrator dialog box. You must set up an Admin user to manage all the other user tasks.

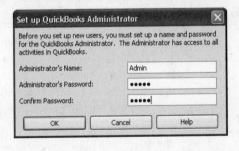

The administrator determines who can use the various features in QuickBooks. It's a good idea to leave the administrator's name as Admin, but you should assign an Admin password. To password-protect the administrator's login, type a password in the Administrator's Password box and then type the same password in the Confirm Password box.

 C A U T I O N : Make a note of the Admin password and keep it in a secure place; consider using a password vault software package or placing the Admin password under lock and key. If you forget the administrator's password, you can call QuickBooks support and arrange to have them recover the password—for a fee.

Creating a New User

When you click OK in the Set Up QuickBooks Administrator dialog box, QuickBooks displays the User List window.

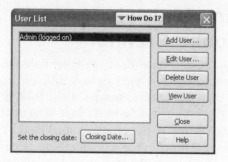

You use this window to add, edit, or delete users.

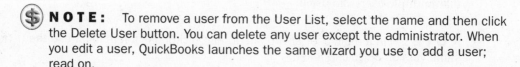 **N O T E :**   To remove a user from the User List, select the name and then click the Delete User button. You can delete any user except the administrator. When you edit a user, QuickBooks launches the same wizard you use to add a user; read on.

To add a new user to the list, click Add User to start a wizard that assists you in setting up the new user.

In the first wizard window, fill in the necessary information as follows:

1. Enter the username; the user types this name to log into QuickBooks.
2. Although passwords are optional, you should enter and enter and confirm the user's password to prevent unauthorized access to those areas in which the user has permission to work.
3. Click Next to set up the user's access to QuickBooks features. See the next section "Setting User Permissions."

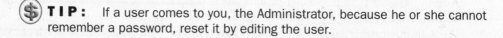 **T I P :**   If a user comes to you, the Administrator, because he or she cannot remember a password, reset it by editing the user.

Setting User Permissions

When you're adding a new user or editing an existing user, the wizard walks you through the steps to establish the user's permissions. Click Next on each wizard window after you've supplied the necessary information.

On the first permissions window, you decide whether you want to give this user access to selected areas or all areas of QuickBooks. If you give the user full permission to do everything, QuickBooks asks you to confirm your decision, and you can click Finish to return to the User List window.

CAUTION: Giving a user full access to all areas of QuickBooks doesn't provide any security. Think that decision through carefully.

If you want to limit the user's access, click Selected Areas Of QuickBooks and click Next. The ensuing wizard windows take you through 10 screens, each representing an area of QuickBooks such as Sales and Accounts Receivable or Purchases and Accounts Payable. On each screen, you can assign one of the following permission options:

- **No Access**   The user is denied permission to open any windows in that section of QuickBooks.
- **Full Access**   The user can open all windows and perform all tasks in that section of QuickBooks.
- **Selective Access**   The user can perform the tasks you select. When you choose this option, you also specify the rights this user should have. Those rights vary slightly from component to component, but generally you're asked to choose one of these permission levels:
  - Create transactions only
  - Create and print transactions
  - Create transactions and create reports

 TIP: You can select only one of the three levels, so if you need to give the user rights to more than one of these choices, you must select Full Access instead of configuring Selective Access.

Two of the wizard windows for setting permissions are not directly related to any specific area of the software: sensitive accounting activities and sensitive financial reports.

Sensitive accounting activities are those tasks that aren't directly related to QuickBooks transactions, such as:

- Making changes to the chart of accounts.
- Manipulating the register for any balance sheet account.
- Using online banking.
- Transferring funds between banks.
- Reconciling bank accounts.
- Creating journal entries.
- Preparing an accountant's review.
- Working with budgets.

Sensitive financial reports are those reports that reveal important financial information about your company, such as:

- Profit & Loss reports
- Balance Sheet reports
- Budget reports
- Cash flow reports
- Income tax reports
- Trial balance reports
- Audit trail reports

Establishing Transaction Rights

If you gave a user selective permission for any area of QuickBooks, you can limit his or her ability to manipulate existing transactions within those areas. You can allow or deny permission to change or delete a transaction, even if the user originally created the transaction. You also can control whether the user can edit or delete transactions dated prior to the closing date.

When you have finished configuring user permissions, the last wizard page presents a list of the permissions you've granted and denied. If everything is correct, click Finish. If there's something you want to change, use the Prev button to back up to the appropriate page.

 TIP: Don't forget that the Audit Trail report will tell you who did what and when they did it. See Chapter 15 for details.

Multi-User Mode Restrictions

When you work in a multi-user environment, it isn't uncommon to find certain activities restricted to avoid damaging your data or creating conflicts. For example, as you'd expect, only one person can adjust payroll liabilities at a time. Table 21-1 lists the activities that only one person can perform at a time.

In addition, there are activities that you can't perform in Multi-User Mode, such as backing up your company file. For these activities, listed in Table 21-2, you need to switch to Single User Mode, and everybody needs to be logged out of the company file so that you can switch to Single User Mode. To switch, choose File | Switch to Single User Mode.

Print 940, 941 Forms	Online Banking Matching
Adjust Payroll Liabilities	Online Mail
Budgets	Pay Bills
Create Paychecks	Pay Liabilities
Assess Finance Charges	Pay Sales Tax
Interviews (for 940, 941, East Step Interview, etc.)	Payroll YTD
Mail Merge	Print Paycheck/Paystub
Sending or Receiving Payroll Service Data	Print Statements
Make Deposits	Update/Autopatch
Online Account Setup	W2, W3 Creation and Printing
Online Banking Download	Batch Printing Checks (By Account)
Online Banking Inset Transaction	

TABLE 21-1   Actions You Can Take in Multi-User Mode One Person at a Time

Backing up, condensing, converting, rebuilding, restoring, or updating the company data file	Signing up for a payroll service
Changing company information, including the closing date	Printing Form 1099-MISC
Setting up or changing preferences	Mapping a network drive from within QuickBooks
Importing or exporting data	Defining custom fields
Merging, deleting, or resorting list items	Linking to QuickBooks from TurboTax
Changing list item fields that interacts with other lists	Accountant's review activities

TABLE 21-2   Activities You Cannot Perform in QuickBooks Premier While in Multi-User Mode

Managing Multiple Users in QuickBooks Enterprise

Most businesses using QuickBooks Enterprise have multiple users accessing their QuickBooks company files, typically in a multi-user network environment.

The new installation process for the QuickBooks 2007 guides you through properly setting up the program to operate in a network environment. For details on this process, see the Startup and Quick Reference Guide that came in the box with your software.

In this section, we'll focus on effectively setting up your company data file so that multiple users can use it securely.

 N O T E :   In a multi-user environment, all QuickBooks users must use the same version of QuickBooks.

Examining Users and Roles in Enterprise

When you want to create or modify users, choose Company | Users | Set Up Users and Roles from the QuickBooks menu bar. The User List tab of the Users and Roles window appears, showing the people you have set up as users in QuickBooks.

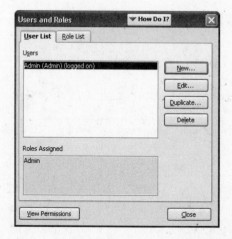

 N O T E :   Access to this window can (and should) be limited using roles, since you can control all aspects of permission to access your data from this window. Occasionally, QuickBooks users will need to know who's logged in to the company; any user can view the list of users in the system by choosing Company | Users | View Users.

You'll also notice that the Users and Roles window contains a Role List tab; QuickBooks Enterprise uses roles to establish sets of permissions. Using a role, you define the type of access you want to grant to any user assigned to that role. Then you create users and assign each user a role; the role you assign determines what that user can and cannot do in QuickBooks. By using roles, you can establish a set of permissions once but assign it many times.

 NOTE: You can assign more than one role to a user.

You'll find 13 predefined roles when you click the Role List tab, and you can click a role to see a description of the role's function, along with users assigned to the role. Using roles, you can control access to all individual lists, to specific report groups, and to information in individual accounts.

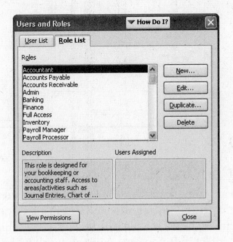

You get a good feel for the way roles work if you select one and edit it so that you can see how it is set up. Don't make any changes; just look. Using roles, you can define a user's permissions in extreme detail. Any filled-in symbol beside an area or activity indicates that the role has full access to that area or activity. When the symbol appears only partly filled in, the role's access to that area is limited, but the way in which the access is limited can vary. For example, in one area, the role may have permission to view information, but not create, modify, or delete. In another area, the same role may have permission to view and create but not modify or delete. You can click the plus sign beside an area or activity—the plus sign changes to a minus sign— to view the role's permissions for that area or activity.

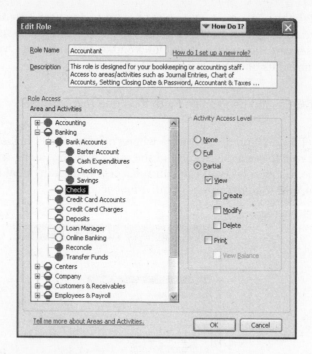

Creating a New Role

If the predefined roles don't work for you, you can create roles that do. I suggest that you start with an existing role and duplicate it; once you've duplicated it, you can modify the duplicate to suit your needs. Using this approach, you leave the original roles intact, but you save yourself work by borrowing permissions from an existing role.

On the Role List tab, select the role that most closely matches the permissions you want to assign to your new role and click Duplicate. QuickBooks displays the Duplicate Role dialog box; the name of the role is the same as the role you selected, proceeded by "Dup1." Simply type a new name for the role that means something to you and modify the description so that, months from now, you'll be able to remember the role's function. Then click the plus sign beside an area or activity in the list on the left side of the dialog box and use the Area Access Level options to set the permissions for the role.

In the Area Access Level, you can select one of the first three options; the one you select determines whether you can select any of the check boxes:

- **None**   The user is denied permission to that area or activity in QuickBooks.
- **Full Access**   The user can open all windows and perform all tasks in that area or activity of QuickBooks.

- **Partial**   The user can perform the tasks you select, and you specify the rights this user should have in relation to those tasks. Those rights vary slightly from component to component, but generally you're asked to make decisions about these permission levels:
  - View and create transactions or reports
  - View and modify transactions or reports
  - View and delete transactions or reports
  - View and print transactions or reports
  - When appropriate, view balance information

When you give partial permission, you can mix and match the options; for example, you can give the role permission to view, create, and modify transactions but not delete or print them.

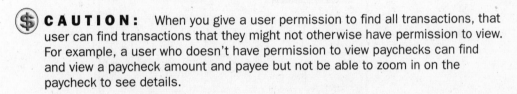 **CAUTION:**   When you give a user permission to find all transactions, that user can find transactions that they might not otherwise have permission to view. For example, a user who doesn't have permission to view paychecks can find and view a paycheck amount and payee but not be able to zoom in on the paycheck to see details.

NOTE: To give a user permission to view and print a memorized report, you must also give the user permission to view the report from which the memorized report was created.

Assigning an Administrator Password

The administrator determines who can use the various features in QuickBooks. It's a good idea to leave the administrator's name as Admin, but you should assign an Admin password. To password-protect the administrator's login, select the Admin role in the on the User List tab of the Users and Roles window and click Edit. In the Edit User dialog box that appears, type a password in the Password box and then type the same password in the Confirm Password box and click OK.

CAUTION: Make a note of the Admin password and keep it in a secure place; consider using a password vault software package or placing the Admin password under lock and key. If you forget the administrator's password, you can call QuickBooks support and arrange to have them recover the password. Standard recovery is free for Enterprise users, but expedited recovery has a fee.

Creating a New User

After you set up the roles you want to use, you can create users. When you create a user, you assign a role and a password to the user.

N O T E :   While passwords aren't required, using them makes your company data file more secure.

To create a new user, click the User List tab and then click New. QuickBooks displays the New User dialog box.

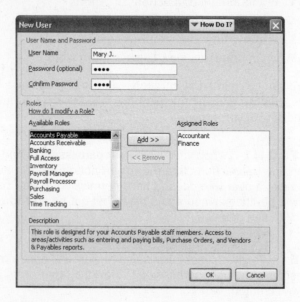

① Enter the username; the user types this name to log into QuickBooks.

② If you want to establish a password for this user (it's optional), enter and confirm the user's password.

 T I P :   If a user comes to you, the Administrator, because he or she cannot remember a password, reset it by editing the user.

③ In the Available Roles list, click a role and then click the Add button. You can repeat this step to assign additional roles to the user.

④ Click OK. QuickBooks redisplays the User List tab of the Users and Role window; the user you just created appears in the Users list. If you click the user, you'll see the roles you assigned to the user in the Roles Assigned box.

 N O T E :   To remove a user from the User List, select the name and then click the Delete User button. You can delete any user except the administrator. When you edit a user, QuickBooks displays the same dialog box you use to add a user.

Reporting on Permissions

You can print a very useful report on the permissions granted to each user; using this report, you can identify modifications you want to make. The report lists all the areas and activities in QuickBooks for which you can assign permissions, along with a column for each user and that user's permission for each area (see Figure 21-12).

To view this report, click the View Permission button on either tab of the Users and Roles window. Then select the users you want to include as columns on the report and click Display.

 TIP: Don't forget that the Audit Trail report will tell you who did what and when they did it. See Chapter 15 for details.

Multi-User Mode Restrictions

When you work in a multi-user environment, it isn't uncommon to find certain activities restricted to avoid damaging your data or creating conflicts. For example,

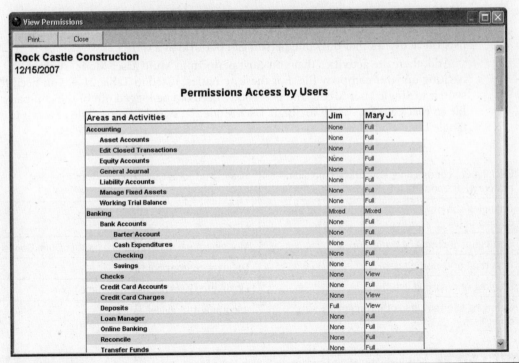

Areas and Activities	Jim	Mary J.
Accounting	None	Full
Asset Accounts	None	Full
Edit Closed Transactions	None	Full
Equity Accounts	None	Full
General Journal	None	Full
Liability Accounts	None	Full
Manage Fixed Assets	None	Full
Working Trial Balance	None	Full
Banking	Mixed	Mixed
Bank Accounts	None	Full
Barter Account	None	Full
Cash Expenditures	None	Full
Checking	None	Full
Savings	None	Full
Checks	None	View
Credit Card Accounts	None	Full
Credit Card Charges	None	View
Deposits	Full	View
Loan Manager	None	Full
Online Banking	None	Full
Reconcile	None	Full
Transfer Funds	None	Full

Rock Castle Construction
12/15/2007

Permissions Access by Users

FIGURE 21-12   Use this report to identify permissions assign to each user you've created

Print 940, 941 Forms	Online Banking Matching
Adjust Payroll Liabilities	Online Mail
Budgets	Pay Bills
Create Paychecks	Pay Liabilities
Assess Finance Charges	Pay Sales Tax
Interviews (for 940, 941, East Step Interview, etc.)	Payroll YTD
Mail Merge	Print Paycheck/Paystub
Sending or Receiving Payroll Service Data	Print Statements
Make Deposits	Update/Autopatch
Online Account Setup	W2, W3 Creation and Printing
Online Banking Download	Batch Printing Checks (By Account)
Online Banking Inset Transaction	

TABLE 21-3   Actions You Can Take in Multi-User Mode One Person at a Time

as you'd expect, only one person can adjust payroll liabilities at a time. Table 21-3 lists the activities that only one person can perform at a time.

And, there are activities that you can't perform in Multi-User Mode, such as backing up your company file. For these activities, listed in Table 21-4, you need to switch to Single User Mode, and everybody needs to be logged out of the company file so that you can switch to Single User Mode. To switch, choose File | Switch to Single User Mode.

Backing up, condensing, converting, rebuilding, restoring, or updating the company data file	Signing up for a QuickBooks Payroll Service
Changing company information, including the closing date	Printing Form 1099-MISC
Setting up or changing preferences	Mapping a network drive from within QuickBooks
Importing or exporting data	Defining custom fields
Merging or resorting list items	Linking to QuickBooks from TurboTax
Changing list item fields that interacts with other lists	Accountant's review activities

TABLE 21-4   Activities You Must Perform in Single User Mode

Managing Your QuickBooks Files

In this chapter:

- Finding transactions

- Creating companies

- Backing up and restore company files

- Using a portable company file

- Cleaning up data

- Updating QuickBooks software

Chapter 22

In addition to performing bookkeeping chores in QuickBooks, you may need to take care of some computer file housekeeping tasks. In this chapter, we'll go over ways to find transactions outside the QuickBooks centers. Then we'll look at creating new companies, backing up and restoring company data files, periodically cleaning up your data, and updating your QuickBooks software.

Finding Transactions

In addition to the Transactions tab of the Customer Center, the Vendor Center, and the Employee Center that you learned about in Chapters 3, 6, and 8, QuickBooks contains other ways to find information in your QuickBooks company file:

- The Simple tab of the Find window
- The Advanced tab of the Find window
- The Google Desktop designed especially for QuickBooks 2007

Performing a Simple Search

Suppose that a vendor calls you and tells you that you haven't paid Bill #10K98L—and you're fairly certain that you did pay the bill. First, you check the Unpaid Bills report and find that the bill doesn't appear, further confirming your suspicion that you paid the bill. If you can find the number of the check that paid the bill, you can double-check with your bank to see if the check cleared.

You can find the check that paid the bill by finding the bill in QuickBooks. You can use the Vendor Center or create a Quick-Report for the vendor to find the bill, but armed with the number of the bill—which the vendor has given you—you can quickly find the bill using the Simple Find window. Choose Edit | Find and then click the Simple tab.

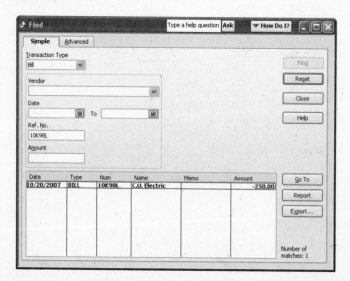

In the Transaction Type list, click Bill and then type the number of the bill in the Ref. No. box. Click Find and QuickBooks displays the results of the search at the bottom of the window. You can double-click the entry to display it in the Enter Bills window. Then click the History button at the top of the Enter Bills window to view details about the check that paid the bill. From the Transaction History—Bill window that QuickBooks displays, you can double-click a payment to display the check in the Bill Payments window or print the check onto plain paper to fax to your vendor.

Performing an Advanced Search

Suppose that you want to look up a customer by his or her address because your service techs forget the name of a customer but can remember the street name. The Advanced tab of the Find window works well for this type of search.

Choose Edit | Find and click the Advanced tab. In the Filter list, click Name Address. In the Name Address box, type the street name. Then click the Find button. QuickBooks will list all the transactions containing the street name you typed—and, of course, you'll see the customer name. If you have more than one customer on the street, you'll have to narrow things down by looking up the complete address.

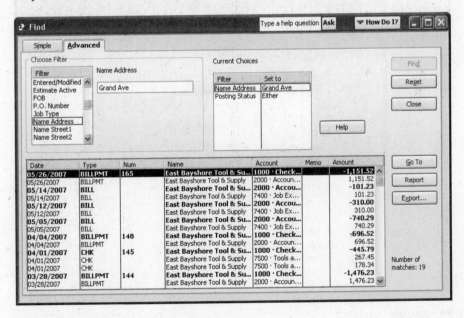

Google Desktop Search

When you install QuickBooks 2007, you can choose to install a specialized version of the Google Desktop search engine that you can use to search your QuickBooks data as well as your computer. To use the Google Desktop search engine with your

QuickBooks data, choose Edit | Google Search from the QuickBooks menu bar to display the QuickBooks Search window shown in Figure 22-1.

You can use the Google Desktop search engine to quickly and easily find transactions and list items in QuickBooks. You use this specialized version of the Google Desktop Search the same way that you use the popular Google search engine on the Internet, searching for multiple words or excluding items from your search results. The more words you include in your search, the more focused the search will be; if you use too many words, Google Desktop Search may not find any information.

When you click the Search QuickBooks button, you search only your QuickBooks company file. When you click the Search QuickBooks and Desktop button, you search your QuickBooks company file and other files on your computer, such as e-mail or Microsoft Word documents. When you use Google Desktop Search inside QuickBooks, you are *not* searching the Internet. And, Google Desktop Search will not display any information that you do not have permission to view; in multiuser environments, *all* users will only be able to see information that they have permission to view.

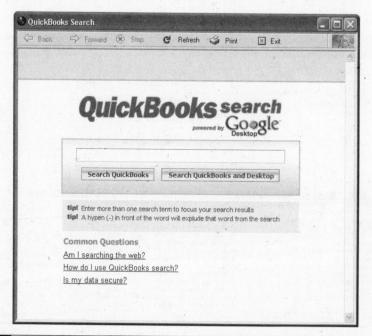

FIGURE 22-1   Use this window to search your QuickBooks data or your computer

In addition to using Google Desktop Search from inside QuickBooks, you may have noticed the Search box that appears on your Windows Task Bar. You can use this Search box to search your computer, but, for added protection, you cannot search your QuickBooks data unless you launch Google Desktop Search from inside QuickBooks. In addition, Intuit has set the preferences for this customized version of Google Desktop Search so that none of your information is transmitted over the Internet or shared with other computers. You can double-check your Google Desktop Search preferences by clicking the Google Desktop icon on the Windows taskbar and then clicking Preferences.

 NOTE: You also can sign up to use marketing tools provided by Google, such as AdWords, Google Maps, and the QuickBooks Product Listing Service. Click the Google Marketing Tools link on any search results page for more information.

Creating Companies in QuickBooks

You can create as many companies in QuickBooks as you wish. You can have your business in one company and your personal finances in another company. If you have enough time and energy, you can also volunteer to run the local community association, open a second business, or keep your mother-in-law's books.

To create a new company, choose File | New Company from the QuickBooks menu bar. This opens the EasyStep Interview you saw the first time you used QuickBooks if you didn't update an existing company file from a previous version. You can go through the EasyStep Interview wizard to create the new company by clicking the button labeled Start Interview.

If you don't want to go through the interview process, you can create the company manually by clicking the button labeled Skip Interview. This provides a shortcut method of creating a company, and it begins with the company information window shown in Figure 22-2.

Fill in the data and click Next to select an organization for your company, such as Sole Proprietorship or Corporation. Select the organization that applies to you and click Next. QuickBooks asks you to select the month in which your fiscal year starts; after you make a selection, click Next. QuickBooks displays a list of industries in the column on the left; when you select an industry in the left column, QuickBooks displays a chart of accounts typically used by businesses in that industry (see Figure 22-3).

Click Next and QuickBooks displays the Create Your Company File screen, which explains that you'll be storing your information in a file QuickBooks calls the company file. Click Finish, and QuickBooks displays the Filename For New Company dialog box in which QuickBooks suggests a location and filename based on your company name.

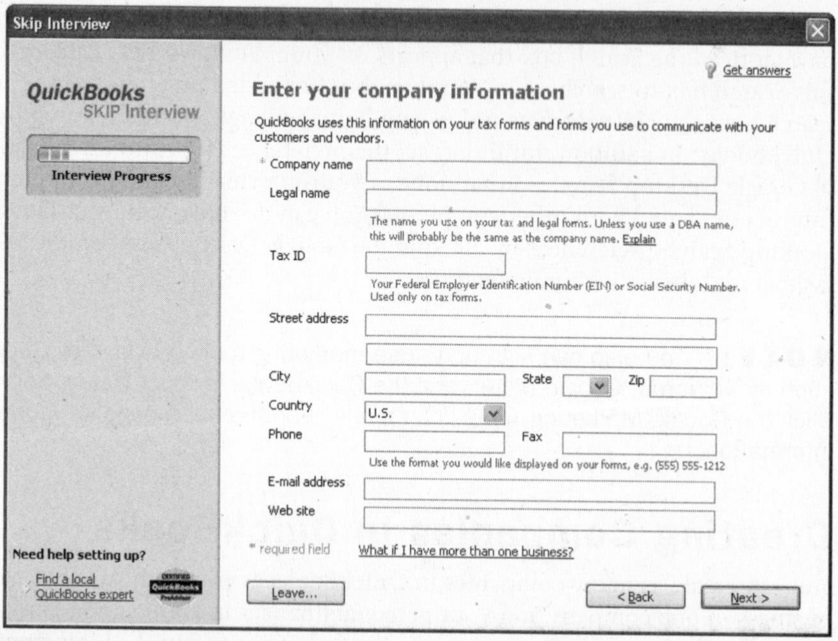

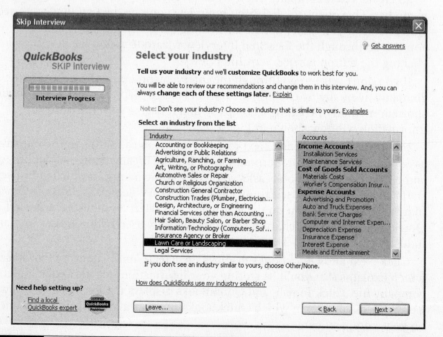

FIGURE 22-2   Fill in the information to create a new company file quickly

FIGURE 22-3   When you select an industry, QuickBooks displays a chart of accounts that works well with businesses in that industry

NOTE: To use QuickBooks effectively under Windows Vista and other Windows operating systems, Intuit recommends that you store company files in C:\Documents and Settings\All Users\Shared Documents\Intuit\My Companies\ or other local locations. Storing company files in the Vista-approved location allows QuickBooks to run as a Windows Standard User instead of requiring Power User or Administrator. When you convert an existing QuickBooks company using QuickBooks 2007, QuickBooks moves your company file to C:\ Documents and Settings\All Users\Shared Documents\Intuit\QuickBooks\My Companies\.

Click Save to create your company file. QuickBooks creates the new company and opens it so that you can view the Learning Center, start setting preferences, entering data, and doing all the other tasks involved in creating a company.

Backing Up and Restoring Files

When QuickBooks performs a backup, it packs your company file and all its ancillary files into a single compressed backup file. By default, QuickBooks names your backup file using your company data file name and the date and time, and all backup files have an extension of .qbb. QuickBooks verifies your data before backing it up, and QuickBooks includes Financial Statement Designer, Letters and Templates, Loan Manager, and other QuickBooks-related files in the backup. To include the files that are not networked, we suggest that you perform the QuickBooks backup on the computer where you work on the non-networked files.

Backing up your QuickBooks data is an incredibly important task and should be done on a daily basis. Using the backup procedure in QuickBooks makes backing up your company file quick and easy. Clients ask me why they need to back up daily; I usually answer by asking them to ask themselves the following questions:

- How much is my data—my customer lists, my purchase history—worth?
- How much will it cost me to reconstruct my finances to do my taxes if I lose my QuickBooks file?

When you think about the effort you put in to record accurate data in QuickBooks, it's hard to find a justifiable reason to risk losing the data to a hard drive failure, an office fire, or a burglary. I can't urge you strongly enough: back up your data daily.

Backing Up

To create a backup of the current company, choose File | Save Copy or Backup from the menu bar to start the backup wizard. On the Save File: Type screen, choose Backup copy and click Next. On the Save Backup: Method screen shown in Figure 22-4, choose Local Backup.

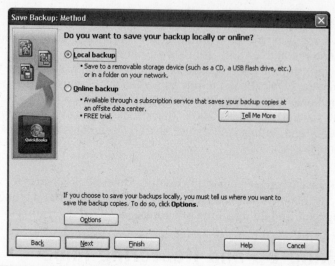

FIGURE 22-4 On this screen, you can make a local backup or use the QuickBooks Online Backup subscription service

The first time you create a backup in QuickBooks 2007, you need to click the Options button to display the Save Backup Copy: Options dialog box.

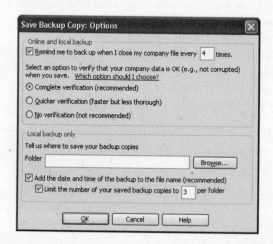

Set Backup Options

If you want QuickBooks to remind you to perform a manual backup, check the Remind Me To Back Up When I Close My Company File Every X Times. If you open and close your QuickBooks files numerous times during the day and you specify a small number, you'll see the reminder at least once every day, which is not a bad thing.

By default during the backup process, QuickBooks verifies the structure of your company data file, helping to ensure that your backup is valid should you need to restore it. QuickBooks 2007 verifies your data faster than earlier versions of QuickBooks, so verifying your data structure shouldn't add significantly to the time you take to back up your data.

Select a default location for your backup; I'll talk more about backup locations in the next section.

By default, QuickBooks adds the date and time information for the backup to the backup filename so that you can tell at a glance when you created each backup. Also by default, QuickBooks limits the number of backups to three per folder.

Choose a Location

You can back up to an external drive, such as a CD drive, a flash drive, or a zip drive; you also can back up to a mapped drive or to a shared folder on another computer on your network. If you're using a zip drive, you cannot set the default unless you put a disk in the drive.

Don't back up onto your local hard drive. If your local hard drive fails, you'll lose both your QuickBooks company data file and your backups.

Periodically—once a week is best, but once a month is essential—make a second backup copy on a different disk and store it off-site. If you live in a disaster-prone area such as California (earthquakes), Arizona (forest fires), or Florida (hurricanes), "off-site" for you means out of state. Then, if there's a catastrophe at your office, your QuickBooks data will survive.

▶▶ FYI

We Use a Tape Drive to Back Up

People usually make this statement when they're trying to explain to me why they don't *need* to know how to use the QuickBooks backup process. I usually respond by asking if they know how to restore from the tape drive. Most of the time, people tell me that the IT person—often an outside contractor—does that stuff. And that means that tape drive users wait for the IT person to restore their data, which costs time and money not only to pay the IT person, but also in lost revenue while QuickBooks wasn't available.

I have one other concern with tape drives; I know very few people who test their tape backups to make sure that they're working properly. On the other hand, I know many people who have discovered that their tape drives were *not* working properly when they tried to restore from a tape.

If you have people in-house who know how to use your tape backup drive and you test your tape backups at least once each week, then the tape drive solution is fine for you. If you can't meet both these conditions, please take advantage of the backup options offered to you by QuickBooks.

($) **TIP:**   You can sign up for the QuickBooks Online Backup subscription service through QuickBooks. Using this service, you back up your company file over the Internet. QuickBooks Online Backup encrypts your data with bank-level security and stores it at two separate data centers to keep it secure. A 30-day free trial is available.

After you finish setting options, click OK to return to the Save Backup wizard, and click Next to display the Save Backup: When screen of the wizard. On this screen, you can choose to make a backup immediately, make a backup immediately and schedule future backups, or simply schedule future backups. We'll discuss scheduled backups in the next section. Insert the backup media of your choice, choose Save Right Now, and click Next.

What happens next depends on the medium you use.

- If you use a CD, QuickBooks writes the backup file to a folder on the hard drive that Windows uses as a temporary holding area. When QuickBooks finishes creating the backup file, a message appears, telling you that QuickBooks has successfully created the backup file but the file hasn't been written to CD yet. If you use Windows XP, Windows Server 2003, or Windows Vista, QuickBooks offers to open the Windows CD Burning wizard; then Windows finishes the burning process. If you don't use Windows XP, Windows Server 2003, or Windows Vista, you will need to use third-party burning software to finish the burning process.

($) **NOTE:**   If your backup file is too large to fit on one CD, you'll need to use a different backup media, such as a DVD-R, which can hold up to 4.3 GB of data, a USB flash drive, or an external hard drive.

- If you use any medium other than a CD, QuickBooks opens your medium and writes the backup file.

($) **TIP:**   When you first start backing up data, once each week, test your backup by restoring it to a location other than your current company data file. By performing this test, you confirm that your backup procedure is working. Once you know the process works, you can reduce your backup tests to once a month. Read "Restoring a Backup" later in this chapter for details.

Automatic Backups

QuickBooks lets you schedule two types of automatic backups:

- Automated backup when closing a company file
- Scheduled backup at a time you specify

To set up automatic backups, follow these steps:

1. Choose File | Save Copy or Backup. The Save File: Type screen of the Backup wizard appears.
2. Click Backup Copy and click Next.
3. On the Save Backup: Method screen, click Local Backup and click Next.
4. On the Save Backup: When screen, click Only Schedule Future Backups and click Next to display the When Should Your Backups Be Created screen (see Figure 22-5).
5. Read the next two sections for details on completing this screen; then click Finish.

Automated Backup When Closing Files

In the Save Backups Automatically section, you can check the Save Backup Copy Automatically When I Close My Company File Every X Times box to automatically create backups based on the frequency with which you close your company, either by exiting QuickBooks or by opening a different company.

Click the Options button to set options for this backup; the options you set are the same as those discussed earlier in the chapter.

Automatic Unattended Backups

You can also configure QuickBooks to perform a backup of your company files at any time even if you're not working at your computer. Take advantage of this cool feature by leaving your computer running when you leave the office. Before you leave,

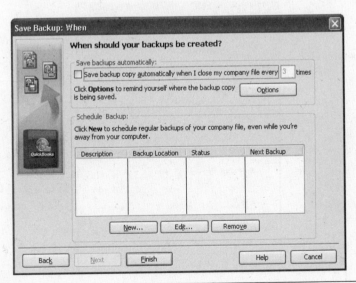

FIGURE 22-5 Use this screen to set up automated backups

make sure QuickBooks is closed so all the files are available for backing up; open files are skipped during a backup.

When you set up unattended backups, QuickBooks uses the Windows Task Scheduler tool to create a hidden task that backs up your QuickBooks data. To set up an unattended backup, click New to open the Schedule Backup dialog box (see Figure 22-6).

Description: Although the descriptive name is optional, supplying a name is a good idea if you're going to create multiple unattended backup configurations.

Backup Location: You can store the backup file on an external hard drive, zip drive, or USB flash drive if you have one. You can't use a floppy drive because your QuickBooks 2007 file won't fit onto a single floppy disk; for this reason, QuickBooks 2007 no longer supports backing up to floppy disks. If you back up to your network drive, use the UNC path (\\servername\sharename) and not a mapped drive because mapped drives are available only when you are logged in to Windows and typically, you'll perform this task in the middle of the night when you're not logged in to Windows. If you set up the scheduled task using a mapped drive, when you log out on Windows, the task will fail. However, if you use the UNC path, the task will succeed.

$ **C A U T I O N :**   Be sure the target drive is available—insert the zip, USB, or other removable drive before leaving the computer, or be sure the remote network computer you're using for backup storage isn't shut down.

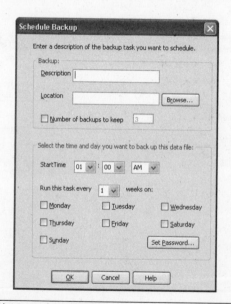

FIGURE 22-6   Set up backups to run automatically

Number of Backups to Keep: Use this option to avoid overwriting the last backup file. QuickBooks saves as many discrete backup files as you specify, each time replacing the first file with the most recent backup and copying older files to the next highest number in the filename, which always begins with SBU_0.

NOTE: Unattended backup files are saved with the filename pattern SBU_0_<CompanyFilename><Date/TimeStamp>. If you specify two backup files in the Number Of Backups To Keep field, the second filename starts with SBU_1_. This pattern continues for the number of backups you specified.

Select The Time And Day You Want To Back Up This Data File: Create a schedule for this unattended backup by selecting a time and a frequency.

If you're working on a network, QuickBooks displays the Set Password dialog box. The password in question is not to your QuickBooks user name and password; it's your Windows network user name and password. If you're familiar with the RunAs feature, this Set Password dialog box works similarly.

NOTE: You cannot use a blank password; if you do, the scheduled task will fail. If a scheduled backup fails for some reason, you should see a message when you open the company data file.

TIP: If you begin to experience performance issues after a period of performing automated backups, perform a backup when you exit QuickBooks. Your QuickBooks company file is actually a collection of three files: the .qbw file, the .nd file, and the .tlg file. Scheduled backups don't reset the .tlg file, so, over time, it may grow and affect performance. Performing a manual backup will reset the file and may improve performance.

When you finish setting options for your scheduled backup, click OK.

Restoring a Backup

There comes a time when you need to restore those backups you've been making so diligently. Perhaps your hard drive failed, or you upgraded to a new computer. Or perhaps you discovered damaged data and you want to roll back to a valid company file. Whatever the reason, restoring a QuickBooks backup is quick and easy.

NOTE: To restore an online backup, follow these steps except, in Step 4, choose Online Backup. Then, follow the on-screen directions.

Here's how to restore a local backup file:

1. If you backed up to removable media, put the disk that contains your last backup into its drive. If you backed up to a network share, be sure the remote computer is running.

2. Choose File | Open or Restore Company from the QuickBooks menu bar. The Open Company: Type screen appears

3. Choose Restore A Backup Copy and click Next. The Restore Backup: Method screen appears.

4. Choose Local Backup and click Next. QuickBooks displays the Open dialog box. The Look In list box displays the backup location you originally selected when you set backup options.

5. Select a backup file to restore and click Open. QuickBooks displays the Restore Backup: To Location screen.

6. Click Next. QuickBooks displays the Restore To dialog box.

7. Select the folder in which to place the company you are restoring and click Save. If you're restoring a company that already exists in this folder, QuickBooks displays a warning that you're about to overwrite the existing file.

8. Click Yes because you want to entirely replace the existing company file with your backup file. QuickBooks asks you to confirm that you want to replace the file.

9. Type Yes and click OK. QuickBooks restores the file.

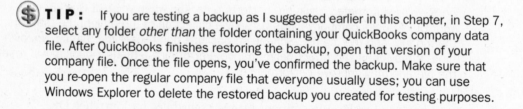 **TIP:**   If you are testing a backup as I suggested earlier in this chapter, in Step 7, select any folder *other than* the folder containing your QuickBooks company data file. After QuickBooks finishes restoring the backup, open that version of your company file. Once the file opens, you've confirmed the backup. Make sure that you re-open the regular company file that everyone usually uses; you can use Windows Explorer to delete the restored backup you created for testing purposes.

QuickBooks displays a message that your data files have been restored successfully. You did it! Aren't you glad you back up regularly? Click OK and go to work!

$ **NOTE:**   If the backup you restored wasn't created yesterday, you must re-enter every transaction you made between the time you created this backup and the last time you used QuickBooks.

Using a Portable Company File

The *portable company file* is a copy of your QuickBooks company file that has been compressed to save disk space; you create a portable file primarily to transfer your QuickBooks data from one computer to another. The portable file extension for a QuickBooks file is .qbm, and a .qbm file compresses to a size of between 1/5 and 1/10 of the .qbw file. Portable files not only take up less room on a disk, but also save download time if you need to attach the file to an e-mail message.

CAUTION: E-mailing your QuickBooks data is not secure. E-mail is like a postcard; anyone who rifles through your mailbox can read it. In addition, even though a .qbm file is much smaller than its .qbw counterpart, if your .qbw file is over 100 MB, it may compress to a 10-MB file, which generally isn't small enough to e-mail.

You can also use a portable company file to move data between computers (such as your home computer and your office computer), so you can work at home, and then bring the updated file back to the office. You could also send the file to your accountant.

Creating a Portable Company File

A portable file is not a backup; it's a smaller version of your company file (the smaller size is the result of the condensing process). The portable filename has the extension .qbm.

To create a portable company file, follow these steps:

1. Choose File | Save Copy or Backup. QuickBooks displays the Save File: Type screen.
2. Choose Portable Company File and click Next. QuickBooks displays the Save Portable Company File As dialog box.
3. Select a folder in which to store the portable company file. By default, QuickBooks chooses the folder in which you store the company file. You can select a zip or USB drive, and take the portable with you so that you can install it on another computer. Or you can keep the default location, and then send the file to yourself (or your accountant) via e-mail.
4. For the file name, QuickBooks supplies the company filename, adds "(portable)" to the file name, and changes the extension to .qbm. There's usually no reason to modify the name QuickBooks suggests.
5. Click Save, and QuickBooks displays a message telling you it must close all QuickBooks windows to perform this task.
6. Click OK. QuickBooks creates the portable company file and, when it finishes, QuickBooks displays a message that reminds you where you stored the file.

Restoring a Portable Company File

You can restore a portable file on your home computer so that you can work at home. After you finish working at home, you can create another portable file that you can take back to the office computer and restore there.

To restore a portable company file, follow these steps:

1. Choose File | Open or Restore Company. QuickBooks displays the Open Company: Type screen.

2. Choose Restore A Portable File and click Next. QuickBooks displays the Open Portable Company File dialog box.

3. Navigate to the folder containing the portable company file you want to restore and select the file.

4. Click Open. QuickBooks displays the Restore Portable File: To Location screen.

5. Click Next. QuickBooks displays the Company File To Save As dialog box.

6. Navigate to the folder containing your regular QuickBooks company file and select it. QuickBooks opens the portable company file and displays a message, telling you that it has opened the portable company file successfully. If you're restoring a company that already exists in this folder, QuickBooks displays a warning that you're about to overwrite the existing file.

7. Click Yes because you want to entirely replace the existing company file with your portable company file. QuickBooks asks you to confirm that you want to replace the file.

8. Type Yes and click OK. QuickBooks opens the portable company file.

Cleaning Up Data

QuickBooks provides a feature that enables you to remove certain data in your company file by replacing transaction details with summary information. Because you lose details about transactions, read on to understand the effects of the feature.

 NOTE: QuickBooks automatically makes a backup of your company file when you start this process; keep that backup file in a safe place and add "Before Cleanup" to the backup file name so that you can recognize it easily.

Understanding What Happens When You Clean Up Data

During this process, QuickBooks deletes closed transactions and replaces them with a journal entry that shows totals posted to accounts. If you subscribe to any QuickBooks payroll services, QuickBooks ignores current year payroll transactions. QuickBooks doesn't remove open transactions, such as unpaid invoices and bills, and estimates that are not marked "Closed."

It's important to understand that QuickBooks doesn't remove any closed transaction that is linked to an open transaction, and this behavior can have a snowball effect. If one open transaction happens to be linked to many closed transactions, that open transaction prevents QuickBooks from removing all of the closed transactions. For example, an open invoice may be linked to a customer payment that partially paid the invoice. The payment is linked to a deposit, and that deposit may contain 20 other payments, all of which are linked to one or more invoices. One open transaction can hold up 100 or more other transactions from being removed. The bottom line here is that cleaning up your data may not reduce the size of your company data file as much as you expect.

During the process of cleaning up, QuickBooks asks you to supply a cutoff date. QuickBooks uses that cutoff date to identify potential closed transactions to remove; QuickBooks will remove all closed transactions dated prior to the cutoff date, as long as the closed transactions aren't linked to open transactions.

During the process, QuickBooks deletes the transactions that meet the criteria of the cutoff date and replaces the details with summary journal entry transactions that show the totals for the removed transactions, one for each month. None of your account balances is changed by removing data, because the summary transactions maintain those totals.

After you clean up the file, you won't be able to run detail reports for those periods before the cutoff date. However, summary reports will be perfectly accurate in their financial totals. You will be able to recognize the summary transactions in the account registers because they will be marked with a transaction type GENJRNL. You can restore the archived file if you need to see the original transaction details.

 NOTE: You cannot delete any of the summary journal entry transactions, and if any of them becomes damaged, you'll need to restore a backup.

Be aware that the Cleanup process can take an extremely long time because of the intensive checking QuickBooks does to determine if each transaction can be removed. As long as you can move your mouse and the hourglass mouse pointer moves, QuickBooks is still cleaning up your company data file, even if the Task Manager indicates that QuickBooks is "Not Responding."

Running the Cleanup Utility

A wizard walks you through the process of cleaning up your data. Choose File | Utilities | Clean Up Company Data. QuickBooks displays the Clean Up Company Data window (see Figure 22-7).

 NOTE: You may see a warning that your budget data may be affected during cleanup because some budgets are based on detailed postings. See Chapter 13 to learn how to export your budgets and import them back into QuickBooks.

The wizard offers two choices for proceeding: Remove Transactions As Of A Specific Date, or Remove ALL Transactions. Choose the first option; QuickBooks automatically displays the last day of the previous year as the cutoff date for this

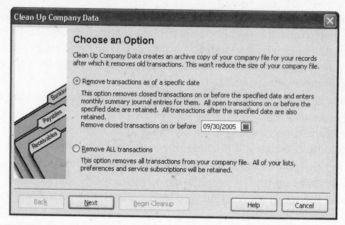

FIGURE 22-7   Select the option you want to use for the cleanup process

option. You can use this date or choose an earlier date (a date long past, so you won't care if you lose the transaction details). Be sure to choose the last day of a month, quarter, or year.

The other option, Remove ALL Transactions, is really an option to wipe all your data so that you can create a new (empty) company file with the same name as your current company file; the new file will retain your list information, preferences, and service subscriptions but none of your data. It's unusual to do this; before you choose this option, make sure that you have a backup that you've tested.

Click Next to see a list of the transaction types that are not removed (see Figure 22-8). You can select any of them to include them in the "to be removed" list, if you know you don't need to keep details about those transaction types.

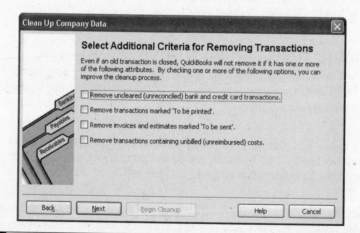

FIGURE 22-8   You can remove transactions that QuickBooks would normally keep, but do so carefully

Click Next and select the lists (accounts, customers, vendors, and so on) you want QuickBooks to empty of unused items.

Click Next to see an informational window that explains the cleanup process. Click Begin Cleanup to start the process. QuickBooks displays a message telling you that it will make a backup of your data file before proceeding with the cleanup process. This is not an everyday backup; it's the last backup of a full data file before information is removed. I suggest that you add text to the name of the backup file to indicate that it's special, such as My Company File (Backup Sep 30, 2005 07 22 PM)-Before Cleanup.QBB. Click OK to start the Backup wizard.

As soon as QuickBooks finishes backing up, it starts removing data. You'll see progress bars on your screen as each step completes. When QuickBooks finishes the job, QuickBooks displays the name of the backup copy of your data file that QuickBooks created, which is intact, so you can open it if you need to see transaction details. QuickBooks calls this copy an archive copy.

Updating QuickBooks

QuickBooks provides an automatic update service that you can use to make sure your QuickBooks software is up to date and trouble-free. This service provides you with any maintenance releases of QuickBooks that have been created since you purchased and installed your copy of the software. A maintenance release is distributed when a problem is discovered and fixed. This is sometimes necessary because it's almost impossible to distribute a program that is totally bug-free, although my experience has been that QuickBooks generally releases without any major bugs, since Intuit does a thorough job of testing.

The Update QuickBooks service also provides notes and news from Intuit so you can keep up with new features and information for QuickBooks.

 N O T E : This service does not provide upgrades to a new version; it just provides updates for your current version.

The Update QuickBooks service is an online service; see Chapter 16 for details on setting up online access for QuickBooks. When you want to check for updated information, choose Help | Update QuickBooks from the menu bar to open the Update QuickBooks window shown in Figure 22-9.

You can set up QuickBooks to automatically check for updates, download them, and install them, or you can set up QuickBooks to download only updates when you manually run the feature. In most cases, automatically updating QuickBooks is the best approach since it keeps your software up to date with no real effort on your part.

However, if you work in an environment where many people are affected by software updates, you may prefer to back up your QuickBooks data and then download updates manually so that you control the process.

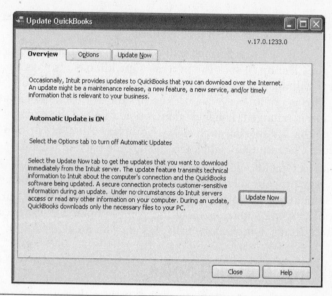

FIGURE 22-9   You can use the Update QuickBooks dialog box to establish update options or to download an update manually

Automatic Updates

If you download updates automatically, QuickBooks checks the Intuit update web site periodically while you're connected to the Internet. QuickBooks doesn't need to be running to check for updates.

If the Automatic Updates feature finds new information, it downloads the information to your hard drive without notifying you. If you happen to disconnect from the Internet while updates are downloading, the next time you connect to the Internet, QuickBooks will pick up where it left off.

Manual Updates

If you turn off automatic updates, you should periodically check for new software files manually. Click the Update Now button in the Update QuickBooks window to select and download updated files.

Setting Up the QuickBooks Update Service

Click the Options tab of the Update QuickBooks window to set up the Update feature. You have several choices for updating your software components. You can always change these options in the future.

Sharing Updates on a Network

If you're using QuickBooks in multi-user mode across a network, set up the Update QuickBooks service to share downloaded files with other users. When you enable this option, QuickBooks creates a subfolder on the computer that holds the shared QuickBooks data files, and the other computers on the network use that subfolder as the source of updated files. The subfolder address appears on the Options tab, and every user on the network must also open his or her copy of QuickBooks and set up the options for Shared Download to reflect the folder location on the host computer.

Selecting Update Types

Select the types of files you want QuickBooks to download when you update. Select Maintenance Releases to ensure that you get all program patches that fix issues or add features.

Determining Update Status

The Update Now tab displays information about the current status of the service, including the last date that QuickBooks checked for updates and the names of any files that were downloaded.

Click the check boxes next to each specific type of update to select/deselect those types of files. Then click Get Updates to tell QuickBooks to check the Internet immediately and download any files. Most of the time, QuickBooks integrates the downloaded files automatically; sometimes an information box appears to tell you that QuickBooks will integrate the files the next time you open QuickBooks.

Part Five

Appendices

Fixed Asset Manager

The values of fixed assets decline over time, and calculating the decline is a thorny undertaking. The calculations for depreciation or amortization are extremely complicated, mostly due to the vast number of IRS regulations on the subject. To make it worse, the regulations change frequently, so keeping up with current rules is a complicated task.

In addition to making sure your depreciation calculations don't cause a problem with the IRS, the amounts involved in depreciation transactions have a direct effect on your business.

- The amount by which an asset is depreciated affects the worth of a business because the net (reduced) current value is used on the balance sheet.
- The depreciation amount affects the business' tax bill (depreciation is deductible).

The QuickBooks Fixed Asset Manager makes it easier to track and depreciate assets, and enter the resulting calculations in both the tax return and the QuickBooks company file.

 N O T E : The Fixed Asset Manager is included in QuickBooks Premier Accountant Edition and in all editions of QuickBooks Enterprise Solutions.

Overview of Fixed Asset Manager

Fixed Asset Manager is a robust, complex program, and I think it's a good idea to help you learn to use it by providing an overview of its features. Here's a laundry list that should help you find your way as you discover all sorts of innovative ways to use the program's power.

- A detailed asset entry screen that you can customize.
- Up to five user-defined classifications for tracking assets.
- Six depreciation bases (Book, State, Federal, Other, AMT, and ACE).
- Projected depreciation calculations.
- Disposition tracking.
- On-screen queries and custom sorting options for the asset list.
- Full calculation overrides (also applies when linking to ProSeries).
- A report list feature that allows you to group commonly used reports for easy access and printing.
- An export feature that allows you to transfer asset information into ProSeries federal tax products.
- A desktop workspace you can customize.
- A toolbar for quick access to common tasks.

QuickBooks Files and Fixed Asset Manager

When you open Fixed Asset Manager in QuickBooks (choose Accountant | Manage Fixed Assets), the currently loaded QuickBooks company file links to the Fixed Asset Manager. You can create a new Fixed Asset Manager client file for this company, transfer prior-year clients from QuickBooks Fixed Asset Manager or ProSeries Fixed Asset Manager to the current year, reconnect Accountant's Review Copy with Fixed Asset Manager, or restore a previous QuickBooks Fixed Asset Manager file from a backup.

QuickBooks Company Information

Fixed Asset Manager must know the type of tax form this business files. To make sure the right tax form is configured for the company file (or, for that matter, to make sure the tax form information isn't blank, which is often the case), choose Company | Company Information and check the data in the dialog box.

Fixed Asset Manager uses other company information (such as the address, EIN, or Social Security number) when it creates the Fixed Asset Manager file, and you can view that information within Fixed Asset Manager. However, you can't edit the information in Fixed Asset Manager, so you must make sure the data is correct in the Company Information dialog box.

Company Fixed Assets List

QuickBooks provides a Fixed Asset Item list, which tracks the purchase date, the description, and the cost of each fixed asset the company owns. When your clients use this list within QuickBooks, the list is inert; that is, it performs no calculations and is not automatically linked to transaction data entry in QuickBooks. When clients purchase or sell a fixed asset, and create the appropriate transaction entry (a check, a loan, or a cash receipt), the information is not automatically transferred to the Fixed Asset Item list.

Even though the Fixed Asset Item list is nothing more than a list, with no ability to interact with standard QuickBooks software calculations, Fixed Asset Manager can read (import) this list. If the Fixed Asset Item list exists in the company file, your work in Fixed Asset Manager is faster and easier. Another advantage of using the Fixed Asset Item list in QuickBooks is that assets in the list are linked to a Fixed Asset account. In a roundabout way, this ensures the QuickBooks company file has one or more Fixed Asset accounts. Fixed Asset Manager can use that account information, which is another efficient time saver.

Fixed Asset Manager Client File Setup

You must create a Fixed Asset Manager client file for each company, and if no file exists for the currently loaded company when you open Fixed Asset Manager, the process of creating the file begins automatically.

If you'd previously set up a Fixed Asset Manager client file for this company, but the currently open company file is an Accountant's Copy, select the option to reconnect the Accountant's Review Copy to Fixed Asset, and a wizard walks you through the task of opening the file.

When you choose to create a new client, the Fixed Asset Manager New Client Wizard launches, and you click Next to move through each wizard window. The first wizard windows display the company information for the client, and you cannot edit that information (see the previous sections on making sure the company information is correct before running Fixed Asset Manager). The wizard then asks you to respond to queries about the following data:

- Current fiscal year
- Prior short years
- Qualification for the "small corporation" exemption from AMT
- Depreciation bases
- Default depreciation method for each selected basis

The wizard offers the chance to import the fixed assets for this company automatically, using the information in the Fixed Asset Item list in the company file. You can also enter the fixed assets manually.

A client summary is displayed on the last wizard window—click Finish to end the client setup and begin using Fixed Asset Manager. (If you automatically synchronized the fixed assets from the client company Fixed Asset Item list, a log appears to report the fixed assets that were imported.)

When you opt to transfer information from client files for the prior-year version of QuickBooks Fixed Asset Manager, or from ProSeries Fixed Asset Manager, into this year's version, the Transfer Client Wizard launches. Click Next to move through each wizard window. Select the client you want to transfer on the first wizard window that appears. The wizard then asks you to respond to the queries about the following data:

- Calculation options
- Qualification for the "small corporation" exemption from AMT
- QuickBooks Asset Synchronization

When a client summary appears on the last wizard window, click Finish to complete the transfer and begin using Fixed Asset Manager.

Importing Data from Other Software

If you've been keeping depreciation records in another software application, you can import client data to Fixed Asset Manager. Once your Fixed Asset Manager client file is set up, the software can import data from a Comma Separated Value (CSV) format file. You must map the fields in the import file to the fields in Fixed Asset Manager. Fixed Asset Manager provides help for this task during the import.

If the other program can't save to a file in CSV format, but can save data in a file format that is readable by Microsoft Excel, open the file in Excel, and then save the file in CSV format.

If you've been managing fixed assets in ProSeries tax software, you can import data directly from that software to Fixed Asset Manager.

Working in Fixed Asset Manager

After the client file is set up, the Fixed Asset Manager software window opens so you can begin your work. By default, the software window opens with the Schedule tab selected. The tabs at the bottom of the window represent the bases you selected for depreciation. Select the Schedule Tab, and as you select each basis tab the data changes appropriately.

Schedule Tab

In the Schedule tab, Fixed Asset Manager identifies the assets using the text in the Purchase Description field of the QuickBooks Fixed Asset Item list—not the text in the Name field. In fact, Fixed Asset Manager doesn't even import the name field from the QuickBooks Fixed Asset Item list.

Fixed Asset Manager assigns a number to each asset, and that number becomes the asset's name (you can think of it as a code) in the Fixed Asset Manager client file. To arrive at the number (code), Fixed Asset Manager reads the text in the Purchase Description field and appends a hyphen surrounded by spaces, followed by the next available number. For example, if the Description text is Workstation Computer, the Fixed Asset Manager name becomes "Workstation Computer - 1." If another asset has the same description (in QuickBooks, only the Name must be unique, and the Name field isn't used by Fixed Asset Manager, so duplicates can occur when synchronizing with Fixed Asset Manager), the next number is appended to the text ("Workstation Computer - 2"). Asset numbers are appended in the order in which they are sorted in the Fixed Asset Item List in QuickBooks (which sorts on the QuickBooks Name field).

You can sort assets differently by changing the criteria in the sort set. In addition, you can choose to edit an existing sort set or create a custom sort set. You can also change the asset list and the columns in the Schedule tab using the View Column Set, Sort Assets By, and Apply Query Criteria controls on the Asset toolbar. To view amounts for any basis supported in a client's file, click the corresponding tab at the bottom of the Schedule tab. The Schedule tab lists all the assets in the Fixed Asset Manager client file. The asset that's currently selected is the asset used when you visit any of the other tabs at the top of the software window.

Asset Tab

Use the Asset tab to enter information about tax forms, the QuickBooks chart of accounts, and other items for the asset you selected in the Schedule tab.

The upper section of the tab is the place to enter general information for the selected asset, including any classification fields. The bottom section of the Asset tab is the Basis Detail section. Enter the cost, date acquired, tax system, depreciation method, recovery period, and other information needed to calculate the asset's depreciation. You can also configure Section 179 deductions here, if appropriate for this asset.

Disposal Tab

Use the disposal tab to dispose of assets. Fixed Asset Manager displays the cost basis and any Section 179 deductions. Enter the sales price, the expense of sale, and any other relevant information about the Disposal.

Select a property type from the drop-down list to determine where the disposal information will appear on Form 4797, Sales of Business Property (for ProSeries client file exports).

Projection Tab

Use the Projection tab to determine the best depreciation method for the selected asset by reviewing its projected depreciation. Use the Bases tabs at the bottom of the window to see the projections.

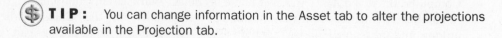 **T I P :**   You can change information in the Asset tab to alter the projections available in the Projection tab.

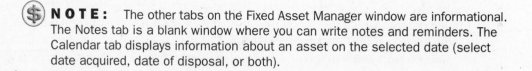 **N O T E :**   The other tabs on the Fixed Asset Manager window are informational. The Notes tab is a blank window where you can write notes and reminders. The Calendar tab displays information about an asset on the selected date (select date acquired, date of disposal, or both).

Using the Section 179/40% Test

To determine whether the Section 179 deductions claimed for the current year are within allowed limits, or to calculate the percentage of assets acquired in the last three months of the year, use the Section 179/40% test. Perform these diagnostics after you enter client asset information and before you print reports or link the file to the client's tax return. To perform these tests, choose Tools | 179/40% test. Review the Section 179 test, then click the 40% test tab to review mid-quarter totals.

Reviewing Section 179 Limitations

The Section 179 test determines the total cost of all eligible Section 179 property, the total Section 179 expense deduction made, and how much of the deduction exceeds federal limits for the active year.

Reviewing the Mid-Quarter 40% Test

Fixed Asset Manager totals the cost of all assets purchased in the active year and all assets purchased in the last quarter of the active year. If the percentage of assets purchased in the last quarter is greater than 40%, you can convert these assets to the mid-quarter convention.

Using the Client Totals Summary

Use the Client Totals Summary to review the accumulated cost and depreciation before and after current-year calculations for each basis supported in a client file. To see the Client Totals Summary, choose View | Client Totals.

Calculating Depreciation

When the selected asset is properly configured, go to the Asset tab and choose Asset | Calculate Asset. If the command is grayed out, Fixed Asset Manager does not have all the information it needs to perform the calculation. Check all the fields to make sure you've entered the required information about this asset.

You can set Fixed Asset Manager to automatically calculate assets after making modifications using the Program Options window. To select this setting, choose Tools | Program Options. Select the Automatically Calculate Assets option, and click OK to save the change.

Posting the Journal Entry to QuickBooks

Fixed Asset Manager automates the process of creating a journal entry for depreciation expense and/or accumulated depreciation. Choose QuickBooks | Post Journal Entry to QuickBooks, and then enter the appropriate information.

Producing Reports

Fixed Asset Manager provides a variety of report options, including preconfigured report templates. You can sort and select the information you want to print, and the order in which you print it. Table A-1 describes the purpose of each predefined report.

Use This Report	For This Purpose
ACE Adjustment Calculation	To determine the total ACE adjustment needed to compute a tax return for a corporation. Assets are grouped by category and sorted by asset number within each group.
Amortization Schedule by G/L Account Number	To see a summary of the activity of the amortized assets. Assets are grouped by general ledger account number and sorted by asset number within each group.
Amortization Schedule by User Defined 1 to 5	To see a summary of the activity of the amortized assets, grouped by one user-defined classification. (There is a report for each user-defined field that you use.) Assets are grouped by the user-defined field and sorted by asset number within each group.
AMT Adjustment Calculation	To print the necessary information for AMT depreciation adjustment reporting (Federal depreciation − AMT depreciation = AMT adjustment). Assets are grouped by category and sorted by asset number within each group.
Asset Disposition by Asset Sale Description	To see a summary of disposition information according to the sale description assigned to each asset. Assets are grouped by asset sale description and sorted by asset number within each group.
Asset, Basis and Disposal Detail Report	To print the asset details for each asset in the Asset and Disposal tabs that you see on-screen.
Assets Acquired in the Current Year	To see a summary of each asset purchased in the current year. Assets are grouped by general ledger account number and sorted by acquisition date within each group.
Depreciation Schedule by G/L Account Number	To see an activity summary for each asset, grouped by general ledger account number. Assets are sorted by acquisition date within each group.
Depreciation Schedule by User Defined (1 to 5)	To see an activity summary for each asset, grouped by one user-defined category. (There is a report for each user-defined field that you use.) Assets are sorted by asset number within each group.
Lead Schedule by Category	To see an activity summary for each asset, grouped by category, in a traditional lead schedule format. Assets are sorted by asset number within each group.
Lead Schedule by G/L Asset Account	To see an activity summary for each asset, grouped by general ledger account number, in a traditional lead schedule format. Assets are sorted by asset number within each group.
Lead Schedule by Location	To see an activity summary for each asset, grouped by location, in a traditional lead schedule format. Assets are sorted by asset number within each group.

TABLE A-1 Description of the Predefined Reports

Use This Report	For This Purpose
Lead Schedule by Tax Form and Property Description	To see an activity summary for each asset, grouped by tax form and property description, in a traditional lead schedule format. Assets are sorted by asset number within each group.
Monthly G/L Accumulated Account Summary	To see the total monthly cost additions and deletions and their beginning and ending balances. This report is grouped by General Ledger Asset Account. Assets without assigned account numbers are grouped by "No Account Number."
Monthly G/L Asset Account Summary	To see the total monthly accumulated depreciation/amortization additions, and deletions and their beginning and ending balances. This report is grouped by General Ledger Accumulated Depreciation and Amortization account. Assets without assigned account numbers are grouped by "No Account Number."
Monthly G/L Expense Account Summary	To see the total monthly depreciation/amortization expense additions and deletions, and beginning and ending accumulated depreciation and amortization balances. This report is grouped by General Ledger Depreciation and Amortization Expense account. Assets without assigned account numbers are grouped by "No Account Number."
Personal Property Schedule by Year of Acquisition	To see a summary of depreciation amounts for assets that you marked as personal property. Assets are grouped by the year each asset was placed in service, and sorted by acquisition date within each group.
Projection by Category	To see a five-year projection for each asset. Assets are grouped by category, and sorted by asset number within each group.
Remaining Basis Over Remaining Life Report	To identify assets that were not fully depreciated. Assets within this report are grouped and subtotaled by category.

TABLE A-1   Description of the Predefined Reports (*continued*)

You can select the reports you want to associate with your client using the Report List Organizer and create a custom report list. Having a custom report list allows you to batch print reports. To organize a report list, choose Reports | Report List Organizer.

Exporting Depreciation Data

Fixed Asset Manager has built-in tools for exporting depreciation data. The export file you create is imported to the appropriate software. The following file formats are supported:

- ProSeries
- Microsoft Word
- Microsoft Excel

- ASCII (text) file
- CSV file

Tax Worksheets

Fixed Asset Manager provides the following tax worksheets that can help you complete the depreciation-related portions of your clients' returns:

- Form 4562 Part I—Section 179 Summary Copy
- Form 4562 Part II & III—Lines 15, 16, and 17
- Form 4562 Part III—Lines 19 and 20
- Form 4562 Part IV—Summary
- Form 4562 Part V—Listed Property
- Form 4562 Part VI—Amortization
- Form 4797 Part I—Property Held More Than One Year
- Form 4797 Part II—Ordinary Gains and Losses
- Form 4797 Part III—Gains from Disposition of Depreciable Property
- Form 4626—Depreciation Adjustments and Tax Preferences
- Form 4626—ACE Worksheet
- Form 4626—Gain/Loss Adjustments

Fixed Asset Manager completes each worksheet automatically using the information in the client's file.

Financial Statement Designer

The Financial Statement Designer (FSD) gives you the power to customize financial statements that are directly linked to a client's QuickBooks data. You don't have to export the data to other programs to create a customized statement; instead, you can produce exactly what you want immediately. QuickBooks includes FSD with the Premier Accountant Edition and in all editions of QuickBooks Enterprise Solutions.

Appendix B

Overview of Features

The Financial Statement Designer includes the following features, all of which provide more control of your financial statements than is provided with standard QuickBooks reports.

- Includes over 30 predefined templates.
- Customize statements by inserting columns or rows to show prior year balances, show percentages and variances between other columns, subtotals, and more.
- Use your customized statement for any client.
- Use the Supporting Document Editor to prepare your title pages, notes to financial statements, and compilation letters.
- Format the statement any way you want using familiar spreadsheet-like tools.
- Save your financial statements and supporting documents for each client to separate file locations.
- Insert rows for subtotals, to group accounts in any way that you want, or even add blank rows for spacing.
- Update your client's statement for the following period in seconds.
- Print a complete set of financial statements and supporting documents by choosing which items you want to print, in the order you want.
- Save as a PDF file.
- Export to Excel.

 N O T E :   With the Financial Statement Designer you can create a standard set of financial statements that are in accordance with Generally Accepted Accounting Principles (GAAP).

FSD and QuickBooks Data Files

As a built-in program, FSD opens from within QuickBooks, by choosing Reports | Financial Statement Designer. The data in the currently open QuickBooks company file is automatically connected to FSD, so open the client company file you want to work with before you launch FSD. When you open Financial Statement Designer in QuickBooks, you can either create a new Financial Statement Designer client file for this company or work on an existing client file you previously created.

Your client's statement data is always connected to the source. This means updating financial statements is easy and efficient, because the balances update automatically. While you're viewing an FSD financial statement, if you use the QuickZoom feature to edit a source transaction, when you return to the financial statement, you'll see that FSD refreshes the statement with the new account balances automatically.

FSD Components

The power of FSD comes from its three main components.

- Financial Statement Organizer
- Financial Statement Editor
- Supporting Document Editor

Using these three components, you can create professional financial statements including supporting schedules, title pages, and compilation letters.

Financial Statement Organizer

The Financial Statement Organizer displays a list of your financial statements and supporting documents. You use the Financial Statement Organizer for the following tasks:

- View the list of financial statements and supporting documents and templates.
- Create a new set of financial statements and supporting documents.
- Edit saved financial statements and supporting documents.
- Create folders to organize your statements and documents.
- Print financial statements and supporting documents in any order you prefer.
- Save statements and supporting documents as PDF files.
- Select a period for which a statement needs to be generated.
- Set the statement basis.
- Select a template for the new financial statement (see the section "FSD Templates," later in this appendix).

To change the location where you save financial statements and supporting documents for the current QuickBooks client, choose Tools | Select File Locations, and select a new location. The new location of the financial statements and documents appears in the Details column in the Saved Financial Statements and Supporting Documents section. You can choose a discrete location for each client file.

FSD Templates

FSD comes with a large selection of customizable financial statement templates. Choose from a wide variety of balance sheets, income statements, statements of cash flows, statements of retained earnings, and financial ratio calculations.

While you can easily create a financial statement from scratch, it's quicker to use one of the financial statement templates as your starting point. You can easily make changes to the template to customize it for your client's needs or your own preferences. Give your altered template a new name so you can use it in the future.

Financial Statement Editor

The Financial Statement Editor is the component you use to design financial statements. The Editor uses spreadsheet-like tools to insert rows and columns, add accounts and formulas, and change the formatting of your financial statements to fit your needs and preferences.

To access the Financial Statement Editor, double-click a financial statement from the Financial Statement Organizer window, or select a financial statement, and choose File | Open Selected.

Editor Toolbars

The Financial Statement Editor includes three toolbars. If you've been using Windows software you'll be comfortable with their functions instantly, because they provide standard Windows toolbar functions.

The standard toolbar provides the normal file operation functions, such as New, Open, Cut, Copy, Paste, Save, Print, Print Preview, Undo, and Redo. In addition to these familiar icons, the Standard toolbar offers a Refresh icon (to refresh the data in your financial statement). The Format toolbar is similar to the Formatting toolbar in a Windows spreadsheet application such as Excel. Use the icons to apply fonts, font color, indentations, alignments, cell underlines, formats (for decimals, percentage, and currency), and AutoSum functions.

Just like the familiar formula bar you use in spreadsheet software, the Financial Statement Editor's Formula bar identifies the current location of the cursor and provides a text box for entering formulas into cells.

 TIP: You can display or hide the toolbars by choosing View | Toolbars and selecting or deselecting the appropriate toolbar.

Properties Panel

The Properties panel appears to the left of the Design Grid in the Financial Statement Editor. This panel consists of four different sections: Column Properties, Row Properties, Cell Properties, and Statement Properties. You can use the Properties panel to quickly view or change the properties for a particular area of the financial statement. If the properties you want to view do not appear in the Properties panel, click the arrows to expand the section. To show and hide the Properties panel, choose View | Properties Panel. If the Properties panel is hidden, you can still access the properties by using the shortcut menus or selecting the properties area you want to change from the Format menu.

Use the Column Properties to set the date range for account balances. For example, you can configure one column for the prior period balances and the next column for the current period balances.

Depending on the area selected in the Design Grid, you can use the Row Properties to repeat column headers on every page, change the account description that appears on the financial statement, quickly add and remove accounts for a combined account row, reverse the sign of an account balance, and print the account row on the printed financial statement even if the account balance is zero.

The Cell Properties let you override the column's date range. (Changing the properties using the Cell Properties section only affects the selected cell.)

The Statement Properties allow you to set the column spacing.

Design Grid

The Design Grid displays the account descriptions, balances, report headers and footers, column headers, and the results of the formulas you've entered. This lets you customize statements by inserting columns or rows to show prior year balances, percentages, and variances between other columns and subtotals. You can also insert rows for subtotals to group accounts in any way you prefer, or add blank rows for spacing.

You can also add more information to a financial statement or document by inserting the following fields:

- **Page Break**   Inserts a page break at the location of the cursor.
- **Page Number**   Prints the correct page number.
- **Current Date and Time**   This selection is actually two separate fields; you must insert both fields to print both on the report.
- **Statement Date**   Prints the statement ending date.
- **Statement Basis**   Prints the statement basis (cash or accrual).
- **Client Information**   Prints the selected field from the Client Information window; includes such fields as company name, e-mail address, URL for the company's web site, and so on.
- **Accountant Information**   Prints the selected field from the Accountant Information window; includes such fields as firm name, e-mail address, URL for the accounting firm's web site, and so on.

Supporting Document Editor

The Supporting Document Editor works like a word processing tool with simple text editing and formatting functions. Use this tool to design documents such as the title page, compilation letters, and audit reports. Templates are available, and you can change those templates to suit your own purposes.

To access the Supporting Document Editor, double-click a document from the Financial Statement Organizer window, or select a document, and choose File | Open Selected.

Previewing and Printing Financial Statements and Documents

You can preview and print a complete set of financials statements and supporting documents. You can export and e-mail the documents, and even save them as PDF files. Previewing financial statements and documents lets you see how they will look when they're printed, giving you a chance to make sure they're formatted correctly. To print a period's financial statement set, access the Financial Statement Designer. Then, enter the statement date, and choose File | Print.

The Options tab on the Print window includes selections that apply to financial statements. You can configure the way account balances appear on the financial statements as follows:

- Divide by 1000
- Use whole numbers (numbers are rounded to the nearest dollar)

If you select the option to use whole numbers, you can select the account to which rounding errors are posted from the drop-down list on the Print dialog.

You can also suppress the printing of accounts with a zero balance.

 NOTE: The settings on the Options tab of the Print window can also be accessed in the Options window of the Financial Statement Editor (choose Tools | Options).

Export Financial Statements and Supporting Documents

You can export your financial statements to an .fst file format, which is the format used by the Financial Statement Editor. You can then import the .fst files into another client's company so statements provided by your firm are all using the same professional organization and appearance.

You can export your financial statements to Excel (.xls) formats. You can print your supporting documents to .rft, ASCII and tab-delimited text (.txt), and comma-delimited (.csv) formats.

Save Financial Statements and Documents as PDF Files

You can save your financial statements and supporting documents to PDF files. These files preserve the text formatting of your financial statements and can be viewed using Adobe Acrobat Reader (which can be downloaded from the Adobe web site http://www.adobe.com).

Of course, like all PDF files, they print beautifully, maintaining the formatting, design, and layout you want.

E-mailing Financial Statements and Supporting Documents

You have the convenience of e-mailing financial statements and supporting documents to another accountant from the Financial Statement Organizer window or the editors. When the recipient accountant receives the e-mail, he or she can save the .fst or .rtf file to a specified location, and then import the statement or document into the Financial Statement Designer.

If you need to e-mail a financial statement or supporting document to a client, save the item as a PDF file that you can attach to your e-mail message.

Index

Symbols and Numbers

: (colon), 10
* (asterisk), 141, 142, 303
2D graphs, 463
#10 business envelopes, 197
40% test, 514–515

A

A/P (accounts payable), bill
payment, 188–215
    choosing what to pay,
      188–191
    credits, applying, 193–194
    direct disbursements, 201–206
    discount account, 193
    discounts, applying, 191–193
    manual checks, 196–201
    options for, 190
    partial payment, 191
    payment amounts, 190–191
    saving information for,
      195–196
    selecting bills to pay, 189–190
    viewing unpaid bills, 188–189
A/P (accounts payable), entering,
150–186
    bills for received items,
      173–174
    date issues when converting
      item receipts to bills, 175
    income accounts for
      reimbursement, 159–160
    invoicing customers for
      reimbursable expenses,
      161–167
    managing item purchases,
      166–176
    mileage expense, 182–186
    purchase orders, 168–170
    receiving inventory items
      without a vendor bill,
      170–173
    receiving items/bills
      simultaneously, 174–176

recurring bills, 178–182
reimbursable expenses,
    157–167
Vendor Center, 150–154
vendor credits, 177–178
A/P (accounts payable), sales tax,
206–215
    adjusting, 214–215
    assigning codes/items to
      customers, 210
    Code List, 43
    codes for, 207–210
    creating tax groups, 210–212
    default codes for, 207–209
    enabling tracking for,
      206–207
    items, 209
    Liability report, 212, 213
    most common category, 209
    multiple sales tax authorities,
      206, 208, 210–212
    payment basis, 209
    payment dates, 209
    preferences for, 467
    for reimbursable
      expenses, 163
    remitting, 214
    reports for, 212–213
    Revenue Summary report,
      212, 213
    Sales Tax Group, 37
    sample codes for, 208
    setting up customer
      information, 21
A/P Account (option), 190
A/P Aging Summary
report, 188
A/R (accounts receivable):
    Aging Detail Report, 132–134
    Aging Summary, 132, 133
    filtering aging reports, 135
    and opening balance, 18
    tracking, 132–150
Access (Microsoft), 373

access permissions, 152, 477,
    482–483
Account By Class report, 325
Account by Customer: Job
    (report layout), 325
Account by Month (report
    layout), 325
Account By Month
    report, 325
Account Is Inactive option, 13
account number, 6–7, 10,
    22, 25
Accountant Information, 523
accountant's copy,
    358–364, 405
Accountant's Edition:
    accountant's copy, 358
    billing rate level, 25
    cash sales, 118, 123
    current availability of
      items, 103
    Fixed Asset Item List, 341
    Fixed Asset Manager, 41
    memorized report, 138
    tracking, 52
Accounting Preferences, 453–455
accounts:
    adding, 12–13
    alphabetizing, 7
    editing, 13
    inactive, 351
    naming, 7–10
    nonposting, 9, 168
    sorting, 9
    splitting expenses among
      multiple, 157
    standards for naming, 7–9
    using numbers for, 6–7, 10
    viewing, 13
    zero-balance, 351
Accounts Affected button, 252
accounts payable (see A/P
    (accounts payable))
accounts receivable (see A/R
    (accounts receivable))

Accounts Receivable Graph, 139
accrual basis, 348–349
Acrobat Reader, 94, 525
activity (Timer), 440–442
Add New Payroll Item wizard, 28, 29
Additional Info tab, 19–23, 25–26, 33
Address and Contact tab, 33
Address Info tab, 18–19
addresses:
    billing, 19
    customer, 19
    employee, 33
    vendor, 24
adjusting (adjustments):
    inventory, 277–280
    prices, 62
adjusting entry, 312, 338–341
Admin user, 475
administrator (Admin) password, 360, 365, 475, 483–484
Advanced Options window, 350–351
Advanced tab (find), 489
aging reports, 464
    A/R Aging Detail report, 132, 133
    A/R Aging Summary, 132, 133
    customizing, 133–137
    definition of, 132
    exporting/importing memorized, 137–139
    filtering, 135
    memorizing, 137–139
    preferences for, 464
    printing, 139
    types of, 132–133
aliases, 391–392
aligning (alignment):
    dot matrix printers, 86
    of forms, 85
    Inkjet printers, 86–87
    laser printers, 86–87
    setting up form, 85
All Open Transactions As Of Statement Date, 146

Allow Background Downloading of Service Messages, 468
Always Ask For A Password Before Connecting, 468
always-on connections, 380
Always Show Years As 4 Digits, 453
Amount (Type of Change), 307
Analyze Financial Strength tool, 328
As Of Invoice Date (sales tax payment basis), 209
assemblies:
    cost of, 272
    creating, 271–273
    disassembling, 275
    finished goods, 273, 274
    item type for, 37
    pending builds, 273–275
    printing components of, 275–276
Assess Finance Charges window, 141, 143
assessment date, 142–143
Asset tab, 514
assets, 513, 514
asterisk (*), 141, 142, 303
ATM withdrawals, 123, 290, 291, 390
attachments, PDF, 94
audit trail, 201, 299, 304, 307, 365–366
Autofill Payee Account Number In Check Memo, 457
automatic invoices, 102
automatic updates, 505–506
Automatically Apply Payments, 111, 466
Automatically Assign General Journal Entry Number, 455
Automatically Calculate Payments, 467
Automatically Connect Without Asking For A Password, 468
Automatically Recall Last Transaction For This Name (option), 452
Automatically Use Discounts And Credits option, 455

Available Financial Institutions, 381, 383, 385
average cost of inventory, 279
Average Costing inventory method, 269
Avg Cost, inventory costing method, 269

B

backdating bills, 175
backorders:
    customer, 62, 78–80
    vendor, 170
backups (backing up), 493–499
    automatic, 496–497
    on closing files, 497
    creating year-end, 409
    location for, 495–496
    online, 496
    reconciled data, 310
    restoring, 499–500
    setting options for, 494–495
    tape drive for, 495
    unattended, 497–499
bad checks (see NSF checks)
balance:
    applying credit, 114–115
    beginning, 306–309
    cleared, 305–306
    differences in beginning, 306–309
    ending, 305–306
    ending different than cleared, 305–306
    total, 139
    unpaid, 22
    zero-balance, 351
    See also opening balance; trial balance
balance sheet:
    Budget Overview report, 325
    budgets, 314, 316
    chart of accounts, 226
    Detail report, 355
    financial reports, 354–356
    Prev Year Comparison report, 356

reporting, 354–356
Standard report, 354, 355
Summary report, 355
year-end report, 399
bank accounts, 284–292
bounced checks, 286–289
default, 457
deposits to, 284–285
entering opening balances for, 335–336
multiple, 126
separate deposits by, 126
tracking cash, 290–292
transferring funds between, 285–286
voiding disbursements, 289
bank accounts, reconciling, 298–312
adding transactions, 301–302
adjusting entry, 312
clearing transactions, 301
correcting deleted/voided transactions, 308
deleting transactions, 302
differences in beginning balance, 306–309
Discrepancy Report, 307–308
ending balance different than cleared balance, 305–306
entering interest income, 299
entering service charges, 299
establishing opening balance, 298
finishing, 304
giving up the search for a reason, 311–312
missing check numbers, 303
pausing during, 304
printing reports, 304–305
reconciling transactions, 300–304
searching manually for discrepancies, 308–309
troubleshooting issues, 305–312
undoing last reconciliation, 310–311
using Begin Reconciliation window, 298–299
viewing last reconciliation report, 309, 310

bank charges, 305, 311, 389
banking services, online, 378–395
basics of, 378
bill-paying services, 383
connecting to your bank, 387
credit card deposits, 126
enabling Direct Connect, 384–385
enabling Web Connect, 385
finding your bank, 381–382
getting bank account data, 385–388
interest payments, 299
matching transactions, 389–392
online transaction reports, 394–395
paying bills, 393–394
QuickReport, 126
receiving customer payments, 395
recording bill payment information, 195
sending data to your bank, 387–388
sending messages to your bank, 387
service charges, 299
setting up, 380–385
transferring money between accounts, 392–393
viewing received data, 387
banks, purchasing checks from, 197
batch:
e-mailing, 92–93, 170
printing, 87, 205
beep, 451
Begin Reconciliation window, 298–299
beginning balance, 306–309
bill(s):
credit card, 295–296
entering, 455
memorized, 178–182
preferences for, 455
recurring, 178–182
bill(s), vendor, 296, 455
behind the scenes for, 176
and credit cards, 296

one-account posting of, 155–157
preferences for, 455
receiving inventory items without a, 170–173
receiving items/bills simultaneously, 174–176
recording, 153–157, 173–174
resolving date issues when converting item receipts to bills, 175
splitting expenses among multiple accounts, 157
warning message, 455
"bill as you go," 71
Bill Of Materials, 271, 272, 274–275
Bill Pay (QuickBooks), 380
bill-paying services, 380, 383, 391–392
bill payment:
backdating bills, 175
choosing what to pay, 188–191
credit card, 296
credits, 193–194
direct disbursements, 201–206
discounts, 191–193
manual checks, 196–201
oldest bill first, 292
online, 378, 393–394
options for, 190
partial payment, 191
payment amounts, 190–191
preferences for, 455
resolving date issues when converting item receipts to bills, 175
saving information for, 195–196
selecting bills to pay, 189–190
viewing unpaid bills, 188–189
Bill To address, 61
BILL transaction type, 176
billing address, 19
Billing Rate Level, 25, 52
Billing Solutions (QuickBooks), 395
birth date of employees, 33, 48
birthdays, 48

Blank Paper (option), 85
bounced checks, 286–289
breakage, 277, 278
budget(s), 314–327
    analysis tools for, 328–329
    automatically increase/
        decrease monthly figures,
        320–321
    basics of, 314–316
    Budget vs. Actual Graph
        report, 327
    Budget vs. Actual report, 326
    Budget window, 315–316
    class, 323
    and cleaning up files, 503
    compound changes, 321–322
    copy numbers across the
        months, 319
    creating, 316–323
    for customers and jobs,
        322–323
    definition of, 314
    deleting, 314–315
    enter budget amount,
        317–319
    exporting, 315, 327–328
    initial tasks to perform, 316
    making two of the same type
        for same time period, 315
    Overview report, 324–325
    Report wizard, 324, 325
    reports for, 323–327
    types of, 314
    using last year's data, 319, 320
    "what if" games, 325
business planning tools, 328–329

C

C corporations, 29, 229, 406
calendar year, 317
capital account, 284
cash:
    drawer, 123–124, 128
    petty, 290–292
    tracking, 290–292
cash basis, 348–349

cash flow:
    configuring report, 464
    financial reports for, 366–369
    Forecast report, 369
    Projector tool, 328
cash register transactions, 123–124
cash sale(s):
    batches of daily, 123
    cash drawer, 123–124
    definition of, 118
    entering information for,
        119, 120
    handling, 118–124
CC field (e-mail), 91
CCH Incorporated, 243
CD (Compact Disc), 496
Change Check Date When Check
    Is Printed, 456
Change New Employee Default
    Settings, 30–31
change orders, 74, 103
changed accounts, 338–339
chart of accounts:
    account numbers, 6–7
    adding, 6–15
    editing, 13
    merging, 15
    naming accounts, 7–9
    Sales Discounts income
        account, 115
    sorting, 9
    subaccounts, 10–11, 13–15
    supporting payroll, 226
    tracking discounts, 115
    window, 10, 11
check amounts, 389
check numbers, 195, 298, 303,
    389, 393
check style, 197, 200
Check 21 wallet checks, 200
checks:
    arranging in numerical
        order, 298
    bounced, 286–289
    depositing individually, 111
    fonts for, 198

locking up, 196
manual, 195–204
missing, 201, 303
NSF checks, 286–289
postdated, 300
printing, 83, 196–201,
    205, 303
purchasing computer,
    196–197
refund, 83
reprinting, 200, 201
standard, 197, 200
unmatched, 390
void/voiding, 201, 241, 242,
    289, 290
voucher, 197
wallet, 197, 200
writing, 195–205, 291, 336,
    456–457
(See also paychecks)
Choose Billable Time and Costs
    dialog box, 163, 165, 464
Choose Multiple Windows, 458
Choose Template For Invoice
    Packing Slip, 466
class(-es):
    all classes in report, 470, 471
    basics, 43–44, 469
    budgets, 323, 325–326
    creating, 469
    editing/deleting/merging, 470
    for payroll job costing, 430
    preferences for, 468–489
    reporting by, 470–472
    single class in report,
        470, 471
    subclasses, 470
    using, 468–489
Class Budget Overview report,
    325–326
Class By Month report, 326
Class List, 43–44, 470
cleaning up:
    data, 502–504
    files, 502–505
cleared balance, 305–306
client file, 511–512

Client Information, 523

Client Totals Summary, 515

Closing Date Exception report, 408–409, 455

closing the year, 407–409

COD delivery, 205

COGS (*see* cost of goods sold)

Collection History, 143, 144

collections, 140 (*See also* finance charges)

Collections report, 139

colon (:), 10

columns:
    changing template, 98–99
    customizing display of, 301
    Reconcile window, 301
    removing report, 134

Combine Activities With The Same Service Items, 426

Combine Reports feature, 372–373

comma separated value file format (*see* CSV file format)

Compact Disc (CD), 496

company, 491–493, 511

Company Preferences, 450, 451, 453–454, 458

Company Setup section, 227–228

Compare Debt and Ownership tool, 328

compounding (in budgets), 321–322

computer checks, 196–197

connecting to your bank, 387

contact information, 139

Contractor (QuickBooks), 25, 52

contractors, 413

corporate officers, 29, 229

corporations, 401, 491

cost, assembly, 272

Cost field (inventory), 269

cost of goods sold (COGS), 39, 193, 273, 356

Create New Budget wizard, 315

credit card(s), 292–296
    billing customer for reimbursement, 294
    charges for, 293–295

creating account for, 293

customer number, 23

deposits, 126

entering charges for, 293–295

entering opening balances for, 335–336

handling merchant card fees, 127–128

as liability accounts, 293–296

opening balances for, 335–336

paying bill for, 296

QuickBooks, 380, 383

reconciling bill for, 295

three-digit security code, 23

as vendors, 292–293

credit limit, 22, 25

credit memos:
    batch printing of, 87
    creating, 81–83
    invoice, applying the credit to an, 83
    issuing a refund for the credit, 82–83
    retaining the credit, 82
    sending, 83–94
    and unreturned merchandise, 81
    using to cancel invoices, 68

credits:
    applying, during bill payment, 193–194
    applying, to different job, 115
    applying, to invoices, 113–115
    and credit memos, 81
    issuing, 79, 81
    and merchandise that is not returned, 81
    payroll, 342
    recording vendor, 177–178
    retaining, 82

Crystal Reports, 373

CSV (comma separated value) file format, 512–513, 518, 524

CTRL-A key combination, 102

CTRL-E key combination, 13

CTRL-I key combination, 58

CTRL-J key combination, 56

CTRL-M key combination, 74, 178

CTRL-N key combination, 102, 210, 268

CTRL-Q key combination, 470

CTRL-R key combination, 195, 284

CTRL-T key combination, 74, 181

CTRL-W key combination, 203, 287

current availability, 103–104

current date, 60, 61, 452

Current Date and Time, 523

current window, 474

custom fields, 21, 48–50, 371

custom item information, 453

customer(s):
    addresses, 19
    assign sales tax codes/items to, 210
    Balance Detail Report, 139
    Balance Summary Report, 139
    billing for credit card reimbursement, 294
    contact information, 139
    Contact List report, 139
    custom fields for, 48
    and e-mailing invoices, 94
    grouping cash, 119
    messages for, 46
    Name field, 18
    notes on, 23–24
    opening balance, 337
    payments, 395
    Phone List report, 139
    records, 23–24
    selecting for statements, 146–148
    tips for entering information on, 16, 18

Customer: Job By Month (report layout), 325

Customer: Job column, 161

Customer & Vendor Profile Lists, 44–47

Customer Center, 10, 16–18, 23–24, 56–58

Customer Type list, 45

Customer:Job budgets, 323

customers and jobs, 15–24
    Additional Info tab, 19–23
    Address Info tab, 18–19
    Budget Overview report
       for, 325
    budgets for, 322–323, 325
    editing customer records,
       23–24
    entering jobs, 39–40
    lists of, 16
    new customers, 16–23
    Payment Info tab, 22
    printing reports for, 139
    reimbursable expenses, 169
    setting up a new customer,
       16–23
    tab for, 56, 57
customizing aging reports, 133–137
    changing header/footer
       information, 136
    changing the cosmetic
       appearance, 136, 137
    and controlling the
       columns, 134
    filtering information, 135
    Fonts & Numbers tab,
       136, 137
customizing columns display
    (Reconcile window), 301
customizing customer statements,
    149–150
customizing forms, 123
customizing QuickBooks
    (see preferences)
customizing templates, 94–101
    additional features for, 103
    changing the columns for,
       98–99
    changing the data in the
       Footer tab, 99
    changing the data in the Print
       tab, 99
    changing the data in the Prog
       Cols tab, 99
    changing the header for,
       96, 98
    columns for, 98–99
    designing a new, 96, 97

    designing the layout for,
       100–101
    editing a predefined, 94–96
    Footer tab, 99
    header, 96, 98
    layout for, 100–101
    Print tab, 99
    Prog Cols tab, 99
    for sales receipts, 120–122
customizing the Icon Bar, 472–474
customizing the Vendor Center, 152
customizing trial balance report,
    348–354
cutoff date, 503, 504

D

daily cash sales, 123
data:
    cleaning up, 502–505
    entering for items, 36, 38
    lists, 437–438
    and memorized reports, 138
date(s):
    and accuracy of reconciliation
       reports, 308
    assessment, 142–143
    birth, 33, 48
    current, 60, 61, 452
    cutoff, 503, 504
    default, 452
    discount, 193
    "dividing date" feature, 3
    entering original, 18
    formats for, 136
    hire, 35
    invoices, 60–61
    issues in converting item
       receipts to bills, 175
    of last transaction, 61, 452
    payment, 209
    release, 35
    sales tax payment, 209
    Warnings, 455
date-driven terms, 46
date range (customer
    statements), 146
days overdue, 140, 143, 146

debits, 342
debts, 288, 289
decimal point, automatic placement
    of, 451
deductions:
    Add New Payroll Item
       wizard, 29
    mileage, 47
    pension, 29
    SUI, 34
    vendor, 29
default:
    bank accounts, 457
    e-mail message, 93–94
    employee information, 30–31
    packing slip, 89–90
    payment terms, 455
    report formatting, 464
Default Name (Timer option), 442
Deleted (Type of Change), 307
deleted transactions, 308, 364–366
deleting:
    a budget, 314–315
    classes, 470
    standard invoices, 67–68
    voiding vs., 67, 68
deposit slip(s), 125–127, 129
depositing income, 124–129
    adding items to the deposit,
       126–127
    cash back from, 128
    choosing which to payments
       to deposit, 124–125
    credit card deposits, 126
    deposit slips, 126, 127, 129
    deposits on bank statements
       but not in QuickBooks, 302
    filling out the deposit slip,
       126, 127
    handling overages/shortages
       for a cash drawer, 128
    merchant card fees, 127–128
    "negative" deposits, 126
    printing deposit slips, 129
    selecting account for, 284
    separate deposits by bank
       account, 126

separating deposit items by payment method, 125

separating items by payment method, 125

unmatched deposits, 390

Depreciate Your Assets tool, 328

depreciation:

    calculating, 515

    exporting data for, 517–518

    Fixed Asset Items List, 41–42

    Fixed Asset Manager, 41, 341, 510, 515

    journal entries for, 339–341

description for inventory items, 268, 269

descriptive name (for backup), 498

Design Grid, 523

Desktop View preferences, 457–458

Details section, 154

dial-up connections, 379, 380

dictionary, 64, 270

Direct Connection, 384–385

    data exchange with, 387

    and online banking, 378

    sending messages with, 387

    two-way messaging, 387

direct deposit, 35, 236, 240

direct disbursements, 201–206

disability withholdings, 27, 28, 34

disassembling assemblies, 275

disbursements:

    direct, 201–206

    recording petty cash, 291, 292

    voiding, 289

Discount (item type), 37

discounts:

    applying, for timely payments, 115–117

    applying, for untimely payments, 117

    applying, to bills, 191–193

    to bills, 191–193

    for early payment, 45, 46

    earned, 193

    invoices, 64, 65

    and partial payments, 117

    as reverse expense, 193

    taking after discount date, 193

    timely payments, 115–117

    untimely payments, 117

    vendor, 115, 193

discrepancies, 308–309

Disposal tab, 514

"dividing date" feature, 3

dollar amounts, 88, 90

Don't Print Items With Zero Amounts, 466

Don't Save The Desktop, 458

Don't Show This Message Again option, 452

dot matrix printers, 84, 86, 196, 198

double-entry accounting, 13

downloaded transactions, 389–392

downloading:

    banking transactions, 385–388

    ODBC driver, 374

    templates, 60

drop-down lists, 451

DSL/cable modem, 380

Due Date column, 248

Due On Or Before (option), 190

DVD-R, 496

E

E-file & Pay, 246

e-mailing (e-mail):

    batch, 92–93, 170

    changing default message for, 93–94

    credit memos, 90–94

    financial statements/ documents, 525

    immediate, 92

    invoices, 66, 90–94

    preferred send method, 21

    purchase orders, 170

    security, 358, 501

    sending customer statements by, 147

    Timer software, 437

    year-end reports, 405

earned discounts, 193

Earnings Item (option), 430

EasyStep Interview, 491

Edit Customer dialog box, 23–24

editing:

    accounts, 13

    classes, 470

    customer records, 23–24

    paychecks, 240–241

    predefined templates, 94–96

    previously entered invoices, 66–67

    time entries, 422

    Timer activity, 441–442

    transactions, 302

EIN (vendor), 25

electronic filing of payroll, 220

employee(s):

    birth date of, 33, 48

    custom fields for, 48

    default information for, 30–31

    Employment Info tab, 32, 35

    entering, 31–32

    gender of, 33

    information on, 225

    modifying record for, 428–429

    pay schedules for, 27

    Payroll and Compensation Info tab, 32–35

    Payroll Setup wizard, 230–231

    personal information, 32–33

    reporting compensation of, 229

    setting up, 230–231, 413

    tax information for, 34

    theft, 277, 278

    tracking time of, 413, 414

    types of, 35

    Workers Compensation tab, 32, 36

Employee, Contractor, or Temp? tool, 329

Employee Center, 16, 30–31, 220–222

Employee Organizer, 31, 33, 241–242

Employment Info tab, 32, 35
Employment Regulations Update
    Service, 241
Enable Compounding option, 321
Enable Sales Orders, 466
encryption of accountant's copy, 360
ending balance, 305–306
Enhanced Payroll Service
    (QuickBooks), 252
Enter Bills command, 176
ENTER key, 451
Enter Sales Receipts window, 120
Enterprise Edition (QuickBooks):
    additional features for, 52
    billing rate level, 25
    cash register transactions, 123
    cash sales, 118
    change order tracking, 74
    change orders saved as
        estimates, 103
    consolidating reports, 372
    customizing templates, 103
    Employee Organizer, 31,
        241–242
    exporting/importing
        reports, 370
    features of, 2
    Fixed Asset Item List, 341
    industry-specific editions of, 2
    managing multiple users in,
        479–486
    memorized report, 138
    multiple reconciliation
        reports, 309
    number of items in lists, 52
    ODBC reporting, 373–376
    Sales Order Fulfillment
        Worksheet, 79
    search fields in Item List
        window, 38
    Timer, 436
    Workers Comp field, 418, 420
Entire Paycheck option, 430
envelopes, 100, 197
equity account, 334
error message, amount of
    payment, 109

estimates, 69–74
    change order tracking, 74
    creating, 70–71
    creating invoices from, 71–73
    duplicate, 70
    by Job report, 72
    marking up, 70
    memorized, 74
    multiple, 70
    preferences for, 69–70,
        460, 461
    and reporting, 72–74
Excel (see Microsoft Excel)
expense account, 191
expenses:
    accounting for, 349
    job, 139
    reverse, 193
    shipping, 69
    splitting, among multiple
        accounts, 157
    (See also reimbursable
        expenses)
Expenses tab, 155
exporting:
    budgets, 325, 327–328
    data lists to users of Timer,
        437–438
    depreciation data, 517–518
    documents, 524
    Financial Statement
        Designer, 524
    Financial Statement
        Editor, 524
    memorized reports, 137–139,
        370–371
    Timer files, 443–445

F

federal forms:
    Employee Organizer, 241–242
    W-2 forms, 35, 220, 258–259
    W-4 forms, 35, 36
    (See also Form...)
FICA, 27, 28

fields:
    displaying template, 98
    using ENTER key to move
        between, 451
files:
    automatic backup on
        closing, 497
    backing up/restoring,
        493–500
    cleaning up, 502–505
    exporting/importing Timer,
        443–447
    finding transactions in,
        488–491
    multiple company, 491–493
    PDF, 94, 309, 310, 405, 525
    searching, 488–491
    unlocking, 364
filtering (filters):
    aging reports, 135
    transactions, 66
    trial balance report data,
        351–352
    unpaid bills, 189
finance charges, 140–144
    assessing, 141–143, 148
    assessment date for, 142–143
    checking collection history,
        143, 144
    customer statements, 148
    overdue finance charges, 141
    preferences for, 140, 141, 459
    printing options, 143, 144
    saving invoices for, 144
    selecting customers with, 143
financial reports:
    audit trail, 365–366
    balance sheet, 354–356
    cash flow, 366–369
    connecting with other
        programs, 373–376
    consolidating for multiple
        companies, 372–373
    exporting/importing
        memorized, 370–371
    ODBC driver, 373–376

process multiple reports feature, 371–372

Profit & Loss, 356–358

sensitive, 478

voided/deleted transactions, 364–366

year-end, 399, 405–407

(*See also specific reports*)

Financial Statement Designer (FSD), 520–525

  basics, 520

  components of, 521–524

  e-mailing financial statements/documents, 525

  exporting documents, 524

  previewing documents, 524

  printing documents, 524

  and QuickBooks data files, 520

  saving as PDF files, 525

  templates, 521–522

Financial Statement Editor, 522–524

Financial Statement Organizer, 521

Financing Activities (cash flows report), 367

finding transactions, 66–67, 488–491

Finish Later button, 227

finished goods, 273, 274

fiscal year, 317

Fix This Error Now option, 230–231

Fixed Asset Item List, 41–42

Fixed Asset Manager, 510–518

  Accountant's Edition, 41

  basics, 510

  client file setup for, 511–512

  Client Totals Summary, 515

  company information and, 511

  depreciation, 41, 341, 510, 515

  exporting depreciation data, 517–518

  files and, 510–511

  importing data from other software, 512–513

  journal entries, 515

New Client wizard, 512

notes, 514

reporting, 515–517

Section 179/40% test, 514–515

tax worksheets, 518

working in, 513–514

flat view (Chart of Accounts), 10, 11

FOB (Free on Board), 47, 62, 465

fonts:

  changing check, 198

  changing trial balance report, 353

  for checks, 198

  customizing aging reports, 136, 137

  editing template, 95

  Fonts & Numbers tab, 136, 137

Footer tab, 99 (*See also* header/footer information)

Forecasts tool, 328

Form 940 (Federal Unemployment, FUTA), 232, 247–248, 258

Form 941 (Employer's Quarterly Federal Tax Return), 227, 257–258

Form 1096 Wizard, 401–403

Form 1099, 25, 400–404, 414, 468

  checking setup for, 401–402

  issuing, 400–404

  preferences, 468

  printing, 403–404

  reports, 403

  troubleshooting with 1099 Options, 403

  vendor, 25

  verifying vendor balances, 402, 403

  Wizard, 401–403

Form 1120/1120S, 406

Form 4797 (Sales of Business Property), 514

forms:

  alignment of, 85

  assigning different printers to, 84

  Inuit Preprinted, 85

invoice, 94

multipart, 84

printer, 84–85

state, 242

tax, 514

(*See also* federal forms)

FoxFire Report Writer, 373

Free on Board (*see* FOB (Free on Board))

FSD (*see* Financial Statement Designer)

.fst file format, 524, 525

Full Access (option), 477, 482

FUTA (*see* Form 940)

future transactions (bank account), 300, 301

G

GAAP (Generally Accepted Accounting Principles), 520

gender of employee, 33

general ledger:

  direct disbursements, 206

  discounts, 193

  entries for invoices, 68

  partial payments, 191

  reimbursable expenses, 166

  vendor credit, 178

Generally Accepted Accounting Principles (GAAP), 520

GENJRNL transaction type, 503

Give Me The Option Of Saving A File Whenever I Download Web Connect, 467

Google Desktop™, 3, 489–491

government reporting, payroll (*see* payroll, government reporting)

grace period, 141, 143

grouping (groups):

  cash customers, 119

  employees by pay frequency, 27

  item type, 37

  memorized bill, 181–182

  reimbursable expenses, 164, 425

  tax, 37, 210–212

guidelines:
    for account names, 9
    for merging list entries, 51–52
    for payroll items, 29

H

header/footer information:
    changing in aging
      reports, 136
    changing template, 96, 98
    default options for, 464
    Footer tab, 99
    trial balance report, 352–354
Heading section, 154
help and advice, 242
hierarchical view (Chart of
    Accounts), 10, 11
hire date, 35
historical data:
    entering, 226–227, 233–236
    payroll, 226–227
    Payroll Setup wizard,
      233–236
history, payroll, 227, 233–236
Home page, 458
hourly workers, 428

I

Icon Bar, 472–474
icons:
    adding, 474
    change graphic/text/
      description, 473
    changing order of, 472–473
    display without text title, 473
    removing, 473–474
If QuickBooks Is Run By My
    Browser, Don't Close It After Web
    Connect Is Done, 467
.iif file extension, 438
importing:
    data from other software to
      Fixed Asset Manager,
      512–513
    downloaded banking data,
      386–387
    Fixed Asset Items list, 511

information to Timer, 440
memorized reports, 138–139,
    370–371
Timer files, 445–447
Improve Your Cash Flow tool, 329
inactive accounts, 351
inactive inventory items,
    270–271, 278
Include Only Transactions Over
    X Days Past Due Date, 146
income:
    accounts, 159–160, 323,
      338–339
    interest, 299
    tracking, 14
    (*See also* depositing income)
Income Account field, 39
income statement, 399 (*See also*
    Year-end Profit & Loss report)
Income Tax Form Used field, 406
Inkjet printers, 86–87, 196,
    199, 200
installing:
    ODBC driver, 374
    Timer software, 436–437
insurance, 33, 338
integrated applications, 459
interest income, 299
interest payments, 299, 305, 311
interest rate, 140
Internet connection:
    dial-up, 379, 380
    network/always-on, 380
    no Internet connection, 380
    online banking, 378–380
    setting up, 379–380
    (*See also* Direct Connection;
      Web Connect)
Internet Service Provider (ISP), 380
Intuit, 2, 197
Intuit Product Invoice template,
    59, 60
Inuit Preprinted Forms, 85
inventory, 262–281
    assemblies, 271–273
    asset account, 273
    creating inventory items,
      262–271

current availability of,
    103–104
inactive, 270–271, 278
items, 337
negative, 175, 281
new items for, 267–270
preferences for, 262–263,
    459–460
receiving, items without a
    vendor bill, 170–173
reporting on, 280–281
Stock Status report, 280
subitems, 270
Units of Measure, 263–267
Valuation Detail Report, 280
Value Summary Report,
    280, 281
warning on unavailable/on
    hand inventory, 77
inventory, counting, 276–280
    adjusting the count, 277–280
    adjusting the value, 279–280
    making adjustments, 277–280
    printing physical inventory
      worksheet, 276–277
Inventory And Purchase Orders Are
    Active, 459
Inventory assembly item, 37,
    271, 273
Inventory Part (item type), 37
Investing Activities (cash flows
    report), 367
invoices:
    adding message to, 65
    additional features for
      forms, 94
    applying a credit to, 83,
      113–115
    applying payments to,
      110–111
    automatic, 102
    batch, 87, 92–93
    behind the scenes of
      customer, 68
    billing rate levels, 52
    calculating total amount
      of, 109
    creating, with timesheets data,
      424–426

creating from estimates,
    71–73
credits to, 83, 113–115
dates on, 60, 61
e-mailing, 66, 92–94
from estimates, 71–73
fee-based sending of, 94
heading for, 60
items on, 36, 37
memorized, 101–102
memorizing, 101–102
older, 110, 111
"pay online" feature for, 94
payments to, 110–111
printing, 84–85, 87, 99
progress, 71, 72, 99
receiving payments for,
    108–115
recurring, 101–102
reimbursable expenses,
    161–167
from sales orders, 77–79
saving finance charge, 144
sending, 83–94
unpaid, 139
invoices, standard:
    adding memo to, 66
    adding messages to, 65
    applying price levels, 63
    creating, 58–67
    editing previously entered,
        66–67
    entering discounts, 64, 65
    entering heading information,
        60–62
    entering line items, 62
    finding missing numbers
        for, 61
    methods for sending, 66
    saving, 66
    shipping costs, 69
    spell checking, 64–65
    voiding/deleting, 67–68
IOU, 291
ISP (Internet Service Provider), 380
Item Estimates vs. Actuals
    report, 74
Item List, 50–51, 267–270

Item Price List report, 139
item purchases, managing, 166–176
    purchase orders, 168–170
    receiving inventory items
        without a vendor bill,
        170–173
    receiving items/bills
        simultaneously, 174–176
    recording bills for received
        items, 173–174
    resolving date issues when
        converting item receipts to
        bills, 175
ITEM RCPT transaction type, 176
item receipts, 175, 176
item types, 36, 37
items:
    adding to the deposit,
        126–127
    current availability of,
        103–104
    custom fields for, 48, 49–50
    definition of, 36
    entering, 36–39, 62
    invoice, 62
    mileage, 183
    sales tax, 209, 210
Items tab, 155

J

job costing:
    and estimates, 69
    payroll preferences for, 429
    payroll reports for, 432–434
    using timesheet data for,
        428–430
Job Estimates vs. Actuals Detail
    report, 74
Job Estimates vs. Actuals Summary
    report, 74
Job Info tab, 39–40
Job Progress Invoices vs. Estimates
    report, 74
job type list, 45
jobs:
    applying credits to
        different, 115
    multiple per customer, 18

preferences for, 460, 461
tracking, 15
(See also customers and jobs)
Jobs & Estimates, 69
journal entries, 332–345
    adjusting entries, 338–341
    boilerplate for, 344–345
    for changed accounts,
        338–339
    creating, 332
    depreciation entries, 339–341
    employer payments, 343–344
    entering opening balance,
        334–338
    Fixed Asset Manager, 515
    for outside payroll services,
        342–345
    payroll liabilites/expenses,
        343–344
    posting withholdings, 343
    previous equity, 334
    reporting on, 345
    reversing entries, 341
    templates for, 344–345
    window for, 332–333,
        344, 345
    year-end, 404–405

K

Keep Previously Saved Desktop, 458

L

labels, printing mailing, 87, 89
laser printers, 86–87, 196, 199, 200
Last FC column, 143
Last Year-to-Date, 354
last year's data, 319, 320
layout, 100–101
Letterhead (option), 85
liabilities:
    paying unscheduled, 251–252
    payment schedules for tax,
        246–248
    payroll, 252, 338, 343–344
    Sales Tax Liability report,
        212, 213
    tax, 212, 213, 246–252

liability accounts, 284,
   293–296, 343
Limited liability companies
   (LLCs), 401
line items (invoice), 60, 62
lists:
      chart of accounts (*see* chart
         of accounts)
      class, 43–44, 470
      customer message, 46
      customer type, 45
      customers and jobs, 16
      drop-down, 451
      employee, 30–36
      Employee Center, 16
      entering items for, 36–39
      fixed asset item, 41–42
      job type, 45
      memorized transaction, 44
      merging entries in, 50–52
      other names, 44
      payment method, 46
      payroll, 26–33
      pick, 105
      price level, 42–43
      sales rep, 44–45
      sales tax code, 43
      setting up other, 40–48
      ship via, 46–47
      Templates, 41
      terms, 20, 45–46
      vehicle, 47–48
      vendor, 24–26, 45
      Vendor Center, 16
      viewing, 10, 11
      workers comp, 44
LLCs (limited liability
   companies), 401
loans, 178, 284
location:
      backup, 495–496, 498
      company files, 493
Lock Net Pay option, 240
locking the books, 407–408
logo, 95, 96, 198

M

mail, 21, 147
Mail Invoice feature, 94
mailing labels, 87, 89
Make Deposits window, 284, 285
Make General Journal Entries
   window, 332–333, 344, 345
Manage Your Receivables tool, 329
manual updates, 506
Manufacturer's Part Number
   field, 268
Manufacturing and Wholesale
   Edition (QuickBooks), 79,
   103, 271
margins, changing, 100, 101
Mark All button, 237
marking up:
      estimates, 70
      reimbursable expenses,
         165–166
Maximum Number You Can Build
   From Quantity On Hand, 273
Measure Profitability tool, 328
Medicare, 27, 28, 241
memo(s):
      adding to invoices, 66
      automatically fill, 453
      and bank charges, 299
      Memo column, 161, 165
      and online bill payment, 394
memorized bills, 178–182
memorized estimates, 74
memorized invoices, 101–102
memorized reports:
      aging reports, 137–139
      customized report, 354
      data and, 138
      exporting/importing,
         137–138, 370–371
      printing several at once,
         371–372
      process multiple reports
         feature, 371–372
      report settings, 326
      user permissions, 483
memorized transaction list, 44

merchant account, 390
merchant card, 127–128, 391
merging:
      accountant's changes, 360,
         363–364
      chart of accounts, 15
      classes, 470
      entries in lists, 50–52
messages:
      adding to invoices, 65
      adding to standard invoices, 65
      changing e-mail default,
         93–94
      for customers, 46
      onetime, 452
      pop-up, 452
      sending two-way with Direct
         Connection, 387
Microsoft Access, 373
Microsoft Excel, 48, 138, 370, 372,
   373, 524
mid-quarter 40% test, 515
mileage, 184
      entering, 184
      by Job Detail report, 185
      By Job Summary report, 185
      By Vehicle Detail report, 186
      by Vehicle Detail report, 185
      By Vehicle Summary
         report, 185
mileage expense:
      for employees, 186
      entering mileage, 184
      mileage rates, 182–183
      reimbursing employees/
         subcontractors for, 186
      reports for, 184–186
      for subcontractors, 186
      tracking, 47–48, 182–186
mileage rates, 182–183
missing transactions, 61, 303, 336
mode restrictions (multi-user),
   478–479, 485, 486
money market account, 285
money orders, 125
monthly figures (budgets), 320–321

most common category
(sales tax), 209
multiple accounts, 157
multiple sales tax authorities, 206
Multiple U/M Per Item,
263–266, 268
multiple users, managing:
administrator password,
483–484
creating new user, 483–484
creating/removing/changing
user information, 475
mode restrictions, 478–479,
485, 486
one person at a time actions
in multi-user mode,
479, 486
in QuickBooks Enterprise,
479–486
in QuickBooks Premier,
475–479
removing user
information, 475
reporting on permissions, 485
setting user permissions,
476–478
transaction rights, 478
unpermitted activities in
multi-user mode, 479, 486
users/roles, 480–483
My Preferences, 156, 450, 451–453

N

names (naming):
accounts, 7–10
custom field for, 48–49
vendor, 24
.nd files, 499
NEBS, 197
"negative" deposits, 126
negative inventory, 175, 281
Net Due In, 45
Net Worth Graph report, 369–370
network, sharing updates on, 507
network connection, 380
Never Update Name Information
When Saving Transactions, 453

New Account dialog box, 14
New Employee dialog box, 31–33
New Item window, 38–39
New Price Level dialog box, 42
No Access (option), 477
nonbillable time, 430, 432
Noninventory Part (item type), 37
nonposting accounts, 9, 168
nonprofit organization, 333
notes:
caution about, 417, 420, 425
customer, 23–24
Fixed Asset Manager, 514
NSF checks, 286–289
Number of Backups to Keep, 499
Number of Days to Remember
Activities (Timer option), 442
numbers:
account, 6–7, 10, 22, 25
check, 195, 298, 303,
389, 393
display of, trial balance
report, 353
finance charges, 143, 144
finding missing invoice, 61
missing check, 201
page, 136, 523
using for accounts, 6–7, 10

O

ODBC (Open Data Base
Connectivity) reporting, 373–376
off-site storage for backup, 495
Office Depot, 197
Officer (employee type), 35
officer compensation, 29, 229,
406–407
one-account posting, 155–157
One Window (option), 457
onetime messages, 452
Online Banking Setup Interview
wizard, 383, 384
Online Funds Transfer box, 392
Online Received Payments
report, 139
Open Invoices report, 139

Open Sales Orders by Customer
report, 79, 80
Open Sales Orders by Item report,
79, 80
Opening Bal Equity account:
deleting adjusting entry, 311
and entering opening
balances, 13, 18–19,
334–337
OBE item for, 337
zero value of, 334
opening balance:
for bank accounts/credit
cards, 335–336
customer, 337
entering, 12, 13, 334–338
establishing bank
account, 298
field for, 18–19
inventory items, 337
and missing transactions, 336
for payroll liabilities, 338
setting, 335–336
skipping when creating
accounts, 12, 13, 18–19, 24
vendor, 337
Operating Activities (cash flows
report), 367
optimization, ODBC driver,
375–376
Other Charge (item type), 37
Other Names List, 44
out-of-stock items, 74 (See also
backorders; sales order(s))
overdue finance charges, 141
overtime, 253
Owner (employee type), 35

P

packing slips, 66, 88–90
Page Break, 523
page numbers, 136, 523
parent account, 7, 10, 13, 454
Partial Access (option), 483
Partial Page tab, 199
partial payment, 117, 191
partnership, 44, 401

passwords:
  accountant's copy, 360
  administrator password, 360, 365, 475, 483–484
  assigning, 483–484
  audit trail, 365
  backups, 499
  blank, 499
  online banking, 388
  preferences for, 468
  resetting, 476, 484
  security, 475, 483, 484
  timesheets, 415
pausing, during reconciliation process, 304
"pay online" feature (invoices), 94
pay schedules, 27, 224–225, 232–232
paychecks:
  direct deposit information, 240
  editing, 240–241
  elements of, 27–28
  printing, 239–240
  reviewing information for, 238–239
  Social Security/Medicare on, 241
  user permissions, 483
  voiding, 241, 242
payment(s):
  choosing which to deposit, 124–125
  partial, 117
  schedules, 246–248
  terms for, 20, 45–46, 455
  (See also bill payment)
Payment (item type), 37
Payment Account (option), 190
payment amounts, selecting, 190–191
payment basis (sales tax), 209
Payment Date (option), 190
Payment Info tab, 22
payment method, 23, 46, 125, 190
payments, receiving:
  applying credits to different job, 115

applying credits to invoices, 113–115
applying discounts for timely, 115–117
applying discounts for untimely payments, 117
applying to invoices, 110–111
behind the scenes of, 117–118
customizing template for sales receipts, 120–122
depositing income, 124–129
handling cash sales, 118–124
handling underpayments, 112–113
for invoices, 108–113
online customer, 395
recording, 108–110
Undeposited Funds account, 111–112
payroll:
  configuring from timesheets, 428–432
  lists, 26–33
  reconciling, 345
  Setup wizard, 28, 227–236
  tax deposits, 246–252
  Transaction Detail report, 432–434
  transferring money to, 342
payroll, government reporting, 246–259
  940 report, 258
  adjusting payroll liabilities, 252
  making payroll tax deposits, 246–252
  paying tax liabilities, 248–250
  paying unscheduled liabilities, 251–252
  preparing annual documents, 258–259
  Quarterly 941 form, 257–258
  state/local annual returns, 258
  W-2 forms, 258–259
  workers compensation, 252–257
payroll, outside services for, 342–345
payroll, running, 218–243
  changing Social Security/ Medicare, 241

chart of accounts, 226
choosing payroll services, 218–220
configuring elements of, 222–223
creating pay schedules, 224–225
electronic filing of, 220
Employee Center, 220–222
employee information, 225
employees, 230–231
historical data, 226–227
payroll items, 224, 228–229
Payroll Setup wizard, 227–236
printing paychecks, 239–240
reviewing employees to pay, 236–238
reviewing paycheck information, 238–239
scheduling tax payments, 232–232
sending direct deposit information, 240
setting up employees, 230–231
taxes, 231–232
vendors, 223
Payroll and Compensation Info tab, 32–35
Payroll Center, 221, 224
payroll items:
  C corporation, 229
  definition of, 224
  entering, 27–29
  Payroll Setup wizard, 228–229
  setting up, 224, 228–229
  Subchapter S corporation, 229
payroll job costing, 428–430
payroll liabilities, 338, 343–344
PDF (Portable Document Format) files, 94, 309, 310, 405, 525
penalty (sales tax), 214
pending builds, 273–275
Pending Builds report, 280
pension, 27–29
Per Item price level, 42, 43
performance (online banking), 499

Periodic Tasks tool, 329

personal identification number (PIN), 380, 382, 383, 388

Personal Information, 32–33

petty cash account, 290–292

physical inventory worksheet, 276–277, 280

pick lists, 105

PIN (see personal identification number)

planning tools, 328–329

pop-up messages, 452

portable computer file, 500–502

postdated checks, 300

posting transactions, 10

Pre-Fill Accounts For Vendor Based On Past Entries, 452

predefined roles, 481

predefined templates, 94–96

preferences, 450–468
    account number format, 6–7
    accounting, 453–455
    Additional Info tab, 19
    aging reports, 464
    bills, 455
    checking, 456–457
    classes, 468–489
    Company, 450, 451, 453–454, 458
    Desktop view, 457–458
    employees, 460
    estimates, 69–70, 460, 461
    finance charges, 140, 141, 459
    general, 451–453
    integrated applications, 459
    inventory, 262–263, 459–460
    Jobs & Estimates, 460, 461
    miscellaneous, 466
    My, 156, 450–453
    passwords, 468
    payments, 109–111
    payroll, 429, 460
    purchase orders, 459–460
    receive payments, 466–467
    reimbursable expenses, 159, 162
    reminders, 460–462
    Reports & Graphs, 462–464

Sales & Customers, 464–467
sales orders, 75–76, 466
sales tax, 467
send forms, 467
service connections, 467–468
spelling, 65, 468
1099 form, 468
time, 417, 468
Timer, 442, 443

preferred payment method, 23

preferred send method, 21

Premier Edition (QuickBooks):
    accountant's copy, 358
    change order tracking, 74
    change orders saved as estimates, 103
    customizing templates, 103
    Employee Organizer, 31, 33
    exporting/importing reports, 370
    features of, 2
    Fixed Asset Item List, 41, 341
    industry-specific editions of, 2
    managing multiple users in, 475–479
    multiple reconciliation reports, 309
    search fields, 38, 267
    Timer, 436
    Workers Comp field, 418, 420

previewing, customer statements, 148–149

previous equity, 334

price levels, 21, 42–43, 63

prices, 139

Print Account Names On Voucher, 456

Print Pay Stubs button, 240

Print Paychecks button, 239–240

Print tab, 99

printer(s):
    assigning different, to different forms, 84
    configuring for check writing, 197–199
    dot matrix, 84, 86, 196, 198
    Inkjet, 86–87, 196, 199, 200
    laser, 86–87, 196, 199, 200
    setting up forms, 84–85

printing:
    aging reports, 139
    aligning, 86–87
    assemblies, 275–276
    batch, 87, 205
    checks, 83, 196–201, 205, 303
    components of assemblies, 275–276
    credit memos, 83–87
    customer statements, 149
    customers and jobs reports, 139
    deposit slips, 125, 129
    direct disbursement checks, 205
    finance charges, 143, 144
    from Financial Statement Designer, 524
    invoices, 66, 83–87, 99
    mailing labels, 87, 89
    memorized reports, 371–372
    packing slips, 88–90
    paychecks, 239–240
    physical inventory worksheet, 276–277
    pick lists, 105
    reconciliation report, 304–305
    the register, 196, 205
    reports, 139, 304–305
    setting up printer forms, 84–85
    single checks, 205
    statements, 149
    1099 Form, 403–404
    weekly timesheets, 422–423

Process Multiple Reports feature, 371–372

Professional (QuickBooks), 25, 52, 103

Profit & Loss budgets:
    Budget vs. Actual report, 326
    creating, 314, 316–317
    for customers and jobs, 322–323
    Overview report, 324–325
    Performance report, 326
    reports, 326

Profit & Loss reports, 226
  By Account And Customer
    Job, 325
  Budget Overview, 324–325
  Budget Performance, 326
  Budget vs. Actual, 326
  By Class, 357, 471
  Detail report, 357
  By Job, 357
  Prev Year Comparison, 357
  Standard report, 356, 399
  Unclassified report,
    357–358, 471
  YTD Comparison, 357
Prog Cols tab, 99
progress invoices, 71, 99, 460
Projection Tab, 514
Prompt Me To Modify Report
  Options Before Opening A
  Report, 462
Properties panel, 522–523
proprietorship, 44, 401, 491
purchase orders, 167–170
  from estimates, 71, 168
  preferences for, 459–460
  receiving inventory items
    without a vendor bill,
    170–173
  receiving items/bills
    simultaneously, 174–176
  recording bills for received
    items, 173–174
  resolving date issues when
    converting item receipts to
    bills, 175
  from sales orders, 77, 168
  using, 168–170
  warning message, 460
purchase receipt, 291
purchasing an ODBC driver,
  374, 376

Q

.qbb file extension, 493
.qbm files, 500
.qbw files, 374, 499
.qby file extension, 360, 363
Quantity Available, 460

Quarterly 941 form (*see* Form 941)
QuickBooks 2007:
  features of, 2–3
  number of items in lists, 52
  pop-up messages, 452
  tax deposits, 246
  updating, 505–507
QuickBooks credit card, 380, 383
QuickReport, 126, 280, 470

R

rates, mileage, 182–183
receipts, online, 378
Receive Payments window, 23,
  108–110, 112, 113, 115, 116
recollecting debt, 288, 289
Reconcile window, 300–302, 306
reconciliation report, 304–305,
  309, 310
reconciling (reconciliation):
  of bank accounts (*see* bank
    accounts, reconciling)
  of credit card accounts, 295
recurring bills, 178–182
recurring invoices, 101–102
redepositing NSF checks, 286–289
refreshing reports, 422, 463
refunds, customer, 79, 81–83
register (bank):
  and bill paying, 201
  deposits, 284
  printing, 196, 205
  and printing checks, 205
  transferring funds, 393
  using, 202–203, 393
  VOID transaction in, 309
Regular (employee type), 35
Reimb Group item, 425
reimbursable expenses, 157–167
  changing amount of, 165
  grouping, 164, 425
  income accounts for, 159–160
  invoicing, 161–167
  marking up, 165–166
  options for managing, 158
  preferences for, 159, 162
  recording, 161, 162

and redepositing NSF
  checks, 288
removing, 165
setting up, 158–160
tracking, 158–160
release date (employee), 35
reminders, 180, 460–462, 494
remitting sales tax, 214
Remove ALL Transactions, 503, 504
Remove Transactions As Of A
  Specific Date, 503
removing, 165, 473–475
rent, 178
Reorder point field, 269
Rep field, 62
rep field (sales rep), 21
reporting:
  balance sheet, 354–356
  budgets, 323–327
  on changed template
    fields, 98
  by class, 470–472
  combine reports feature,
    372–373
  deleted transactions, 364–366
  estimates, 72–74
  and Fixed Asset Manager,
    515–517
  inventory, 280–281
  journal entries, 345
  memorized reports, 370–372
  ODBC driver, 373–376
  online transactions, 394–395
  payroll for cost information,
    432–434
  pending builds, 274
  on permissions, 485
  sales tax, 212–213
  timesheets, 420–423
  trial balance, 348–354
  voided transactions, 364–366
  (*See also* payroll, government
    reporting)
reports:
  accrual vs. cash basis,
    348–349
  and cleaning up files, 503
  default formatting for, 464

format defaults, 464

and inactive inventory items, 271

mileage, 184, 185

preferences, 462–464

refreshing, 422, 463

removing columns from, 134

timesheets, 420–422

(*See also* financial reports; *individual report*)

Reports & Graphs preferences, 462–464

Reports—Show Accounts By, 464

reprinting checks, 200, 201

Require Accounts, 454

Resale Number, 21

resizing panes, 153, 222

restoring:

backups, 499–500

portable computer file, 501–502

Retail Edition (QuickBooks), 79, 103, 118, 123

Retained Earnings equity account, 334

retaining the credit, 82

revenue, 69, 349

reversing entries, 341

roles (user), 480–483

.rtf file format, 524–525

S

Safeguard, 197

salaried workers, 428

Sales Discounts income account, 115

sales forms, 465

sales order(s):

creating, 74–77

fulfillment of, 104–105

Fulfillment Worksheet, 79, 104–105

invoicing from, 77–79

outstanding, 60

preferences for, 75–76, 466

from purchase orders, 77, 168

Sales Price field, 39

sales receipts, 120–122

sales rep, 21, 44–45, 62, 122

sales tax, 206–215

adjusting, 214–215

assigning codes/items to customers, 210

Code List, 43

creating tax groups, 210–212

default codes for, 207–209

enabling tracking for, 206–207

items, 209

Liability report, 212, 213

most common category, 209

multiple sales tax authorities, 206, 208, 210–212

payment basis, 209

payment dates, 209

preferences for, 467

for reimbursable expenses, 163

remitting, 214

reports for, 212–213

Revenue Summary report, 212, 213

Sales Tax Group, 37

sample codes for, 208

setting up customer information, 21

sales tax items:

assigning to customers, 210

creating, 21, 210

definition of, 209

item type, 37

Save Backup Copy Automatically When I Close My Company File Every X Times, 497

Save Current Desktop, 458

Save When Closing Company, 458

saving:

bill payment information, 195–196

finance charge invoices, 144

never update name information when, 453

standard invoices, 66

transactions, 453

Schedule tab, 513

schedules, pay (*see* pay schedules)

scheduling, backups, 497–499

searching:

advanced, 489

files, 488–491

finding transactions in files, 488–491

Google Desktop, 489–491

invoices, 66–67

manually for beginning balance discrepancies, 308–309

simple search, 488–489

user permissions, 483

Section 179 deductions, 514–515

security:

accountant's copy, 358

Admin password, 475, 483

audit trail, 365

credit cards, 23

e-mail, 358, 501

levels of, 2

ODBC driver, 376

online banking, 382, 496

passwords, 475, 483, 484

and user access, 477

vendor information, 152

Select Default Accounts to Use, 457

Select The Time And Day You Want To Back Up This Data File, 499

Selective Access (option), 477

SEND (as check number), 195

send forms, 467

sending:

credit memos, 83–94

data to your bank, 387–388

invoices, 83–94

standard invoices, 66

(*See also* e-mailing; mail)

sensitive accounting activities, 477

sensitive financial reports, 478

service charges (bank), 299

service connections, preferences for, 467–468

service item, 37, 415
service rep, 45 (*See also* sales rep)
Set Up Budgets window, 315–316, 318, 322, 323
Ship field, 62
Ship To address, 61
ship via list, 46–47
shipping addresses, 19
shipping costs, 69
shipping expense, 69
Shipping Manager, 88
Show All Bills (option), 190
Show Envelope Window option, 100
Show Full List Only button, 153, 221
Show Home Page When Opening A Company File, 458
Show Lowest Subaccount Only, 7, 15, 454
Show Time When Minimized (Timer option), 443
sick and vacation pay, 31, 35
single activity, tracking, 416–418
Single U/M Per Item, 263–266, 268
Single User Mode, 478, 486
Social Security, changing, 241
social security number, 25, 32
software, 436–437
Sort Bills By (option), 190
sorting:
    accounts, 9
    assets, 513
    bills, 190
    trial balance, 350
spell checker (spelling), 64–65, 270, 468
Splits button, 203
standard checks, 197, 200
standards:
    for naming accounts, 7–9
    vendor name, 24
Staples, 197
Start With Payee Field on Check, 456
state forms, 241–242
statement charge(s), 144–146
Statement Date, 523

Statement of Cash Flows report, 366–368
statements (customer):
    assessing finance charges on, 148
    creating, 146–148
    customizing, 149–150
    entering statement charges, 144–146
    monthly, 145
    previewing, 148–149
    printing, 149
    selecting customers for, 146–148
    selecting date range for, 146
    sending, 144–150
    skipping, 148
Status column, 248
Statutory (employee type), 35
stopwatch, 418
subaccounts:
    in budget, 324
    creating, 13–15
    and depreciation, 338–339
    displaying, 7, 454
    and merging list entries, 51
    using, 10–11
Subchapter S corporations, 29, 229, 406
subclasses, creating, 470
subcontractors, 413, 414
subitems, 38, 270, 271
Subtotal (item type), 37
SUI, 34
Summary Reports Basis, 464
Supporting Document Editor, 523–524

T

T-account format, 332
TAB key, 142, 202, 317, 451
tape drive, 495
tasks, setting up, 415
Tax Code field, 39
tax forms (*see* federal forms)
tax groups, 210–212
Tax ID, 25, 401

tax line assignments, 405–406
tax rate, state, 208
taxes:
    information for employee, 34
    making payroll tax deposits, 246–252
    paying tax liabilities, 248–250
    paying unscheduled liabilities, 251–252
    Payroll Setup wizard, 231–232
    scheduling payments for, 232–232
    tax code field, 39
    tax liability payment schedules, 246–248
    vehicle mileage, 182
    worksheets for, 518
    year-end reports, 405–407
    (*See also* sales tax)
taxes, federal:
    employee withholding, 27, 246
    vendor, 223
    worksheets for, 518
    (*See also* federal forms)
taxes, state and local:
    employee withholding, 27, 246
    entering manually, 29
    information on, 29
    SUI, 34
    vendor, 223
templates:
    changing the columns for, 98–99
    changing the data in the Footer tab, 99
    changing the data in the Print tab, 99
    changing the data in the Prog Cols tab, 99
    changing the header for, 96, 98
    columns for, 98–99
    copies of, 96, 121
    customizing, 94–101
    designing a new, 96, 97

designing the layout for, 100–101

downloading, 60

editing a predefined, 94–96

Employee Organizer, 241–242

exporting/importing memorized report, 138–139

and Financial Statement Designer, 521–522

Footer tab, 99

header for, 96, 98

Inuit Preprinted Forms, 85

for invoices, 58–60

for journal entries, 344–345

list for, 41

memorized reports, 138–139, 371

predefined, 94–96

Print tab, 99

Prog Cols tab, 99

reporting on changed fields in, 98

Timer activity, 441–443

working with copies of, 96, 121

terms:
    date-driven, 46
    field, 61
    vendor, 25

Terms List, 20

testing backups, 496, 500

theft, employee, 277, 278

time-and-a-half (*see* overtime)

Time By Item report, 421

Time By Job Detail report, 421, 422

Time By Job Summary report, 421

Time By Name report, 421

time entries, 422

time format, 417, 453

Time Tracker, 416

time tracking, 412–426
    creating invoices with timesheets data, 424–426
    editing time entries, 422
    employee time, 413, 414
    other worker time, 414
    and payroll/job costing, 428–434

preferences for, 468

printing weekly timesheets, 422–423

reporting timesheets information, 420–423

setting up, 412–415
    a single activity, 416–418
    the stopwatch, 418

tasks, 415

Time Tracker, 416

timesheets, 31, 415–420

vendor time, 413, 414

weekly timesheets, 419–420

(*See also* Timer)

timely payments, 115–117

Timer, 436–447
    distributing Timer software, 436–437
    editing the activity in, 441–442
    exporting data lists to users of, 437–438
    exporting/importing files, 443–447
    opening for the first time, 439–440
    preferences for, 442, 443
    setting up an activity in, 440–441
    timing your work, 442
    using, 439–442

timesheets:
    and billing rates, 52
    copy of previous, 420
    creating invoices with, 424–426
    efficient use of, 430
    imported Timer entries, 439
    and payroll job costing, 428–434
    printing weekly, 422–423
    reporting, 420–423
    running payroll with, 430–432
    user permissions, 415
    using, 415–420, 428–434
    weekly, 419–420

.tlg files, 499

To Be Printed check box, 87

toolbars, 522

ToolTips, 452, 473

Track Reimbursed Expenses As Income, 466

tracking, out-of-stock items, 74 (*See also* backorders; sales order(s))

Traditional Wallet checks, 200

Transaction List By Customer report, 139

transaction rights, 478

transactions:
    beep on recording, 451
    cash register, 123–124
    cleared, 389
    closed, 502–503
    default data for, 452
    filtering, 66
    report on, for each customer, 139
    tab, 56, 57, 152
    user permissions for, 478
    voiding (void), 308, 309, 364–366
    warnings on, 451–452

transactions, bank account:
    adding, 301–302
    clearing, 301
    correcting deleted/voided, 308
    deleting, 302
    editing, 302
    eliminating future, 300, 301
    matching downloaded, 389–392
    matching unmatched, 389–391
    reconciling, 300–304
    recording missing, 336

Transfer Funds Between Accounts window, 392–393

transferring funds, 285–286

traveler's checks, 125

trial balance:
    accrual vs. cash, 348–349
    definition of, 348
    and opening balance, 334
    reporting of, 348–354

troubleshooting issues, 305–312

TurboTax, 405, 407

Turn On All One Time Messages (Timer option), 442
2D graphs, 463
Type of Change column (Discrepancy Report), 307

U

unattended backups, 497–499
Unbilled Costs By Job, 139
Uncleared (Type of Change), 307
Undeposited Funds account, 111–112, 118, 120, 123, 124
underpayments, 112–113
unemployment, 27, 28, 33
unincorporated partnership, 44
Unit(s) of Measure, 3, 263–268, 460
unlocking files, 364
Unmark All button, 237
unmatched transactions, 389–392
unpaid balance, 22
unpaid bills, 188–189
Unpaid Bills Detail report, 188
unpaid invoices, 139
unscheduled liabilities, 251–252
untimely payments, 117
updating QuickBooks, 505–507
    automatic updates, 506
    configuring service, 506
    manual updates, 506
    selecting update types, 507
    sharing updates on network, 507
    update status, 507
Upon Receipt Of Payment (sales tax payment basis), 209
Use Account Numbers, 454
Use Class Tracking, 455
Use Price Levels, 466
Use Time Data To Create Paychecks, 31
Use Undeposited Funds As A Default Deposit To Account, 467
user information, 475

user permissions, 415, 476–478, 482–483, 490
users:
    creating new, 475–476
    Icon Bar, 472
    removing, 484
    roles for, 480–483
Usual FOB, 465
Usual Shipping Method, 465

V

vehicle list, 47–48
vendor(s):
    addresses, 24
    backorders, 170
    credits, 177–178
    custom fields for, 48
    customer account numbers, 457
    deductions, 29
    discounts, 115, 193
    inventory help from, 277
    lists, 24–26, 45
    naming, 24
    opening balance, 337
    and payroll items, 28
    and petty cash, 292
    report on, 139
    security, 152
    setting up payroll, 223
    and taxes, 223
    1099 form, 25, 400–403
    terms, 25
    time tracking, 413, 414
    treating credit cards as, 292–293
    type list, 45
    (*See also* bill(s), vendor)
Vendor Center, 16, 150–157, 189
vendor credits, 177–178
Vendor Eligible For 1099, 25
Vendor 1099 Review report, 400, 401

Vista (Windows), 493
void check, 201
Voided/Deleted Transactions Detail report, 365
Voided/Deleted Transactions Summary report, 364–365
voiding (voided):
    checks, 201, 241, 242, 289, 290
    deleting vs., 67, 68
    paychecks, 241, 242
    standard invoices, 67–68
    transactions, 308, 309, 364–366
voucher checks, 197

W

W-2 forms, 35, 220, 258–259
W-4 forms, 35, 36
wallet checks, 197, 200
Warn About Duplicate Check Numbers, 457
Warn About Duplicate Invoice Numbers, 465
Warn About Duplicate Purchase Order Numbers, 460
Warn About Duplicate Sales Order Numbers, 466
Warn If Not Enough Inventory to Sell, 460
Warn When Posting A Transaction To Retained Earnings, 455
warnings:
    deleting a transaction/unused data item, 452
    editing transaction, 451–452
    on maximum number of assemblies, 273, 274
    on sales orders, 77
    on unavailable/on hand inventory, 77
"washing" liability accounts, 343
Web Connect, 378, 385–387, 393, 467–468

Weekly Timesheet, 416
When Calculating Quantity
    Available For My Inventory,
    Deduct, 460
window envelopes, 100
withdrawals, 390
    ATM, 123, 290, 291, 390
    unmatched, 390
workers:
    hourly, 428
    other worker time
        tracking, 414
    salaried, 428
    setting up for time
        tracking, 413
Workers Comp field, 418, 420
Workers Comp List, 44
Workers Comp Summary, 256, 257
workers compensation, 252–257
    automatic calculation of, 256
    calculations for more than
        one state, 256

categories, 253
paying, 257
reporting on, 257
setting up tracking for,
    253–255
tab, 32, 36
writing checks:
    appearance, 198
    bank account register,
        202–203
    check styles, 197
    direct disbursements,
        201–205
    manual, 195–204
    missing check numbers, 201
    partial check pages, 199
    preferences, 456–457
    printing checks, 205
    reprinting, 200, 201
    Write Checks window,
        201–204, 291, 336

Y

year, display of as 4 digits, 453
Year-end Balance Sheet report, 399
year-end procedures, 398–409
    backup, 409
    calculating officer
        compensation, 406–407
    closing your books, 407–409
    financial reports, 399
    journal entries, 404–405
    tax reports, 405–407
    1099 Forms, 400–404
    TurboTax, 407
    typical tasks, 398
Year-end Profit & Loss report, 399
    (*See also* income statement)

Z

zero-balance accounts, 351
ZIP code, 148